INFLATION AND RECESSION
IN THE U.S. ECONOMY IN THE 1970s

PÉTER ERDŐS AND FERENC MOLNÁR

INFLATION AND RECESSION IN THE U.S. ECONOMY IN THE 1970s

PRICE, PROFIT AND BUSINESS CYCLES IN THEORY AND PRACTICE

AKADÉMIAI KIADÓ BUDAPEST 1990

This is the English translation of the Hungarian original
Infláció és válságok
a hetvenes évek amerikai gazdaságában
published by Közgazdasági és Jogi Könyvkiadó, Budapest 1982

Translated by
GYÖRGY HAJDU

ISBN 963 05 4780 5

Printed in Hungary by Akadémiai Kiadó és Nyomda Vállalat, Budapest, 1990

CONTENTS

APPENDIX

A METHOD FOR THE ESTIMATION OF THE INCOMES, CONSUMPTION AND SAVINGS OF SOCIAL CLASSES, BASED ON THE STATISTICAL DATA OF THE UNITED STATES OF AMERICA

PREFACE

In his work *Wages, Profit, Taxation* Péter Erdős sought to present the laws, deemed most important by him, of the capitalist economy in the era of state monopoly capitalism on the level of political, that is, of "pure" theory. However, following from the limitations of his genre, he could treat them in only a very abstract manner. He also indicated this fact in the last paragraph of the book, saying that "the theoretical economist, the political economist does not even examine capitalism as it is in practice, only its abstract model." Yet the book ended on an optimistic note, saying that "the work of the political economist is not in vain if, by showing the real laws to be read from the abstract model, he helps others to understand the most intrinsic relations in which the workers of the West are living" (p. 505).

But this is not enough; this stage had to be surpassed. The real, concrete economy, "living capitalism" had to be scrutinized, but in a manner that the results drawn from the theoretical model should serve as road signs for research: either their substance should be proven or it should become clear that some of them should be discarded. Of course, this much was obvious from the outset that the theorems derived from the simplest model prove to be too rigid and in many respects too narrow when confronted with the actual situation of a specific country, with the development of a country in a given period. Only a comparison with concrete reality can reveal whether the model did not abstract from one or another aspect of today's economy, the neglect of which may lead to false conclusions.

The authors of the present book have joined forces if not for completing this work, at least to begin it.

Of course, the investigation could not extend to the whole or even the main characteristics of the economic laws of capitalism and their changes, not even for a given period. Originally we had intended to extend our investigations to a few countries at least, but it soon turned out that even the study of the economy of the United States provides enough lessons to fill a book. Furthermore, the scope of the problems to be investigated had to be restricted as well. These investigations are linked more closely only to the last sphere of problems discussed in *Wages, Profit, Taxation* and, following from the nature of things, to Part Four "Unproductive employment and state monopoly capitalism". But even from this array of problems we only discuss what is promised in the title: the theories of prices, profit and business cycles.

11

Clearly, on the basis of the examination of a single decade of a single country not much can be stated with general validity even about these partial problems of economic theory. What we can say about the US economy need not necessarily hold true for Japan or the Federal Republic of Germany. As a matter of fact, the decade of the American economy investigated here qualitatively differs from the preceding ones in several respects with the coming of a new era. The interpretation and explanation of this changeover would require very thorough investigation from the aspects of growth theory, world economy, sociology and politics, and we were not in a position to undertake such a task.

It would be, for example, highly interesting to point out why inflation did not cause greater difficulties in the sixties, while in the seventies the inflationary process accelerated; why economic growth could be faster in the sixties than in the seventies; to what extent was the large-scale unemployment made tolerable by the social and age composition of the unemployed and by unemployment benefits; what role did the spread of service activities play in the unsatisfactory development of productivity, etc. We had not raised these and similar questions, much less answered them. We took the conditions of the era, relevant to our subject, as given and examined how price level, profit formation and business cycle were linked to each other under these conditions and how all these influenced high-level economic policy. It was precisely this latter aspect, the expected and actual impact of economic policies that constituted one of the focal points of our investigations.

Partly for this reason, our book has become rather heterogeneous. But we could not radically change this situation, since it is in fact the result of our joint work. Together, complementing one another with our different knowledge and reconciling our views in sharp debates, we set to write a book which neither of us could have written alone. Some parts were drafted by one of us, and some by the other. And both of us insisted on including our pet ideas. We only hope that readers will forgive for the unevenness of the book for the sake of the diversity of the material discussed.

Our book consists of four parts and an Appendix.

The first part comprises general remarks on the economic policy of the United States, its nature and possibilities. In writing it we strongly relied on Herbert Stein's *The Fiscal Revolution in America*, which is a standard work on the subject. In the work we separately indicated the places where, in the absence of such indication, our procedure would have almost bordered on plagiarism. In the second and third parts of the book—examining the development of prices and profits—we used analytical methods which, to our knowledge, are our own. We have not found examples of their use in the works of other authors. The fourth part discusses the economic events of the decade in detail and in chronological order. Finally, the Appendix presents the statistical procedure and the hypotheses, with the aid of which the contents of parts two and three could be quantified.

The Authors

PART ONE

PROLEGOMENA CONCERNING HIGH-LEVEL U.S. ECONOMIC POLICY AND ITS INSTRUMENTS

CHAPTER ONE

WAS THE ECONOMIC POLICY OF THE UNITED STATES KEYNESIAN?

1.1 SOME DISTINGUISHING FEATURES OF KEYNES' CONCEPTUAL SYSTEM

It is a rather widespread belief that the economic policy of the United States has been Keynesian[1]—perhaps ever since Roosevelt, but at least after World War II—which at times bent towards the monetarist school hallmarked by the name of Milton Friedman. However, reality is much more complicated than that. But, before going into details, we have to speak about the Keynesian system of ideas itself. This is so also because the proposals concerning the (high-level) economic policy to be followed have to be publicly justified somehow—at least in the United States. Justification has to be made in some system of concepts, categories. The system of concepts introduced by Keynes, and the Keynesian economic "language" became generally accepted and used after World War II. Thus, e.g., the annual reports of the Council of Economic Advisers usually employed Keynesian concepts and, although recently Keynesianism has become rather compromised, these are much used even today. Without a knowledge of these concepts we cannot understand their argumentation.

The Keynesian system of concepts differs from the pre-Keynesian one first of all in that it shifted the emphasis from the problems of relative prices and the quantity of money to those of incomes and outlays. If someone using these ideas wants to know on what the volumes of social production and employment depend, he will inquire how the total demand for goods and services is determined—"effective" demand, since in a not too short period only those things are produced for which there is a demand. Incomes depend on outlays and outlays mainly on incomes: this is a "circular" determination. Still, it is said, in this system of mutual dependence problems arise from one side, from the side of outlays, from that of effective demand. But the Keynesian system of concepts makes a distinction between consumer outlays (thus, consumer demand) and the outlays destined for investment (thus, investment demand). According to the Keynesian theory, consumer outlays depend decisively on incomes; basically, they are growing—or diminishing—together with the national income, but by less than the latter. Investment outlays depend on the expected profitability of the projects on the one hand, and on the cost of interest of the money to be spent on

---

[1] In this context we think mainly of the 1946 Employment Act. It enacted, progressively, a not at all new practice, but by no means amounted to a commitment of the legislation to the Keynesian—and precisely the Keynesian—scope of ideas.

investment on the other—more exactly on the expected rate of interest. The marginal rate of income, the marginal rate of return on capital goods expected for their lifetime cannot fall, under normal conditions, below the rate of interest forecast for any date. Thus the real question is whether investment demand is growing together with the increasing national income to a sufficient extent for making up for the volume of demand by which the increment of consumer demand is lagging behind the increment of the national income.[2]

The Keynesian theory assumes that as long as such capital goods are at hand, or can be produced, the expected rate of profitability which is not lower than the expected rate of interest, there will be also demand for such capital goods. Thus, here the problem again bifurcates: (a) on what does the expected marginal rate of profitability ("marginal efficiency") of capital depend? and (b) on what does the size of the rate of interest depend? The answer to the latter question is one of the most particular, most characteristic products of the Keynesian world of ideas.

It can already be seen from that much that Keynes—as distinct from the vulgar economists of his age—does not equate the return on capital (profit) with interest, nor does he believe that in a balanced situation profit is zero. With him, the relevant problem[3] is not the return of capital, but of money, that is, of banknotes and demand deposits—bank account money. But, he who possesses banknotes or a sight deposit with some bank on his current account, does not draw interest on his money. But he who has (sufficient) money may—unless he buys capital goods—also invest it in securities (e. g., shares, government or private bonds) and these do bear interest. (From this aspect the dividends on shares may be also considered interest.) The higher the rate of interest on the latter, the more income from interest the person who still keeps a part of his wealth in cash (banknotes or account money) has to forgo. This will stimulate him to hold as little money in cash as possible. But in every country and at any time there is a certain amount of cash, which is mostly referred to as M_1,[4] in present-day economic literature, and this amount of money must be held by someone.

Of course, it is not immaterial whether one possesses his own or borrowed money. Interest has to be paid on borrowed money. When speaking about interest on money, we mean the interest which has to be paid after a loan received in cash. But today essentially all money is credit money, thus the total amount of money in circulation is always exactly equal to the sum total of monetary short-term credit extended by the banking system. This amount of money (the quantity of money in circulation) is partly in the hands of those who do not owe it to anyone—e. g., they got it from those raising credit—and partly in the hands of those debtors who have not yet spent the money they borrowed—but it is always in the possession of somebody. According to a popular theory, in the case of a given quantity of money in circulation the rate of interest must be high enough so that people should not want to raise more credit than the actual one, thus increasing the quantity of money in circulation. (If the rate of interest is low

[2] Keynes' answer was that in a rich country it does not grow satisfactorily without adequate government interference.

[3] The adjective "relevant" was inserted for the sake of accuracy. Namely, Keynes knew not only of monetary interest.

[4] The terminology differs somewhat from that in Great Britain.

enough for them to possess more money, securities will be sold: this will bring down the price of securities and, as we shall see, will raise their rate of interest competing with short-term credits.) It is the interest on cash-loans that sets an upper limit to the quantity of money in circulation. On the other hand, it is claimed, the rate of interest must not be too high either, else people would want to reduce the quantity of money in their possession. But the quantity of money sought to be possessed also depends on the size of incomes. Thus, e.g., if incomes are increasing while the bank does not want to boost the quantity of money, the rate of interest has to be raised in order that people should be content with the possession of an unchanged quantity of money in spite of their higher income. (Experience has proven that this theorem is weak indeed.)

Accordingly, in Keynes's system the rate of interest is determined, on the one hand, by the quantity of money in circulation at any time, and, on the other, by the quantity of money which people wish to hold in the case of different rates of interest, also considering the size of their incomes. (To this idea is related the Keynesian concept of liquidity preference.) But, in the case of different price levels the same amount of money has different purchasing power. In this sense, we may speak about the nominal quantity and the real quantity of the money in circulation. Now, it is the nominal quantity of the money in circulation which the "monetary authority"—in the USA the Federal Reserve System (FED)—is able and called upon to regulate in harmony with the rate of interest. It is mostly—but not exclusively—this regulation that is called monetary policy.

This Keynesian scope of concepts and theory is contrasted essentially with the quantity theory of money.[5] The modernized quantity theory of money—as distinct from its version current at the time of the gold standard—does not simply confront the quantity of money existing in the country with the purchasing power of money, but the given quantity of money at any time with the quantity that people wish to possess (it confronts a stock with a stock). This novel quantity theory of money was introduced by today's monetarists. Accordingly, if people wish to possess more money than the existing amount—against the intentions of the FED—their purchases of goods, services and securities will be reduced (thus they will not spend their total income). Thereby prices, and with them nominal incomes, will diminish,[6] while the rates of interest will rise. That is, the real value of money in circulation and the rates of interest will also rise, as long as people are not satisfied with possessing as much money as there is in circulation. Thus, the emphasis here is on the sum of money, and on the demand for money, while in the Keynesian framework matters depend on the treble interrelation between (1) the income of consumers and the level of their outlays on consumption, (2) the rates of interest and the rate of investment, (3) the quantity of money and the rate of interest. (Let us note that thus the quantity of money has an essential role also in Keynes' theory.)

Staying within the scope of ideas of the Keynesians,[7] if we want to know what size

---

[5] Keynes himself lists his own theory with those of the quantity theory. In this matter he was not right. See, e.g., P. Erdős, 1982, p. 186.

[6] Namely, a diminishing sum of prices involves diminishing incomes for sellers, unless, at the same time, the nominal costs of sellers also diminish.

[7] The following brief and precise summary is based on Stein, 1969, pp. 158-159.

the demand (for goods, services and securities) will be, we have to examine the following:
1. the development of government expenditure (and revenues),
2. the factors determining the interrelation between consumers' incomes and their outlays on consumption,
3. the factors determining the expectable profitability of investments,
4. the factors on which the relationship between rates of interest and the money wanted to be possessed depends,
5. the monetary policy determining the nominal quantity of money,
6. the factors determining the relationship between the level of economic activity and prices.

These are the problems on which after World War II the attention of economists responsible for economic policy was concentrated and around which the annual reports of the Council of Economic Advisers conduct their argumentation. It was only with the approach of the current decade, with the accumulating failures of economic policy, that the voice of the counterrevolution of the monetarist school turning against the "Keynesian revolution" has become ever louder. In its most extreme form, coupled with the name of Milton Friedman, this school not only discards the bulk of the Keynesian economic policy measures, but also advances the absurd theory that the smooth development of the capitalist economy can only be secured if the monetary authority steadily increases the quantity of money by the same few per cent every year.

1.2 ON THE PREHISTORY OF KEYNES' AND THE KEYNESIANS' THEORY

Keynes, of course, was not born a perfect Keynesian. At the time of writing his first major theoretical work, *A Treatise on Money*, around 1930, although he had already replaced the quantity theory of money with an income theory of money, he was still a monetarist in the sense that he believed that an essentially smooth development of the economy could only be realized with the aid of monetary policy, by manipulating the rates of interest. It was only around 1932–33, at the height of the Great Depression, that he began to raise doubts about the absolute effectiveness of monetary policy.[8]

It happens at times[9]—so he believed—that the expected profitability of investment becomes highly uncertain, thus investment activity declines and employment and incomes fall even more (through the multiplier effect). In such cases, according to classical theory, wages and prices also should diminish, which would increase the *real* quantity of the nominally circulating money, hence the rate of interest would fall and this would stimulate investment activity. But in reality wages and prices are rigid downwards, thus the purchasing power of money would hardly grow and the rate of interest would hardly decline. But it would not help much even if the quantity of money in circulation were not increased. In such situations, the public would expect interest rates to rise again with improving business. Therefore, they would refrain from buying

[8] More exactly, he expressed such ideas already in 1930 before the MacMillan Comission. See Harrod, 1953, p. 417.
[9] Also in this paragraph Herbert Stein's report was relied upon.

18

securities for their money since—as we shall see—low interest on securities means that they have a high market price. On the other hand, it might be highly uncertain whether there is enough opportunity for profitable investment. In short, at such times the rate of interest perhaps cannot be reduced so much that it should stimulate investment activity securing full employment. In this case, therefore, only the raising of government outlay and such a reduction of the tax burden may be the way out which stimulates sufficiently high personal consumption.

The standpoint of the *General Theory* in 1936 was much more definite. Keynes no longer believed that monetary policy might become unsatisfactory only at times; his faith in an exclusively monetary policy was basically shaken. He saw that not even very low rates of interest can lead the public to invest its money rather in securities, because at such times there is a great danger that the price of securities would fall. (As a matter of fact, the very low rates of interest can easily rise.) This could not be helped, not even by a flood of money. All the less, because, as he put it, with a rising national income consumption would increasingly lag behind income, thus more and more investment goods would have to be produced in order for investment to balance the relative decline of consumption. Furthermore—argued Keynes in the spirit of the marginal productivity school—while the economy of the country is growing, and the quantity of capital is increasing relative to labour, in the meantime the profitability of further investment will increasingly diminish. He believed it was possible that—considering the most developed countries—in the not-too-far future from 1936, the rate of profit would fall below the lowest possible rate of interest. Under such conditions a lasting stagnation would follow and this could only be helped by a lasting budgetary deficit and—to a certain extent—by a reallocation of the tax burden in favour of those with low incomes (thus consuming much relative to their income). (The theory of lasting stagnation, called "secular stagnation" was elaborated not so much by Keynes as by his followers. Before World War II many American Keynesians were more Catholic than the Pope.)

Thus, we can see that although the economic theory of the *General Theory* reckons with the development of the two macroeconomic factors—the quantity of money in circulation and the rate of interest—for which, in principle, the monetary authority is responsible, in the Keynesian arsenal to forestall the evils, it is increasingly the instruments of fiscal policy that come to the fore.

1.3 FISCAL AND MONETARY POLICY

When speaking of the United States of America, a developed capitalist country where state ownership is insignificant, by high-level economic policy almost exclusively fiscal[10] and monetary policy should be understood. Monetary policy affects the economy unequivocally through money circulation and the credit sphere. The scope of fiscal policy is already more complex than that. He who limits his attention to what the size of the total revenue or expenditure of the budget is, how it changes, and what the surplus or deficit of the budget depending on the former is, will first of all notice that

---

[10] By fiscal policy we mean that of the federal government.

with its size and its deficit or surplus the budget itself is an important determinant of the sphere, to regulate which would be, in principle, the task of monetary policy, i. e., of the monetary and credit sphere. But the money outlays of the budget directly affect, through state purchases, the trade in commodities and through government orders (perhaps in connection with public works) also production. Government expenditure includes, in addition to the outlays of the federal budget, the state and local outlays, thus not only of the highest bodies. The federal government can significantly influence the latter—mainly because the source of income of these bodies is to a significant extent the aid given by the federal government.

We mostly identify the notion of high-level economic policy in capitalist countries with the economic policy of state monopoly capitalism—understanding the term "state" rather loosely. Of course, in capitalist countries the "monetary authority" directly responsible for monetary policy is not always part of the state power. Although the official status of the monetary authority of the United States, the Federal Reserve System, is a government agency, and, in principle, it is subordinated to Congress, this subordination is formal in practice. The twelve member banks of the FED are substantially independent of the Federal Reserve Board (the highest body of the FED, in Washington), which is formally independent, and was originally also practically independent of the federal administration. True, in the mid-thirties, and much more during World War II, the FED could give advice to state bodies, it could even argue with them, but in monetary questions the final decision was in the hands of the President. But this did not remain so. After a long fight (and the date can be given fairly exactly), the FED again won its practical independence in 1951.

As a matter of fact, the state power and the FED always must and do find a compromise acceptable to both parties, since both are defenders of the American capitalist system. Furthermore, if we think of the state in the strict sense, we cannot think of a single person or a single authority. The President and the government represent the executive power, while the legislative power belongs to Congress which consists of two houses, the House of Representatives and the Senate, but there may be a Republican majority in one of the houses when there is a Democratic one in the other. It may also happen that the President's party is in a minority in both houses. Party discipline does not bind the representatives and senators, thus they often vote across party lines. It follows that government decisions are not the free decisions of a single person or a single office, but they are always result of compromise. And, in the last instance, there is the Supreme Court which, in the name of the constitution, frequently wilfully interpreted, may declare void even enacted laws, as Roosevelt had frequently experienced. And since the decisions of the FED have a direct macroeconomic impact similar to those of state economic decisions in the strict sense, we shall not be in error if we include the monetary policy directed by the FED in the scope of the economic policy of state monopoly capitalism.

1.4 THE RELATIONSHIP BETWEEN ECONOMIC POLICY AND ECONOMIC THEORY

Returning now to the question of whether the economic policy of the United States was indeed a Keynesian economic policy—leaning at times towards monetarism—perhaps since Roosevelt, at any rate as much can be established as a fact that following the publication of the *General Theory* many of the most authoritative American economists joined the Keynesian school and several of them had an important influence on some policy makers of the time. Further, there can be no doubt that— although not from one day or year to the next—at least since Roosevelt changes have taken place in the U. S. fiscal and monetary policies which may indeed be called revolutionary in their entirety, and the main characteristics of these changes have on the whole coincided with certain economic policy proposals and ideas of Keynes.

But, Keynes' work and ideas could really be understood, even in the best case, by those engaged in economics as a science. And the fact that someone understood them, does not at all mean that he also accepted them. Economic policy decisions are not taken by scholars, but by the President—who is not an economist—and by the main officials of the presidential administration, with the control and approval of Congress, as well as by the heads of the "monetary authority". But the members of Congress are pushed and pulled in the most diverse directions by the influential men of the banks, industry, trade, by the various lobbies and their own interests. And they also have to consider—at least when the next election is drawing close—their voters as well. And the President must do the same. The actual economic policy is not formed simply by the recommendations of this or that economic theory; it takes shape as a result of conflicts of interest and power positions, emerging as a compromise.

True, but the interest and power relations derive from the objective course of the economy. Certain objective facts in the development of the economy—war, unemployment of intolerable size, rapid inflation, etc.—may demand, even without ready and complete theories at hand, such government measures which might follow even from a good theory if such were available. Above and beyond the conflicting views there are the general interests of the capitalist class. In connection with these the state has to appear on the scene, and this is no new phenomenon either, see, e. g., the role of the classical capitalist state in the struggles over workhours. But large unemployment and inflation developing also in peacetime are phenomena of ageing capitalism developed into state monopoly capitalism in the era of imperialism. Keynesianism is the macroeconomic theory of state monopoly capitalism, reflecting the economic needs originating in the interests of the capitalist class as a whole which had had a hegemonic role for some decades. The birth of its proposals regarding economic policy was made mostly possible by the recognition of the same facts and interrelations which forced economic policy to take a similar course—with all its compromises—even without a generally accepted theory.

CHAPTER TWO

MONETARY POLICY AS ONE OF THE INSTRUMENTS OF HIGH-LEVEL ECONOMIC POLICY

2.1 INSTRUMENTS OF MONETARY POLICY

Let us now scrutinize these instruments, first of all the instruments of monetary policy. We shall not discuss them merely in an abstract manner, but also by illustrating them with the actual practice of a given period.

By monetary policy we mean the regulation of rates of interest and the variation of the quantity of money, first of all of the so-called M_1, that is, the combined amount of banknotes in circulation and of bank account money at sight deposits. From the textbooks current in Hungary we can learn about the method of regulating M_1 that it occurs mainly through changes in the compulsory bank reserve rate. Samuelson, however, considers the open-market transactions as the main instruments of regulating the quantity of money in the United States.

Monetary policy aimed at the regulation of the quantity of money may endeavour to both increase and reduce M_1. In the case of a restrictive policy the upper limit to the quantity of money in circulation can indeed be lowered by reducing bank reserves or by raising the reserve rate.

The 1970 report of the Council of Economic Advisers established that in 1969 the FED restrained the rate of increase of money mainly by moderating the growth of monetary debts. (*Economic Report,* 1970, p. 33.)

2.2 THE FIRST INSTRUMENT: THE SYSTEM OF BANK RESERVES

This concisely formulated idea indicates essentially the system of bank reserves. By bank reserves the claims of the banks toward the central bank are meant. A claim for a bank is a commitment for the central bank, or, more clearly, a debt. The debts of the central bank include (though, as regards the substance of the matter, today only formally) the amount of banknotes issued, i. e., the amount of cash. Thus the cash possessed by the banks is similarly a part of their own reserves. Let us add that if the central bank grants credit to a bank on the current account of that bank, this amount will also be added to the claims of the bank. In this sense, it is similarly a claim if an industrial enterprise gets a current account credit from a bank—as long as this current account credit is good. But an industrial enterprise raises credit if it needs it, if it wants to pay with the borrowed money,[11] and thus it will soon remove the credit granted from its current account, as for such credit interest has to be paid. The banks also pay interest on the credits granted them by the central bank, but they will hardly use this sum from the current account, as they need it precisely because it increases their reserves. Namely, the central bank—in the USA the FED—prescribes for commercial banks how many times the sum of deposits in the current transfer accounts of their clients may exceed the sum of their reserves. It is in this context that the reserve rate is mentioned. If the central bank prescribes a higher reserve rate than the previous one, it forces the commercial banks to reduce the stock of deposits, while the reduction of the reserve rate amounts to a permission to increase the stock of their deposits—if they can. But the sight deposit—in other words, the credit in the current transfer account—is, together with the banknotes, money, account money, the main part of M_1. Thus, summing up briefly, if the FED reduces its monetary debts, it lowers the upper limit to the most massive kind of money in circulation—of bank account money—at least when it does not reduce simultaneously the obligatory reserve rate to an adequate extent.

Such a restrictive measure is employed if the FED considers the increase in the quantity of money to be too fast. If it is considered too slow, it will do the opposite: it will increase the amount of bank reserves—if it can—and/or will reduce the obligatory reserve rate, thus easing the raising of monetary credits, offering a possibility for increasing the quantity of money. But nobody can be obliged to raise the credit: the amount of credits raised does not grow automatically with the sum of credit offered. (Though in negative form, this was indicated in footnote 11.) It is relatively easy to suppress the raising of credits, but, under certain conditions, it is much more difficult to expand it. And, as we have seen, both the Keynesian and the monetarist theory couple the problem of the quantity of the actually circulating money with the interest rate policy.

2.3. A BRIEF THEORETICAL DIGRESSION ON THE RATE OF INTEREST OF SECURITIES (FOR THOSE TO WHOM THIS IS NEW)

Before entering into the related complications we have to speak about the substance of rates of interest, since textbooks on political economy treat this subject in a rather superficial manner.

First we have to distinguish the rate of interest on generally short-term loans—given in the form of cash or bank account money—from the rate of interest on interest bearing securities. The rate of interest on cash loans is the simpler, yet a complex concept in itself. A different (lower) interest is paid by banks on credit raised from the central bank; a different (higher) one by the largest corporations, and a still higher one by individuals for the same, and so forth. The situation is similar with the instalment

---

[11] It is a different matter that there is a practice in the United Kingdom, but also known elsewhere, whereby at times of excessive credit supply or too low demand for credit the large banks force their clients (the enterprises) to use full credit limit (right of overdraft), even if this is not needed by the latter, and pay interest on it.

credits mostly granted directly by institutions other than banks. This much is the complication. Yet the matter is simple, because the rate of interest of some credit of such a type is simply as many percent as the borrower pays for it. (A part of the interest is usually accounted as handling charges.)

The concept of the rate of interest on securities is a quite different matter. Of course, the commercial bill of exchange is also a security, and the treasury bills and (treasury) certificates are securities as well. But these are debentures on short-term debts. How their interest rates develop does not essentially differ from the development of rates of interest on cash loans. From our point of view the debenture on a long-term loan is the typical security. The purchase of bonds is a typical case of granting long-term credits, such as, for example, the bonds issued by the enterprises, (large corporations), but also those issued by the state and municipalities, etc. These are issued with an expiry of several or many years or, perhaps, even without expiry—and they are securities with a fixed rate of interest.[12] How can the rate of interest of securities bearing a fixed rate of interest fluctuate? We might think that with generally increasing rates of interest the "fixed" rate of interest of newly issued bonds will be higher than of those issued earlier. This, too, might happen. But, since bonds are traded on the market, the earlier issued bonds with an earlier nominal rate of interest have to stand fast in the competition with those having a higher nominal rate of interest. This only becomes possible if their market price falls. The bond purchased at a lower price—perhaps lower than its nominal value—secures for its buyer a higher, perhaps much higher actual income than the nominal rate of interest. For example, the interest of a bond of $ 100 nominal value bearing nominally a 2 per cent interest, will be actually 2.5 per cent, if it has been purchased for $ 80. (Also, the market price of a newly issued bond may be lower than its nominal value.)[13] That is to say that while the rate of interest or some type of cash loan is as many per cent as the borrower pays for it, the rate of interest on long-term credit granted in the form of purchasing securities is—assuming an identical nominal rate of interest—high or low depending on whether the market price of the security entitling this interest is high or low.

It is not the interest rate written on the bond but the price of the bond (together with the nominal rate of interest indicated in the text of the bond) that determines the true rate of interest (for those who bought the bond at that price). With bonds of a given nominal rate of interest the price of the bond and its true rate of interest are merely two aspects of the same unequivocal interrelation—the two are inseparable from each other. But this is only the first—and very innocent—complication relative to those to be explained in the following.[14]

---

[12] The issuer of the bond promises to pay annually a percentage given once and for all of the nominal value of the bond as interest.

[13] Otherwise, a similar thing happens to the shares: if speculatory factors did not compound interrelations, the price of shares would be the capitalized dividend, thus—leaving this complication out of account—if the interest at which the dividend is capitalized is high, the price of the share is low. To avoid misunderstanings, every transaction is considered speculatory which is motivated by an expected change in price.

[14] Even this first complication is not so simple as it would seem from what has been said. Namely, the price of the bond depends, beyond the nominal value of the bond, not only on the nominal rate of interest on long-

2.4 CONTINUATION OF THE THEORETICAL DIGRESSION: SUPPLY OF AND DEMAND FOR SECURITIES

The price of the bonds determines the true rate of interest, but the role of the price of bonds is not exhausted by that. The price of the bonds is a price. And since the bond is a piece of paper, because, though it is capital, it is a fictitious one, its price does not depend on the quantity of labour necessary for its reproduction. Thus, the trinity of the most vulgar economics—demand, supply and price—asserts itself. The asymmetric law of supply and demand asserts itself: increasing demand raises the price, and an increasing price reduces demand; increasing supply reduces the price and decreasing price increases demand. And, in addition, while the use value of usual commodities is rather unambiguous, the use value of a security is a rather complicated matter. People buy securities because securities are objects much suited for speculation. A speculator as buyer or seller of securities is not interested in the interest on the security but in its price changes. He speculates on a bull or a bear market and wants to gain by the price changes of the security. Also a rentier buys securities who wants to get lasting income with their aid. He is interested in the interest the bond bears and in its price mainly because the percentual size of the interest depends on the purchase price of the bond. The case is similar in many respects even with enterprises: frequently, an enterprise invests its free money capital in long term securities. However, not only the purchase price and the interest on the bond is important for it, but also the current market price, because, if the market price of a security falls—and it does fall if the rate of interest on long-term loans rises—the value of the part of enterprise capital invested in securities will also fall. (This is why an enterprise is also compelled to engage in speculation.) A fall in the price of securities is particularly troublesome when the enterprise appears on the securities market as a seller, thus, e. g., when it wants to acquire additional capital by issuing bonds, or if it is forced to increase its circulating capital in monetary form by selling a part of its portfolio. Furthermore, also the government frequently increases the supply of bonds, at times because it is forced to do so by its budgetary deficit, at times because it intentionally increases its deficit in order to stimulate business. Finally, also the FED regularly sells and buys securities on the open market, either to protect with its transactions the quotations of bonds—in the typical case of government bonds—or to increase or reduce the stock of cash of the private sector.

---

term loans, but also in the "maturity" of the given bond, that is, on the number of years after which the issuer of the bond has to redeem it at face value. A share has no expiry. If it is known of a share valued at $ 100 that year after year a dividend of only 2 dollars is paid on it, while the rate of interest on short-term loans is 4 per cent, the price of the share will not be higher than 50 dollars. But the market price of a bond of $ 100 face value and bearing a nominal rate of interest of 2 per cent cannot fall essentially below 100 dollars if its redemption at face value is due next year.

Theoretically, the interrelation beetwen the P market price of a bond with a face value of 100 dollars and a nominal interest rate of i_n per cent, if the rate of interest on long-term loans i_n per cent, if the rate of interest on long-term loans in i_n and the number of years until redemption is n, is the following:

$$P = \frac{100 + n.i_n}{100 - n.i_n}$$

One thing should be obvious: The realized demand for securities—actual purchase—must always be equal to the realized supply—actual sale—of securities. It holds for every commodity, thus also for securities that sellers always sell the same amount that buyers purchase. If the demand for securities is regulated by the return from interest of the securities (if they are bought for the sake of interest), then this interest cannot, in general, be smaller than other—more easily available risk-free—interest, that is the interest on deposits. This fact roughly determines the possible maximum of the quotation of securities. Similarly, if the supply of securities is regulated by the wish of holders of securities to get liquid monetary assets, and if it is more than a simple wish in the sense that they have to acquire liquid assets, this supply reduces the price of securities, thus raising the rate of interest. And, in general, this rate of interest is not only not lower than the interest on short-term credits, but higher, because it is not quite immaterial for any buyer of securities if the market price of his securities falls. The holding of securities involves risk. And the extent to which the rate of interest on long-term credits exceeds that on short-term ones depends in the last resort on the mostly incalculable development of supply and demand.

2.5. ANOTHER INSTRUMENT OF MONETARY POLICY: OPEN-MARKET POLICY, PRESENTED THROUGH ITS DEVELOPMENT

Our argumentation is not yet complete. We only mentioned one of the most important factors of high-level monetary policy related to bonds: the "open-market" policy of the FED *per tangentem.*Through one of its organs, the Federal Market Committee, the FED stimulated at times considerable excess demand, at other times considerable excess supply in order to influence either the quantity of money or the prices of bonds (and through this the long-term rate of interest). We shall present through an example how the task of regulating the quantity of money and the price of bonds can get into conflict with each other. This will also show the revolutionary changes the structure of the rates of interest and monetary policy in general underwent in the course of merely two or two and a half decades.

At the end of World War II, banks, insurance companies, enterprises and even private persons possessed an extremely large quantity of government bonds issued in order to finance the war. If the private sector wanted to expand its investments and other outlays, it put a part of its long-term bonds on the market. But in those times it became a prime obligation of the FED to prevent a fall in the price of government bonds and thus on such occasions it bought the securities offered. But with this it pumped reserves into the banking system[15] and thus allowed banks to increase their short-term loans by a multiple of the additional reserves thus attained. Hence, not only

---

[15] To wit: the FED purchases a bond from "someone" against a cheque issued by itself. "Someone" forwards the cheque to his bank. The bank credits him with the amount on his transfer account. At the same time the claim of the bank against the FED is increased by the amount of the cheque, and this is a bank reserve. Now the bank can increase the amount of the account money created by it by a multiple of this increment.

26

did the FED not slow the growth rate of money in circulation in this inflation-prone period, but it directly stimulated an increase in the quantity of money.

It thus happened that in 1946, and even in the greater part of 1947, the market price of government bonds was higher than their nominal value, while their true rate of interest was less than 2.5 per cent per annum. This situation could only be maintained with such abundance of money, with which the true rate of interest on short-term securities remained below 1 per cent.

In order to contain the circulation of money, the FED wanted to obtain the possibility for increasing the rates of interest, at least those on short-term loans. Of course, bankers in general prefer higher rates of interest to lower ones. But the matter was not so simple and not only the containment of inflation was at stake. In the last resort a situation had to be devised in which monetary policy ceases to be a mere supplement to fiscal policy and in which it becomes possible to complement the instrumentary of the high-level economic policy with its own means.

And now the fight started between the FED and the Treasury. The former gave its consent only in August 1948 to pay on the newly issued treasury bills, instead of 1 1/8 per cent—*horribile dictu*—1 1/4 per cent interest. In 1950 the Korean War broke out. Then the FED raised the rate of discount and tolerated that the interest on one-year securities should rise to 1 3/8 per cent. As a result the purchase of treasury bills still bearing a 1 1/4 per cent interest became disadvantageous and the private sector refrained from buying them. Their majority was purchased by the FED which sold from its own portfolio treasury debenture bonds at a price conforming to the new higher rate of interest on the market—let us not forget that it was higher merely by 1/8 per cent p.a. There was a general uproar in financial circles, since what actually happened was that though the FED took over the financing of the debt of the budget— and provided money for the Treasury—the loan to the goverement, raised in the last resort from the market was transacted by the FED, on conditions set by itself.

The at most 2.5 per cent rate of interest on long-term government bonds still remained taboo. After further mutual accusations and pseudo-news released in the press (furthermore by the President himself), the FED dared to state, with the willy-nilly consent of the Treasury, only in Spring 1951 that though it will provide for financing the government's needs, it will also take care that the monetarization of government debts[16] should remain at a minimum. This meant that the FED was no longer willing to continue securing the steady quotation of long-term bonds with market transactions. The rate of interest on the latter was maintained in 1951 still at the level of 2.5 per cent; yet this agreement of 1951 declared the independence of the FED. According to opinions voiced in those times this independence should have secured that monetary policy becomes an instrument of general economic stabilization, a partner to fiscal policy.

[16] The role of increasing government debt is increasing the quantity of money in circulation.

27

Let us now see what chaos it leads to if the FED actually uses its powers. Let us jump ahead 18 years, to 1969. Now we have to complement what has been said with an as yet hardly mentioned problem, with grave complications, namely inflation. We have already mentioned that in 1969 the FED pursued a restrictive monetary policy. Interest is the price of using money capital. Being a price itself, it is subject to the impact of supply and demand. It can already be seen from as much that the containing of the quantity of money in circulation—reduction of the money supply—increases, in general, the short-term rate of interest serving to finance circulating capital needs. But in the year 1969, in addition, also inflation was relatively significant, and in the first three quarters of the year the economy also expanded. The growth of the economy itself increased demand for credit, since in order to realize a growing amount of commodities generally more money is needed. And since today all money is credit money, more money in circulation is tantamount to a greater volume of short-term credits, and an increased demand for short-term credits raises—*ceteris paribus*—the rate of interest on credit. But on this occasion the growing quantity of commodities was sold at rising unit prices and for this even more money and thus more credit was needed. Now, from the aspect of those granting the credit at p per cent rate of interest p.a. only means with an i per cent annual rate of inflation a $(p-i)$ per cent interest in real terms, and if i is higher than p, the real rate of interest will be negative. And on a negative real rate of interest only one incapable of doing anything else grants credit.[17] But, from the aspect of those raising the credit, the situation is that he who raises a credit repays his debt later with depreciated money. And he who can invest in saleable commodities the money borrowed fares doubly well: he can sell the commodity bought today later at higher prices. The typical relevant case is the increase of inventories. And, indeed, the increase in the volume of inventories in the first three quarters of 1969 exceeded the rise in the corresponding period of the preceding year by almost 50 per cent, and declined only in the fourth quarter. Thus, demand for short-term credits gradually increased and, because the credit supply was restricted, also the rate of interest on short-term credits increased to an extent unprecedented since the Civil War. Of course, at the same time also the rate of interest on long-term credits soared—and the price of bonds fell.

Already toward the end of 1968 the FED shifted—mainly through reducing its commitments, thus the bank reserves—to a policy of issuing money at a reduced rate in order to prevent the economy from a growth deemed too fast, coupled with inflation. In April 1969 new restrictive steps followed: the FED raised the discount rate for its member banks from 5.5 to 6 per cent, and raised the reserve rate of the member banks by a further half percentage point. The reserves of the commercial banks remained

---

[17] By the institution granting credit not the bank is meant in these sentences, but the individual or enterprise (but not financial institute) who or which lends its free money for interest. Of course this is done, in general, through the mediation of some bank, but in this context the bank only mediates and does not grant credit. And the person who keeps his money saved in the savings bank in lack of better investment does not take out his money from the savings bank even if prices increase annually by a higher percentage than the interest on the deposit, since, if he took out his money, he would lose even this low interest.

practically invariable relative to the raised rate of reserve in the course of the year (one year earlier, in 1968, they increased by 7.8 per cent).

The annual increase of the quantity of money in circulation was 7.2 per cent in 1968. As against that, first of all as a result of measures outlined, the increase of M_1 net of seasonal fluctuations fell in the first half of 1969, at an annual rate, to 4.4 per cent. In the second half of the year, similarly at an annual rate, it was only 0.7 per cent, thus in the course of the whole year merely 0.35 per cent. (The quantity of banknotes circulating outside the banking system withstood the restrictions and its annual increase attained 6 per cent.)

We have thus on the whole indicated what the FED did to brake inflation. But the relationship between the application of monetary instruments and inflation is highly complicated. The monetary impacts had to appear immediately in the credit sphere. They did appear and in the form of a major upheaval.

The money stock of "non-banks" fell, thus the latter withdrew a considerable part of the deposits tied down for a longer time and of savings deposits and invested their money in market securities. (This "stock of money" is not a part of M_1.) This happened also to the deposits accumulated with the Mutual Savings Banks and the Savings and Loan Associations, because the rate of interest payable by them could not exceed a very low minimum. A part of the population, the "households", followed the example of the enterprises not belonging to the category of financial institutions. Thus, in the third quarter of 1969 they spent 29.1 billion dollars (at an annual rate) on the open market purchase of securities. This major part of the securities purchased by them (to the amount of $ 27.4 billion) was made up by debentures of the government and its agencies. The listed purchases of securities increased the demand side, thus they worked in the sense of increasing the price of securities.

This flow had an impact on the financial institutions, as seen in the following data.

The sum of non-sight and savings deposits placed with the commercial banks fell in the course of the year by 5.2 per cent. And the stock of the certificates of deposit on large amounts fell from 22.8 billion dollars in 1968 to 10.8 billion by the end of the year. The non-sight and savings deposit stock of all financial institutions accepting deposits increased in the course of 1968 by $ 33.1 billion, while in the third quarter of 1969 it fell, at an annual rate, by 20.5 billion. (And the owners of life insurance policies had the right to raise a loan from the insurance companies on the basis of their insurance premiums at a 5 per cent interest p.a.) Under the impact of all that also the liquid capital of insurance companies showed a strong decrease. This had grave consequences on the development of homebuilding.

These were then the sources that fed demand for long-term securities.

But the net increment of the supply of securities derived from corporations other than financial institutions. (We have just seen these companies were not inactive on the side of demand either and that on account of this the banks had to pay the piper, but now we are discussing the net result.) In this context we may state by way of introduction that, according to the testimony of econometric surveys, the investments of corporations react, as a rule, with a time lag on monetary restrictions—if they react at all.[18] And this is what now happened. While the assets of corporations usable for

[18] See, e.g., J. Crockett, J. Friend and H. Shavel,1967.

29

self-financing amounted to $ 61.7 billion in 1969, their expenditure on investment attained the level of $ 85 billion. They had to cover the difference from something (in fact they even built up a reserve of $ 5.2 billion in addition). The shortage of money restricted the loans that could be raised from banks and other sources, though the sum of such credits was, in spite of the money squeeze, $ 17.7 billion, i.e., 4.8 billion more than in the preceding year. (True, a considerable part of that was not regular bank credit but came from financing companies, the government, and bankers' bills of exchange.) The shortage was mitigated by the fact that while in 1968 the sum of liquid assets acquired was 10.1 billion, in 1969 this was only 2.3 billion,[19] and, in fact, in the third quarter of the year they reduced the stock of liquid assets by 6.1 billion dollars. Finally, essentially greater amounts than these were acquired by the enterprises through selling long-term securities and those without expiration, that is, bonds, mortgage deeds and shares to the amount of $ 20.8 billion. This increased the supply of securities. Let us add that the 1968 deficit in the balance of government revenues and expenditure turned into a surplus of $ 16.7 bn, which reduced demand for credit. Thus the supply of and the demand for long-term credit could become equal only with a low price, with rates of interest that were then high, above 7.6 per cent.[20]

But interest on short-term credits also soared. Inflation, as mentioned, prompted enterprises to increase their inventories and this kind of investment is financed—being an increase in circulating assets—by short or at most medium-term, credits. Thus, while the rate of interest on short-term credits raised by the wealthiest and most reliable clients moved in 1965 around 4 per cent, in 1969 it hardly remained below 9. Together with it, the rate of interest on other kinds of credit also exceeded the 1965 level by four percentage points. While prices increased, the quotations of bonds dropped.

The behaviour of banks added to the financial tensions. The order which prohibited the banks and similar institutions to pay high interest on deposits did not at all restrict their right to collect high interest. They had to charge high interest, else they would have closed the year with a loss. The bank raises and grants credit. Its net receipts do not depend in absolute terms on whether the rate of interest is high or low, but on the interest margin, the difference between rates of interest paid and collected. From the interest margin it has to cover its costs (these are "pure turnover costs") and above that it has to make a profit. Under conditions of inflation not only the real rate of interest (denoted earlier by (p-i)) has to be greater than zero, but so must the real interest margin, thus the nominal interest margin must be even greater. Then, in order that the interest margin—which cannot be so high that credit should not be resorted to at all— should not only cover the banking costs but also secure a profit, the volume of credits must be sufficiently large. But the FED, in harmony with the intentions of the government, restricted precisely the credit granting possibilities of the banks and thus also slowed down, in the last resort, the growth of bank deposits. It is hardly surprising that they did not want to put up with this situation. They acquired loanable money capital in roundabout ways.

[19] Cash, sight deposits and other deposits, government securities—in their bulk probably treasury notes—open market securities, bonds of state and local organs.
[20] Let us remember that in 1951 the fight between the FED and the Treasury was still about ⅛ of a per cent.

They increasingly raised credits in the Euro-dollar market, although they had to pay on them 10-11 per cent interest in 1969, which also far exceeded the interest on bonds. It can be imagined how high an interest they charged those to whom they granted credit (it does not matter whether under the title of interest or other costs). They concluded buy-back agreements with corporations, meaning that formally it was the corporations that granted the credit from their own means, but so that the bank reserved the right to take over the role of creditor from the companies later. In order to be able to grant further credits they also raised credits from subsidiaries and affiliates.

Seeing this, the government machinery did not remain idle either, but this machinery is cumbersome. It took till late August until also the loans granted in the framework of buy-back agreements became included in the scope of credit restrictions related to bank reserves (and thus eliminated this loophole born out of necessity). Beginning with September similar restrictions were introduced in connection with Euro-credits, too. The banks, on the other hand, increased the sales of so-called commercial papers, and they, too, sold state and communal debentures, thereby further increasing the supply of long-term securities, depressing prices and thus raising the rate of interest on long-term securities.

In conclusion, for the time being we only mention that the outlined monetary policy raised a liquidity panic among large companies and the FED was forced to retreat and lift the monetary restrictions. Thus we can by no means state that the "monetary policy has become an instrument of general economic stabilization" and, in this sense, "a partner of fiscal policy".[21] Or, if it has become one, it has proved to be an unrealiable tool and a dangerous partner.

---

[21] This is how Stein characterized the favourable outcome of the fight between the FED and the Treasury.

CHAPTER THREE

FISCAL POLICY: ANOTHER INSTRUMENT OF HIGH-LEVEL ECONOMIC POLICY

3. 1 THE BEGINNING OF THE FISCAL REVOLUTION: ROOSEVELT AND HIS RELATIONSHIP TO KEYNESIANISM

We now pass to certain questions of principle of the fiscal policy considered as Keynesian. We start with a historical survey: we reach back right to Roosevelt, since it was in his time that the first germs of the "fiscal revolution" emerged. In this retrospect we shall devote particular attention to the question to what extent the actual fiscal policy was Keynesian.

We know that the Great Depression of 1929–1933 was aggravated by the efforts of governments at balanced budgets. The then ruling economic theory demanded such behaviour. In reality, of course, a lasting maintenance of budgetary equilibrium proved impossible. And as regards Roosevelt, he deliberately used the instrument of the budget deficit. He did so for a long time with "principled" reservations. Until 1938, Roosevelt was also of the opinion that at a time of crisis the preservation of trust was of the highest importance. By a possible loss of trust it was meant that in the case of a budget deficit capital could take flight in gold. People might run on the banks and drive them into bankruptcy. The price of government bonds might fall. But in the meantime these fears became at least partially transcended. The first danger was removed in March 1933 by the devaluation of the dollar, the cessation of its free convertibility, and first by the total prohibition and then the restriction on the export of gold. The government also took over the guarantee for bank deposits. Also the rate of interest was so low that the price of bonds could not sink low. But Roosevelt—and with him the majority of economists—were still afraid lest "irresponsible fiscal behaviour" might slow down the growth of private expenditure, mainly of private investment, thereby hindering the emergence from the depression.

At the time of his first presidency, in 1933, Roosevelt could not be Keynesian, if only for the fact that at that time even Keynes himself was at most close to becoming "Keynesian". Never in his life did Roosevelt accept Keynes' system, at most he adopted some of its elements. The American view, counting as progressive, on the causes of Great Depression around 1933 was that in the twenties a too small part of the national income fell to workers and farmers, and too much got into the hands of those who save too great a part of their income. As a consequence, so they believed, investment activity increased so much that consumption, i.e., the purchasing power, no longer allowed full utilization of capacities—and this is how the depression came about. (According to this reasoning, saving determines the size of investment, while in the Keynesian scope of ideas it is investment on which the size of saving depends.)

It was, among other things, this scope of ideas that led to Roosevelt's New Deal, implying the redistribution of national income somewhat in favour of working people. Mainly because of this and furthermore because of his intention to implement a kind of restricted national economic planning, Roosevelt got into a conflict with the representatives of big business who partly demanded to be left alone, and partly such favours which would promote investment. At any rate, it was not the disequilibrium of the budget which led to a sharpening of the conflicts between him and the directors of the conservative "public opinion".

Roosevelt never attained a balanced budget, although demand for it was in those times part of the basic dogma of American economic thinking. But he constantly maintained the *appearance* of striving for a balanced budget. Thus, e.g., in May 1933 he presented an expenditure program of $ 3.3 billion, but introduced new kinds of taxes at the same time. He estimated the expected returns from the latter at 220 million, and the income thus acquired was called upon to serve the purpose of paying the interests due in the existing government debt and some repayment. This proved sufficient for him to be seen as striving for a balanced budget. "He had shown how small an obstacle the budget-balancing ideology was to a pragmatic fiscal policy, if the policy was described in a way that met the formal requirements of the ideology and did not raise opposition on other grounds." (Stein, 1969, p. 47)

Roosevelt's practical fiscal policy was not one dictated by Keynesian theory, but a pragmatic one. He did not repeat the mistake committed in 1932 by Hoover who tried to balance the budget at the time of a depression, nor did he make efforts to make up for the loss of budgetary revenues caused by the depression itself through taxation. No such thing has ever been tried since. Since Roosevelt was seen as an advocate of a "sound budget", he already could make a proposal on a (relatively) lavish handling of the expenditure side of the budget. He did not increase budget expenditures with intention of compensating—according to the Keynesian recipe—the insufficiency of effective demand, creating thereby the conditions of upswing. He simply—and for obvious political reasons—wished to improve the situation of the immediate victims of the crisis with aid, public works, favours granted to farmers, and similar things—at the price of "deficit financing" of an extent then considered significant. But at the time of his first term this budgetary spending could not be significant. This was not made possible by the—according to our present concepts—low rate of tax revenues to the national product.

Under Roosevelt this was also gradually considerably changed. In certain respects the Revenue Act of 1935 was a milestone in this field. It raised the tax rate of high personal incomes and corporate profits (relative to incomes and to pre-tax profits) and the tax on inheritance. As regards the amounts, not much was gained by this measure: it resulted only in about a quarter of a billion dollars tax revenues in a year. But there was loud indignation in business circles and in the press influenced by them. It was the justification of the raising of taxes—implemented in a depression after the crisis—that was worthy of attention. According to it, the raising of the tax would not have a depressive effect since—it was said—it only affected the already high, thus presumably not dynamic incomes and wealth. In the eyes of the President, from the aspect of purchasing power it was the incomes of workers and farmers that were of particular value, from this aspect the incomes of entrepreneurs and capitalists were immaterial. In this case Roosevelt's efforts at reform asserted themselves: through the tax reform he wanted to get nearer to a society in which incomes would be less concentrated. This was the counterpart of the argumentation of Mellon, the Secretary of the Treasury under Hoover, according to whom a reduction of the taxes of poor people would not stimulate the economy as poor people had no choice in the question whether to employ their capital productively.

Yet another event happened in 1935 when Congress approved a one-time grant for veterans, and Roosevelt vetoed it. Also at that time, it was not the size of the amount, but Roosevelt's argumentation that was interesting. According to him, although the amount of the grant would have somewhat stimulated retail trade, it would not have improved the conditions for the development of the industries most afflicted by unemployment. The treasury bills issued for the financing of the grant would quickly return to the banks. The final justification of the act on the grant—said Roosevelt—according to which the spending of money was the most effective way of accelerating the revival, was so much mistaken that it was not worth wasting so many words on it. Congress, he emphasized, never voted in the course of the 1933 or 1934 budget outlays merely so that the spending of money should promote emergence from the depression. They always voted on the basis of a sounder principle: they wanted to prevent people from losing their homes and farms and industries from going bankrupt. They guaranteed the repayment of bank deposits and—what is most important—through public works employment was provided for those struggling with hunger.

3.2 ROOSEVELT'S TURN IN 1938. THE SECOND WORLD WAR: THE EMPLOYMENT ACT

It was only around 1938 that Roosevelt accepted the idea that budget expenses, simply as outlays, have a positive role in emerging from a crisis. Meanwhile, around 1936, output already attained the 1929 level. Prices also started to rise, although they approached the 1929 level only slowly. Also a speculative increase of inventories started. All that was considered, in agreement with Roosevelt, as having already emerged from the crisis, although unemployment still remained very high, around 17 per cent. By 1937 the crisis was there again,[22] and—as a rare exception—not a "Republican", but a "Democratic" one. Even in February 1938 Roosevelt left out of consideration the proposal of the then already perfectly "Keynesian" Keynes—communicated in a private letter—that the outlays of the budget should be increased, mainly in order to finance public works, and that a more conciliatory behaviour should be displayed towards business circles in order to stimulate private investment. (The Revenue Act of 1935, which did not treat business circles kindly at all, did not reflect Keynes' political ideas.) However, by the end of March 1938 shares began to fall, ominously recalling 1929. It was at the same time that Roosevelt received the memorandum of a few people he trusted.

According to the memorandum, the whole past economic development of America had been made possible by the fact that the nation alienated certain of its properties,

[22] Kalecki wrote about this in 1943 that the collapse or the upswing occurred in the second half of 1937 because of the steep fall in the budget deficit. (Kalecki, 1971, p. 145)

34

thereby creating purchasing power for the growing volume of products. First gold was mined and made into coins. Then state lands were given to the railways and settlers: these raised loans from the banks in order to purchase land and this entailed the creation of money. Then companies were given monopolistic rights for certain activities. Also the companies raised loans on their future profits and this, too, entailed the creation of money and an increase in purchasing power. And the memorandum explained that in the given year the creation of a national income of 88 bn dollars would require as much labour that all those seeking employment should find a job, although the actual national income was only $56 bn. If the amount spent on investment or consumption was returned annually two or three times, then an annual 7 to 10 bn dollars of investment or consumption outlays would be needed to secure an acceptable level of employment—whether the additional spending came from private persons or from the budget. But the contribution of the private sector could reach 4 bn at most. Thus the state could choose between two things. It either tries to promote private production in the hope that it creates purchasing power or promotes consumption, thus bringing about more production.

In the given situation this argumentation took effect: the president decided to increase budget expenditures. In June 1938 budget expenditures were raised and so was the sum of loans payable from budget funds. The economic situation soon began to improve. It is highly questionable what the role of the more generous budget was in that—but public opinion began to become firmly convinced that fiscal policy should be accorded a very important role.

Even in 1939 there were 10 million unemployed in the United States. It became ever clearer that private investment would be insufficient to raise the economy to the level of full employment and to keep it there. But the economic policy makers could not bring themselves to the decision to balance the gap in private investment with a lasting budget deficit, nor to resort to the measure proposed by the conservatives in order to stimulate investment directly. But soon World War II came. It created full employment, warded off the immediate danger of secular stagnation, and brought about the most diversified forms of direct cooperations in economic policy between the government machinery and monopoly capital. It bequeathed large government debt and hugely increased both sides of the budget. Without these developments and their lessons the Employment Act, which made it a government task to secure a high level of employment, would have hardly been accepted.

The Roosevelt era, at the beginning of which the germs of the fiscal revolution just began to appear, reached deep into World War II. The post-war USA very much differed from the pre-war one. We continue our story with an important event following the end of the war.

Soon after the war a "Full Employment Bill" was advanced which would have obliged the federal government to secure full employment. From the text of the law approved in 1946 the term "full employment" was omitted.

The law is simply called the Employment Act and it only says that by resorting to fiscal policy the government has to aim at a high level of employment, but this must not be its only aim and fiscal policy must not be the only instrument serving to secure a high level of employment. The same Act set up and institutionalized the Council of Economic Advisers. The members of this Council are, naturally, always economists.

Through the vicissitudes of Roosevelt's economic policy we wanted to make palpable how little it was influenced by Keynesian theory, and much more in the wake of the pragmatic measures forced by the inescapable necessities of the economy that the instruments and practice of the fiscal (and monetary) revolution were created in the USA in the early years, frequently identified, in a simplified manner, with the introduction of the Keynesian revolution. It would take us very far from our proper objective if we subjected the economic ideology and activity of the two presidents following Roosevelt to a detailed examination. We continue our story with the Kennedy era because by that time Keynesian theory had won over most of the leading American economists. It was the economists on the Council of Economic Advisers operating under his presidency (Heller, Tobin and others) who developed the terms of the Keynesian economic policy held as a banner. Such was

1. the "gap". By this they meant the difference between the actual GNP and the one that would result in case of full employment. By the time Kennedy was elected the theorem that in the case of a recession powerful budgetary actions were necessary was commonly held. But by 1961 the recession had ended and still the Kennedy administration contemplated a tax reduction though it would have impaired the balance of the budget. The "gap" approach turned against the view that powerful budgetary stimulation was necessary only in the case of a recession. It should not only be watched, they said, whether the GNP was growing or decreasing, nor would the matter be decided in itself by the fact that it happened to be greater than ever. The essential question was by how much was the actual GNP lagging behind the one possible in principle in the case of a full exploitation of resources, since this was the standard for the losses that can and should be avoided. The number of people seeking employment was growing for simple demographic reasons and in the meantime labour productivity was also growing. If the growth of unemployment was to be avoided, output must grow faster than employment. (It will hardly escape the attention of the reader that this was one of the main concerns also around the late seventies. But by then the danger of a significant and accelerating inflation came to the fore in the official American economic policy relative to the elimination of unemployment as an important objective). But the exact size of the gap remained unclear throughout because the standard was missing that would have given the size of the potential GNP. What percentage could the practically attainable smallest unemployment be? At that time, for lack of a better measure, it was assumed that it might be about 4 per cent, and this was used, although this figure is debatable. (Not to mention that there is no unchangeable ratio between the population of working age and those employed or seeking employment.) Thus computed, the gap in 1961 amounted to 10 per cent of the GNP.

The next concept they wanted public opinion to accept was

2. the "Full Employment Balance", the budget balance in the case of the assumed "full" employment. The prophets of "secular stagnation"—whose number dwindled by the sixties—originally argued that warding off menacing lasting stagnation and high unemployment demanded permanent deficit financing. But, according to the anti-Keynesians—then the conservative wing of economists—if stagnation became lasting

and full employment could not be secured, then there was some specific trouble with the economy and this must not be covered up with the artificial means of fiscal stimulation, but had to be fixed. Lasting deficit financing, involving a lasting and accumulating government debt was to be discarded because it was a medicine that would bring about an intolerable situation.

It was intended to answer this argumentation by the notion of the Full Employment Balance, or more specifically, with that of the "Full Employment Surplus". By this the surplus of budget revenues over the existing ones in the case of full employment—with unchanged programs—was meant. This concept relied on the realization that the American budget is flexible in a certain sense. Namely, on the side of revenues it did not, and does not, prescribe the upper limit of revenues, but the percentual size of the various kind of taxes related to the assessed tax bases. (Thus, e. g., what percentage of incomes the government takes in taxes in the case of the different income brackets, or the percentage of the sales tax in the price of certain products.) Clearly, the size of the tax revenues thus depends on the size of the GNP. But if the government program remains unchanged, the situation is the same on the expenditure side of the budget. If, e. g., the legislature voted the amount of unemployment aid per capita, the sum of the government unemployment benefits actually paid out will depend on the actual size of unemployment.

The idea that the budget is flexible in the said sense can also be formulated from the aspect of deeper interrelations by stating that certain automatic stabilizers are built into the system of the US budget which shift the balance towards deficit in the case of poor business and towards a surplus in the case of good bussiness, while, looking at it from the side of the enterprises and the population, they increase spendable incomes if business is slack and reduce them in an upswing (relative to the situation if these stabilizers did not exist).

Now, the approach of the Full Employment Surplus served as an ace around 1961 in the hands of those who in the interest of faster growth wanted an expansive fiscal policy, since in those times surplus was great. The full employment budget would have been balanced according to the computations even if the programs on the expenditure side of the budget had been essentially expanded or if taxes had been reduced. The emphasis on the concept served to make palpable that acceptance of the Keynesians' program does not necessarily entail a lasting and cumulating budget deficit.

To this scope of ideas a logically unprovable Keynesian prejudice was also attached, namely, that the right recipe was to keep the Full Employment Surplus low or even at zero, that is—and as much was sufficient—the system of budget revenues and expenditures had to be modified in such a manner that, until there was no full employment, the gap was not filled, the annual budget should show a deficit, since only such budget could be of sufficiently incentive power. And it must be sufficiently stimulating, else investment will lag behind the intended saving. Effective demand would not lag behind supply only with a low employment, thus the gap would persist and unemployment would be high, even increasing. This is why a deficit is needed. Logically it cannot be proven that in the case of a budget surplus capitalism cannot at all attain a state of full employment or, conversely, if in the case of non-full employment there would be a Full Employment Deficit instead of a Full Employment

Surplus, it would then attain the desired state.[23] Otherwise, this prejudice—or, if you like, superstition, was not shared by sound Keynesians without reservations, either. The Council of Economic Advisers itself pointed out that if private investment demand was also very brisk, then full employment could be attained even with a very large budget surplus. True, but in 1961 investment demand was not sufficiently brisk and it was under such conditions that the conclusion was drawn that the existing budget had a too strong braking effect. At the same time, the theoreticians of the Full Emloyment Balance lived with the illusion that a stimulating budget would surely bring about the desired result. But the stimulating effect of the budget exercises its effect through increasing demand in relative terms, and the increase in demand stimulates not only an increase in supply but—at least as much—the raising of prices, competing with the former. This fact, which became quite palpable precisely in the seventies, significantly reduced also the effectiveness of the built-in stabilizers. But in the early sixties the Keynesians called attention to quite a different limit to the effectiveness of the system of built-in stabilizers. To this was related the

3. notion of "Fiscal Drag" and its counterpart, the "Fiscal Dividend". The first indicated the tendency whereby with the growth of the economy the budget automatically exerted a restrictive effect. It follows, namely, from the structure of taxation that budget revenues continually increase when the economy is approaching the state of full employment: this holds back the growth of private demand and becomes a shackle on the realization of full employment. The advocates of big business and their economists acknowledged as much that under the conditions of the slow growth of the early sixties the insufficiency of private investment constituted the most essential lag, but they believed that this lag was mainly attributable to the large-scale taxation of profit derived from investment. The Kennedy people—as against the erstwhile stand of Roosevelt—did not discard this view. In 1961 they were inclined to ease the tax burden of profit, but so that taxes not directly burdening profit should be increased. And the Keynesian economists of the Kennedy administration mostly did not argue in the positive way that the lag in the economy had to be fought with the aid of the budget, but in the negative one that the shackle had to be removed which put a brake on the economy in the form of rising taxes. The computations, which showed that in those years the Full Employment Surplus was high, served as a proof that the

[23] The computation of the Full Employment Budget relies on hypotheses. Its computed amount depends not only on the size of the "full employment" assumed, but, so it seems, also on the fact when and by whom this computation is performed. The Full Employment Balance *for 1972* was according to the annual Economic Reports as follows:

Year	bn dollars
1974	− 7.6
1975	− 10.3
1976	− 8.4
1977	− 21.5
1978	− 11.8

The 1974-1977 Reports were submitted under the presidencies of the Republicans Nixon and Ford, the 1978 one under the Democrat Carter. *Sapienti sat.*

given structure of the budget indeed put shackles on development at an adequate rate and, in the course of growth, it would become an ever greater plague if not balanced by a "Fiscal Dividend" of adequate size. This involves the requirement that, if the economy is growing, either budget expenditures ought to be increased, or revenues decreased.

3.4 DIFFICULTIES OF THE ACTIVE—"DISCRETIONARY"—FISCAL POLICY

In the following we wish to illustrate the contradictions between theory and the realized economic policy; more exactly, how cumbersome was the adjustment of the U.S. fiscal policy to some given state of the economy.

Following the enactment of the Employment Act, at the time of Truman's presidency, though there were some Keynesians among his economic advisers, the economic policy could not be called Keynesian. The economic policy of the Eisenhower administration which followed was certainly not Keynesian. We already emphasized that during the Democratic administration of Kennedy his advisers urged a Keynesian economic policy. But Kennedy was no economist. He, too, had to be instructed and educated so as to accept Keynesian theory in principle. Kennedy was a politician and knew that even the most perfect rule in principle cannot be implemented if not supported by those possessing economic and political power. He knew that politics is the science of recognizing the useful steps that can be actually implemented at a given moment. And from this follows the third "but": it is not simply the president who makes economic policy, but it is realized through compromises dictated by the power relationships. Therefore, even an orthodox Keynesian president may be forced at times to propose and implement utterly anti-Keynesian measures. But Kennedy was not an orthodox Keynesian. At any rate, his possibilities were greater than those of Roosevelt. In 1929 the total of the budget had moved around 2 per cent of the GNP, while at the time when Kennedy was elected it was already around 20 per cent. It is mainly not the about 1000 per cent relative increase that indicates the "revolutionary" change in the role of the budget. In itself, it only shows that through the variations of about 2 per cent of the GNP a considerable macroeconomic impact can hardly be released, while 20 per cent already secures multiple possibilities. The substance of the fiscal revolution that actually took place could be illustrated perhaps with the behaviour of the administrations active at two different dates. Unemployment was high in both 1931 and 1962, and so was the budget deficit. Hoover proposed raising taxes in 1931, while in 1962 Kennedy favoured a reduction. But it is precisely this matter of tax reduction that is suited to illustrate how difficult the road is leading to the implementation of the right things needed doing.

"On John F. Kennedy's Inauguration Day in January, 1961, the stage was set for the act which, more than any other, came to symbolize the fiscal revolution. The play had been written, a receptive or at least permissive audience was in its seats, the actors in the wings." (Stein, 1969, p. 372.) The time had come for a tax cut.

It was almost three and a half years since unemployment had been around the 4 per cent frequently mentioned as barely acceptable. On the day of the inauguration it approached 7 per cent. The events of the recent past allowed one to surmise that even the possible next upswing would not result in a statisfactory employment level. Tax rates were so high relative to expenses that a great budget surplus would have resulted in the case of full employment. This would have allowed the reduction of taxes or the raising of expenditures without having to reckon with a full employment deficit instead of a full employment surplus. And the inflationary impact of a tax reduction is weaker than the price raising impact of greater expenditure.

In the course of the 1960 presidential election campaign the Democratic Party proposed a combination of an adjusting monetary policy and a budget surplus for easing unemployment. But the budget deficit was high and the low rate of interest accompanying a permissive monetary policy would have only worsened it and the outflow of capital was menacing. Therefore, in the given situation fiscal policy ought to have been steady and firm.

The combination of three circumstances, i.e., high unemployment, a big employment surplus, a balance of payments deficit, all called for a tax reduction.

Kennedy and his advisers ought to have been the protagonists in the play entitled tax reduction. Kennedy is usually mentioned as the first "modern economist" among the American presidents. But this is true at most for the Kennedy of 1963. He was neither a convinced Keynesian, nor a conservative: in 1961 or in 1962 he followed the traditional line on the question of budget balance. And as regards his advisers, they cared less for the danger of inflation than the Eisenhower people and strongly believed that they could forecast exactly the fluctuations of the economy. But they also believed that, by relying on their forecasts, they could continually apply the instruments of fiscal and monetary policies in such manner that the economy would remain stable—apart from minor fluctuations. But in 1961 even the convinced Keynesians—e.g., Galbraith, Heller, Samuelson, and Tobin—did not have a plan or proposal for a major and lasting tax reduction. The idea matured in them only a year and a half later, under the impression of the events and failures of that period.

But the actual initiative is the task of the president and his administration, not of the advisers. In spite of the existing level of unemployment, the government did not consider the state of the economy in 1961 or 1962 grave enough to endanger its long-term objectives and get perhaps involved in greater conflict with Congress. True, as a consequence of the unsatisfactory development of the previous 4 or 5 years, the "gap" amounted to about 50 bn dollars. It followed that even a possible spontaneous upswing would not lead to satisfactory employment and thus further incentives would be needed. In principle, the government knew this but it was waiting for things to improve by themselves. In early February the president promised that, if it proved necessary, after 75 days he would propose new measures in the interest of an upswing. There was pressure also within the government on the part of the liberal members of Congress and the trade unions that the government should initiate massive public works and reduce taxes—at least temporarily. But then already a certain upswing could be felt. And the president was reasoning along the line that the upswing would prove lasting by itself and Congress would not vote the necessary measures even if they were needed for purely economic reasons. But politics intervened. The level of unemployment persisting at the time of the inauguration of Kennedy was the unemployment of the Republican Eisenhower, while the slight fall in spring was attributed to Kennedy—and Kennedy rested content with that much. A tax reduction would have impaired the chances of his long-term ideas. It was, namely, not the liquidation of unemployment that took first place in his priorities. True to the Democratic traditions, he attributed great importance to the raising of military expenditure and foreign "aid". Furthermore—let us remember this was the time of the "sputnik-shock"—government aid to education had to be increased, and to this were added the costly demands of stopping the obsolescence of towns, the development of backward regions, the retraining of workers and care for the aged.

Also the theoretical views he held at that time dictated caution to Kennedy. According to these views a budget surplus allows a loose monetary policy without also invoking inflation; this would keep rates of interest low and thus stimulate investment—which was highly important. And if in the following budget outlays had to be increased and yet the budget had to show a surplus, then a tax reduction was out of the question. That is, a transitory reduction of tax rates still could have been implemented, but there was no guarantee that a measure intended to be temporary would not become final because of the behaviour of Congress.

What was left was to increase expenditure. But this, too, had conservative opponents in Congress, the Democratic Party and in business circles. They did not like the government support of education, "socialism" in the field of the health service, nor the interference of the federal government in state and local affairs. They would have preferred some tax reduction instead.

True, the period lasted from 1961 to mid-1962 during which the president was an industrious disciple of his advisers who formulated the concepts (and slogans) of the "gap", "full employment surplus", "fiscal drag" and "fiscal dividend". But, as already mentioned, the economy entered the road to an upswing, although a sufficiently high level of employment did not develop. (By the way, there were people already at that time who argued that unemployment could not be eliminated with the aid of stimuli because it was structural, that is, the skills of the unemployed were inadequate, they were too young etc.) Under such conditions, the initial determination of the advisers became increasingly uncertain.

Yet a certain turn did come. At a press conference in late February 1962 Kennedy still declared that there was no chance of a tax cut in 1963. But on June 7 of the same year he promised a net tax reduction for 1963 or even earlier. The level of unemployment then moved around 5.5 per cent, but, although at a slow rate, the GNP also continued to grow, and yet the "gap" was still widening. But the prices of shares were falling since March and tumbled on May 28. Under its impact the advisers were already of the opinion that the risk of a "Kennedy recession" had to be taken seriously. Kennedy was prompted to make this promise by the fact that the slowdown in economic growth followed a dragging development over the preceding five years and that the temporary upswing had stopped far short of full employment. This was a belated answer to a chronic state made when trust in a spontaneous healing of the disease was already vanishing.

But ... and again a but.

What size should the tax reduction be? When Kennedy made his promise they thought about 3 bn. But figures cannot be evaded. The maximum tax rate on personal income was 91 per cent. It should have been reduced at least to 70 per cent to have a palpable "encouraging impact" on business circles. Even if it had been reduced to 50 per cent it would only have meant a tax revenue loss of about 500 mn. But such a

41

reduction was inconceivable politically, if taxes on middle and mainly lower income brackets were not reduced at the same time and at least to the same extent. However, if tax rates on the lowest income brackets had been reduced even by a single per cent, it alone would have deprived the budget of 1.2 bn dollars. Furthermore, the rate of the corporate profit tax was 52 per cent. If this had been reduced to, say, 48 per cent, it would have cost the budget 2 bn dollars. Taken altogether, the full amount of tax reduction could have hardly remained below 10 billion dollars annually.

As a matter of fact, the loss of budget revenues could have been kept around 3 bn if the tax reduction had been counterbalanced by reforms increasing revenues by closing certain loopholes.

That was what the Treasury had in mind. However, loopholes are not there by chance in the tax laws. Someone demanded them and Congress had approved them. How could Congress be expected to vote for their elimination? No, a "reform" coupled with a partial increase of taxes was out of the question. But would Congress approve a tax reduction when, in spite of a considerable full employment surplus, the budget of the given year showed a deficit? The remnants of the fetish of a balanced budget were still alive among the members of Congress. Of course, the members of Congress are not knights of the Holy Grail, nor prisoners of their own deep internal convictions. They heed the behaviour of big business. In a naive way, Stein put it as follows: ". . . there were few congressmen who would believe that the tax cut was morally, economically, and politically unsound if respectable leaders of business and finance said it was not." (Stein, 1969, p. 415) The president himself began to ponder seriously the idea of tax reduction with fuller conviction only when in December 1962 the mostly Republican big capitalists of the Economic Club of New York received his ideas favourably.

The Treasury, the Council of Economic Advisers and the Office of the Budget thus began to work seriously on the proposal to be submitted to Congress in January 1963. But it was not clear how extensive the reform should be and what its elements would be. The scheduling of its introduction was also debated.

We shall not go into more details. In January 1963 the stage was set. The President submitted his proposal to Congress in January 1963. At the end of the same year the full employment surplus was as great as when he took office. On November 22 Kennedy was assassinated. In an atmosphere in which serious opposition to the propositions of the former President would have amounted to indecency, Congress voted for it and the tax reform was signed into law by Kennedy's successor, Johnson, on February 26, 1964. It took "only" three years[24].

[24] For the consequences and analysis of the tax reform in the Hungarian literature, see F. Molnár, 1965.

CHAPTER FOUR

BOURGEOIS CRITIQUES OF THE EFFECTIVENESS OF FISCAL POLICY

4.1 ARTHUR M. OKUN ON THE DIFFICULTIES
OF ECONOMIC POLICY, NEARING FULL EMPLOYMENT

In his book, completed in 1973, R. A. Gordon wrote the following in the second last paragraph of his book: 'In the middle and late 1960s, a question frequently asked was: Is the business cycle obsolete? One does not hear the question asked any more. The business cycle is still with us, particularly in the United States....'' (Gordon, 1974, p. 210) But this book was written at the time of the last great upheaval and, already in its title, it dealt with the instability of the economy.

But Arthur M. Okun, the former chairman of the Council of Economic Advisers, wrote his book *The Political Economy of Prosperity* in 1969. He proudly wrote in November 1969 that the American "nation is in its one hundred-and-fifth month of unparalleled, unprecedented, and uninterrupted economic expansion". (Okun, 1970, p. 31) And then, under the subtitle "Obsolescence of the business cycle pattern", he wrote the following: "Today few research economists regard the business cycle as a particularly useful organizing framework for the overall analysis of business activity and few teachers see 'business cycles' as an appropriate title for a course to be offered to their students... President Johnson was making in 1965 a controversial statement when he said: 'I do not believe recessions are inevitable.' That statement is no longer controversial. Recessions are now generally considered to be fundamentally preventable, like airplane crashes) and unlike hurricanes."

And yet, he went on to say: "But we have not banished air crashes from the land and it is not clear that we have the wisdom or the ability to eliminate recessions." *(Op. cit.,* p. 33) Then he went into the details of the difficulties. He related that in the first half of the sixties, between 1960 and 1965, the American economy managed to exploit its productive capacities. At the time of the upswing the GNP increased by about 5.5 per cent p.a. Following that, an increase faster than 4 per cent already had to increase tensions—but the reduction from 5.5 to 4 per cent also ought to have entailed unfavourable consequences. "...Once full utilization was attained, the range of tolerance for policy error would have to shrink. Because there had been little risk of excessive demand in the early sixties, and growth performance between 5 and 6 per cent could be viewed as qualitatively successfull: it would be fast enough to reduce unemployment and not so rapid as to jeopardize essential price stability. Once the economy is close to target, however, there are necessarily dangers from both inadequate and excessive demand. In the earlier period economists knew what to prescribe, and the medicine worked once the patient was persuaded to take it. But in a healthy, prosperous economy, there was no sure tonic. Like physicians, we can cure pneumonia and look great, but we can't keep our patient from catching cold." (*Op. cit.,* p.55)

In a world where assets are fully utilized "the problem of keeping the economy close to a chosen course is compounded by the uncertainties in choosing the course. The ideal rate of utilization is necessarily a difficult compromise between the objective of maximum production and employment, on the one hand, and the objective of price stability, on the other. We have little experience historically in confronting that hard choice because the nation has so rarely remained on a reasonably satisfactory growth path. Except during wartime inflations, we have not been at full employment long enough to test, under these circumstances, the supply capabilities of the economy, its price-cost performance, or public attitudes towards price increases of various rates." (*Op. cit.,* pp. 60–61)

And then Okun quotes an article by G. Ackley: "It is easy to prescribe expansionary policies in a period of slack. Managing high-level prosperity is vastly more difficult business and requires vastly superior knowledge. The prestige that our profession has built up in the Government and around the country in recent years could suffer if economists give incorrect policy advice based on inadequate knowledge. We need to improve that knowledge." (Ackley, 1966, p. 176)

4.2 R. A. GORDON ON THE PROBLEMATIC NATURE OF DISCRETIONARY FISCAL POLICY AND MONETARY POLICY AND ON THE NECESSITY OF EMPLOYING "NON-TRADITIONAL INSTRUMENTS"

In the second half of the sixties, in connection with the escalation of the Vietnam War pathogenic germs already proliferated in the American economy and in 1967 they already caused a cold, a so-called mini-recession. The 1969–1970 recession may also be considered as a mild cold. But what followed in 1974–1975 was much more than that, at least an inflammation of the lungs, with lasting remainders.

The experiences of the seventies profoundly shook the confidence of the Keynesian economic policy makers. Under such conditions Milton Friedman and his associates could challenge, with no small success, one of the two basic pillars of the conventional armory of capitalist economic policy—of monetary and fiscal policy—namely the fiscal policy. They could even launch a frontal attack. But it can hardly be doubted that a capitalist economy cannot function without resorting to the instruments of fiscal policy. In the last resort the theoretical attacks of those seeking the dictatorship of monetary policy on the (in their view only troublesome, thus unambigously harmful) fiscal instruments, cannot break through. As a matter of fact—and this could already be seen in the example of the economic policy of Roosevelt—the unavoidable necessity sooner or later forces its acceptance even without a coherent theory, even in spite of every theory. Thus, the shaking of the self-assurance of the actual policy makers can only be partial, since also the internal critique of their own theories is also partial at most. It goes only as far as to recognize that the medicaments deduced from the original Keynesian theory are not effective for every illness. Thus they think it is timely

44

to search for new cures. In other terms, and perhaps more accurately formulated: they do not doubt the effectiveness of old medicaments, but it had become evident that the panaceas also have very uncomfortable side effects.

But let us now hear the already quoted Professor R. A. Gordon, who was by no means a Leftist, yet was moderately sceptical. First let us speak about what we discussed a few pages earlier at length the difficulties of the application of discretionary[25] fiscal policy which is of an institutional type but of political origin. "The accelerating inflation after 1965 pointed up some of the weaknesses in fiscal policy, at least as it was being practised in the American setting. Under the American Constitution, only Congress can change taxes. Inevitably, therefore, there are delays before tax rates can be altered, either upward or downward. The delay in obtaining the tax increase in 1968 is a good example. Fiscal restraint would almost certainly have been more effective if the surcharge had gone into effect in mid-1966 instead of mid-1968." (Gordon, 1974, p. 204) The Council of Economic Advisers asked in 1973 "whether the future conduct of fiscal policy could be improved if Congress were to develop expeditious procedures for temporary, limited changes in the level of the particular taxes." (*Op. cit.*, p. 205) But, added Gordon, "it remained to be seen whether Congress would be any more sympathetic to this suggestion than to similar ones made by Presidents Kennedy and Johnson." (*Ibid.*) Well, particularly after the experiences with Nixon, this was hardly likely.

It is also an important lesson that "fiscal policy must have the strong support of monetary policy. . . . Along with the delay in getting the tax increase after 1965, the worst blunder of American stabilization policy in the sixties occurred when the Federal Reserve took its foot off the brakes in the second half of 1968 after the surcharge went into effect. In 1969 a combination of restrictive fiscal and monetary policies brought the boom to an end, although it did not succeed in reducing inflation to an acceptable rate." (*Op. cit.*, p. 204)

The next lesson is that the 1968 surcharge belonged to the category of discretionary fiscal policy. It did not much restrain effective demand. "The rationale underlying the use of discretionary fiscal policy rests in the existence of stable spending functions for the different types of consumption and investment in a Keynesian type of economic model. In particular, for fiscal policy to be effective there needs to be a stable predictable response of consumer spending to a change in disposable income in the short run. The behaviour of both consumer spending (particularly for automobiles) and business investment in 1968 surprised the experts both in and out of government." (*Op. cit.*, pp. 204-205)

And, as regards monetary policy: "In 1970 and the first half of 1971 the Nixon administration relied heavily on monetary policy to speed recovery. It was then that the growing influence of the monetarists experienced something of a setback. Extremely tight credit and a virtual halt in the money supply did not noticeably retard the rise in prices in 1969. Monetary ease in 1970-1971 did not promptly bring about

[25] This is the American term for what in Hungary is called active fiscal policy. By this the changes in the regulations valid for revenues and expenditure are meant.

45

rapid economic recovery. If expansionary monetary policy was effective, it seemed to be so only with a distressingly long lag."(*Op. cit.*, pp. 206)

In the case of monetary policy, one can do something with a much shorter lag than in the case of fiscal policy. "Once the need for action is recognized, very prompt action can follow in the form of open-market operations or changes in the discount rate or in reserve requirements. . . . First of all, . . . open-market purchases or sales or changes in the discount rate do not immediately and in a perfectly predictable way affect the supply of money. The first effects are on interest rates and bank reserves."(*Op. cit.*, p. 206) And the question still remains unanswered "through what channels and with what lags do changes in the money supply affect spending, prices and output?" (*Op. cit.*, p. 207)

It is understandable that Gordon raised the question why one should resort only to the conventional instruments of monetary and fiscal policy in order to implement macroeconomic goals. "The argument for doing so is that this involves the minimum interference with 'the free play of market forces'. But is that always and necessarily an advantage, particularly in a world of highly imperfect competition in both commodity and labour markets? We have chosen to interfere with the free play of market forces in a wide range of macroeconomic areas—agriculture, the environment, minimum-wage laws, industrial safety, social security, education, medical care, and so on. Why not in the field of macroeconomic policy if doing so will bring us closer to our policy targets?"(*Op. cit.*, pp. 207-208.)

But, first of all, it is not clear or perhaps only too clear why Gordon thinks, from among the instruments unusual in capitalism, of the macroeconomic, thus the merely indirect ones, e. g., of a continuous incomes policy that can be eased or tightened as conditions seem to warrant. (*Op. cit.*, p. 208) Obviously, for a high-level control of a national economy, more or less eliminating fluctuations, merely indirect instruments are insufficient. For this a real planned economy would be necessary and a planned economy cannot rest content with only macroeconomic instruments. They are clearly insufficient in a society where the economic units are motivated in the last resort by the profit drive and where from among these units it is the huge national and supranational enterprises that are really important. But it is indeed this "adressed" influencing that a capitalist economy of the American type aims at most when it is in really great trouble, that is, when a smooth and steady capitalist development is indeed out of the question. (See, e.g., the wrangling in 1979 about the surtax on the oil monopolies.)

4.3 EPILOGUE

What can we add to this?

The dream of a smoothly developing capitalism, free of recessions, has collapsed. What remained was the double target of possibly high employment and an acceptably stable development of prices, aggravated by the constraint of the balance-of-payments problem. An expansive fiscal policy coupled with an adjusting monetary policy is sure to increase nominal demand and thus directly raises prices, while its stimulating impact on production is uncertain and mainly indirect. It is highly uncertain to what extent a restrictive monetary and fiscal policy can reduce inflation, as prices are nowadays rigid downward and public opinion expects inflation but—at most with some time lag—it certainly restricts production and employment. The two aspects of the double target are in contradiction: there is nothing to prove that there is today a zone—a narrow one in the best case—proceeding along which the two targets could be on the whole simultaneously and lastingly achieved. It is even less likely that economic policy could keep to this zone—if it exists. In all probability, inflation today is an inescapable concomitant of the capitalist economy. One can learn to live with inflation, but one can hardly live with it without grave problems.

The other aspect of the matter is that though the combined monetary and fiscal measures can increase nominal demand, to some extent they also stimulate real demand, yet they can hardly have a direct impact on private investment. Private investment is increasingly decidedly governed by long-term expectations and these are not derived from the monetary market situation. But under conditions of inflation expectations are particularly uncertain. Yet the capitalist economy is motivated, in the last resort, by profit even today and, in the long run, private investment is a decisive component of profit. But not only that and not only as much. Net investment increases private capital, but it does not increase the number of jobs to the same extent, although the number of those seeking jobs also increases. Chronic unemployment threatens together with chronic inflation. In principle, nominal demand could be increased to an extent that, through the accelerator-effect, investment should also automatically accelerate, but this would increase inflation so much, thus they dare not risk it. The fate of present-day capitalism is not high employment without inflation, but high unemployment coupled with inflation. The situation will be at times easier, at times graver, but it seems that the dilemma cannot be circumvented under contemporary capitalist conditions.

PART TWO

ANALYSIS OF THE INTERRELATIONS BETWEEN THE PRICE LEVEL AND THE EFFECTIVE CONSUMER AND GOVERNMENT DEMAND

CHAPTER FIVE

ON THE INTERPRETATION OF THE p_c FORMULA AND ITS VARIANTS AS WELL AS THE CONCLUSIONS THEY LEAD TO

5.1 THE ORIGINAL FORM OF THE p_c FORMULA AND THE ONE USED IN THE PRESENT WORK

The formula p_c, already well known in Hungary, originally served to explain how modern money divorced from gold can fulfill of the two aspects of value-measuring function—the measurement of relative values and the level of value—the latter one. Put more simply, the question to be answered was how the general price level develops, if a money without intrinsic value, capable of inflation, functions as money. The answer provided by the formula p_c is in fact only a partial one, it concerns the price level of consumer goods. As regards the price level of the means of production, what is clear is that the latter has to adjust on the whole to the price level of consumer goods.

The formula yields the average price of a unit volume of wage goods in the given period. In the modified form used in this book, it states a mere tautology: it is nothing but a fraction whose numerator represents the sum of money spent by wage earners on consumption in a given year, and the denominator represents the volume of consumer goods bought for this money. Of course, the quotient of the sum of money spent on this consumption and of the volume of goods bought for it yields the price of a unit of consumer goods bought by wage earners, while the absolute size of this price depends on what we consider as the consumer good of unit volume.[1]

From what has been said it is not clear why consumer articles should have a distinguished role relative to other commodities—thus particularly to capital goods—since such tautological truth can be also stated for the totality of commodities.

It is true that the fraction with the sum of money spent in some given period on goods and services as its numerator and with the volume of these goods and services as its denominator is identical with the price of an average unit of goods and services. But the price trend of the articles for personal consumption has two essential features distinguishing it from the trend in the price level of other—above all capital—goods. The original form of the formula p_c, simpler than the one used here, with which its author wished to show not a tautologically valid truth, asserting itself in every moment, but a regularity which is deeper, hiding behind the infinite variety of phenomena and

---

[1] The original form of the formula p_c was first reviewed in the Contributions... (Erdős, P., 1971., p. 145) in the special form in which a unit volume of consumer goods means the product of a man-hour. But on pp. 339—40 of the same work it is the quantity of consumer goods bought for a dollar at the 1929 price level that figures as unit volume.

asserting itself in the average of some shorter or longer period, relies precisely on these two particular features. The first feature is that the large majority of articles for personal consumption is composed of wage goods—i.e., goods and services purchased by those living on wages and salaries. A very large majority of wage goods is bought from current wages and salaries. We do not commit a major error if we assume that, at a given moment, the sum of money spent by workers on consumption depends on a single variable, and not on the development of the price level, but on the sum of nominal wages received in a given period (though this nominal wage sum is also a function of other variables, thus mostly also of the price level). As against that, capital goods are only bought by capitalists and the sum of money spent on these is a function of the volume of commodities to be bought and of the price level.

If the price level of consumer articles is higher, workers can buy with their given nominal wages only a smaller volume of consumer articles. If, however, the price level of capital goods rises, this does not force the capitalist class to reduce the volume of capital goods intended to be bought since, by the additional amount spent by capitalists on these goods the money receipts of the capitalist class will also grow.

The second distinguishing feature is that the articles serving personal consumption include, in addition to the totality of wage goods, also the totality of goods and services consumed by the capitalists. And about the latter we may state not only what we said about capital goods, namely, that a rise in their price level does not force the capitalists to reduce the volume of their consumption. (Conversely: nor does it follow from a fall in this price level that the consumption by capitalists will grow, since capitalists buy consumer goods from each other, and if some capitalist pays a lower price, the sales receipt of another capitalist will be smaller.) But, while the volume of capital goods actually bought strongly fluctuates over time, the volume of the capitalists' consumption is rigid. It does grow with the growth of GNP, but its annual fluctuation is negligible.

As mentioned, the simplest, thus simplified version of the p_c formula relies on the accounting for these properties. It was in this form that the formula became known in Hungary. The numerator of the simple formula comprises the nominal sum of wages of workers. Its denominator does not comprise the commodities purchased, but the difference between the volume of consumer articles produced in a year and the volume of the personal consumption of capitalists. (Workers on the whole spend their wages on consumption; the volume of commodities produced and sold do not much differ; and the volume of capitalists' consumption is rigid. It is these three assumptions that lie behind the simple formula.)

In this simple form the formula p_c cannot, of course, precisely yield the actual height of the price level and thus the partial purchasing of money with respect to personal consumer articles. Yet it offers more than a simple tautology. Based on essential interrelations it explains and interprets the medium value, realized in the average of a few years, of the price development of articles serving personal consumption—and with this of the most important partial purchasing power of money.

That much is surely true, at least as long as rapid inflation does not render doubtful even the sense of this medium value.

52

We are not interested now in the average value of the purchasing power of money or of price level, but in their relatively accurate size and therefore we have to expand the formula p_c. This causes first of all formal changes.

To wit, the numerator of the formula includes the wages of workers, the monetary benefits received from enterprises above wages, together with such minor items as the sum of net interests on the savings of workers (the items up to now will be simply called wages). The numerator also includes government transfer payments (pensions, unemployment benefits and similar items), but we have to deduct from the numerator the direct taxes of wage earners, inclusive of similar payments (as social insurance contributions) and, finally, the possible net savings of wage earners have to be deducted (while their possible overspending should be added to the numerator). Two complementary remarks should be made. First, in our actual computations we also include services in the consumer articles. Second, also the purchase of a flat or a home is considered as a consumer outlay.

The denominator of the expanded formula only comprises the difference of two items. The minuend is *not* the volume of the produced but of the purchased consumer articles, and the subtrahend is the volume of consumer articles purchased by capitalists for their own purposes. In connection with the latter, attention has to be called to the fact that this is not identical with the current consumption of capitalists (just as the difference is not indentical with the volume of current consumption by wage earners). A home, or a flat, and the durable consumer goods are, namely, purchased at a definite date, but are only consumed through longer use. This remark is essential because, even if the volume of the current consumption of capitalists is justly held to be rigid, the sum of their purchases aimed at consumption is by far not so rigid, it fluctuates because of the massive or less massive purchases of consumers' durables. At any rate, the quotient of the sums in the numerator and the denominator yields the price coefficient of consumer articles, p_c. Its formula is:

$$p_c = \frac{W + \mathit{Trf} - T_W - S_W}{C_V - C_{CV}}$$

where W = wages, etc.

Trf = government transfers to wage earners

T_W = taxes paid by wage earners

S_W = wage earners' net savings

C_V = volume of personal consumption

C_{CV} = volume of capitalists' consumption.

In this book we use data reflecting the reality instead of the algebraic symbols in the formula. The data may be partly found in official statistics and partly they are our own estimate. The Appendix to the book provides detailed information about the estimation procedure.

At this point we are not interested in the price coefficient itself, but in its annual changes. The formula expressing this change in percentages will be called the Δp_c formula. For the determination of the new indicator we work out, one by one, the annual increment or decrement of the items in the formula p_c and determine what percentage this growth or drop is of the sum of the numerator in the preceding year— or, in the case of the total personal consumption and the consumption by capitalists, of the denominator. Then we compute the algebraic sum of these differences in percentages—separately for the numerator and the denominator. Adding 100 to both sums and multiplying their quotient by 100 we get the annual percentual change in the price level (e.g., that the price level has risen, say, from 100 to 103 per cent). Thus, in 1974 the percentage changes of the factors in the numerator to the sum of the numerator of the preceding year were as follows: wages +11.5, transfers +3.1, savings

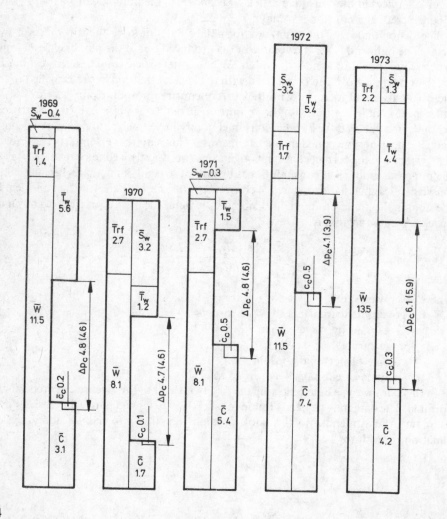

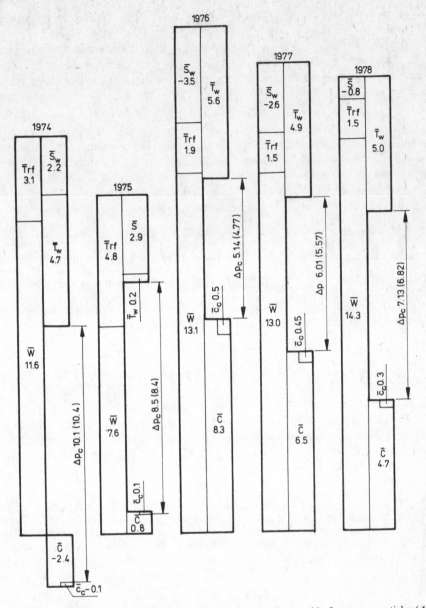

Figure 5.1 Annual percentual changes in the price level and volume sold of consumer articles (Δp_c)
1969—1978

Legend:

W	= wages etc.	T_w	= workers' taxes
Trf	= transfers	C	= volume of consumption
S_w	= workers' savings	C_c	= volume of non-wage-earners' consumption

All items represent percentual changes at annual rate

55

of wage earners $+2.2$, taxes of wage earners $+4.7$; thus the numerator increased relative to the preceding year by 7.8 per cent.[2] The volume of consumption in the denominator decreased relative to the preceding year by 2.4 per cent, while the volume of consumption by capitalists remained unchanged, thus the difference of the two was 2.4 per cent less than in the preceding year. Thus the percentual change was 100 $\times \dfrac{107.8}{97.6} - 100 = 10.4$ per cent.

We wanted to illustrate graphically the changes in the listed factors, more exactly, in their relative weights. But how can we illustrate the relative weights of such factors in the value of a faction which figure as addenda partly in the numerator and partly in the denominator of the fraction? Fortunately, there is a way to illustrate the relative weights of these factors in a simple manner and within error margins of two or three percentage points at the most. It can be, namely, easily proven that a term of the form $100\frac{a}{b} - 100$, in our example $100 \times \dfrac{107.8}{97.6} - 100$, is approximately equal to $(a\text{-}b)$ if the denominator does not much differ from 100—and this condition is always statisfied in the examined cases. (Thus, for 1974, $100 \times \dfrac{107.8}{97.6} - 100 = 1\tilde{0}4$ per cent, and $107.8 - 97.6 = 10.2$, and $10.4 \cong 10.2$) Our Δp_c diagrams in Figure 5.1, illustrating the mutual adjustment of demand, supply and prices rely on this consideration.

5.4 PRICES UNDER PERFECT AND OLIGOPOLISTIC COMPETITION

As has been emphasized, the p_c formula originally served for a rational explanation of the purchasing power of money severed from gold. It fulfilled this task by making it possible to interpret the price level of consumption goods at a given moment of time. That much is true. And because that is so, we feel tempted to say more about it, to state that the percentual change in the value of the expanded fraction p_c—derived from the

[2] For those who reason in terms of formulae, let the terms in the numerator of the Δp_c diagram for the year n (W, Trf, T and S) be $a_{1,n}$, $a_{2,n}$, $a_{3,n}$, and $a_{4,n}$; and of those in the denominator (C_vm c_{cv}) $b_{1,n}$, and $b_{2,n}$. Let further be the numerator of the formula for year $(n-1)$; $\Delta p_{cn\ 1}$: $N_{n\lambda1}$ and its denominator D_{n-1}. With these notations the quantities shown in the $\Delta p_{c,n}$ diagrams are the following:

$$100\frac{a_{k,n} - a_{k,n-1}}{N_{n-1}} - 100 \text{ and}$$

$$100\frac{b_{i,n} - b_{i,n-1}}{D_{n-1}} - 100 \text{ where}$$

k takes the values 1,2,3,4 and
i takes the values 1,2
then

$$p_{c,n} = 100 \times \frac{100 + \sum\limits_{k=1}^{k=4} k,n}{100 + \sum\limits_{i=1}^{i=2} \beta_{i,n}} - 100 = \sum\limits_{k=1}^{k=4} \alpha_{k,n} - i = 2\beta_{i,n}.$$

sum of changes in the individual components in the formula—provide a satisfactory explanation for the causes of the price changes and hence also for those of inflation experienced throughout the period investigated. We, economists are accustomed to think in terms of functions in which the change in price is uniquely determined by the totality of variables regarded as independent. This conditioning is the consequence of the fact that we can rarely get rid of the—sometimes explicit, sometimes tacit—assumption of classical political economy, that an almost perfect competition is prevailing on the market.

Indeed, in the case of perfect competition prices are formed over the heads of economic agents independently of their will, and, in this sense, under the impact of objective forces, though these forces work only through actions not independent of the consciousness of the agents themselves. True, this consciousness adjusts to the objective factors of reality not immediately but through a lengthy process. But it is certainly true that in the case of perfect competition the prevailing prices are "externally" given for the individual agents on the market which they are unable to change individually, or to a perceptible extent.

Let us, however, also consider the other extreme case, that of complete monopoly. In this case the managers of monopolized branches determine the prices of their products at any time, though, of course, not independently of the state of the market, of the recognized market forces. It is also evident that under conditions of lasting inflation they set ever higher prices and, by doing so they set the course of inflation themselves—even if constrained by market forces. Thinking in the framework of such a model, the price changes ought to be regarded as independent variables, and the volumes of goods marketable at those prices become the dependent variables. This is particularly true for the goods for which the p_c formula holds, namely, the articles of personal consumption, since their part consumed by capitalists is inelastic, while the volume of goods bought by wage earners for their nominal wage diminishes with rising prices and increases with falling ones.

In such a model it is almost meaningless to ask what the objective relationships are that cause the price level of consumer goods to rise precisely by such and such percentage. In this case the price depends on expectations which are also influenced by objective conditions. In reality, of course, the market is neither perfectly competitive, nor completely monopolized. Nowadays the market is Janus-faced: a part of it is ruled by conditions similar to perfect competition, while the other part is strongly oligopolistic and we can only guess that it is this second part by which the character of the total market is to a great extent determined.

5.5 THE JANUS-FACED NATURE OF THE Δp_c DIAGRAMS

We should note at this point that the Δp_c diagrams are also Janus-faced. If we regard the volume of consumer goods sold as given, we may consider the diagram to show us the percentual change in the price level made possible by the quantities figuring in the numerator of the formula. From this point of view we may regard the diagrams as indicating changes in the price level (a price coefficient). And conversely: we may say that our diagrams show the percentage change in the volume of consumer goods (in the demand for these goods) made possible by the quantities appearing in the numerator of the formula—if we take the change in the price level as given. From this point of view we may regard the p_c diagrams as depicting and interpreting the change in the volume of real demand for the articles serving personal consumption. In reality, on account of—among other things—the Janus-faced nature of the market, neither the change in the price level nor that in the real demand for consumer goods can be exactly given *ex ante*. What the diagrams really indicate is how the mutual adjustment of the quantities figuring in the formula took place (among the actual spendable money income of wage earners, its unspent part, the volume of sales—realized demand—of consumer goods and the price level)—and this in a period of permanent inflation during which the economy was undergoing not only a mild recession, but even a real crisis.

Our diagrams indicate the extent to which the factors illustrated in them made an increase or decrease of inflation possible with an increase or decrease in the volume of (real demand for) consumer goods. But it does not emerge from the diagrams what factors caused this and to what extent the exact pattern of the mutual adjustment of inflation and real demand, since our diagrams do not and cannot explain the final cause of the phenomena illustrated.

The numerator of the p_c formula does not comprise the total effective demand for consumer goods expressed in terms of money, but only a part of it—although an overwhelming one. This numerator gives us the amount of money which workers spent on consumer goods. This sum of money represents demand in terms of money; its increase raises—*ceteris paribus*—the amount of money paid for consumer goods by the same amount and hence the realizable price-sum as well. If we really wanted to follow up the links of the chain of causes and effects that bring about a change in this demand, then we ought to state precisely why the wage earners' income was as much as it was and why exactly so much flowed from it (or even from credits received) to the market as it actually did. This, however, we did not and cannot do.

Inflation was rampant. Working people tried to defend themselves against the consequences of price increases by attaining a rise in their nominal wages. They led an organized fight for higher wages. They compared expected price increases with expected increases in productivity, they compared their own wages with those of other groups of working people. And they formulated their wage demands on the basis of such comparisons, taking into account also the existing power relations. They succeeded in enforcing that much of their demands, neither more nor less. And this is only the level of wages and not their sum. Besides the wage level, the sum of wages depends also on the rate of employment—and there is nothing to prove that employment had to develop as it actually did. Further, owing to certain institutional conditions also the non-wage incomes of workers increased, and this increase was not independent of the rate of employment either, but also depended on unemployment benefits and other transfers—since these, too, are included. (Unemployment is not simply a function of the rate of employment, but also, e.g., of demographic factors.) It is also a fact that direct taxes took such and such much from the gross money income of wage earners. These are the facts. It was not the working of any deeper law of economics that exactly this and that much had to happen. We are forced to start our analysis by simply accepting these facts and not by attempting their quantitative explanation.

Moreover, the difference between the wage earners' income and the deductions from it is not yet income spent. Between these items and the effective demand we find the net saving or dissaving (overspending) of wage earners. During the years under examination wage earners' savings were rising in "bad" years and diminishing (or turning into overspending) in "good" ones. We think we understand why this happened: in bad years, afraid of the future, of possible unemployment, they effected savings, while in the good ones they made extensive use of consumer credit and mortgages for purchasing homes. (But only as long as this was made possible by the credit market.) This much is probable and understandable, but we do not know why the saving (or dissaving) changed exactly by the given amount.

Let us continue by looking into the changes of the data figuring in the denominator. The terms figuring in this denominator represent volumes. Volumes are derived from data at current prices by using proper price deflators. The latter ones we took from official statistics. With this we already accepted the actual rate of inflation and used it in working out the denominator.

Among the data in the denominator is the change in capitalists' consumption. This was estimated by ourselves. The change in this volume is anyway insignificant— however accurately or approximately we estimated it. Thus we need not worry much about it. The volume of total personal consumption is, however, a more intriguing problem.[3]

Indeed, why did the volume of consumer goods sold during the individual years of the period investigated increase or decrease exactly by the amount it did?

5.6 ON THE MUTUAL ADJUSTMENT OF THE PRICE LEVEL AND THE VOLUME OF COMMODITIES SOLD

In trying to answer this question we can only venture explanations. This will be complicated but essential and—unfortunately—we have to begin somewhere with Adam and Eve. We should go into these explanations in different ways, depending on whether we set out from one of the extreme cases, that of perfect competition, or from the other one, that of a completely monopolized market.

In the case of perfect competition producers cannot directly regulate either the unit price of products, or the total amount of commodities entering the market. It is obvious that both the price level and the volume of commodities sold are each other's functions. We cannot know either without knowing the other (and some further complementary data).

---

[3] In its original form the p_c formula comprised in C not the volume of consumer goods sold, but that produced. It was absolutely logical that, in order to arrive at the real consumption of workers, we subtracted the capitalists' consumption from C. In the modified form of formula the same procedure seems to be unjustifiably circumstantial. Namely, now C is the sum of the purchases by capitalists and wage earners, and the latter is seemingly independent from the size of consumption by capitalists. In reality it is not independent of the latter, since, if capitalists' consumption—which is little dependent on price—is of an unusually high volume, higher prices can be set than in the opposite case, and this will diminish the volume of consumer goods bought by workers.

The neoclassical school "solves" this dilemma by determining separately the amount of commodities produced by each producer with the help of the completely erroneous theorem that with such an amount produced the market price of the product and its marginal cost will coincide. But such a train of thought still leaves the problem of price level unsolved.

Overall demand for the total amount of wage goods—expressed in terms of money—which makes up the overwhelming part of consumer goods in general, is *ex post* always a given sum. It is not completely independent of the volume of consumer goods produced, since total demand is *also* a function of the wages paid in the consumer goods producing sector. But a change in the volume of production modifies the sum of spendable income only negligibly-other things being equal. It follows that if producers unable to coordinate their volumes of production bring commodities to the market and also wish to sell them, then, other things being equal, they are forced to reduce the prices of their goods relative to wage costs. But is there an upper limit to this increase in production? The existing capacities—and sometimes the labour situation as well—do set such an upper limit. Within this limit a fall in the price level may be stopped if marginal producers were forced out of business and this would reduce supply. However, studying individual years, theory has to take into account a factor of uncertainty, a band within which the behaviour of producers is not determined by coercive economic interrelations. In respect of this band we can only state *ex post* that this happened and that's all.

In real life, however, complete monopoly is rare, while oligopolistic situations are quite common. It is reasonable to assume that on the market of consumer goods oligopolistic behaviour by producers and sellers is significant. And as far as present-day oligopolistic competition is concerned, the commonplace statement is valid that competition is practised whenever possible not through prices but through the volume of production. (This statement holds more for competition within rather than between branches.) We would say too little if we wanted to reformulate this by stating that is a downward rigidity of prices, as nowadays prices are rising. (The case of computers and similar products is an exception and easy to explain.) At any rate, oligopolistic prices are always manipulated prices. However, with prices given—other things being equal—the marketable volume of consumer goods is also given. The question arises how producers and sellers enjoying an oligopolistic position calculate and fix their prices. Obviously, a role is played here by the relationship among the price level of consumer goods, their volume sold and the profit gained from these sales.

5.7 INTERRELATION BETWEEN THE VOLUME OF CONSUMER GOODS SOLD AND THE PROFIT MARGIN

Assuming "pure" capitalism, Péter Erdős, in his *Contributions*... and *Wages, Profit, Taxation,* arrived at the conclusion that in the case of an unchanged price level and relatively inelastic capitalists' consumption, if workers spend exactly the amount of their current income on purchases, the share of marketable products of Department

II within the GNP can only rise if the price level of these products falls. In this case the percentage of profit realizable from consumer goods also diminishes.[4]

We have to check to what extent the above theorem maintains its validity under the conditions of present-day capitalism.

For this purpose we constructed a two-sector model. Sector I produces investment goods, Sector II consumer goods and both sectors also produce the raw materials for their own use. Besides those actually paid in these two sectors, the sum of spendable wages comprises also government wages and transfers. Wages in Sector II belong partly to the changing, partly to the constant costs of production. We assumed that the changing part of wages moves proportionately to the output of consumer goods. (If, instead, we had assumed that the wage-like marginal costs increase with growing production, our conclusions would mostly hold *a fortiori*.) We assumed an unchanged price level and also that wage earners spend exactly their wages on consumption.

It was not difficult to find the rule in the two borderline cases: when capitalists' consumption changes proportionately to the volume of consumer goods production and when this type of consumption is completely inelastic. But, for intermediate situations we often arrived at unmanageable formulae. Thus, instead of producing exact proofs, we had to rely on simulation methods. We performed numerous simulation experiments, changing the parameters within broad limits, far beyond the limits we assumed would actually occur in practice.[5] The results obtained were unequivocal. Namely, the price level of consumer goods decreases parallel to an increase in the volume of consumer goods sold, except in the unlikely case when consumption by capitalists is so elastic that with a plus or minus 8 per cent deviation of consumer goods production from its average value, capitalists' consumption rises above or falls below its average by about 40 per cent. Thus, the price level of consumer goods falls—other things being equal—when the production of consumer goods increases, and rises—other things being equal—when the production of consumer goods diminishes. This is congruent with the statements of the two books mentioned.

---

[4] For a short summary of that see: Erdős, P., 1977, p. 244.

[5] The model was the following one:

The number of direct producers employed in Department II equals n. For a sum wages equalling n money units they produce an n volume of consumer goods and the volume of personal consumption is also exactly n. The difference between the total amount of wages (and other wage-type income) paid in the whole economy and wages paid in Department II is B; the total constant costs of Deparment II is K. The volume of capitalists' consumption $c_o = f(n) = \alpha_n + \beta$, so that $\alpha n^* + \beta = 0,1^*$, where n* is the volume of production in Department II regarded as an average one. The independent variable of the system is n, while B, K, α, and β parameters which we varied in a band that was somewhwat wider than the limits considered realitic.

In this model the price coefficient of consumer goods is $p_c = \dfrac{B+n}{n-f(n)}$; the price sum of goods sum of goods

for personal consumption $= n \dfrac{B+n}{n-f(n)}$; their production cost $= K+n$, and the volume of profits at current

prices is $= n\dfrac{B+n}{n-f(n)} - (K+n) = \dfrac{f(n) \times (n+K) + n(B-K)}{n-f(n)}$ the profit margin

$= \dfrac{\text{amount of profits at current prices}}{\text{price sum}} = \dfrac{f(n) \times (n+K) + n(B-K)}{n(B+N)}$ while volume of profits at constant prices

is arrived at by deflating the amount of profits with the corresponding p_c value.

61

5.8 PARADOXICAL RELATIONSHIP BETWEEN THE PRICE TREND OF CONSUMER GOODS AND THE VOLUME OF PROFIT THAT CAN BE EARNED FROM THEIR SALE

It may, however, be regarded as a new and important result that the volume of profit (expressed at constant prices) increases when the production of consumer goods grows and falls when the latter diminishes. Thus, a reduction of the price level of consumer goods increases and its raising reduces this volume of real profit. The same cannot be said about the amount of profits expressed at current prices. If n is the volume of consumer goods sold and if capitalists' consumption changes somewhat more elastically with the changes in n than what would correspond to the function f(n) = 0.8 n-10, then the amount of profits expressed at current prices also grows and diminishes with n; With a less elastic capitalists' consumption, the contrary is true. (A rising price level is coupled with a falling production, hence profits expressed in money terms may increase, while the real value of profits is reduced.)

The above outlined model experiment has shown that the theorems stated for "pure" capitalism and mentioned above also hold for the present-day conditions of capitalism. Meanwhile, we also revealed a hitherto unknown relationship: with the increasing volume of consumer goods sold within the GNP, that is, if the price of consumer goods is reduced, then *ceteris paribus* also the volume of the real profit increases in Department II.[6]

From this new theorem has also become evident that we indeed face a paradoxical situation. If oligopolistic conditions really prevail in the production (or sale) of consumer goods, if this sector can really manipulate its prices and can adjust its production to the demand determined by these prices, then the paradoxical situation arises that if this sector raises its prices in order to protect its profit margin, this simultaneously reduces the volume of its real profits.

The capitalists of the consumer goods producing sector do not act, of course, as one man. And if individual enterprises have a free hand in any respect, then to the extent depending on the degree of their monopolistic position—called the "degree of

---

[6] It is easy to prove the theorem also with exact methods for a very probable case when $B-K$ is greater than zero.

Namely, since real profit is the quotient of profit measured in terms of money and the price coefficient, real profit

$$= \frac{f(n) \times (n+K) + n(B-K)}{n - f(n)} : \frac{B+n}{n - f(n)} = \frac{f(n) \times (n+K) + n(B-K)}{B+n}.$$

The derivative of the latter with respect to n:

$$= \frac{[(n+K)f'(n) + f(n) + B - K] \times (B+n) - f(n) \times (n+K) - n(B-K)}{(B+n)^2}$$

The denominator here has a positive value and the numerator can be brought, after having performed the operations indicated, to the following form: $f'(n) \times (B+n) \times (n+K) + (f-K) \times [f(n) + B]$. We know that f(n) increases together with n, thus in the relevant domain $f'(n)$ is greater than zero, and if also B is greater than K. All terms in the numerator will have a positive value. Thus the theorem holds for the case when the above mentioned conditions hold (but, within certain limits, it would also be true in the unprobable case when $B-K$ *is less than zero*.

62

monopoly" by Kalecki[7]—this will show in their relative freedom in price setting. But the demand for their products at the prices set by them does not depend on them absolutely. Moreover, the above stated theorems hold for the sector as a whole, but not for its individual enterprises. The prices of products with inelastic demand can be raised without a significant drop in sales. At the same time, this price draws away demand from other products. But also the opposite case often occurs: demand for some products may grow also in a manner that more is sold without a reduction of the attainable profit margin. In connection with the purchase of dwellings and certain durable consumer goods it is particulary true that the saleable volume depends not so much on their prices as rather on the availability of credits. At any rate, under inflationary conditions there is considerable pressure to raise prices since at such times—contrary to the assumptions of our model—the level of wages also rises. By assuming that both sectors produce their own raw material, prices disappear. This problem, however, is a very real one for individual branches and enterprises. It is all too real especially when a considerable part of raw materials and energy is imported. (This type of inflation is rightly called a cost-push one.) Hence enterprises do raise their prices and they may easily raise them so much that through their behaviour—and this is the substance of the paradox—they curtail the growth of the volume of real profit (or even reduce its volume).

We also have to keep in mind that at the time when entrepreneurs calculate their prices by simply adding the profit margin to the costs, then not only wages and the future price level of the raw materials are uncertain, but also the size of overhead costs per unit of product, since the latter depends also on the volume of products to be sold, which is *ex ante* uncertain. That is, the calculation of costs is itself based on rather uncertain assumptions.

It is true that prices are also changed during the process—while such actions of entrepreneurs are governed partly by changes in costs, partly by the behaviour of competitors, and partly by changes in demand. Moreover, during the same course of events there also are changes in the government deficit, and in wage earners' propensity to save. Besides changes in the level of raw material prices and wages there will also be changes in interest rates and credit conditions. Everything will change and affect profits and profit margins. That much remains true that neither individual capitalists nor producers of consumer goods as a whole are in a position to adjust themselves— from the point of view of their own interests—optimally to the changing environment, since they cannot even know what the optimal would be if everybody acted optimally or in case everybody acted as they actually did. In other words, the behaviour of capitalists either in forming a price policy or in their production decisions contain a great many unforeseeable, random elements. We can, however, state quite

[7] What is said here about the Kaleckian "degree of monopoly" should be taken with a grain of salt. As a matter of fact, Kalecki applied his concept to microeconomics. He gives a formula for determining the amount by which an enterprise, depending on its "degree of monopoly" can set its prices above its prime costs. It is, namely, evident that this attainable profit margin is not independent of the state of business. In times of recession the profit margin falls and this can hardly be formulated in the terms that the "degree of monopoly" has also diminished.

accurately—again only *ex post*—the relative share of the sales increment or decrement of a given year in the price increase or decrease in that year, if we consider sales as the independent variable.

5.9 THE Δp_c DIAGRAM WHICH ALSO TAKES INTO ACCOUNT GOVERNMENT PURCHASES

The changes in the price level of consumer goods are considerably influenced by changes in government revenues and expenditures. In our Δp_c diagrams this effect appears partly in the changes in government wages included in the numerator of the formula and partly in the changes in government transfers. We can obtain a deeper insight into the effect of the government sector on the price level by expanding the numerator of the p_c formula to comprise also the price sum of government purchases of goods and services and the denominator to comprise the volume of these purchases. With this, we reach beyond the category of personal consumption. The few formula taking into account also government purchases is akin to the p_c formula, but also differs from it. Therefore, to distinguish it from p_c, we shall denote it by $p_{\ast}$. It is computed according to the following reasoning.

The volume of total consumption (R_v) equals the volume of consumer goods[8] purchased by wage earners, capitalists and the government: $R_v = c_{wv} + c_v + c_{gv}$. The price of this volume is also composed of three items: the price sum of government purchases c_g, the price sum of capitalists' purchases of consumer goods and the price sum spent by wage earners on consumer goods. The latter is the sum of wages paid by business (W_b)[9] and by government (W_g) plus government transfers (trf), less direct taxes paid by wage earners (T_w) and less net savings by wage earners (S_w).[10]

If now, giving a simplified image of reality, we assume that the price of a unit of all three components of R_v is uniformly $\Delta p_{\ast}$, then the following equation holds:

$$(c_{wv} + c_v + c_{gv})p_c^* = c_w + c_c + c_g + W_b + W_g + trf - T_w - S_w \tag{1}$$

On the right hand side of the equation we may write $c_{cv}p_c^*$ instead of c_c, and thus the second term can be cancelled on both sides. It is also true that

$$W_g + trf + def + GE_r + def \tag{2}$$

where GE_r stands for the part of government expenditure covered by revenues and *def* for government deficit. Hence, from (1) and (2)

$$p_{\ast} = \frac{W_b + GE_r + def - T_w - S_w}{c_{wv} + c_{gv}} \tag{3}$$

[8] The volume of consumer goods purchased by government includes here the purchase of all kinds of goods and services by the government, from the ink consumed by bureaucracy through school construction to intercontinental ballistic missiles. But, contrary to official statistics, it does not comprise the services provided by government employees and purchased by the government (e.g., police services).

[9] Including private transfers and some minor items.

[10] More exactly, from the numerator also a smaller "others" item has been subtracted, as not only wage earners receive government transfers. Furthermore, a part of government outlays are paid to foreigners. This correction is taken into account in our figures under *def*.

64

The volume of personal consumption is $c_v = c_{cv} + c_{wv}$, hence $c_{wv} + C_c - c_{cv}$. Substituting this into the denominator of (3) we get the final formula:

$$p_c^* = \frac{W_b + GE_r + def - T_w - S_w}{C_v + c_{gv} - c_{cv}} \qquad (4)$$

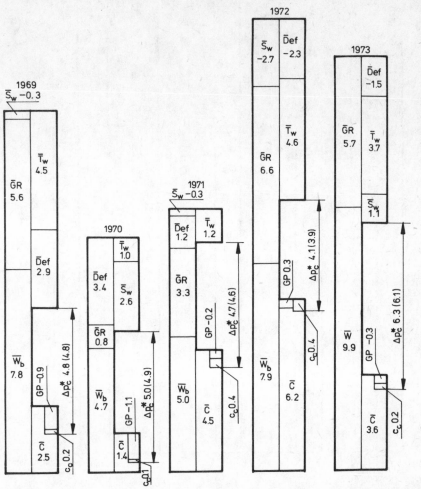

Figure 5.2. Annual percentual changes in the volume and price of personal and government consumption (Δp_c^*) 1969—1978

Legend:

W_b	= wages etc. paid by business	def	= Govt. domestic deficit
GR	= government expenditures covered by receipts		
		C	= volume of personal consumption
S_w	= workers' savings	GP	= govt. purchases
T_w	= workers' taxes	C_c	= volume of non-wage-earners' consumption

All items represent percentual changes at annual rate

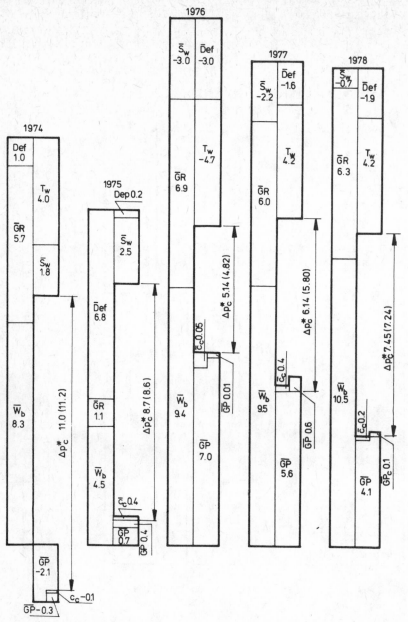

Fig. 5.2. (Cont.)

The second series of our diagrams was drawn on the basis of this formula, so that, similarly to the Δp_c diagrams, they illustrate the yearly percentage *changes* in the price level. Also, the diagrams approximate the price level as the difference between the

66

numerator and the denominator, instead of the exact value given by the quotient of the two.[11]

Anything else we should have to say about the interpretation of these series of diagrams—whether they show final causes or simply register facts *ex post*—we have already related, *mutatis mutandis*, in connection with the Δp_c diagrams.

The Δp_c^* formula reveals that, other things being equal, the government expenditures raise the price level—with the exception of expenditures covered by direct taxes levied on wage earners (and of quantitatively insignificant "other" items). The values received for Δp_c^x are higher than those for Δp_c not only owing to this fact, but first of all because, as indicated clearly by the official price deflators of government purchases, the government pays higher prices—mainly for military equipment—than the private business sector. (We do not know of any objections ever raised by capitalists protesting these covert premia.)

5.10 THE PROFIT MARGIN IN THE UNITED STATES IN THE YEARS UNDER EXAMINATION

It would be fine if we could check with the aid of actual figures the truth of our hunch that capitalists, through all the ups and downs of business fluctuations, want to defend their profit margins, and, if so, to what extent. In the official statistics there can be found data on the profit margins in individual industrial branches, but, unfortunately, we could not make use of them, because the method of calculating them was changed exactly in the critical year of 1974 and we were unable to construct a link between the two series calculated with different methods. Neither could we make direct calculations ourselves, since we do not know, e.g., the changes in the raw material costs of enterprises and branches.

Table 5.1

The profit margin at GNP level, 1968—1978
(as percentage of the price receipts less indirect taxes of the business sector)

Profit margin	1968	1969	1970	1971	1972	1973	1974	1975	1976	1977	1978
Net pre-tax profit margin	26.1	24.3	22.9	21.9	22.5	22.4	19.2	19.3	20.2	20.8	20.7
Net after-tax profit margin	16.8	15.4	14.2	14.4	14.8	14.9	12.0	12.4	12.8	13.3	13.2
Gross pre-tax profit margin	35.6	34.1	33.4	32.6	32.7	32.4	30.2	31.3	32.1	32.3	31.9
Gross after-tax profit margin	26.2	25.2	24.7	25.0	25.0	25.0	22.9	24.5	24.7	24.8	24.4

[11] The reader can easily write the formulae for the components in the Δp_c^* diagrams and for the Δp_c^* formula on the analogy of footnote 2 (p. 56).

We had to be content with "proxy" indicators, outlining only certain trends, with such as are indifferent to changes in raw material prices. We thus had to construct indicators using GNP (value added) categories.

Under profit margin on the GNP level we understand the percentage ratio of total profits in the economy to the price sum of total commodity output by private business enterprises. GNP is the price sum of services and goods not undergoing further processing (in the given year and the given country) less the costs of materials. In the U.S. statistical system, GNP exceeds the output of the private business sector, because it also includes the services of government employees rendered to the government. Therefore, the item "compensation of government employees" has to be deducted from official GNP data, and thus also from the denominator of the formula of profit margin. We decided also to exclude indirect taxes from the denominator, since they do not really constitute an income for enterprises; in this respect the latter act merely as tax collectors for the government. Profits in the national economy, figuring in the numerator, have been, however, taken into account in four different variants: we used both gross and net profits, both before and after taxes. Thus we obtained four time series (see Table 5.1).

It was evident from the outset that gross profit margins are considerably higher than net ones, and that before-tax margins are higher than after-tax ones. It was also expected that net profit margins would show greater fluctuations than gross ones, and, owing to the effect of the corporate profit tax as built-in stabilizer, before-tax margins would fluctuate more than after-tax ones.

Table 5.2

Average*profit margins and the maximum and minimum deviations from it

Profit margin	Average	Maximum	Minimum
Net pre-tax profit margin	21.8	+ 19.7	− 11.9
Net after-tax profit margin	14.0	+ 20.0	− 14.3
Gross pre-tax profit margin	32.6	+ 9.2	− 7.4
Gross after-tax profit margin	24.8	+ 5.6	− 7.7

* = Unweighted arithmetical mean

The data in the first two lines of the table slightly refute our expectations, as the spread of the net, after-tax, profit margin was greater than of the net, before-tax one (+ 20.0 and − 14.3 per cent respectively as well as + 19.7 and − 11.9 per cent respectively around the mean values). We have no clear explanation for this anomaly. The cause might have been that in 1974, when the rate of inflation was exceptionally high, the corporate profit tax as a built-in stabilizer turned into a destabilizing factor. (Corporate tax liabilities are affected also by the unrealized profits originating in the inventory valuation and capital consumption adjustments.) The question arises whether the smoothest course of gross, after-tax profit margin is simply due to arithmetical causes, or has some deeper, really economic cause. Maybe, it does.

Namely—if we are right in accepting Kalecki's thesis—enterprises add their calculated profit margins to calculated prime costs, but, of course, in a way that it should cover their overhead costs as well. This is tantamount to the statement that enterprises calculate their prices by taking into account not net but gross profits. (Depreciation is a part of overhead costs.) At any rate, the course of gross profit margins, particularly those after taxes, is astonishingly smooth.

We have to mention that these profit margins, calculated at GNP level, are much higher than the profit margins of enterprises. Namely, the formula of the enterprise profit margin is interpreted as a percentage of price receipts, not as of prime costs is $\frac{pr}{c+v+pr} \cdot 100$, where c is the sum of materials used and of depreciation; while in the numerator of the formula given above for profit margin on GNP level the numerator also comprises the sum of enterprise profits, but the denominator comprises, besides enterprise wages and profits, only the sum of enterprise depreciations, while it excludes the sum of material costs.

CHAPTER SIX

SOME CHARACTERISTICS OF PRICE MOVEMENTS IN THE UNITED STATES IN THE 1969-1978 PERIOD

6.1 QUALITATIVE CHARACTERIZATION OF THE PRICE-LEVEL-MODIFYING EFFECT OF THE FACTORS IN THE Δp_c AND Δp_c^x FORMULAE

Relying on Figs 6.1 and 6.2 as well as Tables 6.5 and 6.6 serving for their basis we shall attempt to outline the main characteristics of price movements in the period under investigation. To avoid a too complicated formulation, we shall treat in the following—in a rather simplified way—the formulas Δp_c and Δp_c^x as if they unequivocally showed the components of price developments. The reader will understand that our statements relate, more exactly, to the changes which rendered possible the sale of the volumes, or their increments in the denominator of the formulae, at the prices indicated in the formulae.

For a starting point let us scrutinize the following two tables (6.1 and 6.2) in which we summarize the qualitative impact of the components of the two price level indicators (Δp_c and Δp_c^x) on the development of prices in the years under examination, whether they increased or decreased the price level relative to the preceding year.

To avoid repetitions, we present the lessons to be drawn from these two tables together.[12] First of all, it is striking that there were components which affected the price level during the entire period "consistently", that is always in the same direction, while the impact of the others was positive in some and negative in some other years. The amounts of wages and transfers and also of government expenditures increased year in year out and, as they figure with positive signs in the numerators of the fractions, their growth affected the price level of the volume of products sold consistently in a positive, i.e., price-raising sense. (Even at these higher prices they rendered the sale of more products possible.) We only find a single component with a consistently price reducing effect: the taxes paid by wage earners. Not even the tax cut of 1975 nor the increase in unemployment altered this, since, due to inflation, a considerable part of working people got into higher tax brackets. With the exception of a single year (1974), also the effect of changes in the volume of consumer goods sold was price-reducing. The same holds for the effect of changes in the volume of total consumption (the sum of personal consumption and government purchases).

The effects of changes in capitalists' consumption (a part of total consumption) had anyway an insignificant effect on prices and—since we used our own estimated data—

---

[12] The two tables have necessarily a few common features, since their components are partly identical.

Table 6.1

Effects of changes in the components of the Δp_c formula on the change in price level, 1969—1978
(+ indicates a price-level raising, − a price-level reducing effect)

Years Components	1969	1970	1971	1972	1973	1974	1975	1976	1977	1978
1. Wages	+	+	+	+	+	+	+	+	+	+
2. Transfers	+	+	+	+	+	+	+	+	+	+
3. Taxes paid by wage earners	−	−	−	−	−	−	−	−	−	−
4. Net savings by wage earners	+	−	+	+	−	−	−	+	+	+
5. *Numerator*	+	+	+	+	+	+	+	+	+	+
6. Personal consumption	−	−	−	−	−	+	−	−	−	−
7. Capitalists' consumption	+	+	+	+	+	+	+	+	+	+
8. *Denominator*	−	−	−	−	−	+	−	−	−	−
9. *Addendum:* Direction of the change in Δp_c	+	+	+	+	+	+	+	+	+	+

Table 6.2

Effects of changes in the components of the Δp_c^* formula on the price level, 1969—1978
(+ indicates a price-level raising, —a price-level reducing effect)

Years Components	1969	1970	1971	1972	1973	1974	1975	1976	1977	1978
1. Business wages	+	+	+	+	+	+	+	+	+	+
2. Government expenditures covered by receipts	+	+	+	+	+	+	+	+	+	+
3. Government deficit	−	+	+	−	−	+	+	−	−	−
4. Taxes paid by wage earners	−	−	−	−	−	−	−	−	−	−
5. Net savings by wage earners	+	−	+	+	−	−	−	+	+	+
6. *Numerator*	+	+	+	+	+	+	+	+	+	+
7. Personal consumption	−	−	−	−	−	+	−	−	−	−
8. Government purchases	−	−	−	+	−	+	+	−	+	−
9. Capitalists' consumption	+	+	+	+	+	−	+	+	+	+
10. *Denominator*	−	−	−	−	−	+	−	−	−	−
11. *Addendum:* Direction of the change in Δp_c^*	+	+	+	+	+	+	+	+	+	+

it is not absolutely certain that we gave correctly even the direction of changes for every year. If, however, our estimations are correct, we are able to state a characteristic fact: changes in the volume of capitalists' consumption and total consumption worked consistently against each other. The effects of changes in savings by wage earners, government deficit and the volume of government purchases altered—contrary to those mentioned above—their signs quite often. Already this qualitative investigation shows a very characteristic feature of the decade examined very plastically.

Under "normal" conditions, that is, when the capitalist economy is growing without disturbances, the effect of the numerator in our formula is price raising, since, parallel to an increasing GNP, the amount of wages paid is also growing. Conversely, in such cases the denominators in the formula have in themselves generally a price-reducing effect, since the volume of consumer goods sold is usually growing, not only because of the usual increase in employment. In a recession the price reducing effect of the denominator will diminish, in times of a crisis it might turn into its opposite and become a price-raising factor. That is exactly what happened in 1974.

Recessions and crises, of course, are not exactly what we would call "normal" conditions. But earlier, also these abnormal conditions ran their normal course. Thus, a slowing down of GNP growth usually brought about a slowdown in the sum of wages paid and a fall in GNP, a decrease in that sum. And this usually more than counterbalanced the price-raising effect of the decrease in the value of the denominator.

In the decade under review the numerators of our formulae fulfilled, of course, their function as price raisers excellently, and even more than that. They grew at an unusually rapid rate; and the growth of the denominators did not neutralize the effects of this unusually rapid growth. Conversely, in 1974, under the conditions of inflationary expectations, the momentum of wage increases—together with the mostly induced growth of transfers—did not allow a decrease of the numerator, while the behaviour of the denominator was typical in that year, its decrease worked similarly towards raising prices. (Tables 6.1 and 6.2)

6.2 ANALYSIS OF THE PRICE CHANGES BETWEEN THE TWO END POINTS OF THE 1968-1978 PERIOD

Let us now pass to the quantitative analysis of the events and first of all have a look at the numerical changes characterizing the price levels, and their components between the starting and the closing year of the period.

It becomes apparent from the table that Δp_c^* (which comprises about three quarters of GNP without imputations), increased somewhat faster than the price level indicators of consumer purchases did. One of the causes was already mentioned on p. 65. Another aspect of the same phenomenon may be understood from a closer investigation of the changes in the composition of the realized volume of commodities, i.e., of the denominator. Changes in the denominator of the formula Δp_c^* counterbalanced less the price-raising effect of the numerator than those of the denominator of the Δp_c formula and this was clearly due to the changes in the volume of government purchases, because—as it is shown by column 4 in row 17 of Table 6.3 B—their volume

Table 6.3

Changes in price-level indicators and their components 1978/1968

Components	Absolute change, bn dollars*	Percentage contribution**		Percentage change	
		Total	Yearly average	Total	Yearly average
		A: Δp_c			
1. Wages	749.3	175.8	10.7	152.3	9.7
2. Transfers	158.5	35.1	3.1	280.5	14.3
3. Less: taxes paid by wage earners	273.2	60.5	4.8	199.9	11.6
4. Less: net savings by wage earners	−21.5	−4.8	−0.5	−210.8	−12.0
5. *Numerator*	101.1	155.1	9.8	155.1	9.8
6. Personal consumption	249.4	46.5	3.9	41.8	3.6
7. Less: capitalists' consumption	17.0	3.2	0.3	28.9	2.6
8. *Denominator*	232.4	43.3	3.7	43.3	3.7
9. Δp_c	18	18.2	5.9	78.2	5.9
		B: Δp_c^*			
10. Business wages	659.9	118.8	8.1	154.1	9.8
11. Government expenditures covered by receipts	422.3	76.1	5.8	154.6	9.8
12. Government deficit	−14.8	−2.1	−0.3	−648.1	−11.9
13. Less: taxes paid by wage earners	273.2	49.2	4.1	199.9	11.6
14. Less: net savings by wage earners	−21.5	−0.4	−0.04	−210.8	−12.0
15. *Numerator*	802.0	144.5	9.4	144.5	9.4
16. Personal consumption	249.4	37.7	3.2	41.8	3.6
17. Government purchases	−4.6	−0.7	−0.06	−3.7	−0.4
18. Less: capitalists' consumption	17	2.6	0.3	28.9	2.6
19. *Denominator*	227.8	34.4	3.0	34.4	3.0
20. Δp_c^*		81.9	6.2	81.9	6.2
Addendum					
21. Government wages	18.2	3.3	0.3	13.8	1.3
22. Total government expenditure (11 + 12)	407.5	73.4	5.7	15.3	9.7
23. Total consumption (16 + 17)	244.8	37.0	3.2	33.9	3.0

* Current dollars in the numerators; constant, 1972, dollars in the denominators
** In the strict sense: percentage contribution to the change in the numerator, respectively denominator. Due to the fact that the denominator is significantly bigger than 100, the method of subtraction instead of division is not applicable.

changed in a way somewhat raising prices (to the extent of 3.7 per cent) instead of reducing them. How much the behaviour of this component of the more comprehensive price indicator differed from that of the two components during the whole period is especially clearly illustrated by curve No. 6 of Fig. 6.2.

The data presented in Table 6.3 illustrate well the relationship that the impact of any individual component on the movement of the price level or, more accurately, on the mutual adjustment of price level and sales volume, is determined, on the one hand, by its relative weight in the numerator, respectively the denominator, and, on the other, by its percentual change. Thus, among the components of the numerator of the Δp_c indicator the amount of transfers showed the fastest growth. Yet the one affecting the change of the numerator most was the sum of wages, since its absolute amount was much bigger than that of transfers. Similarly, although taxes paid by wage earners increased faster than wages (by 199.9 and 152.3 per cent), their price-reducing impact for the period as a whole was only slightly bigger than the price-raising effect of transfers.

Examining the components in the numerator of Δp_c^* we find a phenomenon that is to some extent similar. Although government expenditure (B: row 22) grew somewhat faster than business wages, the impact of the latter was—due to their bigger weight— much stronger (118.8 and 73.4 per cent contribution to the increment of the numerator). It is worth mentioning that the government deficit (the part of government expenditure not covered by revenues), although showing the highest growth among all components, had an almost negligible effect on the change in the price level between the two extreme points of the period.[13] It is not without interest for theory that the changes in the price level between the two end points of the period were considerably influenced only by the total amount of government expenditure, not by the government deficit which latter may be regarded, in a sense, only as the tip of the iceberg. This observation helps put into proper place the demand for a permanently balanced budget, nowadays much in the fore in the United States—meaning, in addition, only the federal budget.

Concerning the denominators, we find that their changes, and thus, in the final analysis, their impact on the price level were decisively determined by the developments in the realized personal consumption. (The role of changes in capitalist's consumption was, of course, minimal in this respect.) It is, however, surprising that this is equally true for both denominators. We might, namely, expect that the impact of government purchases was much stronger, since their sum in the opening year of the period, 1968, was almost one fifth of the denominator in the Δp_c^* formula. Owing, however, to special circumstances, the volume of government purchases moved throughout the whole period around the same level.

Let us first have a look at the curves related to the price level indicator Δp_c. It is immediately evident that after 1973, that is, in the last five years of the period, the curve rises more steeply than in the preceding five years. This is numerically reflected in the fact that its average yearly growth was 7.2 per cent in the later period against 4.7 per cent in the preceding one. The curves also provide information on which of the components played a major role in this jump of the rate of price increase. In Fig. 6.1 it can be well recognized that while the curve of the numerator rises somewhat more steeply after 1973, that of the denominator becomes flat. (The more important data that cannot be read from the figure are that the former rose between 1968 and 1973 by 8.9 per cent on a yearly average, and by 10.7 per cent between 1973 and 1978, while the latter by 4.1 per cent in the earlier and by 3.3 per cent in the later period.) Accordingly, both changes in rates worked in the direction of speeding up the increase in the price level. While, however, the increase in the rate of 1.8 percentage points of the former

---

[13] This statement is not true for price changes in some individual years of the period.

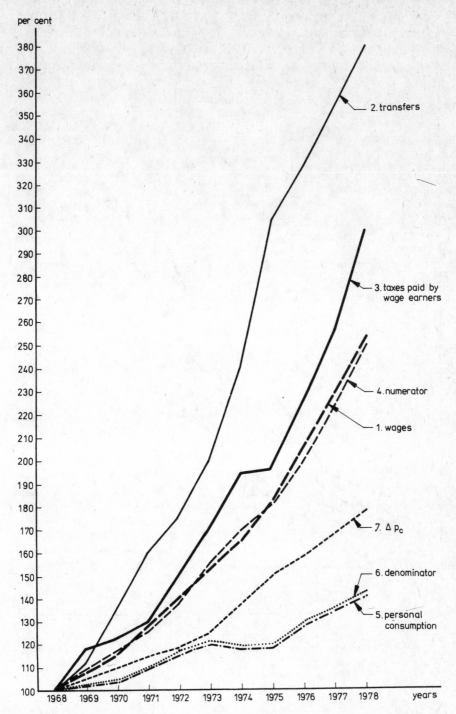

Figure 6.1 The price level indicator Δp_{ξ} and its major components, 1968—1978, 1968 = 100

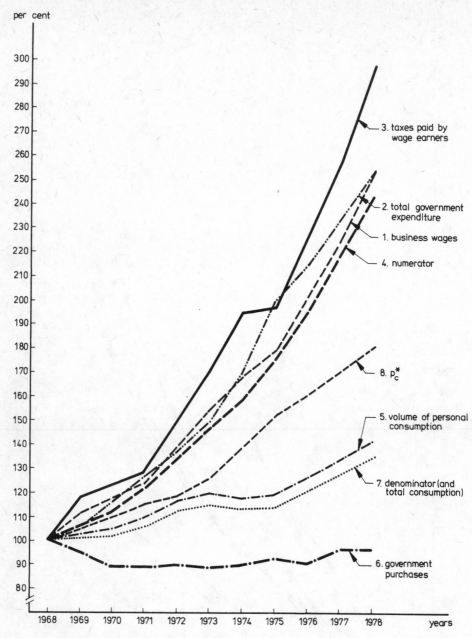

per cent

300
290
280
270 — 3. taxes paid by
        wage earners
260
250
240 — 2. total government
        expenditure
230 — 1. business wages
220
210 — 4. numerator
200
190
180
170 — 8. p_c^*
160
150 — 5. volume of personal
        consumption
140
130 — 7. denominator (and
        total consumption)
120
110
100
90 — 6. government
        purchases
80

1968 1969 1970 1971 1972 1973 1974 1975 1976 1977 1978   years

Figure 6.2 The price level indicator Δp_c^* and its major components, 1969—1969, 1968 = 100

corresponded to an about 20 per cent increase in the growth rate, the decrease of 0.8 percentage points in the latter represented a 20 per cent fall in the growth rate. Looking closer at the curves of the denominators it may also be immediately established that the declining growth rate was unequivocally a consequence of the fact that in 1974–75 these curves show a decline and in the next year a minimum rise, though in 1976–1978 the growth rate was on the whole the same as in the years prior to 1974.

As far as the movement of the individual components within the numerator is concerned, it is worth mentioning that in 1974–1975 the curve of wages ran below, while in 1976–1978 above that of the numerator. Transfers rose steeply steadily, especially in 1974–1975 as a result of a fast growth in the sum of unemployment benefits paid as a consequence of the crisis and the expansion of unemployment. The sharp break of the curve showing taxes paid by wage earners is also a highly conspicuous phenomenon. This was brought about by the great tax cut introduced as an anti-recession measure in April 1975.

Quite a number of the curves presented in Fig. 6.2 for Δp_c^* and its components are identical in the two indicators of price level. Of course, this is not discussed again. Also the curve of Δp_c^* rises faster after 1973 than before. The jump in the growth rate of the price level from 4.8 per cent to 7.5 per cent is here even more pronounced. This derives from the fact that the growth rate of the numerator increased from 7.9 to 10.8 per cent, while that of the denominator only from 2.9 to 3.1 per cent. The fact that the denominator of the Δp_c^* formula increased to a minimum extent, while that of the Δp_c formula decreased, can be traced mainly to the development of the volume of government purchases. Although, as has been already indicated, the volume of government purchases of goods and services essentially stagnated over the period as a whole; in the earlier five years it showed a rather mild decline and in the later ones a rather mildly rising tendency, and the latter worked towards a rise in the whole of the denominator. It is worth noting that in this figure, as distinct from Fig. 6.1—the denominator's curve is situated below that of personal consumption, as it is pulled down by the curve of the stagnating volume of government purchases. Curve no 7. on the figure is otherwise the curve of both the denominator and the volume of total consumption, (personal consumption plus government purchases) as the values of their indexes almost coincide.

Concerning the curves of the components in the numerator of Δp_c^* it seems worth mentioning that the growth of wages paid by private companies slowed down discernibly in 1975, more than that of total wages. Government wages were less affected by the recession. We also notice that the numerator of the Δp_c^* formula showed a higher rate of acceleration after 1973 than that of the Δp_c formula. As for the components of the two numerators, responsibility for this phenomenon lies evidently with government purchases, since the other two components from the three of total government expenditure, i.e., government wages and transfers, figure in the numerator of the Δp_c formula as well. We have just mentioned that the volume of these purchases showed a slightly upward trend in the last four years of the period—contrary to the development of the first five years. The upward trend is, of course, even more pronounced when these purchases are expressed in terms of money. Herein lies the explanation for this numerator's faster growth.

Events during the two years of the crisis (1974 and 1975) deserve particular attention. In these two years price developments appear especially paradoxical when compared with those during the preceding two boom years. Even the overall data are startling. During the two years of the overheated period (1972–1973) the narrower price indicator showed a 9.9 per cent, the wider one a 10.3 per cent rise, while in the two years of recession they showed 19.6 and 20.7 per cent, respectively. We can get a closer look into the circumstances of this as yet unparallelled phenomenon with the aid of Table 6.4.

In the Δp_c formula the price increasing effect of the numerator was reduced from 22.1 per cent in 1972–1973 to 17.7 per cent in 1974–1975, yet the rise in the price level was for

Table 6.4

Changes in price level, 1973/1971 and 1975/1973

(per cent)

	1973/1971		1975/1973	
	change	contribution*	change	contribution*
A: Δp_c				
1. Wages	22.9	26.5	17.0	19.8
2. Transfers	26.4	4.2	50.0	8.2
3. Less: taxes paid by wage earners	33.2	10.3	14.7	5.0
4. Less: net savings by wage earners		−1.7		5.3
5. *Numerator*	22.1	22.1	17.7	17.7
6. Personal consumption	10.7	11.9	−1.5	−1.7
7. Less: capitalists' consumption	7.3	0.8	−0.3	0.0
8. *Denominator*	11.1	11.1	−1,6	−1.6
9. Δp_c	9.9		19.6	
B: Δp_c^*				
10. Business wages	23.9	18.8	16.4	13.2
11. Government expenditures covered by receipts	28.2	12.9	14.1	6.9
12. Government deficit		−3.9		8.5
13. Less: taxes paid by wage earners	33.2	8.6	14.7	· 4.2
14. Less: net savings by wage earners		−1.5		4.5
15. *Numerator*	20.5	20.5	19.8	19.8
16. Personal consumption	10.7	10.0	−1.5	−1.4
17. Government purchases	0.0	0.0	4.3	0.6
18. Less: capitalists' consumption	7.3	0.7	−0.3	0.0
19. *Denominator*	9.4	9.4	−0.8	−0.8
20. Δp_c^*	10.3		20.7	
Addendum				
21. Government expenditures (11 + 12)	18.7	8.9	32.6	15.4
22. Total consumption (16 + 17)	9.2	10.0	−0.7	−0.8

* Percentage contribution to the changes in the numerator and the denominator.

the latter two years double that of the two former ones. It thus seems obvious that the "blame" for this big rise should be unequivocally put on the change in the denominator (a decrease of 1.6 per cent). The matter is, however, not quite so simple nor unequivocal.

We could just as well argue in the following manner: 1974 and 1975 were recession years and in a recession both GNP and sales usually fall. Indeed, the volume of personal consumption also dropped this time, thus obeying the "rule" valid for crises. Had the volume of personal consumption been growing—other things being equal—also in this period by about 11.1 per cent instead of the decline of 1.6 per cent, then the price rise would have amounted to 5.9 per cent, not to 19.6, that is, much less than between 1971–1973. This train of thought leads to the conclusion that the "culprit" for the unusually high rate of inflation was the denominator, that is, the drop in the volume of commodities sold. As much is true that under the conditions of an almost 20 per cent rise in price level only a smaller volume of consumer goods could be sold. But an increase in the denominator of only 7.5 per cent would have been sufficient, instead of 11.1, to bring about a price rise not higher than the one between 1971–1973. i.e., 9.9 per cent.

But would it have been possible at all to sell 7.1 per cent more consumer goods in 1974–1975 than that sold in 1972–1973? The answer can only be yes, and we cannot even exclude that this could have been done without a rise in output, since stocks increased even during 1974 considerably, and the inventories of retail trade increased somewhat even in 1975. But, if it had been intended, production also could have been increased as there was abundant labour available and capacities were underutilized. However, capitalists would have answered this argument by saying that a price rise of only 9.9 per cent would not have even compensated for the increase in costs. It certainly would not have been sufficient for that, although an increase in output could have, at least to some extent, reduced the increase in unit costs (during the crisis—mainly in consequence of it—there was a drop in productivity). And, as we have seen on pp. 62–64 an increase in sales could also have augmented the real profits of those producing consumer goods. But why could costs not have risen faster than sales prices? This is an almost redundant question since, in fact, they did increase faster. This is also proven by the changes in the profit margin. Namely, we have seen that the net profit margin after taxes fell from 14.9 per cent in 1973 to 12 per cent by 1974 and the gross, after-tax profit margin from 25 per cent in 1973 to 22.9 per cent by 1974, (to rise again to 24.5 per cent in 1975). There are too many variants for the forms in which the sales volume of consumer goods could have increased by 9.9 per cent instead of falling by 1.6, so that we are unable to tell exactly what consequences this would have involved. According to our estimate the net, after-tax profit margin might have been around 10 per cent. It could have reached a somewhat higher value than that of net capital investment, the balance of foreign trade, government deficit and the savings by workers had remained at their actual levels of 1974–1975.[14] But, in spite of the rough estimation, we should not think that prices would have been too low to cover costs. And if we make the same

[14] The ratio of profits and the sales' volume of 1973 multiplied by 0.984 equals 12, if the ratio of profits and the sales' volume of 1973 multiplied by 1.099 is x, then x = 10.7.

estimation for the gross, after-tax profit margin, we get a value of 20.5 per cent, thus one that is only 10.5 per cent (2.4 percentage points) less than the actual one.

In other words, it is true, and if so, to what extent, that the denominator was the "culprit" for the astonishing rise in prices? The numerator increased while the denominator decreased, hence the "guilt" of the denominator is also clear, though both changes increase the price. But why did the denominator fall? Obviously not because the nominator increased. It fell, because, as long as it could, capital defended its usual profit margin. If the numerator had risen more strongly, it would have become possible to sell more goods even at the administered, 20 per cent higher, prices, the denominator need not have decreased at all, or only slightly (though it is not clear whether the profit margin would not have fallen to an even lower value).

Who could justly and reasonably expect capitalists not to defend their profit margins? But who would have expected what happened before it actually happened, namely, that prices would soar by 20 per cent in two years in a time of crisis? "The time is out of joint", said Prince Hamlet. And we cannot blame unequivocally either the numerator or the denominator; it would not be justified to speak unequivocally either about cost-push or demand-pull inflation. We have three aggregate variables: the numerator, the denominator and the price level. Our diagrams show how and with what paradoxical result their mutual adjustment took place. The mutual adjustment of the price level and the volume of sales (realized demand) produced turmoil. This was the price to be paid for the "success" of capitalists, as sellers exploiting their oligopolistic position, to shift the burden of their production-cost increases onto their customers—consumers and the government—brought about to a considerable extent by the explosion in oil prices and the rise in raw-material prices in general, that is, by random shocks originating mostly outside of the American economy. For this "success"—in our opinion, justly placed between quotation marks—capitalists had to pay with a drop in their sales volume and, as will be seen in the next part of this study, consequently with a considerable drop in their profit volume as well. The same phenomena are reflected (with some modifications not uninteresting themselves) by the data describing the developments in the components of the more comprehensive price level indicators in part B of the table. Here, too, we find an inversion of the normally price-reducing function of the denominator. This corroborates our previous statement about the failure of the adjustment process. But the "responsibility" of the denominator is somewhat smaller, as its price-raising impact is only about half as much of what we have found in the Δp_c formula. We can trace the cause if we scan row 8 of part B of the table: the volume of government purchases did not play any role whatever in the changes having occurred between 1971 and 1973. In the next two years, however, it had a price-level-reducing effect of 0.6 per cent.

Within the Δp_c^* formula, however, the numerator is not "innocent" either. Its price-increasing impact decreased even during the two years of sluggishness only negligibly in comparison with that during the boom. The explanation for this small difference can be found in row 12 of the Addendum, where it turns out that the price-increasing effect of government purchases has grown significantly (from 8.9 to 15.4 per cent). Within this, the change in the role of government deficit might be considered important both quantitatively and qualitatively. This component, which, in the long run, might be deemed relatively negligible in comparison to the total government expenditure, has now gained considerable significance. Row 3 in table B shows that while its change had a price-reducing effect between 1971 and 1973, in the following two years this was transformed into a price-raising one of considerable quantitative importance. More than half of the price-raising impact of the total government expenditure originated in the fact that the government balance, instead of the 1973 surplus, showed in 1975 the highest deficit of the whole post-war period. The same phenomenon finds its reflection—on the other side of the coin, so-to-speak—in the fact that the price-raising effect of government expenditure covered by revenues fell simultaneously by almost its half.

It is also worthwhile taking a closer look at the other components of the numerator. We have mentioned that the price-raising impact of the numerator of the Δp_c formula weakened between 1973 and 1975, and that this was expectable in times of sluggish business. Yet this weakening of the price-raising effect was not as pronounced as might be judged adequate during a crisis. Let us see how the price effect of the spendable income of wage earners (wages plus transfers less taxes) changed. The results will hold for both price indicators, since these terms figure in the numerators of both. As a result of declining business the rate of increase in the sum of wages slowed down considerably; so did that of total wages, but even more—understandably—of business wages (by 5.9, resp. 7.9 percentage points). Accordingly, also their price-increasing effect was moderated (by 6.7 and 5.6 percentage points). The paradoxical phenomenon that although the growth rate of business wages was considerably reduced, this was accompanied by only a slight drop in its price raising effect, is attributable to the fact that the relative share of these wages is much less in the numerator of the Δp_c^* formula than that of total wages in the Δp_c formulae.

Transfers present a peculiar but logical picture. Their growth rate which, even in years of good business, is usually higher than that of wages (a consequence of the usual swelling of sums paid out in the scope of the different social welfare programs), showed an unparalleled jump in the years of the crisis—by 50 per cent in two years. This was almost threefold of the growth rate of wages, and thus also its price-raising effect almost doubled. This jump was brought about by the swelling of unemployment benefits, that is, of the operation of a built-in stabilizer. This was useful for maintaining the purchasing power of the workers who lost their jobs, but it was detrimental to the expected mitigation of inflation through the sluggishness of business, since it almost completely neutralized the effect of the drop in the growth rate of wages. This is clearly proven by the data: between 1971 and 1973 the combined price-raising impact of the two components was 30.7 per cent and in the next two years it still remained at 28 per cent.

The price-rise-mitigating effect of the changes in taxes paid by wage earners was quite considerable, 10.3 per cent, in the boom years. But this impact fell in the two years 1974–1975 to less than half, 5.0 per cent. It is commonly known that the progressive income tax is also regarded as one of the built-in stabilizers, as in times of good business it mitigates the growth of disposable income, while in a recession it softens its reduction. But now this proved to be only partially true. Namely, the fast rise of taxes did indeed mitigate the boom, but during the recession it did not exert the expected stabilizing effect because, while trying to keep up with inflation, many moved into higher tax brackets owing to their higher nominal wages. Thus they had to pay higher taxes although their real income did not increase at all, and indeed might have even fallen. The government thus thought it opportune to take a one-time discretionary measure and cut taxes in April 1975. This reduced the price-mitigating impact of the tax by half. Finally, the combined price-raising effect of the above-mentioned three components showed an increase in 1974–1975 in comparison with that experienced during the boom: it went up from 20.4 per cent to 23.3. Thus it is generally true that both the built-in stabilizers and those brought about by discretionary decisions more or less contribute to damping the business cycles, but—since they either expand or reduce nominal demand—they also have an inflationary or deflating effect. In these two years their combined impact was inflationary. A well-working built-in stabilizer and an indeed poorly working one, coupled with a discretionary measure of great impact were to be blamed for the fact that in times of a crisis inflation even accelerated in comparison with its rate in the preceding boom.

But a little while ago we have written that the price raising effect of the numerator in the Δp_c formula did palpably diminish. This is, naturally, true. It may be attributed to the change in the fourth component in the numerator, i. e., the savings by wage earners, as can be read from row 4 in part A of the table. The impact of this component turned into its opposite during the transition from boom to bust — in a manner characteristic of the period: a price-raising effect of 1.7 per cent in 1973–1974 and a price-reducing one in 1974–1975. Thus the behaviour of the working people was—at least from the point of view of fighting inflation—more rational than that of the built-in stabilizers and discretionary measures devised by the experts. This effect was, of course, not conscious, since the replacement of overspending by saving was forced upon them by justified fear from unemployment and other consequences of the crisis. Several Western economists were astonished at the rise in personal savings even under the conditions of growing inflation. So much is, however, true that if saving occurs massively, the final result will be a moderation of the price rise, and everybody's money will lose less of its value than would have been the case without such behaviour.

6.4 OLIGOPOLY, PRICE TRENDS, ACCELERATING INFLATION

In the first two sections of this chapter we have been reasoning in terms of the relationships illustrated by the formulae Δp_c and Δp_c^*, that is, the mutual adjustment of nominal demand, the price level and the volume of sales. We were investigating, for example, whether in a given case the numerator or the denominator of the formula were to be blamed for the increase in prices. According to this reasoning the change in the price level seems to be simply a function of the nominal demand and the volume of product sold, (i. e., real supply), that is, the fact becomes lost that the majority of today's prices are formed in an oligopolistic manner. These prices are formed relatively autonomously by the oligopolies in view of the estimated costs and the calculated profit margin. And the formulae used above do not even include costs or the profit margin. Though in section 3 of this chapter the profit margin was mentioned, it only occurred in a special context, namely, what would have happened to it in 1974–1975, had the volume of sales not declined then. But today the category of the profit margin has a highly important role: it is that factor of oligopolistic price formation that is determined—of course, within certain error margins—by the oligopolies themselves.

Of course, non-oligopolistic business branches can also be found in the United States. But presumably also the overwhelming part of the products of the latter reach the final users through oligopolistic distribution networks. Thus we hardly commit a grave mistake if we try to interpret the inflation of the seventies by reasoning along the lines of the model of oligopolistic price formation.

The price of a unit volume of product is the sum of the prime cost and the profit margin, and the change in price the sum of changes in these two components. The statement that oligopolistic industries can on the whole regulate the profit margin means more exactly that in the oligopolistic industries there usually are one or two such outstanding firms which initiate the change in price, that is, add some calculated profit to the cost unknown precisely in advance but at any rate estimated. It determines the price on this basis and the others follow it in respect of price. (This does not mean that the profit margin will be the same with the other enterprises as with the price leader.)

But the price leader or the individual oligopolistic groups can influence only little the level of costs. They are capable of that only to the extent they can save living or embodied labour (apart from the case when they obtain materials or labour exceptionally cheaply).

But the development of the price level of the cost elements is independent only from the behaviour of the individual oligopolistic groups, but not from that of the ensemble of oligopolies. To wit it is not independent of the fact that the price system of the country bears the imprint of the large weight of the oligopolies.

As regards the wage level, even an enterprise in an oligopolistic situation cannot decide freely how high it should set at the most the wage level of its workers. It is not only that the trade unions have an effective say in the matter, but in respect of the wage level every enterprise has to keep pace with the others and with other industries, or else its workers will leave. But, in lack of particularly inhibitive causes the ensemble of the oligopolies is not forced to exert great resistance against the wage-raising demands of the trade unions, since, in general, they are able to shift the higher wage costs onto their buyers. But materials and services are also brought about by labour. In the last resort—if they are of domestic origin—also their costs are reduced to domestic labour costs and thus their increment can also be shifted. (As much is, however, true that the rise in material prices appears in the rise of product prices usually only with a certain time lag.) On the one hand, the shifting of cost rises through prices is made possible by the fact that the wage is a cost only for the enterprise while for the one receiving the wage it is income, the overwhelming part of which soon becomes effective demand. (The intervention of the state only makes this interrelation more complicated, but does not alter the substance.) On the other hand, the possibility of shifting the costs becomes a fact only because the oligopolies also regulate the volume of products released and thus the actual supply of their products, that is, they prevent—with rather more than less success—unwanted unsold inventories from accumulating while they themselves set the prices. In other words, the oligopolistic group can well adjust its own supply to the global effective demand coming about in the case of a price level regulated on the basis of oligopolistic principles, while, of course, the individual firm makes efforts to increase demand for its own products through advertising, product differentiation, additional services and the like. Thus, the cost level may have and does have a rising tendency. But the situation is different with the profit margin. This surely deserves a more thorough examination.

Alfred S. Echner, one of the leadig personalities of "post-Keynesian economics"—now perhaps the most progressive non-socialist school of economics—is of the opinion that he has succeeded in finding a unique, matematically defined solution to the problem of how high is the profit margin calculated by oligopolies. An essential element of his relevant argumentation is his statement that demand for the commodities of a typical oligopoly is sufficiently inelastic for the enterprise (or group of enterprises) to be able to increase also its total profit by increasing the profit margin. (See. e.g., Eichner, 1980., pp. 113–114.)

With this theorem Eichner wished to estasblish his idea that the oligopolies have more or less a free hand in shaping their total profit, thus also in increasing their total profit through a higher set profit margin—although restricted by the danger of the entry of new enterprises and government intervention. (He explains these ideas using a terminology different from ours.) But this can be only true in the case of microlevel changes. That it might be true also for the case of individual groups of products was shown in this book in section 8 of chapter 5 (pp. 62–64). But in sections 7 and 8 of the same chapter it was also pointed out that in respect to real profit it is not true for the aggregate of consumer-goods producers, in fact—with the possible exception of special transitory states—the opposite is true.

We cannot go here into the details of Eichner's ideas about the determination of the profit margin, explained in over 200 printed pages. In a highly simplified manner and translated into our own terminology we can say that according to him the oligopolies set the profit margin so high—and not higher—that their own means deriving from the resulting profit—after the satisfaction of their shareholders—should allow the implementation of so much investment in the next period for which investment plans considered justified are prepared.

Eichner reached this conclusion through observation of a few oligopolistic groups. It is also true that enterprises indeed spend the overwhelming part of their undistributed profits sooner or later on investment—though we are of the opinion, with good reason, that with a not negligible part of the profit they increase their own liquid reserves and augment their portfolio. Nor is it clear that if the wider profit margin indeed involved a greater amount of profit, why should the investment propensity be a more objective determinant of the profit making efforts of the oligopoly than the size of future attainable profit would be of investment intended to be realized through self-financing. This is particularly unclear if we consider that a growing number of enterprises extend their activities to new fields and the expansion of the scope of activity is investment-intensive.

But, however, matters should stand, it is clear that those planning prices and investment have some *ex ante* idea about how big their total profit will be in the case of a certain profit margin, but it would testify to an unlikely great naivety if they were sure of the realization of their ideas. As a matter of fact, though monopolies reason in terms of the profit margin when setting the price level, they actually set the latter and not the profit margin. Nobody can know the profit margin *ex ante*. In the last but one paragraph of section 8 of chapter 5, in this book we have already discussed why the future prime cost of a unit volume of product is uncertain *ex ante*. To wit, not only the future price level of wages and raw materials may cause surprise, but the prime cost also depends on the development of the general overhead costs per unit of product, and the latter on the, for the time being uncertain, saleable volume of the product. The enterprise could not know this volume *ex ante*, even if it could well estimate to what extent the change in price level would modify—*ceteris paribus*—the volume of sales. The volume of sales does not adjust to *ceteris paribus* assumptions, but depends, among other things, on demand, thus on the size of government revenues and expenditure, on the balance of trade, on the savings or overspending of workers — and not only of workers. And conversely, it is not revealed by the actual, observable (*ex post*) profit margin what the target was, and less the size of the hoped for volume of profit.

Further, it is a fact that the correlation between investment and the course of the business cycle is positive in spite of the fact—and this will be discussed in our book at some length—that today the changes in investment follow the changes in business with a time lag. Greater investment increases—*ceteris paribus*—the profit and thus improves business while smaller investment lessens it—*ceteris paribus*. Our data show (see Table 5.1) that the profit margin was higher in times of good business than in times of bad business. What should we then believe? Did the profit margin diminish in times of bad business because the enterprises wished to moderate the investments within the time horizon of their own planning, or was it the bad business and the accompanying moderation of the increase in nominal demand that forced them to moderate their prices, to accept — intentionally or necessarily — a lower profit margin. In our view, the latter explanation is the one closer to the truth.

We need not necessarily think that the oligopolies would agree with what has been said about the drawbacks of a too high profit margin. The too high inventories and the increase in the relative weight of fixed costs entailed by the moderation of production are costly affairs. Also an enterprise in an oligopolistic situation has to strive to produce by well exploiting its capacities, and watch that its share of total turnover (that is, not only in the turnover of the products marketed by it) should not diminish, and it will thus think twice before further raising its prices if it sees that the realized profit margin is lower than planned. It seems we can draw the conclusion that though the oligopolies can directly influence the price level through planning the profit margin, yet the real development of the profit margin does not depend on their investment intentions but above all on the development of demand and supply.

We believe that in our Δp_c and Δp_c^* diagrams and the related analyses we have sufficiently pointed out the direct causes which determined the changes in nominal demand in a given year and by comparing the changes in price and the profit margin we could also make deductions concerning costs—at least on the GNP level.

It turns out from our diagrams that the relative weight of those factors the combined impact of which determines the mutual adjustment of nominal demand, the price level and the volume of products sold was different in each year and their totality affected the price rise or made it possible to different degrees from year to year. Thus, the price development in individual years was considerably affected by random factors from the viewpoint of the theory of inflation—which has yet to be born, in fact. But it cannot be doubted either that the average increase of prices exceeded in the seventies that experienced in the sixties and it is also a fact that in the decade examined both economic policy makers and public opinion were much more worried about inflation than in the preceding decade.

However, this must not be exaggerated either. It is shown by our diagrams that inflation did not continually accelerate in the examined period. Thus, e. g., the rate of price increase exceeded the annual 4.5 per cent already in 1970, while even in 1976 it moved around 5 per cent and in 1972 it hardly attained 4 per cent. Nevertheless, particulary in the second half of the decade, we not only see irregular fluctuations but also note definite acceleration trends, and the cause or causes of the tendency are hardly explained by our diagrams satisfactorily.

It seems clear that in the acceleration of inflation several one-time events, to be considered random from the viewpoint of the general theory, have played a role, but we can hardly rest content with that. We must further confess that we also cannot solve the problem the solution of which escaped all others. We cannot list in a systematic and, mainly, exhaustive manner the lasting impacts which had to lead necessarily to this change—thus not in a random way.

But we can say something about them. We start with a negative statement. Inflation did accelerate because the oligopolies and monopolies raised the profit margin exorbitantly high above costs. It turns out from Table 5.1 that the profit margin at GNP level was highest in the period examined precisely at the end of the sixties, in 1968 and 1969. It has not attained that level and it was lowest precisely at the time of the highest price rise, in 1974 and 1975. The profit margin increased somewhat in 1976, thus precisely when the lowest price rise of the second half of the seventies was experienced. Following that the rise in price level again accelerated, while the profit margin on the whole stagnated (the net profit margin increased somewhat, the gross declined a little). As much is clear that whenever the profit margin diminishes, the rise in prices lags behind the increase in costs. In connection with the latter the problem arises whether the acceleration of inflation should be considered a cost-push or a demand-pull phenomenon. Obviously, we cannot give an unambiguous "either/or" answer, since we also understand that what is an additional cost for one agent of the economy, is additional receipt for another and thus a source of potential additional demand. This particularly holds for wage costs, since wage earners always spend the bulk of their wages, that is, raise demand with them.

A not negligible part of wages are not paid by enterprises, but potentially all wages can become demand. As regards consumer goods, the overwhelming part of demand derives precisely from wages. Thus the question arises whether a regular parallel development can be found between the demand-increasing impact of the additional wages spent on consumer goods and the extent of change in the price level of consumer goods. The relevant data are to be found at the end of the chapter in rows 1 and 10 of Table 6.5. The contents of the first row, wage incomes, is the percentage with which wages paid would have increased demand in the given year relative to the nominal demand in the preceding year, had the other components of demand remained the same.

From the data it is first of all obvious that wages paid out increased demand (modified, of course, by transfers and savings) every year by a bigger percentage than the increase in prices. If we only reported on tendencies, there would be nothing surprising in that, because, *ceteris paribus*, a wage increase does not raise prices, if labour productivity similarly increases. The surprising thing is that it appeared each year, although the productivity of labour did not at all develop satisfactorily each year.

But we have also seen that the data called "wage incomes" moved parallel to Δp_c in only four years, more exactly, in 1971 both remained on the level of the preceding year, in 1973 and 1978 both increased, in 1975 both diminished, and in 1970 the percentual price-raising effect of wage incomes declined, while Δp_c remained on the earlier level. In a further four years they moved in the opposite direction from the previous year, so that in 1972 and 1974 wage incomes increased, but Δp_c diminished, while when the inflation rate was fastest, that is, in 1974, the price-raising impact of wage incomes exceeded that of 1972 by a mere one tenth of a per cent — when inflation was lowest. In 1977 the inflation rate was again faster than in 1976, yet the impact of wage incomes fell by one tenth of a per cent.

Naturally, the total wages received are not the only determinant of the total demand raised by workers, since this demand is increased by transfers and the overspending by workers, but is reduced by taxes on wages and savings. The percentual increase in the

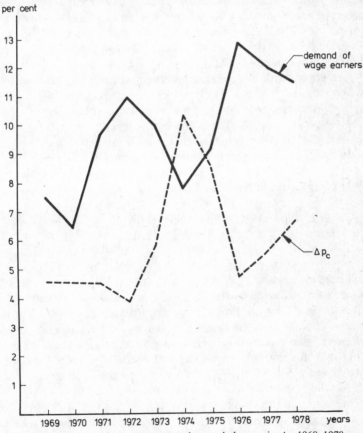

Figure 6.3 Demand of wage earners and annual changes in Δp_c 1968–1978

87

total nominal demand by workers relative to the previous year is shown by the numerator of the Δp formula. This has to be confronted with the development of inflation. The data can be found in rows 5 and 10 of Table 6.5, but, in order to make it palpable, the two rows are illustrated in Fig. 6.3.

We find a startling picture. The line indicating the percentual changes in the nominal demand of workers over the preceding year jumped in 1970 and 1971 rather erratically, while the line of the rate of inflation remained horizontal. Beginning with 1972 the two lines moved each year in the opposite direction: inflation accelerated when the pulling effect of the total earnings of workers diminished in percentages relative to the preceding year. And inflation slackened when the increment of nominal demand effected a relatively bigger pull percentually. We are of the opinion that this provides us with a rather weigthy argument for stating that the inflation of the seventies must not be declared to have been mainly a demand–pull inflation.

But we also see something else. Regarding the tendencies, not only inflation increased, but so did the pulling effect of the demand of workers, facilitating the raising of prices-but this is self-explanatory. Production should fall catastrophically if the growth of nominal demand did not acceletare with inflating prices. Growing demand, of course, also contributed to inflation, since there can hardly be found an inflation, which would not be influenced by both sides—demand and costs—pulled or pushed by them. The question is whether one can establish which aspect's impact was decisive. There is every indication that in the years examined it was that of costs.

A few paragraphs earlier we said that if the profit margin diminishes, price will lag behind the growth of costs. Reversing the theorem we arrive at the following, similarly correct statement, namely, that also in the case of rising prices a diminishing profit margin indicates costs rising faster than prices. In the seventies the profit margin never reached the 1968 or 1969 levels. Therefore, in this decade costs rose faster than prices compared to the late sixties. This was also a lasting phenomenon.

Let us see from what date did inflation accelerate! Consumer prices increased, measured by the consumer basket of urban wage and salary earners by the following percentages, computed on the basis of official data (e.g., *Economic Report*, 1978, p. 314):

1960	1961	1962	1963	1964	1965	1966	1967	1968	1969	1970
1.6	1.0	1.1	1.2	1.3	1.7	2.9	2.9	4.2	5.4	4.9

As can be seen the price index increased somewhat beginning with 1962, but up to 1965 this growth remained below 2 per cent, after which inflation accelerated. By the last year of the decade, measured by the consumer–price index, it was already somewhat faster than what is shown for 1969 by our Δp_c formula.

We have not yet investigated in detail—nor can we—what the reason or main reason was for the acceleration of inflation in the second half of the sixties. It has to be taken into account that, for example, beginning with 1961 President Kennedy pursued an expansive budgetary policy. In 1961, 1962 and 1964 the government balance closed with a deficit, while— partly also on this account—by 1965 full employment taken in the then prevailing official sense was attained (with a 4.5 per cent rate of unemployment). The Vietnam War also contributed to this and its increasing costs made it practically impossible to restore the balance of the budget with the prevailing tax rates. Government expenditure increased between 1961 and 1964 by 5.1 per cent on the annual average, well exceeding the rate of inflation. Between 1965 and 1969 the average annual increase of the deficit was already 8 per cent, and this, too, was much higher than the rate of the already accelerating inflation. In vain did President Johnson propose to Congress in 1966 and 1967 to raise the tax rates—and this is how the record deficit of the post-war period, $14.2 bn, was attained in 1967. But it turned out that the "full" employment of 1965 was not really full: uneployment continued to diminish and fell to its lowest in 1969 with 3.5 per cent.

The increase in government expenditure not covered by wage taxes is a factor contributing to inflation from the side of demand. And the increment of the wage tax, if it is not accompanied by a corresponding reduction of after-tax wages, stimulates inflation from the side of costs, since the costs of enterprises are the gross (pre-tax) wages. But a reduction of the after-tax wage level is quite unlikely under the conditions of full and even tense employment.

We listed only two—probably important—causes of inflation from among the many probable ones, but for the time being we only want to emphasize—with some explanation added—that inflation started to accelerate already beginning with the mid-fifties, and this is a very important fact for understanding what follows.

Namely, the most general cause of inflation and its acceleration is the consolidation of inflationary expectations, or inflation itself.

In the first half of the sixties, under the conditions of increasing employment and rising real wages workers did not much feel the inflation that was less than 2 per cent a year. But when prices start to grow more significantly and when it turns out that this is a lasting tendency, in order to preserve their share of the national income workers start a stronger counter-offensive. And similarly to the price leaders among oligopolies, among the representatives of workers' interests, the trade unions, there also are powerful ones which lead the fight for raising wages. Collective contracts are becoming frequent which take into account the expected increase in productivity, but also the expected rate of inflation. The trade unions face the oligopolies and, as had been pointed out, keeping the wage level low is not a top priority of the oligopolies since they simply shift the costs to the buyers. (At some stages of his attempt at wage control, President Nixon thought it was necessary that the rise in wages should be maximized by the state itself.) As much can be seen from this line of reasoning that a wage rise won under conditions of inflation works—as regards its effect on demand and costs—at least towards preserving the earlier rate of inflation. But much more is likely to be true. We know from Hungarian experience that if wages grow where productivity increases, then—in order to avoid insupportable disproportions and a strong migration of labour, wages have to be increased also where productivity has not increased, e.g., in certain unproductive jobs. (The disproportionate rise in the price level of certain services is chronic.) This works towards accelerating inflation. Enough said about wages in connection with inflationary expectations.

Another aspect of the same phenomenon is related to the price policy of oligopolies. We have already seen that the profit margin did not rise in the course of inflation. But when an oligopoly sets its prices for a coming period, it adds the no higher profit margin to the future cost calculated according to the rate of inflation. Naturally, this too works towards maintaining the inflationary processes and, in an accelerating inflation, it itself accelerates.

The cost per unit of product is reduced by a rising labour productivity only when other things are equal. But in the seventies the productivity of labour developed unfavourably. Between 1968 and 1978 it increased by merely 1.6 per cent on the annual average, while the average over several years had been 2–2.2 per cent, and even a decline occurred. Of course, this development also spurred inflation from the side of costs. And this was accompanied—as will be related later—by an unsatisfactory investment activity. With a slack investment activity the productivity of labour could not, in all probability, have increased satisfactorily. But most bourgeois authors also link the slackening of investment activity with inflation itself. They generally argue that, as a result of inflation, enterprises become hesitant in their calcutions and fear possible but unforeseeable government interventions. It seems to us that it is precisely the fact of inflation itself that makes a certain kind of calculation rather safe. If a fixed asset is to be discarded, say, after five years, then under normal conditions enterprises have to save from their gross profits the cost of future replacement in five years. On the other hand, if the annual rate of inflation were only 5 per cent, in five years they would have to pay 28 per cent more for similar new equipment to replace the old one. But the current rate of inflation is higher than 5 per cent, and the depreciation allowance

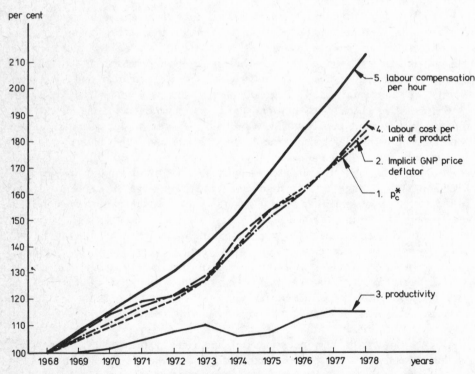

Figure 6.4 Movement of the Δp_c^* price level indicator and some factors influencing price changes, 1968—1978, 1968 = 100

Table 6.5

Percentage contributions of the components figuring in the numerator and the denominator of the Δp_c formula to the total percentage change in the price level indicator Δp_c, 1969—1978

(per cent)

Components	1969	1970	1971	1972	1973	1974	1975	1976	1977	1978
1. Wages	11.5	8.1	8.1	11.5	13.5	11.5	7.6	13.1	13.0	14.3
2. Government transfers	1.4	2.7	2.7	1.7	2.2	3.1	4.8	1.9	1.5	1.5
3. Less: taxes of wage earners	5.6	1.2	1.5	5.4	4.4	4.7	0.2	5.6	4.9	5.0
4. Less: net savings by wage earners	−0.4	3.2	−0.3	−3.2	1.3	2.2	2.9	−3.5	−2.6	−0.8
5. *Numerator* (1—4)	7.7	6.4	9.7	11.0	10.0	7.8	9.2	12.9	12.1	11.6
6. Personal consumption	3.1	1.7	5.4	7.4	4.2	−2.4	0.8	8.3	6.5	4.7
7. Less: capitalists' consumption	0.2	0.1	0.5	0.5	0.3	−0.1	0.1	0.5	0.5	0.3
8. *Denominator* (6—7)	2.9	1.7	4.9	6.9	3.9	−2.4	0.7	7.8	6.1	4.5
9. Δp_c (5—8)	4.8	4.9	4.8	4.1	6.1	10.2	8.5	5.1	6.0	7.1
10. Δp_c (5/8)	4.6	4.6	4.6	3.9	5.9	10.4	8.4	4.8	5.7	6.8

Table 6.6

Percentage contributions of the components figuring in the numerator and the denominator of the Δp_c^* formula to the total percentage change of the price level indicator Δp_c^*, 1969—1978

(per cent)

Components	1969	1970	1971	1972	1973	1974	1975	1976	1977	1978
1. Business wages	7.8	4.7	5.0	7.9	9.9	8.3	4.5	9.4	9.5	10.5
2. Government expenditures covered by receipts	5.6	0.8	3.3	6.6	5.7	5.7	1.1	6.9	6.0	6.3
3. Government deficit	−2.9	3.4	1.2	−2.3	−1.5	1.0	6.8	−3.0	−1.6	−1.9
4. Less: taxes paid by wage earners	4.5	1.0	1.2	4.6	3.7	4.0	0.2	4.7	4.2	4.2
5. Less: net savings by wage earners	−0.3	2.6	−0.3	−2.7	1.1	1.8	2.5	−3.0	−2.2	−0.7
6. *Numerator* (1—5)	6.3	5.3	8.6	10.3	9.3	9.3	9.7	10.7	11.9	11.4
7. Personal consumption	2.5	1.4	4.5	6.2	3.6	−2.1	0.7	7.0	5.6	4.1
8. Government purchases	−0.9	−1.1	−0.2	0.3	−0.3	0.3	0.4	−0.05	0.6	0.1
9. Less: capitalists' consumption	0.2	0.1	0.4	0.4	0.2	−0.1	0.4	0.5	0.4	0.2
10. *Denominator* (7—9)	1.5	0.3	3.9	6.1	3.0	−1.7	1.0	6.5	5.8	4.0
11. Δp_c^* (6—10)	4.8	5.0	4.7	4.1	6.3	11.0	8.7	5.1	6.1	7.5
12. Δp_c^* (6/10)	4.8	4.9	4.6	3.9	6.1	11.2	8.6	4.8	5.8	7.2

allowed would not cover the replacement. (Namely, it is regulated by law what percentage of the purchase price can be written off as depreciation. What would result above that is taxed as profit.) It is highly doubtful whether, if enterprises invest the accumulating replacement fund into securities, their interests make up for the loss otherwise caused by higher prices. (If there were no inflation, the attainable, say, 5 per cent annual interest would be pure profit.)

Further, in the sixties the United States enriched itself through the inordinately overvalued dollar at the expense of the whole world. This process came to an end in this form by the early seventies and the dollar became steadily and significantly devalued. The United States imported significantly less commodities for the same amount of dollars. If the more expensive imported commodity is further processed, this considerably increases costs relative to the earlier ones, while the additional receipts corresponding to the additional costs are enjoyed by other countries.

This problem has become extremely acute because of the oil price explosion and the parallel, though smaller, increase in the prices of other imported materials. True, immediately after the oil price explosion price rise directly caused by it was estimated only at about 2 percentage points. But in the period examined the average annual price rise was 6 per cent, while between 1965 and 1969 it was 3.4 per cent. The difference is only 2.6 percentage points, but oil prices continued to increase considerably even after the price explosion.

Perhaps this necessarily very defective list—comprising many commonplaces—is sufficient so that we do not stand perplexed at the sight of accelerating inflation.

To conclude this part we show in Fig. 6.4 the movement of the price level indicator Δp_c^* and of some factors influencing the price level. The close correlation between the labour cost per unit of product and the development of prices is particularly worthy of attention.

PART THREE

ON PROFIT

CHAPTER SEVEN

PROFIT AND PAPER PROFIT

Having looked in part two into the changes in profit margins, we have already touched on what constitutes the subject of the third part. We are going to discuss profits in connection with business fluctuations.

Profit is a central concept in the political economy of capitalism. Profits and the chase after profits are regarded by buorgeois political economy culminating with Ricardo and by Marxian political economy as the main motor of capitalist economy. In olden times the automatic economic mechanism of capitalism shaped profits, while changes of the latter were fed back, similarly automatically, into the economy, controlling simultaneously also the process as a whole. Today, however, the state also interferes with the development of profits through its monetary and fiscal policies.

In this part we shall investigate what factors influenced the development of profit between 1968–1978 in the United States.

Since among these factors capital investment on the one hand, and government budget, on the other, carry a special weight and, within the latter, government deficits and surpluses are of exceptional importance, we will pay special attention to the relationship between changes in the budget and in investment.

7.1 THE COMPONENTS OF PROFIT

Similarly to the second part of our book, this third part will carry a few illustrative diagrams. These diagrams will illustrate the movement of gross, after-tax profit—that is, also including depreciation allowance—but in a peculiar manner, by its "components".

First of all, we have to clarify what we mean by the components of profit. Not that profit is "composed of" entrepreneurial gain and interest. But, if from nothing else, from Kalecki's macro-economic balances (Kalecki, 1970, pp. 78–83) we know that profit equals the sum of investment, capitalists' consumption, export surplus, government deficit and dissaving by wage earners. These addenda will be called profit components.

In the Appendix to this book we deduce, essentially with formal mathematical methods, Kalecki's theorem on the size of profit from the US statistics balance sheets of GNP. (Based on the National Income and Product Accounts.) However, it seems useful to discuss it also in this place. In the following reasoning, at least as a starting point, we are reasoning not in terms of GNP, but of net national income (product), and thus by profit we mean net instead of gross profit, and by investment net investment.

At the moment of their coming into being, goods belong to the capitalist class and also it is the capitalists who sell the services—except those rendered by government employees and treated in US statistics as a separate item—as if those were their property the way that goods are. A part of these goods only replaces worn out material capital. This part is not income; it is nobody's income. The remaining part is already income. True, by income we usually understand money, and goods or service is not money. In this sense, therefore, by income we mean material income, at least one existing in physical form. In a closed economy there are three types of income: the income of capitalists (profit), the income of the government, and that of workers (wages). In the case of an open economy we have to take into account, in addition to the three, also the possible income of the rest of the world originating in the given country. The part of the goods and services, which at the time of their origin are the property of the capitalist class, that are not to serve replacement, the capitalists have to transfer to others—to the state, the workers, perhaps to the rest of the world. But they may keep a part, that destined for their own consumption or for accumulation, that is, for themselves. Arguing in this manner, we might arrive at the conclusion that exactly this latter part, this set of goods and services makes up profits or, in other words, the physical form of profits. This train of thought facilitates the understanding of the fact that it is not the sum of capitalists' consumption and accumulation that depends on profits, but the other way round, the amount of profits depends on the part retained and meant for accumulation and capitalists' consumption. This train of thought is only approximately true, it is not sufficiently accurate. It was, namely, missing from our train of thought that the produced goods also have to be sold: these goods have to assume a money form instead of their natural form. The set of goods and services remaining the property of the capitalist class and destined for its personal consumption and for accumulation does not represent realized profits at the moment of its birth: in order to be realized they have to take the form of money. And this modifies the amount of profit considerably.

7.2 MATERIAL AND PAPER PROFITS

With this we have come across a paradoxical phenomenon: the paradox related to the process of the transformation of commodity into money form and the latter again into the form of commodity. On the one hand, it is true that the net national product is a sum of goods and services. These goods and services are at the same time the physical, natural form of the incomes accrueing to capitalists, workers and the government. (To this may be added the income received in physical form by the rest of the world from the country in question.) The net national product only comprises goods and services, money does not constitute a part of it. (It would also comprise money, if gold were to function as money and if it were mined in the given country. In such a case the amount of gold mined in a given year and functioning as money would be an integral part of the volume of goods produced in the

96

given country, hence a part of the net national product as well; and the total accumulated gold would be a part of the country's real wealth.) Contemporary money is, namely, credit money. Some people or organizations can have money only because others have the same amount of debt. If someone gets more money than he owned before, the debt of somebody else will grow by the same amount. The wealth of society as a whole will not increase on this account. Money cannot be consumed and any income not consumed increases the wealth of society. An increase in the amount of money in circulation does not increase, however, the wealth of society at all and, thus, money cannot represent more income for the society. This is one side of the coin.

The other side of the coin is that money still does slip, through a back door, into the notion of net national product. The commodities making up NNP take money form when they are realized and the total NNP is measured by the price sum into which NNP as a set of goods is transformed when it has been realized. The measure of NNP is the price sum of commodities making up the NNP. And the theorem that money is not a part of a country's wealth only holds for the nation as a whole (foreign claims being exceptions) but not for individual economic units or their groups. Anybody's wealth may exist either in the form of commodities or in the form of money.

The person who has his wealth in the form of commodities to be sold, transforms these commodities into money and after this transaction his wealth will be in the form of money. At the beginning of any period some people already do have money. Some of them will let this money or part of it out of their hands in exchange for commodities— this is their money expenditure, but, at the same time, money receipt for others, the sellers. Thus the sum of all expenditures and all receipts is always exactly equal. If, during any given period, the expenditures of government and wage earners equal exactly their receipts, and also the balance of trade of the country is zero, then also the expenditures of the capitalist class must necessarily equal their receipts. This is the case when the amount of profits exactly equals the sum of capitalists' consumption and investment, both in physical and money forms.

On the other hand, in order to transform this profit into realized profit, its components—investment goods and consumption goods for capitalists—have to undergo the process of transformation into money form. A capitalist who has money buys investment goods or consumer goods from another capitalist. Thus the other capitalist has effected the sale of his commodity, the money of the first capitalist has flowed to him. No income has come about through this transaction. The first capitalist had money, in exchange for which he obtained goods (or a service), the price of which equalled the sum of money paid. And the other capitalist had in his hand an amount of money equal to the price sum of his own commodity (or service).

By what right then can we say that the total amount of investment goods and consumer goods bought by capitalists still constitutes income, that is, profit? (gross investment gross profit, net investment net profit). We can arrive at this conclusion through two different ways of argument. According to the first train of thought, goods and services consumed by capitalists and investment goods they acquired constitute that part of NNP which the capitalist class did not let out of his hands. The other part of NNP gets into the hands of others: this second part constitutes the natural (physical) form of the production and circulation costs of the capitalist class, including now also taxes regarded as costs. The goods and services which ended in the hands of others constitute the total costs of the capitalist class; there are no other costs whatsoever over and above these. The part they retained is the part over and above their costs, hence it constitutes their profit. This is the first line of argument formulated in physical terms.

We formulate the second train of thought by reasoning, instead of physical terms, in those of money and we reach the same conclusion.

Namely, when selling the goods and services the members of the capitalist class obtain money. They have to sell all their products and thus they acquire a sum of money equal to the price sum of these products. On the other hand, they also have expenses. A part of these expenses cover their costs. The difference between costs and money receipts is their profit expressed in terms of money. But if, besides them, everyone else—both government and wage earners—have spent an amount of money exactly equal to their receipts (and if foreign trade was also balanced), then the capitalist class also had to spend the difference between their money receipts and costs, that is, the sum of money equal to their profits. On what did they, on what could they have spent this money? Not on covering their costs, since this we have already deduced from their receipts. The class as a whole also bought from itself—one capitalist from the other—consumer goods and investment goods. The price sum of these goods and services constitute profits in terms of money.

When government spending exceeds revenues, a deficit results. When wage earners spend more than their income, this results in negative saving. The balance of trade might show a surplus; in this case the rest of the world has spent on goods and services originating in the given country more than the revenues received in exchange for its goods and services from the country concerned.

If the algebraic sum of the trade surplus, government deficit and overspending by wage earners is greater than zero, that is, if these three agents have spent more than their money receipts, then the capitalist class had to spend less than their money receipts by the amount of this overspending. In such a case every capitalist has sold his product—to the government, to wage earners, to the rest of the world, and to each other—for money. But they also had costs and these were monetary expenses. The products sold ended in the hands of workers, government, other capitalists, and the rest of the world. A part of the price of these products just covered the costs incurred by capitalists. The price of another part of the same products—that of investment goods and consumer goods serving the consumption of capitalists—was also spent by the capitalists who bought such goods. Capitalists had no other costs, but an amount of unspent money had to remain in their hands, and they had to acquire thus surplus money also through the sales of their products.

This sum of money might be hoarded by capitalists in its original form, but they also might buy domestic or foreign securities with it, or they might as well invest it abroad. Whichever they are doing, we will call this part of their profits *paper profit*.[1]

[1] According to one of the national economic balances of Kalecki (Kalecki, 1970 p. 83) the saving of capitalist society is $S = I + Exp + Def$. If we denote the saving by capitalists by S_C and deduct from both sides of the equation S_W, we get $S_C = I + Exp + Def - S_N$. By saving, the part of income not spent on consumption is meant. The capitalists only spend the I part of their saving (not on consumption, but on investment). Accordingly, the sum $(Exp + Def - S_W)$ is unspent capitalist income, that is, paper profit.

It seems that we are facing some enigma, since this unspent money apparently constitutes receipts by capitalists over and above their costs, hence it is profit, that is, income. But we just stated a few paragraphs earlier that a transaction in which somebody sells his commodity for money and thus somebody else gives money for a commodity cannot be the source of any income. This enigma is, however, not an insoluble one. The general, theoretic solution of the enigma was given by Marx. On an abstract level we can put it in the following way: surplus value and hence profit is not brought about by circumventing the process of transforming commodities into money and *vice versa*—not without the mediation by circulation, and yet not in the circulation process. Reasoning in an abstract model of the capitalist society it originates in the fact that national income as a set of goods and services is produced by labour, but not only labour (i.e., the working class), but also "capital", (the capitalist class) share in it. It is natural that the latter also have a share, since the entire volume of goods (and services) constituting the national income is owned by capitalists at the moment of their coming into being and they can obviously retain a part of it. The capitalist class shares the NNP with the working class. This sharing, however, takes place through the mediation of circulation, through money. The working class acquires its share for its money wages. Formally, also the worker sells his own commodity, i.e., his labour power (as regards the substance, the work of the worker will be the capitalist's). We do not usually regard the wearing out of labour power as costs incurred by the worker. We look upon the wage as the income of the worker, although, in the pure theoretical case, in the true sense of the word, it is only a money receipt covering the costs incurred, that is, the using up of labour power. The difference between the goods and services (i.e., their prices) produced by the labour of the worker and the amount of products necessary to restore the labour power (i.e., the price of the latter) is in every sense the income of the capitalist, his profit. The size of this difference expressed as a price, in terms of money, depends, however, not only on the way these goods are shared, but also on the price level. This is tautologically the amount of money paid for a unit of the goods and services sold.

Let us assume that there is neither government, nor foreign trade, only (productive) workers and capitalists. Let us also assume that there is no net accumulation either, that the consumption of capitalists is zero and, in addition, let us also assume that workers spend all of their wages for no more on consumption. (All these assumptions could only exist simultaneously if the part of national income—conceived as a set of goods— called accumulation had not been produced at all.) In this case the total NNP is made up of consumer goods and their price sum is exactly equal to the sum of wages paid. Thus the price receipts of capitalists do not exceed their costs and hence their profit is zero. As a second case, let us assume that—all other conditions constant—now also capitalists consume a part of the unchanged volume of consumer goods. In this case the price sum of NNP equals the sum of wages plus the price sum of capitalists' consumption. In comparison with the first case the price sum of NNP is higher, and the amount of profits expressed in terms of money is equal to the capitalists' consumption. As a third case, the situation should be the same, but workers should spend more than their wages—using their previous savings or credit. In this case, the price sum of NNP will equal the sum of capitalists' consumption, wages and overspending by workers. The amount of wages spent by workers equals the sum of wages they have received and this latter is part of the cost of capitalists, thus wages spent do not increase the profits of capitalists. But the price sum of capitalists' consumption is, also in this case, profits, as is the sum of money received by capitalists as a result of overspending by workers. This part of the profits is unspent profit, paper profit, since it is a surplus over and above the sum of receipts accrueing to capitalists to cover their costs and expenditures on investment (now assumed to be nonexistent) and on their own consumption. Its immediate cause is not that workers and capitalists now share in the goods produced in a way different from that in the second case. The mode of sharing is the same. The direct cause is the fact that the overspending of workers has raised the price level compared to the second case, but it has not increased the costs of capitalists.

It is also possible that also the amount of products changes from case to case; it is possible and even probable that the production of consumer goods will also rise. This, however, does not alter the correctness of our argument. We may also assume about the increased amount of consumer goods that (1) all of it goes to workers for their wages; (2) only a part of it goes to them for their wages; and (3) that workers buy the part going to them not entirely for their wages. Nevertheless, the previous argument remains valid.

As cases four, five and six let us now combine each of cases one, two, and three with the assumption that now also goods intended for net investment are produced, but everything else remains unchanged. Thus, in all these cases profits will be higher by the amount of net accumulation by capitalists in comparison with the earlier cases one, two and three.[2] Profits in all these cases will equal the price sum of accumulation and capitalists' consumption plus the overspending by workers as paper profit.

Let the government now intervene! If there are government revenues and expenditures and if they are balanced, then the government expenditures—inclusive of the compensation of government employees and transfers—increase the price sum of NNP. (Since, as a matter of fact, these expenditures are finally spent on the purchase of goods and services constituting a part of NNP.) At the same time, they constitute costs for capitalists, hence they do not bring about any paper profits. (Direct taxes of wage earners are also capitalists' costs: they go to the treasury from gross wages paid by capitalists.) These government expenditures actually have a price raising effect, that is, on their account the price sum of capitalists' consumption and accumulation will also increase, but paper profits will remain unchanged relative to case three. But the distribution of goods constituting NNP will also be changed. When there is no government, they are only shared by capitalists and productive workers, while now also government and its employees will have their share of it. Neither will the correctness of our argument be impaired when, owing to the existence and activity of government, also the amount of NNP as a sum of goods and services has been increased. If, however, the government also spends more than its revenues, this

---

[2] More exactly, now the wages of the workers—previously not employed—producing investment goods raises the price of consumption goods, thus also the price of the volume of consumption goods consumed by the capitalists. But the latter price sum is part of the price sum of profits. Nominal profits will be higher than what appears from the above text.

additional spending, the deficit, will also turn into additional—and unspent—income, that is paper profit of the capitalist class, as did the overspending by workers.

If at last we also take into account the rest of the world as well, we can only repeat in a slightly modified form what has been said above. If the rest of the world buys more than it sells, this difference will also raise the price level, thus also the paper profit of capitalists as well. In the first case the workers buy more consumer goods through overspending and consume them. In the second case it is the rest of the world which buys a part of the domestic NNP as a set of goods and this part is lost to the country as if it had been consumed. This difference does not cause any essential change in the character of profit and paper profit.

To illustrate the above we have a diagram for the year 1975, based on current dollar data, and indicate its characteristic points with the letters A–F.

As our data represent quantities expressed in terms of actual prices, profit is the difference between two sums in money terms, capitalists' money receipts and costs,

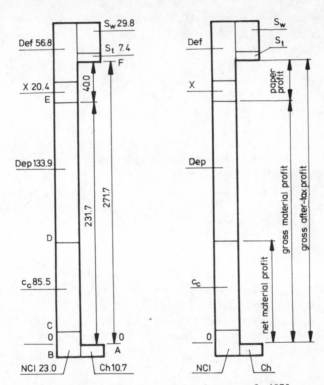

Figure 7.1 Components of the after-tax profit, 1975

Legend:

Ch	= changes in inventories	X	= net exports
NCI	= net fixed capital investment	Def	= domestic government deficit
C_c	= consumption of non-wage earners	S_w	= savings of wage-earners
Dep	= depreciation (capital consumption)	St	= statistical discrepancy

101

while gross profit is higher than that by the amount of depreciation allowance. If the former one is net profits, then the components of gross profits are capital consumption allowance and net profits.

The components of net profits are: (1) change in inventories, (2) net fixed investment, (3) capitalists' consumption and (4) paper profits. We get gross profits by adding capital consumption allowance to these items.[3] Gross profits are thus the sum of paper profit and profits in the tangible form of goods and services. From among the parts of the latter one gross fixed investment was present in material form, but in 1975 the total profit present in material form was smaller than that, owing to a decrease in inventories that year (the amount AB). The part of profits indicated by the distance CD, that is, capitalists' consumption, was spent by them on consumer goods and services. This part is not present either in money or in material form, it does not survive the end of the year.[4]

Let us now have a look at paper profit.

Its amount is the algebraic sum of net (positive or negative) exports, the (positive or negative) difference between government revenues and expenditures and the (positive or negative) savings by wage earners. (A statistical discrepancy also figures in our chart, but this item does not "necessarily" exist.) This algebraic sum can also be negative: for example, in the chart for 1974 such a negative amount of paper profit is found. The existence of negative paper profit implies that capitalists are forced in the given year to sell securities, reduce other claims or increase their debts.

We cautiously refrained from calling the not merely paper profit part of profits real profits without quotation marks. Instead, we spoke about profits in the tangible form of goods and services. Henceforth we shall call it, rather loosely, material profit. The distances AF denote, even apart from paper profits, not the volume of profits, but their amount in terms of money. It should be evident, however, that although capitalists are certainly happy when their profits in terms of money are increasing, the measure of their real income is real profit. In a certain—not unessential sense we can even speak of the real amount of paper profit: we may interpret it as the volume of goods which can be potentially bought for it.

7.4 PROFIT TAXES, DEFICIT FINANCING AND IDLE CAPITAL

It seems appropriate at this point to clarify a common misunderstanding for those readers who have not yet recognized it.

The majority of Marxist economists likely think that mature capitalism left to itself is prone to stagnation and that this becomes manifest, among other things, in the fact

---

[3] Gross capital investment is an actual figure, in our diagrams this is sum of the distances AC + DE. Also the depreciation DE is an official datum, and if in reality this exceeded the physical replacement of capital, then the diagramm overestimated the net fixed capital investment by this difference. The sum AC + DE does not hide, anyway, paperprofit, but is a part of gross profit taking material form in its entirety.

[4] Again, for the sake of accuracy, we have already mentioned that the purchase of consumer durables and homes is considered consumption. They were treated as if these goods had also been consumed by the end of the year. In reality, of course, they have not been consumed, they increased the personal wealth of the population, in this case of the capitalists.

that capitalists do not want to make use of their profits in a positive manner, that is, invest them. Thus idle capital in money form is hoarded by them, and this sum is lacking from total demand. Here is where the government steps in: with one hand it takes money from capitalists in the form of profit taxes and spends it with the other one, thereby creating additional demand and channelling it back into the economy. And if even this proves insufficient, the government spends more than its revenues. It makes use of a deficit or resorts to deficit financing.

But let us now assume that in a given year the export surplus, government deficit and saving by wage earners were exactly zero. Under such conditions the paper profit had to be zero as well. Let us now assume an increase in the deficit to an extent that it should not be offset by a simultaneous increase in the other two items. Then a positive amount of paper profit will come about. Of course, this deficit increase has not drawn away idle capital from the capitalists (or paper profit, which may also be conceived of as idle capital). It may be assumed that capitalists had at the beginning of the year some idle money in their hands (or, what is almost the same, some fictitious capital), accumulated in previous years. The existence of government deficit, however, that is, deficit financing, has not drained the idle capital; on the contrary, the latter has been increased.

For our statement to be correct, we need not assume that in the given year the capitalists' investments or their consumption have remained unchanged. Whether these two items increased or not in comparison with the previous year, there certainly was an increase in the idle paper profit, the idle money capital of capitalists, and exactly by the amount that the increment of government deficit was greater than the incidental decrease in the export surplus and the increment of wage earners' savings. And if this difference increases—say, in the following year—paper profits, that is, the idle money capital of capitalists, will also grow by the same amount. Reality is just the opposite of the common ideas about the effect of deficit financing draining idle capital.

Perhaps it is worthwhile to direct the attention of readers to the fact that—owing to their special nature—paper profits represent a part of profits particularly sensitive to inflation. It might remain in cash, or take the form of different claims, but, contrary to invested or consumed profit, it is subject to slower or faster depreciation depending on its form. This might be somewhat modified but hardly annulled by interests received on paper profits taking the form of securities or bank deposits.

The value of paper profit may be positive or negative in any year. The amount of material profit is always positive. The latter is a part of the profit, primarily appropriated by the capitalist class always in money form, constituting real values. As such it represents transaction already executed, and thus belongs to the unalterable past, while the paper profit in its volatile form, is only a minor reserve fund destined for as yet unspecified but possible future acts. In spite of its merely auxiliary role, its actual existence is important for its owners since, being an unquestionably genuine part of total profits, it may serve corporations as a source of future dividends. It ensures liquidity, the possibility of subsequent freer action for all those sharing in it.

But how big in reality is the capitalists' share in the total GNP which, according to theory, is the main motive force of the capitalist economy?

In Table 7.1 the data relating to the respective shares of total profit, material profit and paper profit in GNP are presented.

Table 7.1

The share of profit in GNP

(excluding imputations, based on data computed in 1972 dollars)

per cent

Components	1968	1969	1970	1971	1972	1973	1974	1975	1976	1977	1978
Total profit	20.6	19.7	19.2	19.4	19.6	20.0	18.3	18.8	19.1	19.1	19.0
Material profit	18.7	19.4	18.4	18.2	18.9	20.2	19.2	16.0	17.3	18.2	18.7
Paper profit	1.9	0.3	0.8	1.2	0.7	−0.2	−0.9	2.8	1.8	0.9	0.3

In the period under review the average (unweighted arithmetic mean) share of total profits was not much less than one fifth of GNP, amounting to 19.3 per cent. The overwhelming part of this was material profit, 95.7 per cent of total profit, while the value of paper profit was merely 4.3 per cent of the total.

Considering the whole of the period investigated the share of total profit shows a declining tendency. This is confirmed by a linear regression computation as well.

From among the figures mentioned here, those for total profits and material profit indicate gross values, that is, they include depreciation allowance as well. The amount of profits in the strict sense, that is, net profits, is rather uncertain since it is impossible to establish unambiguously which part of gross investment really constitutes net investment. Nevertheless, putting aside our doubts and accepting the official data we computed this item as well and publish it below. The shares of net profits in GNP are, of course, considerably lower than those given above and, accordingly, the share of paper profit in net profit is greater than in gross profit.

Table 7.2

The share of net profit in GNP

(excluding imputations, based on data computed in 1972 dollars

per cent

Components	1968	1969	1970	1971	1972	1973	1974	1975	1976	1977	1978
Total net profit	13.2	12.1	11.1	11.2	11.6	12.0	9.7	9.7	10.2	10.5	10.6
Net material profit	11.3	11.8	10.3	10.0	10.9	12.2	10.6	6.8	8.4	9.6	10.3
Paper profit	1.9	0.3	0.8	1.2	0.7	−0.2	−0.9	2.8	1.8	0.9	0.3

Thus, net profits were on the average 11.1 per cent of GNP. The average share of net material profits was 92.1 per cent of net profits, and 10.2 per cent of the GNP, while the paper profit was on the average 7.9 per cent of net profits. Therefore, the average share of the paper profit is not too important in net profits, either.

We could have already noticed in connection with gross profits that their share in GNP fluctuated less than that of material profits. The difference between the highest and the lowest values for the former was 2.3 percentage points, while for the latter 4.2.

The data in the table indicate that the share of gross profits has in 1978 remained lower than in either 1968 or 1969, although 1978 might already be regarded as a prosperous year. But 1978 shares, both for total and material profits, lagged behind the average of 19.3 per cent mentioned and hardly exceeded 18.4 per cent. But it is even more striking that the share of gross material profit in that year was lower than in 1974, although that was the first year of the crisis. This, however, does not hold for total gross profits.

The difference between the highest and the lowest shares was 3.5 percentage points for net profits, while it was 5.3 for net material profits. As the latter relate to a lower percentage, we can say that the above described greater fluctuation of material profits than of total profits appears to be more accentuated in this case.

Also the decline of total net profits between the two final points of the period appears to be more pronounced than in the case of total gross profits. Also the share of net material profits in 1978 lags behind the average of the 11 years, and even behind that of 1974, which was a year of crisis.

In this part of our book we do not discuss the impacts of monetary policy on the economy and thus on profits. They will be dealt with in Part Four of this book. Here we are primarily interested in the impact of fiscal policy on prices, profits and GNP.

As far as profits are concerned, the changes in material profits are determined by the decisions of capitalists, although their behaviour itself is influenced by many circumstances beyond the power of the individual capitalist. On the other hand, changes in paper profit are quite independent of the behaviour of capitalists, but not of the government's fiscal policy since government deficit is an important element of the latter. Simplifying the existing interrelations we may even put it in the following terms: government fiscal policy affects total profits through the difference between its revenues and expenditures, that is, through the deficit and thus through the paper profit. The impact of changes in the deficit on profits are, of course, Janus-faced. On the one hand, *ceteris paribus,* it contributes to profits by its own amount. On the other hand, it has an inflationary effect, and thus it also diminishes the real value of the part of paper profit created by itself. (In the above two tables paper profit was also given in real terms.) Further, it is also true that another factor, similarly independent of the behaviour of capitalists, regularly crosses the impact of government deficit, because the same cause which increases the deficit through the mediation of built-in stabilizers, namely, recession or crisis, increases the savings by wage earners—at least it increased them in the period under investigation—and this reduces the nominal amount of paper profit and, simultaneously, through its deflationary effect, somewhat raises the real size of the decrease.

Nevertheless, we could already observe in Table 7.1 that the share of material profit showed greater fluctuations than that of total profits, and this phenomenon indicated that changes in total profits acted, during most of the period under review, against the changes in material profits, thus paper profits acted as an anticyclical factor. This is well illustrated in Figure 7.2

Figure 7.2 reveals that from an increase or decrease of the indicator of profit shares in GNP correct conclusions on the general state of business or its phases—although this is one of the favourite tools of routine analysis—may only be drawn with due circumspection, taking other factors into account as well.

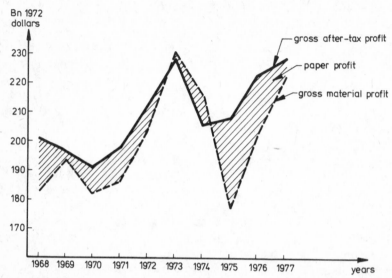

Figure 7.2 Gross after-tax profit, gross material profit and paper profit (bn 1972 dollars)

Thus, for instance, total profits in 1975, relative to the very low material profits, were raised significantly by the considerable export surplus, while the total profit in 1977 remained relatively low primarily due to the fact that the export surplus turned into a deficit. The data for the same year (1977) show that it is not even true that the share of total profit within GNP necessarily increases with improving business. In that year the share of profit fell somewhat in spite of a pronounced improvement in business. On the other hand, Figure 7.2 also shows that the real size of total profits consistently increased with improving business and deteriorated with a declining one. It is, however, true that the whole of 1975 was nevertheless a bad year. But its second half showed many signs of improvement and profits developed in a manner characteristic of recovery. In one of the preceding paragraphs we said that the amount of material profit is always positive.[5] The average size of the paper profit was, as mentioned, only

[5] If we wish to be very exact, we must add that our statement regarding consumption by capitalists always holds, thus also for the whole of investment, since we investigate gross profits and thus also gross investment (inclusive of depreciation). But it does not hold for the element of change in inventories, which may be negative in the case of a reduction. Nor does it hold for net investment. In a grave crisis net investment may

4.3 per cent of gross total profits in the period. Behind this overal value we find considerable fluctuations. The share of paper profit was highest in the second year of the crisis, 1975, attaining 15.2 per cent, and it was lowest, −0.6 per cent, at the peak of the overheated boom. The year 1973 was one of two in which paper profit as a whole had a negative sign. As far as individual elements of paper profit are concerned, net exports were similarly negative in two years, while there was a government deficit in four years and the savings of wage earners were negative in five years.

Indeed, saving and overspending by wage earners balanced each other to such extent during the eleven years under study that, in the final analysis, merely 1.9 per cent of capitalist profits (expressed in terms of 1972 dollars) originated from overspending by wage earners. In eleven years this overspending amounted altogether to 43.7 bn dollars (in 1972 dollars), and this was merely 0.2–0.3 per cent of wage earners' incomes. This is so tiny a sum that it is evidently within the margin of error in our computations. In other words, the assumption that wage earners spend what they earn has been proved valid in practice for the whole of the period investigated. (This is providing that our method used to compute the amount of taxes paid by wage earners is not completely misleading.)

7.6 FACTORS INFLUENCING THE COMPONENTS OF PAPER PROFIT

It seems worthwhile investigating to what extent paper profit and its individual components are in reality independent of the decisions of capitalists.

Capitalists engaged in foreign trade, of course, make decisions on the timing and amount of the export and import of a particular commodity or on whether to export or import at all. Such decisions, however, do not result in themselves in either a trade surplus or a deficit and thus do not produce profits on the macro-level either. In contrast, investment and consumption decisions result in themselves and immediately in a part of profits in the macroeconomic sense, too. This part of the paper profit is influenced to a not insignificant extent by changes in the terms of trade, which themselves depend on exogenous factors such as the state of business in the rest of the world, the activity of capitalists in foreign countries (e.g., the launching of an export drive on the markets of the given country), or measures by governments influencing the development of foreign trade, etc. All these have direct impacts as well. As far as factors within the given country are concerned, the economic policy of the country's government, its measures intended to influence trade in a certain direction (e.g., the measures taken by the Carter administration in October 1978 to foster trade). True, the capitalist class can influence the economic policy of the government, but this influence is not simple and much less unambiguous. Capitalists as a class were not reared on Kaleckian economics and thus they are not aware of the fact that an export surplus is

---

even be negative, the value of the capital stock may diminish. This happened in the early thirties. But it has not occurred since the Second World War. As a matter of fact, in principle, even the whole of gross investment might be negative, namely, in the extreme case if net investment were zero or negative and the reduction of inventories exceeded the physical replacement of fixed capital. This cannot occur in practice since the maximum decline in inventories is 10–20 bn, while the annual replacement is of order of 100 bn dollars.

necessarily profit. And even if they were, profits originating in an export surplus accrue to the capitalists as a class on the macroeconomic level, but on the micro-level only to a few capitalists, and are certainly not shared by all of them. There are, however, capitalists or groups of capitalists, and quite a few of them, who are interested in higher imports (e.g., those using cheap foreign materials), and thus they try to influence the government's economic policy in the interest of reducing the export surplus. Thus the decisions determining the changes in this component of the paper profit are partly completely beyond the reach of the capitalists in the given country, and partly, though they can be influenced by them, this occurs in a very complicated manner, through transmissions, and only as a result of counteracting forces.

It is obvious that changes in the other component of paper profit, that is, in the domestic government deficit, cannot be directly determined by the decisions of individual capitalists. The balance of government revenues and expenditures depends partly, and to a greater part, on the government programs and on the automatism of the built-in stabilizers, and partly on the discretionary measures of the government. These factors work on both sides of the balance.

The impact of objective (i.e., automatic) factors on the balance of government revenues and expenditures consists in that an improvement in business conditions tends to diminish the deficit through the workings of the built-in stabilizers, while deterioration in the same increases it. Profits are affected in the same sense. Capitalists, of course, do have an influence on discretionary government measures, but in a very contradictory manner, similarly to that mentioned in connection with the balance of trade.

It hardly needs explaining that the amount of the savings by wage earners is independent of the intentions or behaviour of the capitalists, although they do have a say in the possible net overspending of workers. However, the changes in this latter component of paper profit are so important and characteristic that their discussion will come later in this study, where we shall lay particular stress on their analysis.

First we have to say a few words about the internal interrelations of the elements of profits.

7.7 THE COMPONENTS OF PROFIT ARE NOT INDEPENDENT OF EACH OTHER

In a static sense—or, more properly, *ex post*—it is certainly true that the total amount of investment, consumption by capitalists, the balance of the government budget, the balance of foreign trade, and also the difference between the wage earners' income and outlays are at any time parts of the amount of profits and that profits are exactly the sum total of these components. But *ex ante,* taking into account the changes, it is the dynamics we should always keep in mind—changes in any of these components are not independent of changes in another component or components. On the contrary, they often directly involve changes in other components.

In some cases, this is easy to understand. Thus, for example, Kalecki[6] stressed that increased exports or a greater deficit—when these involve an increase of production as

[6] See Kalecki's study in "Foreign trade and 'domestic export' " which was written a year later than his profit equation. (Kalecki, 1970, pp. 15–25)

well—or higher investment finally do not increase profits by the total amount of their increment, since an increase in production usually also entails greater imports and, consequently, capitalists lose on the swings a part of the profit gained on the rounds. It is also easy to understand that an increase in government deficit brought about by a rise in transfer payments could—*ceteris paribus*—augment profits by its own amount, assuming also that this increment of transfers also increased the real consumption of wage earners, only if the part of GNP consisting of consumer goods also grew and if this did not involve greater imports. (If the increment of the real consumption of wage earners is not accompanied by a corresponding increase in the production of consumer goods, it will entail a disinvestment in inventories and thus a reduction of profits.)

The same holds for the case when increased government purchases involve a rise in the deficit, the only difference being that in this case government consumption substitutes for the consumption by wage earners. Or, if an increase in wage earners' consumption is financed by their dissaving (overspending), then the output of consumer goods also has to grow in order that this overspending raise profits by its own amount.

We can say about the three cases quoted as examples that at least a part of the increase in profits may be attributed to the adjustment of production.

We could list several examples in which, in certain cases when the volume of output (GNP) remains unchanged, a change in one of the profit components is neutralized by a change in another one. Thus, for example, profits do not increase at all if the increment of investment is made up exclusively of imported investment goods, or if the overspending by wage earners is directed towards imported consumer goods (e. g., spent on imported cars); or when the government spends more than before, but on imported armaments. The increment of investment, the overspending by wage earners and the government's additional spending would raise profits if these increments were not neutralized by increased imports.[7]

But profit may increase by a change in one of its components even without increased production. Let us study this problem in more general terms. Four parties have a share in GNP: capitalists, wage earners, government and the rest of the world. With an unchanged volume of GNP a decrease in the net income of any of these four participants entails a rise in the net income of one or more of the others. And this "other" may be the share of the capitalists, that is, profits.

For Marxists it seems evident *a priori* that with an unchanged GNP any decrease in the real income of wage earners increases the volume of profits by the same amount. But let us take a closer look. Let us assume that the share of the rest of the world and also net government revenue (the difference between revenues and expenditures)

---

[7] This is not so mysterious at all: the government imports armaments at the expense of the deficit. This does not produce paper profit for the domestic capitalists; profit remains unchanged and also the sum of real wages remains unchanged. The GNP does as well, since it is the sum of investment, personal consumption, net exports and government purchases, i. e., of four items of which the first two have remained unchanged and the changes of the other two have balanced each other. The question may be put: Is it a fact that government has now received more from an unchanged GNP, but wherefrom and from what? The correct answer is that it has now received more of material goods at the expense of the rest of the world. At the same time, the rest of the world received money at the expense of the state. From the aspect of the size of income it is the same whether the parts of GNP are received by those receiving them in material or money form.

remain unchanged, but the real income of wage earners falls. Let us assume, for instance, that the real amount of government transfers falls, but government purchases grow by the same amount. Hence the net income of government remains unchanged but the real income of wage earners diminishes. Thus there is also a drop in the volume of consumer goods they can buy (without resorting to previous savings or to credit). As a consequence, the inventories of consumer goods will grow and this counts as an increment of investment. Profits will rise, but, for the time being, they have not been realized!

The situation is the same if there is an increase in taxes paid by wage earnes, but government purchases increase at the same time. And it is the same also in the simplest case, when the real value of wages paid by the business sector drops.

If, on the other hand, there is a change, for example, a drop in net government income, we have to distinguish two different cases. When the government deficit falls because of a drop in profit taxes, but government expenditures remain unchanged, the profits will grow. If, however, the increase in government deficit is caused by a decrease (in real terms) in direct taxes paid by wage earners, but government spending remains unchanged, then the deficit will grow, which has a profit-increasing impact. But the purchases of wage earners reduce inventories and this entails disinvestment, a drop in profits. Thus profits remain unchanged.

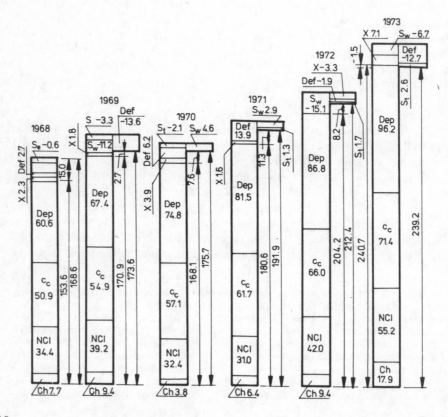

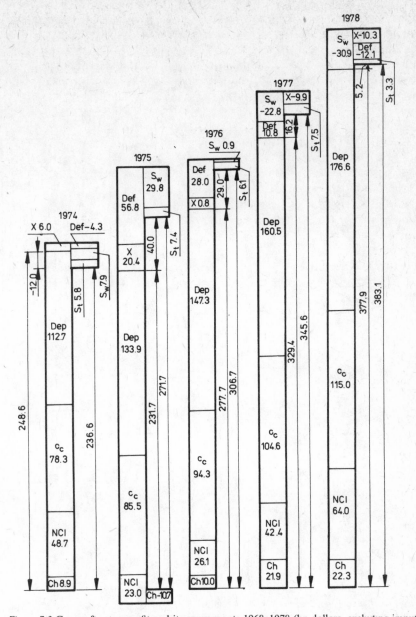

Figure 7.3 Gross after-tax profit and its components 1968–1978 (bn dollars, excluding imputations, at current prices)

Legend:

Ch	= changes in inventories	X	= net exports
NCI	= net fixed capital investment	Def	= domestic government deficit
C_c	= capitalists' consumption	S_w	= saving by wage earners
Dep	= depreciation (capital consumption)	St	= statistical discrepancy

It does not pertain to paper profit, and thus it is a case somewhat different from the above when, although net export remains the same, the share of capital goods is increasing within exports and the share of consumer goods grows within imports. In such cases, *ceteris paribus,* gross domestic investment ought to diminish, and if this reduction is not neutralized by some other profit component—e.g., capitalists' consumption—profits also have to drop.[8]

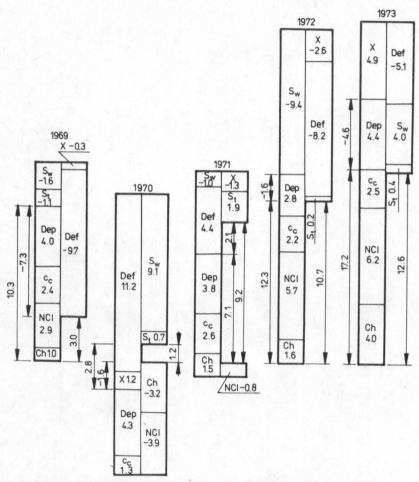

Figure 7.4 Percentage contributions of individual profit components to the total percentage in gross after-tax profit, 1969—1978 (bn dollars, excl. imputations, at current prices)

Legend:

Ch	= changes in inventories	X	= net exports
NCI	= net fixed capital investment	Def	= domestic government deficit
C_c	= capitalists' consumption	S_w	= saving by wage earners
Dep	= depreciation (capital consumption)	St	= statistical discrepancy

[8] See Kardos, 1980.

112

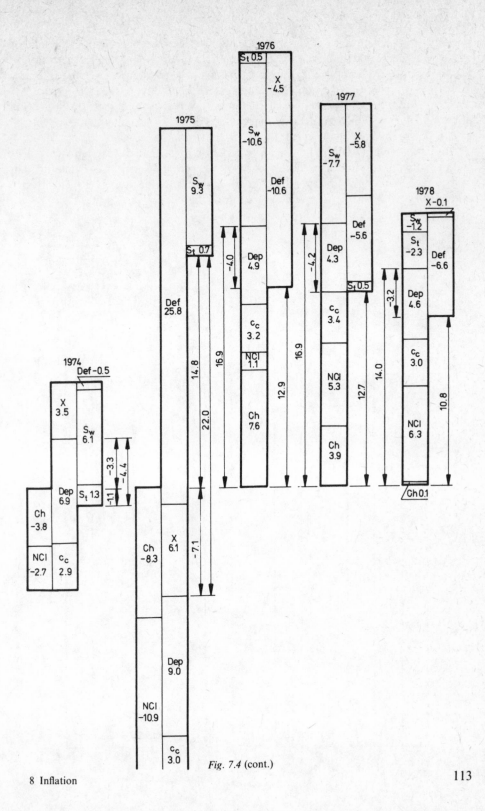

Fig. 7.4 (cont.)

Many similar examples could be given without further particular gain, but, of course, we have to forego this. We judge it opportune to draw our readers' attention to the above outlined complications in order to avoid a possible simplifying interpretation of our tables and diagrams. Having said this, let us have a look at Figures 7.3—7.6. From among them 7.3 and 7.5 on profits are given at current and constant (1972) prices, and 7.4 and 7.6 give the percentual changes over the preceding year of profit and its components (similarly at current and constant prices).

This *caveat* is all the more justified as the period investigated was highly turbulent and the different turnabouts were the results of very complex processes—among them of the mutual impact of changes in profit components. Let us illustrate this with two examples taken from the economic situation of the period.

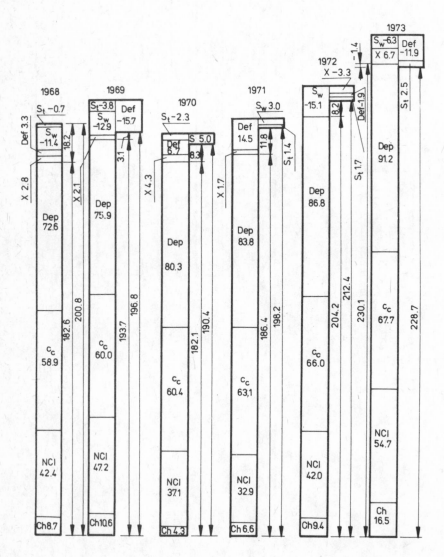

114

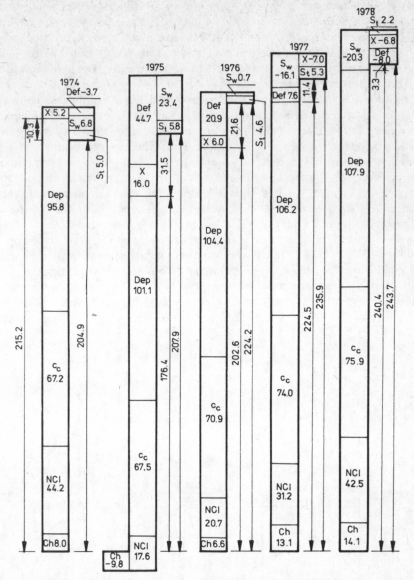

Figure 7.5 Volume of gross after-tax profit and its components, 1968–1978 (bn 1972 dollars, excl. imputations)

Legend:

Ch	= changes in inventories	X	= net exports
NCI	= net fixed capital investment	Def	= domestic government deficit
C_c	= capitalists' consumption	S_w	= saving by wage earners
Dep	= depreciation (capital consumption)	St	= statistical discrepancy

What actually happened in 1975, the year of the through of the recession, and also the year of business upturn. Profits already increased somewhat (by 3 bn 1972 US dollars) that year. This was the result of a 41.8 bn dollar increase in paper profit which overcompensated a 38.8 bn dollar drop in material profits. Over a quarter of the increase in paper profit originated in the 10.8 bn dollar improvement in the balance of trade. This improvement was attributable—as shown by a statistical data—to a considerable drop in imports. Nobody deserves to be called an economist who doubts that the pronounced drop in investment played a significant role in this fall in imports. On the other hand, the decrease in investment and the growth in savings by wage earners also helped to release goods for export. Thus it became possible to double the volume of net exports of durable goods in spite of a drop in production compared to the previous year. It is thus evident that the increase in one of the profit components— net exports—was made possible by the changes in the two other components (investment and wage earners' savings), with the final result that although the two latter ones had a negative impact on profits, profits still increased.

Our other example relates to the period of the overheated boom preceding the recession. In 1972, both investment and wage earners' overspending showed strong increases and partly this led—through its impact on both exports and imports—to a 5 bn dollar deterioration in the balance of trade. In the following year, due to monetary restrictions, overspending by wage earners fell significantly (with a profit-diminishing impact of 8.8 bn 1972 dollars). To a considerable extent this was the cause of the 10 bn

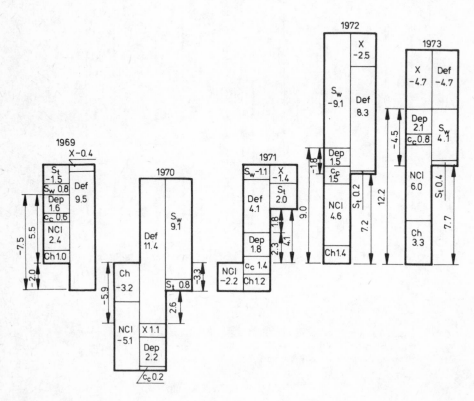

116

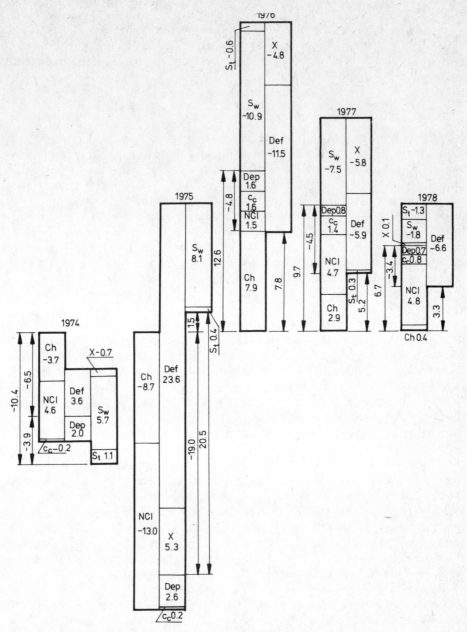

Figure 7.6 Percentage contribution of individual profit components to the total percentage change in gross after-tax profit 1969—1978 (At 1972 dollars, excl. imputations)

Legend:

Ch	= changes in inventories	X	= net exports
NCI	= net fixed capital investment	Def	= domestic government deficit
C_c	= capitalists' consumption	S_w	= saving by wage earners
Dep	= depreciation (capital consumption)	St	= statistical discrepancy

dollar improvement in the balance of trade. This is corroborated by the fact that 3 out of the 10 bn were made up by an improvement in the trade balance of *durable goods,* in spite of the fact that a continued investment boom was a serious burden on this balance.

7.8 THE SPECIAL ROLE PLAYED BY THE SAVINGS OF WAGE EARNERS

In the above examples, in both the fictitious ones and those taken from reality, a change in one of the components of profit brought about a change in some other one almost by technical necessity. The GNP also had to change owing to such necessity in order to bring about an increase of profits equal to the total amount of the original change. In some other examples given, the secondary changes described had to take place exactly as they did because we assumed that wage earners spend their total income on consumer goods. But this assumption goes "too far" since in reality there is always some S_w different from zero. The increase or decrease in the saving by wage earners is in no way technically connected with any change in some of the other profit components. But, as we have already stated, the size of the positive or negative saving by wage earners is to a very great extent independent of the behaviour of individual capitalists, too.

It is not the capitalist who decides whether the worker should put his small savings into the bank or buy a car on credit. Evidently, this is a part of profit, the amount of which is determined by decisions of a class antagonistic to the capitalist one, that is, of the working class (more exactly of wage and salary earners), exactly in the same manner as decisions on investment and on capitalists' consumption are made by the capitalists themselves. Nor are wage earners guided in their decisions on saving or overspending by macroeconomic theorems relating to the amount of profits. We have said that their behaviour in respect of savings was determined in the period under review mainly by the state of business. Their overspending, the main form of which is the purchase of consumer durables and homes on credit, accompanied good business, while their saving, motivated by the fear of a drop in income and of unemployment, accompanied sluggish business. But it was considerably influenced by monetary policy as well, namely, through the impact of the latter on the availability of and the interest on mortgage and consumer credit. Finally, capitalists also had a certain influence on it, since wage earnes have to turn to capitalists (finance institutions) for credit. Of course, the decision on whether or not a credit should be granted is not motivated by the consideration that its granting increases the profits of capitalists, but by the evaluation of the applicant's creditworthiness and by whether the institution grantig the credit judges the transaction profitable or not. Thus the influence of the capitalist class on the changes in this profit component can be anyway but indirect and contradictory.

In the last few paragraphs we have only cleared a debt. We finished what had to be said about the problem whether or not the changes in paper profit are independent of the behaviour of the capitalist class. We can summarize our answer as follows: changes in paper profit are not directly dependent on capitalists' decisions. They are determined above all by factors exogeneous from the point of view of capitalists, such as developments in the rest of the world, government economic policy decisions, and the behaviour of wage earners. They are considerably influenced by the state of

118

business, while the influence of capitalists themselves can assert itself only very indirectly and in a contradictory way.

The most important thing, however, that we have to say about the changes in saving by wage earners is not just this.

As already mentioned, although an economic recovery is usually accompanied by an increase in profits, while a sluggish economy is accompanied by a fall in the same, there is no unambiguous relationship between the changes in GNP, that is, the volume of production (including services) and profits. An unchanged GNP is compatible with different amounts of material profits. This is true *a fortiori* for paper profit, since changes in the latter cannot be directly influenced by capitalists. The so-called built-in stabilizers of the economy influence changes in profit exactly through the mechanisms which bring about paper profit. Usually the system of taxes, unemployment benefits and the like are meant by built-in stabilizers. According to established theory, these bring about their stabilizing effect by relatively increasing effective demand when the economy becomes sluggish and by relatively reducing the same when the economy prospers. An increase in effective demand can indeed have a stimulating impact on the growth of real GNP. However, insofar as this increase in real demand originates from the demand of wage earners—but not from their overspending—it leaves profits unchanged, at least as regards its direct impact, but leads, to a deterioration of the rate of surplus value. However, if the decrease of demand is mitigated by the built-in stabilizers, the balance of government revenues and expenditures cannot remain unchanged, but shifts towards a deficit. This will increase profits, to wit, paper profits. And if it is true that the economy is governed in the last resort by profits, then we can find the really stabilizing effects of built-in stabilizers primarily in this mechanism.

When the business situation is deteriorating, government deficit will, as a rule, increase. This raises profits and thus it works against a further deterioration in business. In an improving business situation the opposite will happen. In a less definite manner, the same might be said about the second component of paper profit, net exports. It seems that an increase in GNP is usually accompanied by an increase in the relative weight of imports. This diminishes paper profits and hence it will have a negative impact on growth. Of course, the opposite will happen when business turns sluggish.

During the business cycle, the third component of paper profit, saving by wage earners, influences changes in profit which run exactly against the one discussed above. Under good business conditions it becomes negative and this increases profits. That is, while changes in government deficit and mostly also in net exports have a negative, that is, stabilizing feedback effect, the changes in wage earners' savings are fed back into the economy in a positive sense, that is, they will have a destabilizing effect. Only the last few months of the boom are exceptions, since in this period, owing to the strained financial situation, overspending by wage earners necessarily slows down. This, however, can hardly be regarded as a stabilizing effect as it rather hastens the oncoming recession.

From among the components of gross profit the depreciation allowance and capitalists' consumption may be regarded as growing along a trend-like path. The movement of the sum of the two over time is illustrated by an almost straight line. (See Figure 7.7)

Changes in net investment and in saving by wage earners showed a cyclical movement, that is one synchronous with business fluctuations. (The curve of the sum of these two is also shown in Fig. 7.7)

Finally, government deficit and net exports moved anticyclically. The only exception in the period under review was the year 1974. In that year the paradoxical behaviour of the deficit contributed considerably to the unfolding and deepening of the crisis. It may be regarded as a random development that the change in net exports did not move anticyclically only in a single year, in 1973.

Since the two main components of paper profit, government deficit and overspending by wage earners, moved consistently in a contrary sense in relation to each other, that is, they weakened each others' impact, the fact already stressed is rather surprising that the movement of cyclical changes of net investment and of that in paper profits were contrary in sense only in two years, that is, total paper profits also moved generally in an anticyclical manner. (See Table 7.3.) One of the exceptional years was 1974, as already mentioned, while the other was 1971. But the latter proved exceptional only at current prices, at 1972 prices the change was regular.

Although exceptions to the rule that anticyclical effects of changes in total paper profits were rare, we still cannot trust too much the regularity of this "rule". That much is true, for example, that in the two years of favourable business conditions, in 1972-1973, paper profit was only 1.5 per cent of gross profit, while in the two years of recession, 1974-1975, it was 5.1 per cent, that is, about three times as high. In the two prosperous years, however, government deficit (more exactly, the surplus), reduced profits by 3.1 per cent, but net saving by wage earners increased it even more, by 4.9 per cent. In the two bad years, however, the share of the deficit was greater (+ 9.9 per cent) and that of wage earners' savings smaller (− 7.3 per cent). In these two latter years the data on paper profit are rather uncertain, because the statistical discrepancy amounted to 2.6 per cent of gross profits. In other words, exceptions could have been even more frequent.

This role of paper profit which makes the development of total profits smoother and moderate, the amplitude of the fluctuations is numerically indicated by the following figures. The yearly changes of gross material profits fluctuated in the nine years following 1968 between + 12.7 and − 18.0 per cent, while those of total profits only between + 7.7 and − 10.4 per cent. As regards net profits, the corresponding percentual changes are + 30.3 and − 36.9 per cent for material profit and + 9.9 and − 20.7 per cent for total profits. From these data we can draw two further concrete conclusions regarding the mitigating effect of paper profit on fluctuations. Namely, (1) in respect of gross profit this mitigating effect is more pronounced in the case of negative fluctuations (decreases); (2) the mitigating effect is, of course, stronger in respect of net profits. (It narrows the 67.2 percentage points difference between the

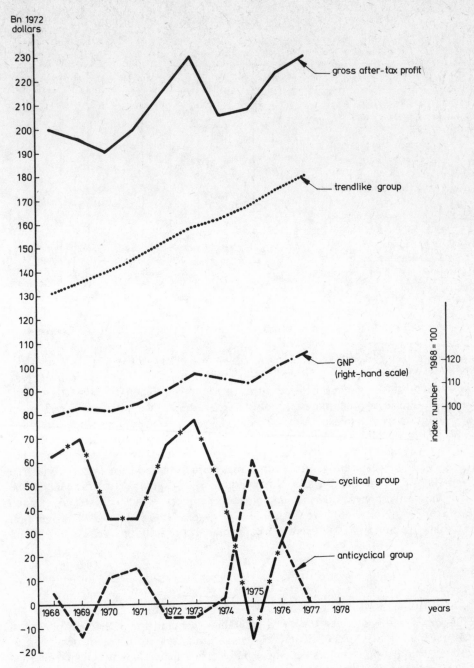

Figure 7.7 GNP (excl. imputations), gross after-tax profit, and trendlike, cyclical and anticyclical groups of profit components

Table 7.3

Annual changes in total profits and the impact on it of changes in individual profit components
(+ profit-increasing—profit-decreasing impact, based on data in 1972 dollars)

Items	1969	1970	1971	1972	1973	1974	1975	1976	1977	1978
1. Gross after-tax profits	−	−	+	+	+	−	+	+	+	+
2. Gross material profit	+	−	+	+	+	−	−	+	+	+
3. Gross investment	+	−	+	+	+	−	−	+	+	+
4. Depreciation (capital consumption)	+	+	+	+	+	+	+	+	+	+
5. Net investment	+	−	−	+	+	−	−	+	+	+
6. Change in inventories	+	−	+	+	+	−	−	+	+	+
7. Net fixed investment	+	−	−	+	+	−	−	+	+	+
8. Capitalists' consumption	+	+	+	+	+	−	+	+	+	+
9. Paper profit	−	+	+	−	−	−	+	−	−	−
10. Net exports	−	+	−	−	+	−	+	−	−	+
11. Government deficit	−	+	+	−	−	+	+	−	−	−
12. Net savings by wage earners	+	−	+	+	−	−	−	+	+	+

extreme values to 30.6, while in respect of gross profits from 30.7 to 18.1 percentage points.)

In conclusion, it will be perhaps worthwhile to draw readers' attention to the following. If we compare the capitalists' consumption with net material profits, it may be found astonishing that the former constitutes a rather great part of the latter. Thus, for example, in 1975 net material profits were made up by almost nothing else than consumption by capitalists. Over the whole 11-year period capitalists' consumption amounted to 59.4 per cent of net material profits and to 54.7 per cent of total net profits. Keeping in mind that the *raison d'être* of capital is not consumption but accumulation by capitalists, these proportions seem rather odd, too high as compared to our *a priori* concepts. We should not forget, however, that under this heading the consumption of a great many others (non-wage earners) is included. (See Appendix, pp. 275–287.) Nor should we forget that, in spite of this, capitalists' consumption amounts to about 9.5–10 per cent of total personal consumption. (See Tables 7.6 and 7.7 on pp. 131–132.)

7.10 A FEW CONCLUDING REMARKS

It will, perhaps, do no harm to restate a few ideas at this stage.

According to Keynesian theory, if capitalists' demand for investment plus total consumer demand is not sufficient to secure a satisfactory level of employment, then, in order to create supplementary demand, a budgetary deficit, that is, deficit financing has to be employed. We also said that the idea in the minds of many economists was false, according to which the government's expansive fiscal policy would increase demand by draining, in the form of taxes, the capitalists' money capital which would have otherwise remained idle and by channeling it back into the economy in the form of its

122

own expenditure. The idea is erroneus in the sense that the money taxed away from capitalists—whether it was idle capital or not—returns in the case of a balanced budget to the capitalists as their income. In fact, if government expenditures exceed revenues and a deficit emerges, soon idle money capital—surplus money capital coming about in the form of paper profit—will accumulate in the hands of capitalists. If we could justifiably continue this last thought by stating that if the balance of government revenues and expenditures shows a deficit over a series of years then annually new amounts of paper profit must come into being; thus the idle money capital in the hands of capitalists must accumulate, then from the point of view of business fluctuations the coming into being of paper profit should be regarded as a sort of waste produced by expansionist fiscal policy. This, however, would be already an erroneous idea. The money profits that capitalists cannot spend in the year they came about can be used in the following year and even in a productive manner and, consequently, capitalists would need less external financing to continue or expand their activity. The coming into being of paper profit improves their liquidity. But it is, of course, also possible that paper profit is cumulating year after year, in which case paper profit would really be a "waste product" of fiscal policy.

These last statements relate to the year or years following the onset of a government deficit. In the year when it comes about, the deficit, *ceteris paribus*, increases total demand in terms of money in spite of the fact that the supplementary amount of money thrown into circulation by the government in the form of the deficit gets stuck, at least until the end of the given year, in the hands of the capitalists.

Here our train of thought touches on certain Keynesian theorems on two different planes. The theorem of fiscal drag relates to the demand-increasing or decreasing role of the budget. This theorem refers to the fact that with improving employment government revenues rise automatically, while there is an automatic drop in certain government transfer payments, that is, with improving business conditions there is a tendency for the budget deficit to diminish or even to turn into a surplus. True Keynesians, however, drew from this indisputable fact the conclusion that while unemployment exists, government revenues and expenditures should not be brought into balance, even under improving business conditions. On the contrary, a deficit is to be maintained, since if this were not done, unemployment could not be brought down to the desired level owing to the tendency of diminishing deficit and its change into a surplus. (Hence, if business conditions improve but unemployment is still considerable, and the budget is balanced, expenditures should be inreased and/or taxes should be cut.) But we could not find a single Keynesian who could have convincingly explained the amount of deficit (or, perhaps, surplus) the budget has to show in order to attain relatively full employment. Thus the Keynesian theory leaves its own fundamental question unanswered.

But the degree of emloyment attainable in a capitalist society certainly does not depend merely on the amount of budget deficit or surplus with such a level of employment. The theory oi fiscal drag does have a rational core. A too big surplus, very rare indeed, may really stifle demand, while a deficit, if explicit inflationary expectations do not intervene, certainly boosts real demand and hence is likely to increase employment as well. But we have to regard the above outlined "orthodox" Keynesian argument as a mere pragmatic catchword feigning only exactness which, if it found credence, might produce a backlash in the case of inflationary expectations in the form of galopping inflation.

The other touching point of our train of thought with Western theories is much more evident than the former one. It concerns the multiplier theory. A budgetary deficit or its increase pump supplementary demand into the economy and, according to the multiplier theory, such "autonomous" excess demand increases GNP in the final outcome by a multiple of its own value. According to a well-known opinion of Keynes we can even tell how many times the increment of GNP will be bigger than the additional demand created by the government. (At other places of his main work Keynes, 1936. chapters 20 and 21, we can find a more realistic but much less known theorem as well.) According to Keynes, this multiplier is a function of the "marginal propensity to consume", while the latter may be regarded as constant with a given GNP or national income.

Having read this explication, readers will be hardly surprised to find that this extremely simplified theory, taught by the followers of the neoclassical school, was not at all corroborated by the events of the period under review.

The multiplier theory to be found in the textbooks would be too primitive even if "related to normal circumstances". And for the years studied in this book it is especially true that, first of all, even disregarding the role of the budget, national income did not change simply according to the usual automatisms of capitalism as more than once monetary policy also deeply interfered with this process. It was also strongly influenced by the international economic situation, and primarily by the changes in the balance of payments. Nor could the multiplier theory take into account the intense fluctuation in investment influenced significantly by the above mentioned factors, too. Nor was there room in the textbook multiplier theory for the pro-cyclical behaviour of wage earners' saving (that is, their propensity to consume was not constant by far), nor for the fact of permanent inflation while, as a matter of fact, in times of inflation a substantial part of the increment of demand takes the form of price increase instead of that of production.

Nevertheless, what can we say about the positive impact if budget deficit on production over and above its improving the liquidity position of enterprises?

Profit gets bigger if to a given amount of investment and capitalists' consumption—these two components of material profit—paper profit is also added than it would be without this addition. The addition leaves unaffected the costs incurred by capitalists. As a consequence the price sum of GNP has to become bigger, *ceteris paribus*, than in the case when the paper profit—that is, government deficit not completely counterbalanced by the savings of wage earners and the trade deficit—does not exist. A given amount of paper profit entails, other things being equal, a given amount of additional price sum, and an increasing surplus of paper profit, that is, an increment in government deficit not completely counterbalanced by the other two components, increases the price sum of GNP. If the volume of GNP remains unchanged, the profit realizable in a unit of product, that is, the profit margin, will increase. But an increasing profit margin somewhat enhances the increase of production and hence of GNP even under inflationary circumstances. It need not increase GNP but stimulates its growth. For this stimulation to become effective supplementary investment is not absolutely necessary as long as there are unutilized capacities. The output of consumer goods can

124

increase without it. If such an increase takes place, it counteracts the increase in price level that would occur without it under the impact of the increase in the value of sales. Thus, in the last instance, the price level need not necessarily increase (though the price sum increases). As a result, the sum of real wages and to some extent their level will be higher.

It cannot be proven, however, that this stimulating impact would increase output to such an extent that the price level should not rise at all. The experience of the decade examined shows exactly that this would also fuel inflation, and this sooner or later leads to a deflationary government policy. If this latter fact were not a fact, we might argue that the production-stimulating impact of the deficit sooner or later would bring about an increase in fixed capital investment. Yet the anti-cyclical fluctuations of economic policy raise doubts whether this effect could be a significant one. We shall see that for the period under study our doubts in this respect are very well founded.

The question arises in what sense we can speak about an economic policy in respect of the changes in the budget during the period under review. In principle a distinction is made between two types of fiscal policy. One is called the anticyclical variant, while the other is labelled the growth-oriented or full-employment variant. The full-employment variant, based on the theory of fiscal drag, proposes a budget deficit even under improving business conditions. Going beyond this, an even more ambitious theory stresses the necessity and possibility of fine tuning, that is, that the government can always work out some sophisticated economic policy which would reduce fluctuations to a minimum. But today this is already an outworn concept. Furthermore, even the application of a growth-oriented policy is made dependent on the development of inflation. The period investigated was characterized by inflation and, regarding the period as a whole, the actual fiscal policy followed could not at all be considered as the growth-oriented variant—at most as one of the anti-cyclical type. But even this was characterized by automatisms built into the budget system. Economic ebb and tide caused by the Vietnam War—that is, by an essentially not directly economic but a political factor—changed the expenditure side of the budget essentially, but the more important elements of the budget, e. g., the tax system were modified owing to purely economic motives only exceptionally. Actual fiscal policy was generally passive and, instead of active measures, it relied more on the built-in automatisms.

Figure 7.8 shows the changes in GNP, profit and its components at unchanged prices.

We can see that the direction of changes in GNP were, with the exception of the years 1971 and 1975, contrary to that in government deficit. The two exceptional years might indicate that in those two years the increase in deficit, combined with other factors, resulted in an intended increase of GNP. The direction of the changes in material profit and deficit was contrary to each other in every year without exception. Whenever this profit increased, government deficit diminished, and, according to established theory, such a drop has a restrictive effect. Whenever this form of profit showed a drop, there was an increase in government deficit, and, according to established theory, such an increase has a business-boosting impact. With the exception of two years, the changes in the budget worked against the changes in GNP, and each year without exception they worked against the changes in profits. This is anticyclical fiscal policy at work.

Of course, in present-day capitalism the fluctuations in GNP are never great. But

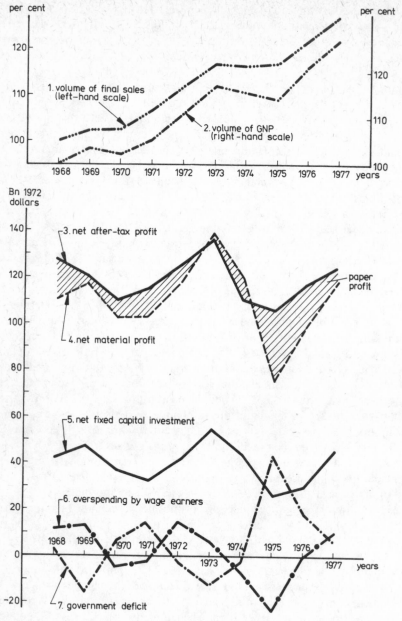

Figure 7.8 The volume of GNP, final sales, profit and its components (upper part: index numbers, 1960 = 100, lower part: bn 1972 dollars, excl. imputations)

those in unemployment and net profit are considerable indeed, and this is the main cause also many Western economists regarded 1974–1975 crisis years aggravated by inflation, even if they do not say so explicitly. (We could speak of a really successful anti-cyclical policy only if, as a result of economic policy, the changes in net profit, that is, of net investment could be kept within narrow limits. In that case also fluctuations in government deficit could be kept within narrow limits.)

In the years under study, however, net investment and government deficit not only moved in opposite directions but both showed violent fluctuations as well. The counter-movements are conspicuous. Looking at the figure one gets the impression as if one is a mirror image of the other. The deficit diminished or perhaps turns into surplus exactly when net investment increases and gross when net investment drops.

Clearly, although fiscal policy was consistently working against changes in investment, it was unable to stop the considerable fluctuation in invesment. But did it perhaps still have some positive impact on investment?

Let us not draw any hasty conclusions. The possibility still exists that changes in investment follow those in fiscal policy with—relatively regular—time lag.

We can check this on Fig. 7.8. Do we not find a positive correlation between the prevailing fiscal policy and the volume of investment one year later? From 1968 fiscal policy turned towards restriction and from 1969 to 1970 the volume of investment actually fell. We know from elsewhere that monetary policy had an important role in this drop. But fiscal policy turned expansive from 1969 to 1970 and a year later investment still continued to fall. The former case would indicate a positive, while the latter a negative correlation—if we really found a correlation between the two variables. And in the following years—obviously by chance—these phenomena are repeated with a near incredible accuracy. The budget remained expansive from 1970 to 1971, the volume of investment increased—a positive correlation. One year later, from 1971 to 1972 the budget aimed at restriction, but, in spite of this, the volume of investment showed a fast growth from 1972 to 1973—a negative correlation. A restrictive economic policy followed in 1973 and there was a slight drop in investment in 1974. Fiscal policy became expansive from 1973 to 1974 and there was a considerable drop in investment from 1974 to 1975. Seemingly positive and negative correlations followed each other alternately, proving that fiscal policy did not have a verifiable stimulating or restrictive impact on investment. Of course, it follows from the demonstrated improbably regular, alternately identical and opposite changes that we can find a parallel movement with a two-year time lag between fiscal policy and investment, but this regularity is in our judgement also a random occurrence like the identical and opposite movements assuming a one-year time lag. We think it would be naive to believe that changes in one year's budget directly affect changes in investment two years later.

It is also imaginable that changes in investment took place as a reaction to changes in the deficit with a time lag shorter than a year. In order to check this assumption we also present in Fig. 7.9 the changes of the above variables by quarters and below the graph we also show the quarterly changes of the same variables (smaller, bigger, of identical or opposite directions) symbolized by shorter or longer arrows. We could not discover any reliable positive correlation with any time lag between fiscal policy and the volume of investment—not even in a quarterly breakdown.

127

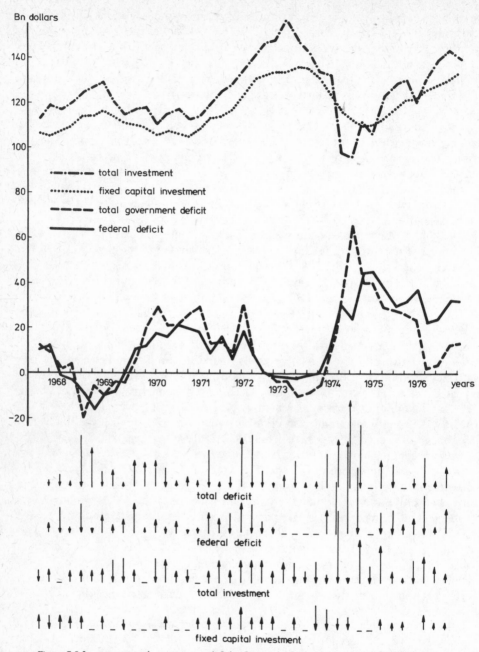

Figure 7.9 Investment and government deficit (Quarterly data at annual rate, bn 1972 dollars)

The size of the arrows is approximately proportionate to the changes in the amount of deficit expressed in billions of 1972 dollars, while a (−) sign indicates an insignificant change

128

Table 7.4

Gross after-tax profit and its components, 1968–1978
(billions of dollars at current prices, excl. imputations)

Items	1968	1969	1970	1971	1972	1973	1974	1975	1976	1977	1978
1. Gross after-tax profit	168.6	173.6	175.7	101.9	212.4	239.2	236.6	271.7	306.7	345.6	282.9
2. Gross material profit	153.6	170.9	168.1	180.6	204.2	240.7	248.6	231.7	277.7	329.4	377.9
3. Gross investment	102.7	116.0	111.0	118.9	138.2	169.3	170.3	146.2	183.4	224.8	262.9
4. Capital consumption allowances	60.6	67.4	74.8	81.5	86.8	96.2	112.7	133.9	147.3	160.5	176.6
5. Net investment	42.1	48.6	36.2	37.4	51.4	73.1	57.6	12.3	36.1	64.3	86.3
6. Changes in inventories	7.7	9.4	3.8	6.4	9.4	17.9	8.9	-10.7	10.0	21.9	22.3
7. Net fixed capital investment	34.4	39.2	32.4	31.0	42.0	55.2	48.7	23.0	26.1	42.4	64.0
8. Capitalists' consumption	50.9	54.9	57.1	61.7	66.0	71.4	78.3	85.5	94.3	104.6	115.0
9. Paper profit	15.0	2.7	7.6	11.3	8.2	-1.5	-12.0	40.0	29.0	16.2	5.2
10. Net exports	2.3	1.8	3.9	1.6	-3.3	7.1	6.0	20.4	8.0	-9.9	-10.3
11. Government deficit	2.7	-13.6	6.2	13.9	-1.9	-12.7	-4.3	56.8	28.0	10.8	-12.1
12. Less: Net savings by wage earners	-9.4	-11.2	4.6	2.9	-15.1	-6.7	7.9	29.8	0.9	-22.8	-30.9
13. Less: Statistical discrepancy	-0.6	-3.3	-2.1	1.3	1.7	2.6	5.8	7.4	6.1	7.5	3.3
14. *Addenda:* Net after-tax profits	108.0	106.2	100.9	110.4	125.6	143.0	123.9	137.8	159.4	185.1	206.5
15. Gross fixed capital investment	95.0	106.6	107.2	112.5	128.8	151.4	161.4	156.9	173.4	202.9	240.6
16. Net material profit	93.0	103.5	93.3	99.1	117.4	144.5	135.9	97.8	130.4	168.4	201.3

Table 7.5

Contribution of profit components to the percentage changes in total profits, 1969—1978
(based on current dollar data, excl. imputations)

per cent

Item	1969	1970	1971	1972	1973	1974	1975	1976	1977	1978
Gross after-tax profit	3.0	1.2	9.2	10.7	12.6	-1.1	14.8	12.9	12.7	10.8
Gross material profit	10.3	-1.6	7.1	12.3	17.2	3.3	-7.1	16.9	16.9	14.0
Gross investment	7.9	-2.8	4.5	10.1	14.6	0.4	-10.2	13.7	13.5	11.0
Capital consumption allowances	4.0	4.3	3.8	2.8	4.4	6.5	9.0	4.9	4.3	4.6
Net investment	3.9	-7.1	0.7	7.3	10.2	-6.5	-19.2	8.8	9.2	6.4
Changes in inventories	1.0	-3.2	1.5	1.6	4.0	-3.8	-8.3	7.6	3.9	0.1
Net fixed capital investment	2.9	-3.9	-0.8	5.7	6.2	-2.7	-10.9	1.1	5.3	6.3
Capitalists' consumption	2.4	1.3	2.6	2.2	2.5	2.9	3.0	3.2	3.4	3.0
Paper profit	-7.3	2.8	2.1	-1.6	-4.6	-4.4	22.0	-4.0	-4.2	-3.2
Net exports	-0.3	1.2	-1.3	-2.6	4.9	3.5	6.1	-4.5	-5.8	-0.1
Government deficit	-9.7	11.4	4.4	-8.2	-5.1	-0.5	25.8	-10.6	-5.6	-6.6
Less: Net savings by wage earners	-1.1	9.1	-1.0	-9.4	4.0	6.1	9.3	-10.6	-7.7	-2.2
Less: Statistical discrepancy	-1.6	0.7	1.9	0.2	0.4	1.3	0.7	-0.5	0.5	-1.2
Addenda: Net after-tax profits	-1.0	-3.1	5.4	7.9	8.2	-8.0	5.8	7.9	8.4	6.2
Gross fixed capital investment	6.9	0.4	3.0	8.5	10.6	4.2	-1.9	6.1	9.6	10.9
Net material profit	6.3	-5.9	3.3	9.5	12.8	-3.6	-16.1	12.0	12.6	9.4

Table 7.6

Gross after-tax profit and its components, 1968—1978

(billions of 1972 dollars, excl. imputations)

Items	1968	1969	1970	1971	1972	1973	1974	1975	1976	1977	1978
1. Gross after-tax profit	200.8	196.8	190.4	198.2	212.4	228.7	204.9	207.9	224.2	235.9	243.7
2. Gross material profit	182.6	193.7	182.1	186.4	204.2	230.1	215.2	176.4	202.6	224.5	240.4
3. Gross investment	123.7	133.7	121.7	123.3	138.2	162.4	148.0	108.9	131.7	150.5	164.5
4. Capital consumption allowances	72.6	75.9	80.3	83.8	86.8	91.2	95.8	101.1	104.4	106.2	107.9
5. Net investment	51.1	57.8	41.4	39.5	51.4	71.2	52.2	7.8	27.3	44.3	56.6
6. Changes in inventories	8.7	10.6	4.3	6.6	9.4	16.5	8.0	−9.8	6.6	13.1	14.1
7. Net fixed capital investment	42.4	47.2	37.1	32.9	42.0	54.7	44.2	17.6	20.7	31.2	42.5
8. Capitalists' consumption	58.9	60.0	60.4	63.1	66.0	67.7	67.2	67.5	70.9	74.0	75.9
9. Paper profit	18.2	3.1	8.3	11.8	8.2	−1.4	−20.3	31.5	21.6	11.4	3.3
10. Net exports	2.8	2.1	4.3	1.7	−3.3	6.7	5.2	16.0	6.0	−7.0	−6.8
11. Government deficit	3.3	−15.7	6.7	14.5	−1.9	−11.9	−3.7	44.7	20.9	7.0	−8.0
12. Less: Net savings by wage earners	−11.4	−12.9	5.0	3.0	−15.1	−6.3	6.8	23.4	0.7	−16.6	−20.3
13. Less: statistical discrepancy	−0.7	−3.8	−2.3	−1.4	1.7	2.5	5.0	5.8	4.6	5.3	2.2
14. *Addenda:* Net after-tax profits	128.2	120.9	110.1	114.4	125.6	137.5	109.1	106.8	119.8	129.7	135.8
15. Gross fixed capital investment	115.0	123.1	117.4	116.7	128.8	145.9	140.0	118.7	125.1	137.4	150.4
16. Net material profit	110.0	117.8	101.8	102.6	117.4	138.9	119.4	75.3	98.2	118.3	132.5

Table 7.7

Contribution of profit components to the percentage changes in total profits, 1969—1978
(based on 1972 dollar data, excl. imputations)

per cent

Items	1969	1970	1971	1972	1973	1974	1975	1976	1977	1978
Gross after-tax profit	-2.0	-3.3	4.1	7.2	7.7	-10.4	1.5	7.8	5.2	3.3
Gross material profit	5.5	-5.9	2.3	9.0	12.2	-6.5	-19.0	12.6	9.7	6.7
Gross investment	5.0	-6.1	0.8	7.5	11.4	-6.3	-19.1	11.0	8.3	5.9
Capital consumption allowances	1.6	2.2	1.8	1.5	2.1	2.0	2.6	1.6	0.8	0.7
Net investment	3.4	-8.3	-1.0	6.0	9.3	-8.3	-21.7	9.4	7.6	5.2
Changes in inventories	1.0	-3.2	1.2	1.4	3.3	-3.7	-8.7	7.9	2.9	0.4
Net fixed capital investment	2.4	-5.1	-2.2	4.6	6.0	-4.6	-13.0	1.5	4.7	4.8
Capitalists' consumption	0.6	0.2	1.4	1.5	0.8	-0.2	0.2	1.6	1.4	0.8
Paper profit	-7.5	2.6	1.8	-1.8	-4.5	-3.9	20.5	-4.8	-4.5	-3.4
Net exports	-0.4	1.1	-1.4	-2.5	4.7	-0.7	5.3	-4.8	-5.8	0.1
Government deficit	-0.9	11.4	4.1	-8.3	-4.7	3.6	23.6	-11.5	-5.9	-6.6
Less: Net savings by type earners	-0.8	9.1	-1.1	-9.1	4.1	5.7	8.1	-10.9	-7.5	-1.8
Less: Statistical discrepancy	-1.5	0.8	2.0	0.2	0.4	1.1	0.4	-0.6	0.3	-1.3
Addenda: Net after-tax profits	-3.6	-5.5	2.3	5.7	5.6	-12.4	-1.1	6.3	4.4	2.5
Gross fixed capital investment	4.0	-2.9	-0.4	6.1	8.1	-2.6	-10.4	3.1	5.5	5.5
Net material profit	3.9	-8.1	0.5	7.5	10.1	-8.5	-21.6	11.0	8.9	6.0

Thus we dare venture our conclusion that during the period reviewed fiscal policy in the United States had no verifiable direct impact on changes in investment. We cannot get rid of the feeling that this conclusion might be generalized. Changes in the government budget increasing or cutting a deficit or a surplus hardly influence changes in investment—these are decisively influenced by factors quite different from said changes. But the trend of changes in profit—freed of short-term fluctuations—depends primarily on investment and we do not have any reason to abandon the basic Marxist theorem that a capitalist economy is directed by profit. If this is true, how could we believe that fiscal policy is able to ensure a smooth development of the economy?

PART FOUR

ECONOMIC POLICY AND BUSINESS CYCLE (CONTRIBUTIONS TO THE THEORY OF BUSINESS CYCLES)

PHASE 1

THE RECESSION OF 1969–1970

CHAPTER EIGHT

A FEW WORDS ABOUT THE ANTECEDENTS

This part of our book follows in chronological order the main events of the US economy through an eleven-year period. The studied period starts with 1969. Nevertheless, we cannot completely leave out of account what happened before January 1, 1969, since in the course of examining the development of the economy we cannot usually draw sharp dividing lines without the danger of missing important causal relationships. Furthermore, important circumstances of the historical and economic historical development of the United States compel us to review the antecedents, that is, economic development in the sixties, at least in its main outlines. From the point of view of economic history, the compelling circumstances are that the events of the first half of the seventies are more closely related to developments in the preceding years than is usually the case. What followed later might also be considered as a reaction to the foregoing through the mediation of government economic policy. Besides, and the coincidence may be random, it was almost simultaneously with the turn of the decade, in November 1969 exactly, that the longest economic expansion in American history, lasting two months short of nine full years, came to an end. During that time the GNP increased every quarter without interruption. And the date ending the decade found the economy of the country amidst a mild recession. This is also a reason why we start the detailed discussion with 1969 instead of 1970. But we have not yet finished characterizing the antecedents of 1969.

The historical and political circumstances which similarly direct our attention to the antecedents are the following. As a result of the Republican victory, after eight years of Democratic administration, in January Nixon, beaten by Kennedy in 1960, became president. This was in no small part due to the fact that voters were turning against the Vietnam War and seeking a change gave their votes to the Republican candidate. This committed the new president politically to end the Vietnam War or, at least, to de-escalate it. This was done and, as we shall see, it entailed important economic consequences.

Let us then start at the beginning—meaning the early sixties. Kennedy's inauguration in January 1961 was an important turn. Namely, while under the preceding Republican administration (1953–1960), and particularly under the second Eisenhower term, the main concern of economic policy had been the fight against rising prices and the deterioration in the balance of payments—even at the price of neglecting the problem of unemployment—Kennedy brought with him a group of economic experts (Heller, Tobin and others) who took quite a different stand on economic policy problems. They interpreted and applied the Keynesian theory in a very active manner. Let us repeat what we have already said about that in the words of A. F. Burns, who in many respects opposed them: "The central doctrine of this school is that the change of the business cycle has little relevance to sound economic policy; that policy should be growth-oriented instead of cycle-oriented; that the vital matter is whether a gap exists between actual and potential output; that financial deficits and monetary tools need to be used to promote expansion when a gap exists; and that the stimuli should be sufficient to close the gap—provided significant inflationary pressures are not whipped up in the process." (Burns and Samuelson, 1967, pp. 31–32)

Accordingly, in the first half of the sixties the Democratic administration pursued an expressly growth-oriented economic policy with the aim of reducing and later closing the gap between potential and actual output[1] that had been wide open under the Eisenhower administration.

To this end, several important economic policy measures were taken. From among them we have to mention, even in such a brief survey, the liberalization of depreciation allowances, the introduction in 1962 of a tax rebate on account of investment and, especially, the tax reform[2] implemented in 1964 after three years of indecision. The positive impact of the latter on economic growth is usually acknowledged; exceptions to this are only the monetarist Milton Friedman and his followers.

As much is a fact that the half decade following 1961 was the fastest and most balanced growth period in post-war American economic history. We may agree with the statement, too, that "discretionary fiscal policy, in the form of deliberate use of tax reductions to stimulate the economy, had apparently brought the economy back to full employment [as far as 4 per cent unemployment may be considered full employment— *authors' note*] with only a modest rise in prices during the first half of the 1960s". (Gordon, 1974, p. 142). This is also borne out by the data: the volume of GNP rose in five years by 30 per cent (5.4 per cent on annual average), unemployment fell from 6.7 per cent to 3.8, while prices (measured by the implicit price index of GNP) increased by merely 2.1 per cent annually. The gap between potential and actual GNP was eliminated.

The last years of the Democratic Johnson administration already bore the imprint of the economically also grave consequences of the Vietnam War. The economy was unable to bear without serious disturbances the tensions deriving partly from the costs of the war and partly from the demand-expanding impact of the increased budget deficit owing to increased social policy expenditures.

Let us have a look at the relevant figures. The balance of the revenues and

---

[1] Potential GNP is, as a matter of fact, a measure of productive capacity. In the early sixties, the GNP producible with a 4 per cent unemployment was considered potential GNP. The as yet not exaggerated growth rate was estimated at 4 per cent p.a.; this would follow from a 2.5 per cent increase in productivity and 1.5 per cent increase in employment. (For the measurement and importance of the concept, see Okun, 1970, pp. 132–145.)

[2] For more detail in the American literature, see Okun, 1968, pp. 25–49, Stein, 1969, Chapters 16 and 17, and in the Hungarian literature, Molnár, 1965.

138

expenditures of the federal government, which in the preceding five years had shown a deficit of only $ 12.4 bn, closed in 1967 alone with a deficit of 13.2 bn, that is, more than in the preceding five years combined. In 1968, the peak year of the Vietnam War expenditures, the deficit amounted to 5.8 bn. In the last two years of Democratic administration the price rise was already 2.9 and 4.5 per cent. This was considered rather high at that time. The rise in taxes aimed at the mitigation of overheated demand (a surtax of 10 per cent was levied) could be only implemented in mid-1968 owing to political wrangling. Economic policy aimed at the moderation of overheated business had already been initiated by the Democratic administration—with the aid of both fiscal and monetary instruments. The last *Economic Report* of the President dated January 1969 pointed out that the economy had to be cooled down with satisfactory effective restriction and the relaxing of inflationary forces had to be made possible. It also emphasized that such a cooling down was to be avoided—which had already occurred—that would push the country into a recession. It equally warned against an overdose of fiscal and monetary restrictions, the introduction of compulsory price and wage controls and against passivity in face of the wage–price spiral. (*Economic Report, 1969, pp. 7–10*) These were, of course, nice principles, but provided no orientation as to their implementation.

Table 8.1

Major indicators of economic growth
(Average yearly percentual change)

Items	1953—1960 Republican	1961—1968 Democratic
	administration	
GNP[a]	2.6	4.6
Personal consumption[a,b]	3.2	4.3
Fixed capital investment[a,b]	3.0	6.3
Consumers' investment[c]	3.6	5.2
Government purchases[a]	1.0	5.2
Material production[a]	2.2	4.4
Industrial production	3.4	6.1
Productivity	2.7	3.6
Implicit price index of GNP	2.1	2.1
Consumer price index	1.4	2.1

[a] The changes in volumes are computed—except for industrial production—on the basis of 1972 dollar data (incl. imputations)
[b] Without the purchase of homes
[c] Sum of the purchases of consumers' durables and housing construction

It was under such circumstances that the Republican administration of President Nixon took charge of economic policy. But even before its representatives had shown their hand in economic policy, knowing certain facts, one could judge with some certainty what the American economy and wage earners could expect from the new administration. This was also indicated by the composition of the new President's "team". The position of chairman of the Council of Economic Advisers was filled by McCracken, a previous member of this board during the second Eisenhower term. The chairman of the board of governors of the FED was the same Burns, who, as chairman of the same board under Eisenhower, had been largely responsible for the grave consequences of that period's conservative economic policy.

But, persons aside, anyone who compared the economic developments of the previous Democratic and Republican administrations (see Table 8.1) could feel that the following four years did not promise much good.

The data are quite unequivocal: under the Democratic administration economic growth was in every respect of a much higher rate—in some respects 2–3-fold—than under the Republicans, but the rate of inflation was also slightly higher. And we have also mentioned that inflation rather accelerated in 1968.

Although economic policy-makers had to face grave problems in early 1969, the incoming McCracken declared in an interview in *The New York Times* that the Johnson administration had bequeathed an economic policy heading in a right direction.[3] In our opinion, the class character was aptly characterized by P. A. Samuelson, the respected and later Nobel-Prize winning economist, who wrote in his usual New Year's article, assessing and forecasting the economic situation: "Ours is still a class society and it warms the cockles of the heart of our business community to have the Republicans back in the White House." (Samuelson, 1969)

[3] *International Herald Tribune*, Jan. 25–26, 1969.

CHAPTER NINE

THE YEAR 1969

9.1 INFLATION OR UNEMPLOYMENT

In 1969, unemployment reached its lowest with 3.5 per cent. But inflation accelerated and between 1965 and 1969 the implicit price index of GNP rose by 3.9 per cent on the annual average. This did not entail a fall in real wages since in these four years hourly nominal wages plus extras increased by 6.8 per cent on the annual average.

True, the rise in prices took much away from the real wage level that wage earners hoped to attain through a rise in their nominal wages. Nor was it immaterial for them that in the course of the four years in question the rate of interest on mortgages rose 34.4 per cent, while the rise in the gross weekly wages was 16.6 per cent and the price index of housing construction went up by 21.3 per cent. Nor were capitalists happy; they had to put up with not only a more than 30 per cent rise in their wage costs, but also with an unfavourable trend in the balance of payments.

At any rate, the new Nixon administration declared war on inflation in 1969.

In those times the so-called Phillips curve was held in high esteem by Western economists. Relying on the data of earlier years, Phillips thought to have proven that there was an unequivocal inverse relationship between the annual rate of wage increase and the extent of unemployment. On this basis, they spoke—and are still speaking—about unavoidable trade-offs between the rate of inflation and unemployment, or, as Nixon put it in his February 1970 *Economic Report:* "...the price of finding work for the unemployed must be the hardship of inflation for all". (*Economic Report,* 1970, p. 3.)

True, Nixon continued the sentence by saying that he did not agree. He ventured that price stability could be attained even with approximately full employment.

This was nothing more than affirming a statement instead of proving te truth of the statement. He did not so much wish to reassure himself as to win trust for his economic policy. However, the question is not whether he himself believed in the possibility of simultaneously solving the double task. (The earlier reasonings quoted from Okun, deriving from Ackley, already threw some light on why the promise had to remain just that even in the best case. See Ackley, 1966, p. 176.)

In the begining of 1970—that is, *post festum*—the Council of Economic Advisers outlined in President Nixon's name the interrelations between the economic policy initiated in 1969 and the results they hoped to attain with it.

1.The federal government would reduce its share of purchases of goods and services in GNP and would strive to reduce the growth rate of purchases by states and local governments by allocating them less from its own budgetary means. Further, the tax reduction provided for mid-1969 would not be implemented.

2. It would support the restrictive monetary policy of the FED. Thus a credit squeeze would come about: interest rates would rise and this would slow down the growth of purchases. This mesaure would affect primarily the credit-financed outlays—home building, state and local construction, business investments not self-financed, and the purchase of consumer durables. But the amount of money in circulation would also diminish relative to incomes and turnover. The price of other non-tangible assets—bonds and the like—would also fall (because of the high interest rate). All that would reduce the spending propensity of the business sector and consumers, although it could not be known in advance to what extent and from what date.

3. Looking at it from the other side, the decelerating growth rate of purchases means a decelerating growth of sales. Thus either inventories would swell, or prices would be reduced, or the growth rate of production would be curbed. But inventories cannot grow sky-high, and costs and prices had been already rising for years, thus it was hardly believable that prices would suddenly be reduced. Thus, in all probability, the growth rate of production would decelerate or—temporarily—output would decline even in absolute terms. Under the given conditions this would anyway entail a decreasing capacity utilization, which would have an anti-inflationary impact.

4. Enterprises would first endeavour to keep their staff, but this would entail loss of productivity and rising unit costs—and a smaller profit margin. True, firms could also raise prices, but—so it was claimed—market conditions would hardly allow the maintenance of higher prices. Thus they would save on costs, reduce employment and overtime, and lay-offs would become more frequent.

5. Experiencing a decline in the profit per unit of product, firms would resist even more any demands for raising money wages and—in the shadow of menacing un-employment—workers would also be more modest, all the more since they would not be able to justify their demands by referring to rising profits. In the last resort, the growth rate of nominal wages would be modified.

Finally, a point radiating optimism which it is worthwhile quoting *verbatim*:

6. "While, as already indicated, the unfavourable development in profits would create some incentive to mark up prices, more sluggish market conditions would encourage business to pursue temperate pricing policies, especially, as this influence began to be reinforced by a slowdown in the rise of wage rates and unit labor costs. The reductions in wage and price increases would tend to reinforce each other. The longer price increases moderated, the weaker would become the expectation of further inflation. In turn, business and labor would be increasingly inclined to respond to the waning inflation by making appropriate price and wage adjustments, in preference to

accepting a lower volume of production and less emloyment. With this change the economy would be on the road to regaining full employment without setting off another round of inflation."

These points can be read—under subtitles instead of numbered paragraphs—in the Report of the Council of Economic Advisers to the President (pp. 25–26). It is worthwhile stressing the cynicism of the first two points, from which it turns out that we were unjust a few paragraphs earlier to the 1969 ecomomic policy of the Nixon administration, but in the President's favour. We wrote that the administration was essentially passive towards unemployment. The fuller truth is that it was passive toward the unemployment it had caused itself intentionally. And point 6 is particularly beautiful in comparison with the preceding five in that its apparent logic is devoid of logic: it repeats, as a matter of fact without argumentation, merely with an optimism aimed at reassuring the reader—although point 3 already forecast the possibility of the opposite—that for a considerable mitigation of inflation even a moderation of the growth rate of unemployment would be sufficient, that is, the attainment of the target did not necessitate an absolute decline in employment. Besides, under the given conditions unemployment would have grown, even if this unfounded prophecy had come true, because of the growth in the number of job-seekers on account of the demographic growth.

9.3 THE FISCAL AND MONETARY RESTRICTIONS

After these preliminaries we can now look into what really happened in the USA in the fields of fiscal and monetary policy in 1969. Let us first see the actual restrictive measures of fiscal policy aimed at curbing inflation.

The expenditures of the federal government exceed those of the preceding year by only $ 7.8 bn in 1969, while in 1968 spending increased by 16.9 bn. The total expenditure of the federal government, corrected for the allocations to state and local government, increased over the preceding year by $ 16.7 bn in 1969, and by 26.5 bn in 1968 over 1967.

The picture still shows an increase. About one-third of this increase may be attributed to the raising of government employees' salaries in July 1969. From the American point of view this raise was a part of the government purchase of goods and services, as American statistics classifies the salaries of government employees as purchase of services. Further, the sum of the government purchase of goods and services increased in 1969 by merely 1 bn dollars over the preceding year, that is, the sum of federal purchases, other than of government employees' services, fell considerably even at current prices. This decline was mostly due to the drop in military expenses; the de-escalation of the Vietnam War was already under way and government constructions also diminished. However, other federal government expenditures kept increasing at a hardly decelerating rate. The social security outlays, other transfers, allocations to state and local governments cannot and could not be cut back at will. Owing to the general rise in rates of interest, the net interests paid by the government increased particularly fast.

This then is what happened to the expenditure side of the balance of government revenues and expenditures.

The revenue side of the balance depends even less on govenment intentions. At any rate, government also took one or two *ad hoc* discretionary measures to increase its revenues. Only a single active measure was taken which in the last resort hit wage earners: with January 1, 1969 the rate of social security contribution was raised from 8.8 to 9.6 per cent and for 1969 this resulted in an additional 3 bn dollar revenue. In the passive sense, as already mentioned, government did not introduce the tax reduction originally planned for mid-1969. More exactly, the general 10 per cent surtax, introduced earlier, in June 1968, remained in force till the end of the year. (This surtax contributed significantly to getting the approximately 25 bn deficit of the *fiscal* year ending on June 30, 1968 to turn into a surplus already in 1969.) Another measure abolished in April 1969 was the 7 per cent investment tax credit in force since 1962. This had meant that the enterprise could deduct 7 per cent of its expenses on real investment from its profits otherwise liable to taxation every year.[4] Lastly, it may be mentioned that also the planned moderation of the sales tax on cars was postponed.

Finally, the combined efforts at reducing budget expenditure and increasing revenues resulted in the following figures:

The federal budget closed in 1968 with a deficit of 5.8 bn, and in 1969 with a surplus of 8.5 bn, while the balance of total government expenditure and revenues showed a deficit of $ 5.5 bn in 1968 and a surplus of $ 10.7 bn in 1969.

Summing up, it may be established that the fiscal policy of 1969 was definitely of a deflationary nature. We already reported on the monetary instruments employed in 1969 to complement the deflationary fiscal policy on pp. 28–32 of the first part of this book, where we also reviewed the financial troubles thus produced.

9.4 THE RISING PRICES OF CONSUMER GOODS

How successful was at least the fight against inflation? As a matter of fact, this question was already answered in Part Two with the Δp_c diagrams reviewed there (pp. 54–55, 75, 87). Nevertheless, let us review in some detail the elements of the Δp_c diagram relating to the year 1969.

1. The sum of wages and salaries in 1969 increased by $ 44.3 bn over the preceding year. This is a rise of 9.6 per cent, and 9.9 per cent of the sum spent by wage earners on consumption in 1968. The growth was a result of changes in two factors. The wage per full-time earner increased by 6.8 per cent, while employment in terms of full-time employment increased by 2.9 per cent. (In the *ex-post* prophecy of the 1970 Report of the President we find the following: "After a sustained period of expansion and labor shortages employers would tend to maintain work forces, and pay-rolls would tend to be fixed." *Economic Report,* 1970, p. 26) (As can be seen, the first part of the prophecy promised too little, the second too much.)

2. Other labour incomes increased by 3.1 bn (12 per cent), amounting to 0.7 of the consumption expenditure of wage earners in 1968.

---

[4] This right of deduction also related to the investment goods ordered but not yet received and thus its abolition might have caused a minor investment cycle. Indeed, orders were increased by those firms which wanted to make use of the tax rebate at the last moment.

3. Government transfers increased considerably, by 14 per cent of the consumption by wage earners in 1968.

4. The sum of deductions also increased. Personal taxes and social security contributions increased for two reasons: nominal income also increased, and the rate of social security contributions was raised. (It also worked somewhat towards increasing personal taxes that the surtax mentioned was in force in 1968 only for the three quarters after April 1, while in 1969 it already affected the whole income of the year.) The increment was 4.8 per cent of the consumption expenditure of wage earners in the preceding year.

5. Finally, according to our estimates, the sum of wage earners' savings was negative even in 1969; in fact, considering the whole year, overspending increased by 1.9 bn.

Thus, in the last resort wage and salary earners spent 7.7 per cent more than in the preceding year.

Let us now take in turn the quantities in the denominator of the formula.

The volume of consumer goods sold increased by 2.8 per cent. According to our estimates, the increase in the purchase of consumer goods by wage earners was 2.9 per cent.

Accordingly, the price index of consumer goods (inclusive of services and the purchase of homes) comes to $107.71/102.92 \times 100 = 104.7$. Sellers were "modest" in their price strategy, raising consumer-goods prices by only 4.7 per cent, while the net after-tax profit margin fell from the record level of 26.1 per cent in 1968 to 24.3 per cent (cf. Table 5.1). This restraint was rewarded, it allowed them to sell 2.9 per cent more consumer goods to wage earners (in terms of volume).

We cannot directly confront our own price index with the official one because there does not exist such an official price index that would relate to consumption without imputations. For information we also give the 1969 changes of some offical price indexes. That of the implicit price index of GNP was 5.0 per cent, of fixed capital investment 4.8, of housing construction 8.6, of wholesale prices 3.9, the consumer price index (based on a consumer basket of town dwellers) 3.5, and the implicit price index of global personal consumer expenditure 4.5 per cent. As regards its contents, the latter is nearest to our own index number, the accounting for imputed outlays causes an upward bias, the neglect of home-purhases a downward one in comparison to our own price index. Thus, as regards the anti-inflationary campaign of the Nixon administration just coming into office, that provoked the recession, we make the summary statement that in the course of 1969 it ended in complete failure, even if we take into account that the rate of price increase somewhat slowed down by the last quarter of the year. The implicit price index of GNP (at annual rate and corrected for seasonal fluctuations) showed the following quarterly changes: 1st: 4.4, 2nd: 5.8, 3rd: 6.4 and 4th: 5.0 per cent.

9.5 PRODUCTION OF AND DEMAND FOR GOODS AND SERVICES

Let us now look more closely at the price of their failure. From the most frequently quoted time series of official statistics, the most comprehensive indicator of business fluctuations, we can learn the following. The growth rate of the GNP at current prices decreased—as we know, in line with government intentions—almost every quarter:

from 8.1 per cent in the first quarter it fell to 2.7 by the fourth. But this nominal growth of 2.7 per cent corresponded to a 2.2 per cent decline in terms of volume.

According to statistical practice, the quoted figures are data projected to the whole year ("output would have grown by that much in the course of the year, if its growth rate had corresponded to the growth rate in the given quarter"). But they are also "seasonally adjusted" and this means, e.g., the following: production usually increases in the fourth quarter because of Christmas purchases. The slowdown and fall in the fourth quarter mentioned in the preceding paragraph is to be understood in comparison to this, for seasonal reasons usually higher rate of growth. In reality, the GNP increased at current prices in the fourth quarter by 5.2 per cent relative to the third—not at the annual rate. This means an increase of about 4 per cent in real terms, although this year it was smaller than usual.

It is with a knowledge of these facts that the view becoming general in the USA is to be judged, namely, that the beginning of the recession was in the fourth quarter of 1969. It is not a statement that cannot be challenged, as the real beginning of a process that does not start with sudden rapidity can be stated unambiguously only in rare cases. Otherwise, the above quoted data relate to an indicator summarizing the development of several partial factors into a single figure, and these partial factors did not in the least develop synchronously.

Unfortunately, American statistics are basically of an income and demand approach, sales rather than production are in the fore, with production itself relegated to the background. The data on gross output can only be found by large aggregates: durables, non-durable goods, services and construction. (There are also data on several industries, but they cannot be aggregated into gross output according to the four main categories of the GNP.)

About the domestic purchases of the goods produced the following can be said.

From the durables, the volume of consumer durables sold attained its peak already in the first quarter of 1969, while in the fourth it was merely 2 per cent lower than the peak. Also the purchase of motor cars diminished less than the production of cars: the latter was −9.5 per cent, the former only −1.5 per cent.

The purchase of durables for investment also reached its peak in the first quarter of 1969 and relative to that diminished by merely 0.7 per cent in the fourth.

The volume of home purchases was also highest in the first quarter and fell by 11.1 per cent by the fourth.

It deserves separate stressing that—brought on not by business forces, but by political factors—the reduction of military expenses had started in real terms already in the fourth quarter of 1968, and continued steadily, reaching −7.6 per cent by the last quarter of 1969.

We have already mentioned that productive investment within private fixed capital investment was essentially stagnating beginning with the first quarter. But the volume of total private fixed capital investment inclusive of investment construction peaked in the third quarter and declined relative to this by 0.9 per cent by the end of the year.

The third component of private investment activity, the accumulation of inventories, peaked (in terms of volume) together with the GNP in the third quarter with $ 13.4 bn; by the fourth, it fell to 6.8 bn (and dwindled to merely 2.9 bn by the first quarter of 1970, to be considered the trough of the recession). Although at a decelerating rate, inventories continued to grow for a long time. It was in the first quarter of 1975, the trough of the 1974–1975 recession that inventories actually first diminished. (We again note that, unless otherwise stated, every quarterly data should be understood as projected to the whole year and seasonally adjusted and inclusive of imputations.)

Deducting from the official volume data the sum of government wages and salaries deflated by the price index of personal consumption purchases we get the result that federal purchases culminated in the second quarter of 1968. Following that they steadily diminished, primarily because of the reduction of military expenditure.

Total government purchases started to decline also following the second quarter of 1968. The fall in federal purchases was 14.7 per cent by the fourth quarter of 1969; that of total government purchases was 8.9 per cent.

The volume of personal consumption did not fall in the course of the year, in fact, in the last quarter of 1969 it was even 2.8 per cent higher than a year earlier. The same holds for the real value of disposable (that is, not actually spent) personal incomes. This, too, increased every quarter and somewhat faster than the former; in the fourth quarter of 1969 it was 3.2 per cent higher than a year earlier. But this official data related—as opposed to the concept applied in our own computations—not to the disposable income of persons remaining after payment of their interest obligations.

Finally, two important things should be kept in mind.

Civilian employment attained its peak in August 1969, with 79.6 mn people emloyed, exceeding the level of the previous year by 2.9 per cent. In September this fell by about one and a half million for seasonal reasons, starting to rise slowly afterwards again. The level of unemployment was lowest in May 1968, only 2.9 per cent of the civilian labour force. Then it basically stagnated with minor fluctuations, and,

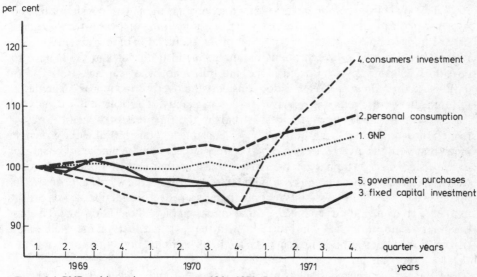

Figure 9.1 GNP and its main componenets, 1961–1971 (Based on data in 1972 dollars, first quarter of 1969 = 100)

regarding the whole of the year, it remained by one-tenth of a percentage point lower than the average of the preceding year. (Namely, in that year the reduction of armed forces was still relatively negligible.) This was the lowest value ever since the Korean War.

Accordingly, the start of the provoked decline is not concentrated on a single date. Both fixed capital investment and GNP attained their peak in the third quarter of 1969. The purchase of consumer durables and home construction, however, peaked already half a year earlier, in the first quarter of 1969, and were already falling when fixed capital investment still continued to grow.

Looking half a year ahead, we can report on a similar time lag. GNP passed the trough after the first quarter of 1970 and the purchase of consumer durables started to rise together with it. These were followed later by a quarter, thus following the second quarter of 1970, by an upswing in housing construction, while fixed capital investment started to rise only in the first quarter of 1971.

For an easier survey we illustrate with a graph (Fig. 9.1) the movements indicated in the above text—but for a somewhat longer period.

9.6 SOME REASONS WHY THE CLASSIC MODEL OF THE BUSINESS CYCLE BECAME OBSOLETE

What was said above in many respects contradicts some more or less known theorems. In Kalecki's theory of business cycles the leading role unequivocally belongs to investment, though, of course secondarily, the volume of investment is itself a function of the general course of business.

Indeed, if we stated without any reservation that the expansion or reduction of investment unambiguously depends on the high or low rate of profit, we might reason as follows: apart from certain modifying factors, profit is the sum of consumption and investment by capitalists. Since the capitalists' consumption is of low elasticity, we may state without committing a major error that profit is a function of investment: the two are moving in a strictly synchronous manner, thus also output and GNP have to develop synchronously with profit. True, but this is not what happens.

In his *Contributions*... Péter Erdős considers the overproduction of capacities as the immediate cause releasing downturn or, more exactly, the crisis. In this context he leaves two possibilities open: the first is that by the time excess capacities cause a reduction of investment, the production of consumer goods has already grown so much that with the given prices an excess supply appears on the market of consumer goods. (Tibor Erdős emphasized particularly this possibility, saying that this is when we can speak of overproduction crisis in the classical sense of the word (T. Erdős, 1976. pp. 90–91)). The other possibility is that there is no overproduction as yet on the market of consumer goods and fixed capital investment is still on the decline. The first possibility is not in formal contradiction with the fact that in 1969 the decline in a certain kind of consumption preceded the fall in fixed capital investment. We may just as well accept this fact.

But it was already mentioned in *Contributions*... and *Wages, Profit, Taxation* establishes it with particular emphasis in discussing the crises of a classical type that

148

recovery has to start from the side of investment. In this context the following argument deserves special attention.

Changes in investment, it is said, have a positive feedback effect in the system. Its increase raises—*ceteris paribus*—the profit margin and (relative to wages) also prices; its reduction, however, involves a decline in all these. Thus a change in investment sets off a self-intensifying process. In contrast, a change in the production of consumer goods has—*ceteris paribus*—a negative feedback effect on the system: its growth reduces prices (relative to wages), diminishes the profit margin and, probably, also the rate of profit. Thus—goes the argument—if at the trough level the production of consumer goods increased, the process would soon throttle itself. This, of course, does not exclude that also investment should take an upswing with a small time lag, and then this investment might further kindle the upturn process. But in our case, in 1970–1971, the upswing in investment was considerably late relative to the growth in the sales of consumption goods and, in spite of that, no decline occurred.

The quoted theorems related to crises of the classical type, and one of their characteristics is that they are brought about by the self-movement of the economy, that is, they are results of a spontaneous processes. The material basis of their periodic repetition is the massive, periodic renewal of fixed capital, concentrated in time, which either leads to intermediate crisis or to the excess production of fixed capital.

But the 1969–1970 recession was not released by an overproduction of fixed capital, nor by overproduction of capacity. In 1969, the degree of utilization of productive capacities was high. The recession was a product of restrictive government policy. The spontaneous forces of the economy withstood this pressure for half a year. (Fixed capital investment could not be stopped overnight, projects begun are usually completed.)

But, ever since the Great Depression of the early thirties, beyond the increased inclination of the state to interfere with the economy, and beyond its increased investment possibilities, there have been several changes also in other institutions which more than challenge the present validity of the theorems about the course of classical crises.

The theorem, quoted a few paragraphs earlier, about the negative feedback of the production of consumption goods was proved, regarding the substance of the matter, according to the following line of reasoning. In its simplest from, the p_c formula is $p_c = \dfrac{\Sigma W}{C - c}$ where ΣW is the sum of wages paid in the period in question. If in the production of investment goods n_1 and in that of consumption goods n_2 number of workers are employed, and the nominal wage of a person is b, the formula may be written as $p_c = \dfrac{n_1 + n_2}{C - c}$ where the volume of consumer goods produced (C) changes on the whole parallel with n_2, but is independent of the size of n_1. Thus, if n_2 increases relative to n_1, considering the relative rigidity of the consumption of capitalists (c), the denominator increases faster than the numerator, thus the price level declines. From this already follows the above statement regarding the profit margin and even the rate of profit.[5]

[5] In this line of reasoning the production of raw materials is classified with the class in which the materials are used.

But this reasoning partly needs refinement since, among other things, it relies on the tacit assumption[6] that every kind of capitalist consumption is very rigid. On the other hand, it needs changing because it relies on the assumption, no longer valid in the short run, that wage earners always spend their wages and only that. (Not to mention the fact that also their incomes other than wages, e.g., from transfer payments, may be considerable as well.)

Now, as regards refinement, the outlays of capitalists on consumer durables, primarily on home purchases, are not nearly as rigid as their other outlays on consumption. As regards the radical changes, the theorem about the negligible size of net savings by wage earners is still valid today on the average of a few years—with few exceptions—but not for every year and at every date. In Chapter 7 of this book an estimate is published of the savings of wage and salary earners (positive and negative) in the years of the seventies. We have found rather large sums, though not large relative to their disposable income, that leads us to see that if a possible overspending by wage and salary earners flows in its bulk onto the market of consumer durables—or, in the reverse case, is missing therefrom—then, taking into account also the significant fluctuations in the similar spendings by capitalists, we find a satisfactory explanation for the phenomenon that in the newer cycles the movement of investment follows the changes in the demand for consumer goods with some time-lag. That is, we should not speak simply of the demand for consumer goods, but of that for consumer durables, regarding the substance of the matter. Namely, the role of consumer credits has much grown in recent years. Homes, household electronics, cars are usually bought on credit.

In those years when the purchase of consumer durables and of homes is around the peak level, the net savings of wage and salary earners become negative. In such times, not only the additional wage of the increment in the n_2 employment flows to the market, but the surplus of consumer and mortgage credits as well. The numerator of the p_c formula augmented by the credits raised may at least grow together with the denominator of the formula. The price level of consumer goods need not fall in the short run relative to wages, thus neither the profit margin nor the rate of profit need to do so.

In the period under discussion demand for owner occupied homes was strong indeed. But the number of housing units started falling back between 1966 and 1968 to a level lower than required by the potential demand released by the creation of new households and the replacement requirements of obsolete homes, i.e., a significant unsatisfied demand accumulated. This state of affairs was largely a consequence of the 1966 credit restrictions. The number of vacant dwellings remained low, the price of new and old dwellings kept increasing and housing rents continued to rise at an accelerating rate. In the meantime, in the second half of 1968, following the introduction of the surtax, credit terms eased somewhat because the government hoped that the introduction of the surtax would allow a certain expansion of credits. Accordingly, the number of new housing units started increasing from 1.4 mn in the

---

[6] It belongs to the assumptions that the inventories of consumption goods do not change, consumer goods are neither exported nor imported, etc.

second quarter of 1968 to 1.7 mn by the first quarter of 1969. (Again, these are seasonally adjusted data at annual rate.) This was followed by a decline.

We find the cause of decline in monetary and credit restrictions. The rate of interest on mortgage credits remained below that of other—long-term—securities. It followed—as we have seen earlier, in Part One, p. 29—the agencies financing housing construction, primarily the savings institutions, shared in the flow of savings with greater difficulty and under less favourable conditions; they even invested their capital in securites bearing interest rates instead of mortgages. Housing construction was throttled not only by the very high rates of interest for ordinary people, but by the fact that credit for housing construction was not at all available to many of them. The number of housing units started to fall by the second quarter to 1.5 mn, by the third to 1.4 mn and by the fourth to 1.3 mn (at annual rate, seasonally adjusted). And that the decline had been caused by the credit squeeze was proven by the fact that as soon as the recession ended (and investment had not even reached bottom) the volume of housing construction started to rise again as a result of easier access to mortgage credit. Similar arguments apply, of course, also for the purchase of consumer durables.[7]

9.7 THE LAG IN THE PRIVATE INVESTMENT CYCLE

We have already reported (Part One, pp. 29–30) what it was that made it possible for enterprises to keep fixed capital investment at a relatively high level in spite of monetary and credit restictions. But the possibility does not yet explain why they in fact availed themselves of it.

We might as well say that it was the momentum acquired in the course of the years— business optimism becoming almost natural—that carried investment forward. The 5.8 per cent increase of fixed capital investment in 1969 over 1968 was only the continuation of a process almost uninterrupted for eight years.

Originally, the raising of the tax rate also had been planned for only one year, and investors pay greater attention to long-range prospects than to such temporary effects. Amidst inflation, the endeavour to put a brake on rising wage costs by labour saving investment also played a role. We also meet with such opinion in the Western literature that the experience of the then recent past may have had a role, namely, the fact that the mini-recession of 1967 was followed by a new upswing, mainly because of livelier commodity trade and an increasing profit margin. But this explanation raises the pseudo-problem of the hen and the egg: was the livelier investment activity the cause and the rising profit the consequence or conversely? There can be no doubt, however, that also the monetary ease introduced in the second half of 1968, already mentioned, contributed to the lasting and lively investment activity. It is a fact that the interviewed enterprise managers at the end of 1968 planned record-high investment for 1969. (In the end this optimistic intention was not implemented.)

[7] In the work already quoted, R. A. Gordon writes, in connection with the housing construction boom which started in the second half of 1970, the following: "By now we are familiar with the typical cyclical behaviour of residential construction—the tendency to decline as money becomes tight in the late stages of a boom followed by a rapid rise during the subsequent business recession and early stages of business recovery as credit becomes easy and mortgage funds again become readily available." (Gordon, 1974, p. 174)

But there was also a special sectoral cause behind the lively investment activity. Towards the end of the sixties, the electricity, gas and telephone companies raised extraordinary demand for capital goods. As distinct from other industries, their investment continuously and considerably increased year after year. The frequent breakdowns necessitated the creation of additional capacities. The high rates of interest did not disturb their investment activities much, partly because they were service companies and the demand for services is continuously rising, and partly because the authorities allowed them to shift their higher costs onto consumers. It is, of course, also true, that overheatedness in an indication of an impending general decline. Naturally, the state of business at any time impacts on investment: the role of investment in guiding self-movement is not one-sided, but is realized under conditions of mutual dependence. There may be, however, also such kinds of investment on which the state of business has little impact.

CHAPTER TEN

THE YEAR 1970

10.1 THE LIQUIDITY CRISIS AT THE BEGINNING OF THE YEAR

We could see that in the course of 1969 the government pursued, "together with the monetary authority", a very resolute restrictive economic policy in order to curb inflation.[8]

Because of the relative independence of the FED, Nixon's advisers were in trouble to a certain extent. They were, namely, rightly of the opinion that in order to actually attain a diminishing inflation, the disinflationary measures must be lasting. As a matter of fact, it was said, if people are not convinced by their own experience that inflation does essentially diminish, but, on the contrary, they expect it to continue, then this expectation becomes a self-fulfilling prophecy. The 1970 Report of the Council of Economic Advisers mentioned it as a deterring example that "in 1966 monetary tightness had contributed to a damping of the economy and of the inflation, but the economic slowdown led in turn to a shift back to highly expansive policies in 1967 and to resurgence of inflation. It was commonly thought [in 1969] that this pattern might be repeated (p. 23)." And it declared that it was not self-evident that the new, tighter monetary policy would be sufficiently lasting.

As if by magic, the advisers saw into the future. They almost prophesied what they would advise in one or two months' time. Indeed, hardly had the printers' ink dried on this report submitted to Congress, when FED already eased the monetary restrictions and the administration also adopted a more expansive fiscal policy. But they saw the future correctly even in a longer perspective: indeed, inflation could not be stopped.

But suddenly they had a more urgent task than to stop inflation. In the fourth quarter of 1969 the recession began. Was this that frightened them? Hardly, since, in spite of every seemingly optimistic promise its occurrence was foreseen. Nor was the election date so close that on its account the unemployment problem should have gained priority. Nor was the recession deep; the decline in GNP did not exceed one per cent—at annual rate—even at its bottom. Perhaps we are not far from the truth if we surmise that it was not the recession and not even the increase in unemployment that acted as a deterrent. It is likely that the pressure the government could not and did not

---

[8] Nixon took care that the FED should not proceed all too independently. He was also fortunate in that the mandate of the Chairman of the Federal Reserve Board just expired and he nominated his own man, the conservative Burns. Burns was removed at the end of 1978.

want to resist started from the large companies. By early 1970, the large companies were threatened by a liquidity crisis. Some of them *in principle* became bankrupt, though government interference warded off *open* bankruptcy. (The best known case was that of the Penn Central Railroad in mid-1970.)

The various measures of enterprise liquidity indicate in some manner how easily a company can meet its payment obligations on maturity. The practically applied measures of liquidity are highly diverse, if only because the liquidity requirements of the various industries are also highly diverse, and liquidity tactics of enterprises in different industries are very different.

At any rate, the liquidity position of firms showed a diminishing tendency in the two decades between 1948–1969. In the times following World War II, the liquidity of enterprises was firm, and in those times the initial decline in liquid assets simply indicated an adjustment to the post-war situation. Further, the fact that no grave depression occurred after the war encouraged firms to reduce their liquid assets relative to total capital. The firms were tired by the possibility of converting a part of their monetary assets into inventories and other circulating assets. Also, the newer forms of handling financial enterprise reserves encouraged them to prefer, under the impact of rising rates of interest, the negotiable short-term securities to cash. Then, after 1965, under the impact of increasing inflation, they increasingly converted their money and securities into inventories and other physical capital goods, since in the course of inflation the real price of securities falls, and that of material assets increases. As a result of this trend, from the two, perhaps most characteristic, indicators of liquidity of manufacturing firms with more than 100 mn dollar assets, the so-called "current ratio" fell from the 1949 peak by 32 per cent and the "quick ratio" by 78 per cent. (The former relates to the assets turning into money (or that can be turned into money) within a year to the obligations maturing within a year, while the latter compares the sum of cash, inclusive of account money, plus state bonds and treasury bills to the sum of debts maturing within a year.)

But the restrictive fiscal policy had started already in 1968. The liquidity indicators of firms continuously deteriorated from early 1969 to the first quarter of 1970 and levelled off there. During this time the current ratio fell by 6.5 per cent on the average, but this indicator also treats inventories as current assets. But the fall in the quick ratio approached 26 per cent (although, as mentioned, it had already fallen by 78 per cent until 1969).

The restrictive monetary policy of the second half of 1969, the fall in enterprise profits in the first half of 1970, the high level of fixed capital investment in 1969 and early 1970, the measures taken by managers at safeguarding the value of enterprise reserve assets all contributed to the deterioration in liquidity. We already reported that in the credit squeeze large corporations, in the interest of securing their growth, reduced their cash and government bond stocks also in absolute terms. In the period under discussion the inventories of large corporations increased by 16.6 per cent, while the growth of all other liquid assets was only 6.7 per cent. The firms were ready to increase their inventories, in the hope of selling later at higher prices, and some of them simply fell into the trap of high inventories when demand for their commodities fell.

The above data were taken by those preparing the 1971 Report of the Council of Economic Advisers from the publications of the Federal Trade Comissions and the

154

Securities and Exchange Commission. It is contained in Appendix A to said Report, which ends with the following conclusion: "This study suggests that the deterioration of corporate liquidity during 1969 and 1970 has been generally moderate for the groups of large manufacturing corporations analyzed... To the extent the sample of large manufacturing firms is not completely representative of all business firms, this general conclusion might have to be qualified. Small businesses as well as firms in some nonmanufacturing industries may have had more liquidity problems than is indicated in this analysis. Furthermore, the severe difficulties experienced by some of the large manufacturing corporations in the analysis are concealed within the general averages. Nevertheless, under the period under review, when there was growing public concern about business liquidity, the responsibility for evaluating the situation and taking the necessary policy actions needed to avert a genuine liquidity crisis was assumed by the appropriate agencies of the Government." (*Economic Report,* 1971, p. 178)

This is what happened. Misgivings and pressure on the part of big capital—the lobby—took care that "public opinion" should get exaggerated information about the difficulties of the corporations, prompting or forcing the government to reverse beginning with 1970 most of the measures taken in 1969 and planned to last. The menace of the liquidity crisis was averted from the second quarter of 1970.

10.2 MONETARY AND FISCAL POLICIES ARE BECOMING MORE EXPANSIONIST

The greatest change occurred in monetary policy. (Although R.A. Gordon, already quoted several times, wrote that the Nixon administration, which refrained from a highly expansionist fiscal policy in 1970, would have gladly accepted an even looser monetary policy. (Gordon, 1974, p. 175))

First, in January, and more resolutely in February, the FED Open Market Commission moved. The stock of money (M_1) which had been kept in the second half of 1969 at an almost unchanged level, was allowed to rise in 1970 at an average rate of about 5.5 per cent. The averting of the liquidity crisis may be attributed mainly to that (although in 1970 the paper profit also increased somewhat relative to 1969). In this context the Report of the Economic Advisers boasted mainly of the development of interest rates, saying that the increased supply of credit "produced a dramatic decline of interest rates" (*Economic Report,* 1971, p. 24). In reality, the picture was more mixed than that. After some decline at the beginning of the year rates of interest on long-term loans again increased by June, in fact, e.g., the interest rates of corporations' bonds rose above the record level of late 1969, because—as is stated in the Report (p. 63)—the tensions increased because of the Vietnam War and the insolvency of the Penn Central Railroad increased demand for liquid assets. Following that, however, the rates on bonds also began to diminish. The rate of interest on the best corporate bonds fell by the end of the year by one-tenth of a percentage point below the 1969 peak, but that of the second-rate bonds exceeded the level of one year earlier by about one and a half percentage points even in December 1970. But as regards the short-term loans, it is actually true that, relative to the peak at the end of 1969, their rates of interest fell by about three percentage points.

Of course, a decline in interest rates also has its drawback. Thus, e.g., the *Economic*

Report of 1972 established that "the decline in U.S. interest rates relative to interest rates abroad in the early part of the year (1971) sharply increased the outflow of funds from the United States" (p. 22).

Fiscal policy also became more expansionist.

In two consecutive steps the surtax, the elimination of which had been already planned a year earlier, was abolished. A further significant decline in income was caused by slackening business, although mostly only in relative terms, since the continuing inflation worked against the decline as it increased tax revenues also with unchanged tax rates. In the final analysis the revenues of the federal government still diminished by 4.9 bn dollars. The decline in corporate taxes owing to the recession significantly contributed to this fact. On the other hand, the expenditures of the federal government increased by 15.8 bn over 1969. The 2.8 bn reduction of military expenses was more than counterbalanced by increasing other expenses. The increase in unemployment assistance alone amounted to 1.8 billion.

It followed that the balance of the federal government turned from a 8.5 bn surplus in 1969 into a 12.1 bn deficit in 1970. A similar change occurred on the total government budget level.

It should be noted, however, that this turn was not quite intentional, but occurred mostly automatically owing to the economic recession and its consequences, as well as to earlier commitments in social programs. Thus, e.g., the budget surplus of the federal government started to diminish already in the third quarter of 1970. Then the deficit kept growing for eighteen months almost without interruption, but this was no longer independent of government intentions.

10.3 PRODUCTION OF AND DEMAND FOR GOODS AND SERVICES

The year 1970 was marked by two events. One was the unfolding of the recession started in the last quarter of 1969, the other the strike lasting for several months in the largest corporation of the country, General Motors, which contributes one half of the output of motor cars. These two factors had an important role in that the volume of GNP somewhat diminished in 1970 compared to the preceding year. Let us immediately add that the strike mentioned had a greater role in this than the recession, at least numerically. Namely, the decline of the whole GNP was, in 1972 dollars, about 3.5 bn, while the fall in the volume of car production was 7.5 bn dollars. As a matter of fact, this recession was the shortest and mildest of the six in the three decades following World War II. GNP declined only in two quarters (from the third quarter of 1969 to the first quarter of 1970). This decline amounted to 9.8 bn 1972 dollars, corresponding to 0.9 per cent. In the last quarter the decline attained one per cent on account of the strike in the car industry. (Seasonally adjusted quarterly data at annual level.) In the wake of the easing of monetary and fiscal restrictions beginning early in the year, the volume of production and sales started to grow in the second and third quarters, but the process of upswing was considerably held back by the strike. There was a certain interrelation between the recession and the protracted strike. On the one hand, namely, the decline in demand for cars, on the other, the lasting high rise in prices made the standpoint of the two parties rigid during the strike. This led to a lengthening of the strike and aggravated its negative impact on the economy.

Table 10.1

GNP and its components, 1969—1970
(Quarterly data at annual rate, based on data computed in 1972 dollars)

Item	Decline				Total decline	
	Between 3rd qu. 1969 and 2nd qu. 1970		Between 3rd qu. 1968 and 4th qu. 1970		in quarters	per cent
	bn 1972 dollars	per cent	bn 1972 dollars	per cent		
GNP	9.8	100.0	12.0	100.0	5	1.1
Personal consumption	−8.6	−87.8	−11.2	−93.3	1	0.8
Durables	1.9	19.4	7.1	59.2	4	2.7
Non-durables	−3.5	−35.7	−9.0	−75.0	no decline	
Services	−7.0	−71.4	−9.3	−77.5	no decline	
Gross private investment	16.9	172.4	18.8	156.7	2	9.8
Fixed capital investment	6.3	64.3	8.6	71.7	5	5.4
Fixed capital investment other than homes	3.6	36.7	9.2	76.7	5	8.0
Structures	1.8	18.4	2.5	20.8	9	8.5
Productive investment	1.8	18.4	6.6	55.0	7	9.5
Housing construction	2.7	27.6	0.8	6.7	5	15.3
Changes in inventories	10.5	107.1	10.1	84.2	2	78.4
Net exports	−2.0	−20.4	−0.9	−7.5	no decline	
Government purchases	3.5	35.7	5.4	45.0	7	4.5
Federal purchases	5.4	55.1	12.6	105.0	22	27.4
Military purchases	9.0	91.8	11.8	98.3		
State and local purchases	−1.8	−18.4	−7.3	−60.8	no decline	
Final sales	−0.6	−6.1	1.8	15.0	3	0.2
Material production	17.9	182.7	22.5	187.5	5	3.7
Production of goods	10.9	111.2	18.9	157.5	5	3.8
Durable goods	10.5	107.1	25.8	215.0	5	13.4
Non-durables	0.4	4.1	−7.0	−58.3	2	1.1
Structures	7.0	71.4	3.6	30.0	4	9.5
Services	−8.1	−82.7	−10.6	−88.3	1	0.2
Consumers' investment	4.6	46.9	6.6	55.0	5	4.8
Auto product	8.2	83.4	18.3	152.5	5	43.9
Disposable personal income	−8.6	−87.8	−26.8	−223.3	1	0.6

Table 10.1 illustrates how the recession and the strike affected the various fields of production and sales, as well as disposable incomes. From the data of the table the following main changes in economic processes may be stressed. The most conspicuous is that the recession—similar to earlier post-war recessions—did not extend to the volume of personal consumption,[9] in fact, the latter even increased during the

[9] This statement holds equally for the data not including and for those including the purchase of homes as consumption.

recession. This happened in spite of the fact that the purchase of consumer durables significantly diminished (amounting to almost one-fifth of the decline in GNP), and fell even more in consequence of the car industry strike.

This is a rather curious phenomenon and it seems to contradict certain theoretical statements of this book. What might explain it? The growth of the amount of wages lagged behind and that of transfers increased relative to the preceding year and the combined growth of the two was 2.2 percentage points lower than that in 1969. Additionally, the savings of wage earners also increased by 3.6 percentage points. Altogether this would have mitigated the increase in demand by 5.8 percentage points, but the sum of direct taxes on wage earners diminished by 4.4 percentage points in comparison to the preceding year and this mitigated the slowdown of the increase in demand to 1.4 percentage points. In other words, the nominal demand of wage earners nevertheless was higher than in 1969 by 1.4 percentage points mainly on account of the considerable reduction of taxes directly inflicting them. At the same time, this kind of tax behaved as an effective stabilizer. Considering the other side of the interrelations, what happened was that while capitalists did not accept a lower percentual rise in sales prices even under the impact of the recession, they did not raise them by more either, although the 1969 net pre-tax profit margin fell as a result from 24.3 per cent to 22.9 by 1970. With such prices they could still increase their sales to wage earners by 1.6 per cent—of course, lagging behind the 2.9 per cent rise in 1969. (All this can be directly seen from the Δp_c diagram for 1970; see Part Two, p. 54) And their modesty in respect of price rises was justified mainly by their wish to get rid of accumulated inventories. We shall see that something similar happened in 1975. Indeed, the main factor in the decline of GNP was, as usual in post-war recessions, a considerable fall in the accumulation of stocks. The absolute size of the fall in stocks even exceeded the fall in GNP. In contrast, the final use (the difference between GNP and the change in inventories) continued to grow during the recession and only fell at the time of the strike mentioned. A further important factor in the decline of real demand during the recession was the fall in fixed capital investment, which was responsible for more than one third of the fall in GNP. Owing to the monetary restrictions discussed the decline in housing construction was also significant.

In constrast with the experiences of previous post-war recessions, consumer investments (housing construction and the purchase of durables) had a greater part in the reduction of total real demand than the decline in business fixed capital investment. Since, however, housing construction began to recover at an earlier date because of the turn in monetary policy, while the decline in fixed capital investment continued even after the trough of the cycle, the opposite of this statement is true if we consider the internal proportions of the fall in GNP between the third quarter of 1969 and the fourth of 1970.

It is an interesting feature of the 1969–1970 recession, and in general of the development of the economy in 1970, that in earlier recessions the growth of government purchases mitigated the recession and considerably counterbalanced the decline in other real sales, in the recession now under review there was an uninterrupted decline in government purchases, thus they expressly increased the difficulties of realization. The reduction of military expenditure, started after mid-1968 and now increasing, came into conflict with the intended change in direction of fiscal

158

policy, but it was an unavoidable concomitant of the de-escalation—forced by both internal and external political factors—of the Vietnam War. The importance of this process is well illustrated by the fact that the reduction of military purchases during the six months of the recession exceeded 90 per cent of the total decline in GNP, and in the period between the third quarter of 1969 and the fourth of 1970 it almost attained 100 per cent of that decline.

Regarding the production side, within GNP it was material production (that of goods) that was affected most gravely by the recession. The decline in the production of goods was almost twice as much as in total GNP. This large decline was counterbalanced by the growth in the volume of services. To characterize the recession and economic development of 1970, it should be added that the volume of disposable personal income (inclusive of imputations and payable interest) did not diminish even at the trough mark of the recession. A minimum decline, 0.6 per cent, was perceivable only in the fourth quarter of 1970, but that was the time of the car industry strike. Considering the whole of 1970, the amount of real disposable personal income exceeded the one in the preceding year by 4.1 per cent.

10.4 EMPLOYMENT AND UNEMPLOYMENT

The number of wage and salary earners (excluding agriculture) peaked in February 1970; after that it declined with minor fluctuations till November of the same year (from 71 to 70 mn), but the automobile industry strike had a major role in this. Employment increased even in the half year of recession. In manufacturing, however, employment peaked in July 1969, then diminished almost every month until November 1970, following which it started to rise with minor fluctuations attaining its earlier peak only in October 1973. Within manufacturing, fall in employment was particularly sharp in the production of durable goods: following the peak of September 1969, its decline also continued until November 1970 and in the course of subsequent growth it similary attained the earlier peak in November 1973. Employment continued to increase in the half year of the recession, e.g., in trade, financial institutions, services, that is—as usually happens in recessions—in several unproductive branches.

Unemployment showed quite a different picture. In 1969 it remained generally on very low level and even at the end of the year was not higher than in the spring (3.5 per cent). Essentially, it started to increase in early 1970, and jumped to 6 per cent by the last month of the year, rising steadily month after month (the car industry strike also had a role in that). In absolute terms unemployment increased between September 1969 and March 1970 by half a million, by the end of 1970 by another 1.4 million. In the period between the end of the recession and the beginning of the strike in the car industry the increase was 870,000, and in the three months of the strike another 560,000.[10]

It is worthwhile to discuss separately the interrelations between the reduction of

[10] The sources of the data on employment and unemployment: *Economic Report* 1971, pp. 224 and 229; *Economic Report* 1972, pp. 222 and 227; *Economic Report* 1973, pp. 222 and 227; *Economic Report* 1975, p. 283.

military expenditure and unemployment. According to the data and forecasts of the Department of Labor of the U.S.A., the employment induced by the Pentagon (military personnel and civilian employees connected with defense, as well as employment in private industry related to military orders) fell from 8.1 mn in fiscal year 1968 to 6.4 by 1971 and, within that, employment in private firms from 3.6 mn to 2.3 mn. According to the same source, in the third quarter of 1968 1.4 million people had performed work directly related to the Vietnam War in private industry (of which almost 1 million, or 5 per cent of total industrial employment, was in manufacturing). (*Economic Report*, 1975, pp. 44–45)

10.5 PROFITS IN 1969 AND 1970

Let us have a look also at corporate profits.

The total *pre-tax* profits of corporations originating from the domestic economy—without depreciation—diminished following the third quarter of 1968 almost every quarter (at current prices) and attained the trough in the fourth quarter of 1970. During the five quarters the decline was 27 per cent, but 55 per cent of the total decline was concentrated in the two quarters of the recession proper. In the two quarters following the end of the recession profit started to grow slowly and was only depressed again by the strike.

The profits of the financial corporations continued to rise almost throughout the whole period, while that of non-financial ones fell by 34 per cent between the second quarter of 1968 and the fourth of 1970. Of this, 49.4 per cent fell to the two quarters of the recession and 21 per cent to the period of the strike.

Corporate after-tax profits fell during the two years 1969–1970 by almost 20 per cent. The profits of domestic origin fell more—by 22.6 per cent in the two years. The decline concentrated strongly in the manufacturing industry, from the 9.7 bn dollar reduction of total profits in these two years 7.7 bn was in manufacturing. The profits of the financial institutions increased by 0.4 bn during the same period.

According to our own computations, the decline in total—not only corporate—net after-tax profits was quite negligible at current prices: the sum was $ 111.6 bn in 1968 and only 1.4 bn less in 1969. This may be surprising for those who believe it axiomatic that monopolies should always fare better. But let us not forget that the category of profits employed in our own computations comprises the net incomes of all non-wage-earners, while a great part of the net income of millions of small entrepreneurs may be conceived as their wages. It is unlikely that their wage level should lag behind that of wage earners, at least not substantially, in a recession. The essential correctness of our computations is confirmed by the official data according to which in the period under review "proprietors' incomes" increased from 61.9 bn to 64.7 bn, and also the sum of net interest increased by 9.8 bn.

Thus, as a partial explanation for the surprising fact we may offer that (1) the decline in military purchases affected mainly the corporations and (2) the profits of non-corporate firms even increased. The profits in agriculture, representing only a fraction of the whole economy, showed an outstanding increase of 18 per cent.

Reality, however, is more complicated. To wit, the sum of profits computed by us comprised in 1968 a large amount of paper profit, 9.3 per cent of total profits at current prices. (A higher paper profit than this, 15.7 bn, was found in the period investigated only in the quite abnormal years of 1975 and 1976.) In 1969, paper profit was only 3.5 bn. Thus the profit spent on goods and services increased more than could have been surmised from our above "explanation". This increase was $ 17.3 bn, and half of it was contributed by the 6.8 bn increase of net fixed capital investment and the 1.7 bn increment of inventory accumulation, while the increment of capitalists' personal consumption contributed almost a quarter, 4 bn.

We should note here that, although corporate profits diminished, their material investments also increased. This was allowed partly because they availed themselves of large amounts of external financing (52 bn in 1968 and 56.9 bn in 1969), and partly because they used their own reserves for this purpose to a considerable degree (as already mentioned in connection with the menacing liquidity crisis). This latter statement is substantiated by the fact that the bulk of the 1969 decline in profits consisted of a decline in paper profits. This decline followed mainly from the turning of government surplus into a deficit; this turn took 16.7 bn dollars from the paper profit.

The paper profit of the capitalist class would have become negative had overspending by wage earners not increased as well, since the export surplus also diminished. (The exactness of our data on paper profit is impaired by the fact the statistical data also include a non-negligible "statistical discrepancy".) In the next year, 1970, corporate profits and the total profits computed by us moved in the same direction. The domestic profits of corporations fell by 17.1 per cent that year, while inclusive of profits from abroad the decline was somewhat milder, 15.5 per cent. In this year the bulk of the decline was suffered by the manufacturing industry, while the profits of financial institutions were hardly affected at all. But only the direction of the movement of corporate and total profits was the same, not the extent of the movements.

Total net after-tax profits diminished from $ 110.2 bn to 105.4 bn. But within that the decline in profits also appearing in goods and services was much more significant: this "material" profit declined from $ 106.7 bn to 96.8 bn, that is, by 9.3 per cent. This was mitigated by a 2.2 bn increase in the consumption by capitalists, but gross investment fell by 5 bn. The fall in net fixed capital investment was 6.5 bn, and the 60 per cent fall in inventory increase was particularly outstanding. Nevertheless, the gross material profit at current prices, inclusive of depreciation allowance, hardly diminished, because a 7.1 bn increase in depreciation was added to the increased consumption by capitalists.

Thus, while material profit had increased in the preceding year, now it diminished. And while in the preceding year paper profit had fallen, this year it increased and by almost two and a half-fold, from 3.5 bn to 8.6 bn. This was again due to the fact that the balance of government receipts and expenditure turned from a surplus into a deficit. This added 20 bn to the paper profit and the increase in the export surplus also worked in the same direction. But the two effects were considerably moderated by the fact that instead of overspending wage and salary earners saved a part of their income due to the recession, and this shift reduced paper profits by 15.8 bn.

There are no data on the real size of profits. There cannot be any since the official data on profits are composed of various net kinds of capitalist incomes, that is, of differences between receipt and the expenses on acquiring them, thus of mere money amounts. In this concept it remains, of course, hidden why profit was as much as it was, as is shown by computations, but it also remains hidden on what profit was spent. Not knowing the use of profits, there is no way of getting exact computations of real profit either, since the use of one or another price deflator would be completely arbitrary. Of course, the real problem is not what profit is spent on; the real interrelation is its opposite. If not total profits, at least material profits depend on what and how much is spent by capitalists. We understand and know that the volume of material profits is the sum of the consumption and accumulation by capitalists. (Not the profit of individual capitalists, but of the class as a whole.) The development of material profits can be and is given also at unchanged prices. The real size of paper profit, not too large relative to the material profit, can also be estimated. From among its elements the trade surplus is available from official statistics also at unchanged prices. But we proceed somewhat arbitrarily by computing the savings of wage earners with the implicit price index of consumer expenditure for the given year—among other things, because by the time this amount will be spent the price level will be already higher. Government deficit (and the statistical discrepancy) were converted to real value—for lack of a better one—with the implicit price index of GNP.

The net profit at constant, 1972, prices was $ 128.4 bn in 1968 and $ 120.0 bn in 1969 (a reduction of 6.5 per cent). Within net profit net real profit also increased at unchanged prices, from 109.2 bn to 117.1 bn dollars. Within that, the increase of net investment was 10.6 per cent, and within the latter net fixed capital investment rose by 8.4 per cent and inventories jumped by 21.6 per cent. The fall in paper profit may be put, at 1972 prices, at 15.2 bn dollars.

In the next year, 1970, the volume of net profit fell from $ 120.0 bn to 110.6 bn, i. e., by 7.8 per cent. Net investment fell by 26.8 per cent. The decline in net fixed capital investment was not as steep, 19.8 per cent. But the fall in inventory accumulation was almost 60 per cent. The "volume" of paper profit rose from 0.4 bn to 6.6 bn dollars.

10.6 CONCLUDING REMARKS

Let us now summarize the impact of the high-level, federal government and FED economic policies in 1969–1971.

When already the data for the whole year showed a fall in investment, i.e., in 1970, monetary and fiscal policies already turned mildly expansive. In the *American Economic Review*, M. J. Bailey criticized economic policy sympathizingly, "generalizing the experience from a theoretical point of view".

"As a deliberately engineered attempt to cool off the economy, this recession may disappoint and embarrass the Administration...." But there was no particular reason for embarrassment, because "whenever fiscal and monetary restraint combine to choke back aggregate demand... business sentiment resists the restraint at first, and then turns around sharply in a virtual stampede."

(Bailey, 1971, p. 520)

The notion of aggregate demand in the text essentially means the GNP. We have just seen that in the first three quarters of 1969 both GNP and gross private investment "heroically" withstood the attack of government and the FED. Then came the decline. But the decline in total demand in terms of volume—i.e., the fall in GNP—did not involve any panic-like sharp turn, the volume of total demand declined insignificantly up to the second quarter of 1970, to exhibit later a steady rise, only interrupted by the strike in the automotive industry. In this respect a sentence a few paragraphs after the above quote seems to be apt: "By the time any ordinary recession goes far enough to leave no reasonable doubt of what it is, recovery is so near that the fiscal remedy, after normal delays of appropriation and execution, is likely to prove ill-advised." (Ibid.)

As regards gross private fixed capital investment, the "panic-like" turn seems already more appropriate, but the second quotation from Bailey is not at all applicable, the upswing in fixed capital investment was not near in spite of the efforts of the government: it came only in the fourth quarter of 1971. (In this respect the slight recovery after the great fall at the time of the strike can be left out of account.) True, the part of budgetary expenditure depending on the economic policy decisions of the administration, or simply on its decisions motivated by political considerations was of a rather restrictive nature throughout the whole period and even in 1971, since the volume of federal purchases of goods and services almost steadily diminished and—though at a much slower rate—total government purchases also declined, apart from the third quarter of 1971.

This being so, if neither private investment nor government purchases had a stimulating effect, what is the explanation for the fact that after the stagnation in the second quarter of 1970 the GNP started to rise already in the third quarter?

It may be attributed first of all to the increase in personal consumption. It was a highly important factor in this growth that after the lifting of monetary restrictions housing construction immediately started to rise steeply. If the peak in the first quarter of 1969 is considered 100, the trough in the second quarter of 1970 is 84, rising uninterruptedly from then on and attaining 125 points in the fourth quarter of 1971. Also the purchase of consumer durables showed a similar increase (changes in purchases on credit have a positive feedback effect on the economy), and—though at a much slower rate—the volume of total personal consumption also increased, apart from the quarter in which the strike in the automotive industry took place.

PHASE 2

1971–1973: THE END OF THE BRETTON WOODS ERA
THE PERIOD OF PRICE AND WAGE CONTROL
THE EVE OF THE RECESSION

CHAPTER ELEVEN

GENERAL CHARACTERISTICS OF THE PERIOD AND
DEVELOPMENTS IN THE FIRST TWO YEARS

11.1 SOME CONTRADICTIONS OF THE PERIOD UNDER REVIEW

The approximately three years between the mildest recession in the post-war economic history of the United States and its gravest crisis constitute perhaps the most contradictory, and in many respects the most complicated period of the past three decades, with many pitfalls, making it not at all easy for the analyst attempting to investigate the economic processes that took place.

It will be worthwhile outlining in the introduction the most conspicuous contradictory tendencies characterizing the period as a whole. Let us start with the statement that it was a period of relative peace. (Only relative, as the de-escalation of the Vietnam War resulted in an actual armistice only at the end of 1973.) Understandably, the military goods and service purchases of the federal government also gradually diminished. Total purchases by government showed a similar development. The weight of government purchases as a source of income diminished. This seems to indicate that a factor was pushed to the background which is usually considered a source of inflation. And yet the government felt it unavoidable to introduce, precisely in this period, with the aim of curbing inflation, economic control measures unprecedented in peacetime and to maintain them with varying rigour between August 1971 and April 1974.

The decline in the volume of government expenditure is illustrated by the following table.

Thus both the weight of direct commodity purchases by government and that of derived incomes (with the exeption of transfers) which originate directly from the government showed an unambiguous decline. And the point is not only that private demand increased in the period analyzed, and thus also the sum of personal consumption, export surplus and investment, while government demand diminished relative to these. Not at all. In several respects, particularly as regards federal government purchases, an absolute reduction took place. Only two examples: in the period under review government purchases of durables fell by no less than 38 per cent and wages paid by government (inclusive of the military payroll) by more than 7 per cent in real terms. Beginning with mid–1968 a steady decline, lasting more than five years, started in the volume of federal government purchases, closely related to the slow de-escalation of the Vietnam War, and those described above should be regarded as a part of this process.

Table 11.1

Government purchases and incomes from government in percentage
of the respective kind of demand or income
(based on data computed in 1972 dollars)

Items	Fourth quater of	
	1970	1973
GNP		
Government purchases, total	22.4	20.3
Federal purchases	10.1	7.8
Purchase of goods		
Total government	8.1	5.4
Federal	5.2	2.6
Durables		
Total government	11.5	4.3
Federal	8.8	2.7
Non-durables		
Total government	6.2	4.9
Federal	3.3	1.7
Structures		
Total government	27.2	23.5
Federal	3.2	3.4
Personal incomes		
Total government	24.4	23.4
Federal	13.5	13.2
Compensation of wage and salary earners		
Total government[a]	19.0	16.8
Federal[a]	7.2	5.7

[a] Inclusive of armed forces

We find contradictory tendencies in the fact that although these three years were characterized by good business conditions, at the same time also tensions became acute. This is, of course, not an exceptional phenomenon—we may rather say that it is usual concomitant of upswing in the capitalist countries.

Indeed, if we judge this three-year period by the most comprehensive indicator of economic growth, i.e., the volume of GNP, we find it a really successful one. In the average of the three years this indicator testifies to a real growth of 4.8 per cent p.a., and this is much faster than the average of the three years following the 1958 recession (3.6 per cent). What is more, a result of this growth being faster than the long-term trend was that the more than $ 30 bn lag (in 1972 dollars) behind the potential GNP of 1970 was made up for. In fact, in 1973 GNP exceeded the value reckoned with earlier as potential maximum by almost 7 bn (in 1972 dollars).[11] A similar phenomenon was experienced

[11] This shows, of course, that the potential maximum GNP had been computed on the basis of uncertain data. Indeed, the economic exports of the Nixon administration modified the possible highest percentage rate of unemployment upwards and this modification was also accepted by the Council of Economic

for the last time in the period of overheated business related to the Vietnam War (1966–1969). But tensions rose precisely on this account. And to these were added essential external circumstances. Yet this seemingly successful period ended in the 1974–1975 recession of a magnitude not seen since 1938.

Furthermore, we may find a conspicuous contradiction between the large-scale active government interference with the economy, quite unusual for a Republican administration and its highly ambitious and very upbeat economic policy, and the actual results of this policy.

Last but not least, the foreign economic relations of the country had a much greater—and we may immediately add, an unfavourable—impact on economic policy and the course of the economy than at any time in the preceding quarter of a century.

11.2 THE ECONOMY AND NIXON'S ECONOMIC POLICY BEFORE THE ANNOUNCEMENT OF THE NEW ECONOMIC POLICY (JANUARY–AUGUST, 1971)

But let us proceed chronologically and examine the development of the economy, economic policy and its results more closely.

The year 1971 started as befits the time of an upswing after a mild recession. Government was full of optimism. In his *Economic Report* written in February the President promised price stability and full prosperity. Regarding the methods with which he intended to secure these, he said that "...we are going to do it by relying upon free markets and strengthening them, not suppressing them. Free prices and wages are the heart of our economic system; we should not stop them from working even to cure an inflationary fever. I do not intend to impose wage and price controls which would substitute new, growing and more vexatious problems for the problems of inflation." (*Economic Report*, 1971, p.7) But as the months passed in 1971, it became increasingly obvious that the reality of economic life would not develop according to the rosy forecasts and the grandiloquent promises. The Joint Economic Commission of Congress pointed out already in March that the growth targets set by government would hardly be realized. In the same month, Secretary of the Treasury John Connally[12] was compelled to acknowledge that the government was "ropewalking" as far as the economy was concerned and in the near future a change in economic policy had to be reckoned with in spite of the successes (*Wall Street Journal*, March 10, 1971). But Nixon's optimism remained unbroken, at least publicly. At the end of April he announced that "the worst of inflation is behind us" (*International Herald Tribune*, April 26, 1971). Of course, it is easy to be clever knowing what happened in the following 3–4 years, but it is a fact that this declaration was not well founded back then either. The most comprehensive indicator of the development of price level, the price

---

Advisers taking office with President Carter. (See *Economic Report* 1978, pp. 83–85.) The potential GNP was reckoned by taking into account a 4 per cent unemployment in 1958, while in 1966 the latter was put at 4.5 and in 1973 at 4.8 per cent.

[12] Though a Democrat, Connally joined the Nixon team. He became Secretary of the Treasury, although he was not engaged in financial matters before. As Governor of Texas he was with Kennedy in the car and was wounded when the president was assassinated.

deflator of GNP rose in the first quarter of 1971 by 6.2 per cent (at annual rate) and this was higher than the average of 1970 and in the preceding three quarters. But the expected stronger upswing did not ensue in the next months in spite of the on the whole stimulative fiscal and monetary policies applied by the government.[13] Although the growth rate of GNP rose high in the first quarter of the year (to 9.2 per cent at annual rate), this only reflected the impact of the large strike in the automobile industry, the efforts to make up for the missing output, and in the second quarter the growth rate fell to 3 per cent. The volume of fixed capital investment still continued to lag significantly in the second quarter of 1971, by 7 per cent, behind the peak prior to the recession. (Let us remember that investment could not be curbed in time with the 1969 restrictions.) Thus in the whole first half of the year the level of unemployment became stabilized around 6 per cent, that is, higher than the level of the 1969–1970 recession. In the meantime, the rate of price increase accelerated, first of all regarding wholesale prices, which did not promise much good for the future. (In the first half of the year it moved around 6 per cent on the annual level.) This would partially justify the declaration of the President at the end of June that he did not intend to take new measures to stimulate the economy.[14] But at the same time he also emphasized that he did not want to interfere with the development of wages and prices either, although in this respect even such an economic policy-maker as Burns urged action. The President also remained true to his stand-point emphasized several times (this would last exactly forty-six days longer) that this call for voluntary wage and price controls was not effective anyway, while a compulsory control would be a nightmare for the administration, involving unequal treatment and result in the disillusionment of the public.

But facts, known to be stubborn, proved stronger. After the said forty-six days, government itself lost faith in its own economic policy, which—as it soon turned out—had been doomed to failure by its exaggerated optimism, by the setting of unattainable tasks. On the night of August 15, 1971, tens of millions of Americans watching television witnessed the unprecedented about-face of President Nixon. This about-face, the proclamation of the "new economic policy", simultaneously meant the acknowledgement of the failure of the original Nixonian "game plan".[15] It was definitely a game plan reflecting the ideas of the monetarist school hallmarked by the name of Milton Friedman from Chicago. What was involved was not only the failure of the economic policy of a government, but in a certain sense it was reality's critique of the views of a theoretical school. The government itself was compelled to acknowledge that "it may well be that more has been promised than can be delivered with existing knowledge and instruments (*Economic Report,* 1972, p. 112).

[13] The deficit of the federal government was (at annual rate) $ 20.1 bn in the last quarter of 1970, 21.2 bn in the first half of 1971 and 22.8 bn in the second half. The quantity of money in circulation (M_1) increased (at annual rate) by 5.2 per cent in the second half of 1970 and by 10 per cent in the first half of 1971.

[14] The suspicion of the economic commentator of the *International Herald Tribune* (July 1, 1971), L. Dale, seems justified that Nixon took this decision because "much of his natural constituency has suffered more from inflation than from unemployment".

[15] President Nixon was an ardent football fan, and of a Washington team. This is why the economic policy conception of the new Republican administration was also called "game-plan", similarly to the plan worked out by the coach of a football team prior to a game.

A liberalized monetary policy, the quickly rising quantity of money (see footnote 13 on p. 167) ought to have secured a satisfactory growth rate, and still the result was growing unemployment and rising inflation. The Phillips curve turned upside down! The building of the initial Nixon economic policy collapsed with a great crash, and the crash produced a greater echo in the whole of the capitalist world than in the United States itself. The international monetary system based on the limited convertibility to gold of the dollar, founded twenty-five years earlier, collapsed.

11.3 THE COLLAPSE OF THE BRETTON WOODS SYSTEM

The monetary system of Bretton Woods had been exposed to tensions particularly since 1965, but in this respect 1970 was still quiet, or so it seemed. But in the first half of 1971 the money markets became increasingly perturbed, and a massive outflow of dollars from America began.

If the currency of a country with convertible currency lastingly flows out of the country, it means that the country's balance of payments has turned unfavourable, i.e., the country is running into debt. This state of affairs cannot be maintained for long, something must be done about it—if at all possible. But this does not hold in the same manner for the country whose currency is the key currency, and thus it did not hold for the United States before 1971 (and the quarter of a century preceding it).

By key currency we mean an international reserve currency, i.e., the currency in which the other countries hold their monetary reserves serving international payments. But the countries of the world could possess dollar reserves only because in the past more dollars had flowed out from the United States than flowed back. The dollar reserves of the world could not increase if the balance of payments of the United States were not in the red. Formally, the deficit in the US balance means the indebtedness of America towards the other countries, but this may well be a debt they do not want to collect. True, a part of the dollars leaving the United States went abroad in the form of aid and similar payments, but a considerable part served foreign purchases: commodities, factories, firms were bought. The FED and the banking system created money out of nothing—paper and printing ink: and the rest of the world became a happy owner of this money created out of nothing. Yes, happy owner since it could make purchases with it if it wanted to. But if it had spent these dollars, it would have deprived itself of this reserve—thus, after so many years of dollar-hunger it did not want so much. This is how the laws of capitalism ensure that the richest become even richer. But the dollar-hunger was followed by a flood of dollars, and this became hardly sustainable around August 1971.

In the sixties, similarly to earlier years, the United States financed its international ventures—military expenses abroad, trade transactions, development aid, capital exports—by issuing dollar debentures regularly. But in the sixties, this flood of dollars increasingly exceeded demand. A structural disequilibrium was developing. Of course, purchases could have been made in the USA with the surplus. But between 1965 and 1969 the American wage, price and productivity proportions significantly deteriorated relative to those of the potential trade partners. Thus also the competitiveness of American commodities deteriorated, the dollars could have been spent only at

168

unfavourable prices. This signalled that the American balance of payments would further deteriorate. In the mild recession year of 1970, the surplus of the American balance of trade was unusually low, although, as was mentioned several times, recessions in America are usually accompanied by an improving balance of trade. It seemed obvious that the upswing would already entail a deficit—further impairing the US balance of payments. In addition, in 1970 and then also in 1971—this time through the widespread use of monetary incentives—the interest rates of money markets fell essentially lower in the United States than in the other countries, thus there was a massive outflow of capital. This was all the more so because, as it is perhaps remembered, during the liquidity crisis of 1970 the American economy availed itself of substantial amounts of Eurodollars, but in 1971, in an essentially easier liquidity position, the American banks mostly repaid the credits raised in 1970 to their foreign affiliates.

All of this suddenly condensed in the summer of 1971. The devaluation of the dollar seemed increasingly inevitable, and a change in this sense resulted in two kinds of major flows of dollars: dollars flowed from American private hands into foreign private ones, while foreign banks and non-financial firms changed their dollar reserves into other currencies (the dollar reserves were customarily deposited with American banks).

These developments affected the FED gravely insofar that it was compelled to sell gold for a part of the foreign dollar surpluses to the central banks at the absurdly low price of $ 35 announce. Though the banks were cautious in exchanging their dollars for gold, since the total of their dollar claims far exceeded the FED's reserves, yet from the beginning of the year to the end of August the FED lost an amount of gold which was equivalent to more than 40 per cent of the amount it still possessed in August. This in itself would have been sufficient reason for suspending and abolishing the convertibility of the dollar into gold, and this in fact happened on August 15. But in an abstract sense the abolition of conversion into gold is different from the devaluation of the dollar. But this also occurred. On December 8, the Nixon administration committed itself, within the framework of the Smithsonian Agreement, to raise gold to $ 38 per ounce—depending on approval by Congress. (In itself this was simple window-dressing since it is all the same whether the treasury does not sell gold for 35 or for 38 dollars an ounce.) But also a *de facto* devaluation of the dollar began after August.

If market forces can act freely, they take care that if the supply of some currency exceeds the demand for it at a given rate of exchange, then the latter should diminish. As long as it was in force, the Bretton Woods monetary system set obstacles to the free assertion of market forces. But if disequilibrium proves lasting, the market forces always get the upper hand. But in the case of the international reserve currency many things are different in this respect, too.

If in a capitalist country a private person fears the devaluation of the dollar, he sells his dollar claims, that is, converts them into another convertible currency, and thus escapes the loss otherwise accompanying devaluation. But banks were obliged to purchase dollars at the rate fixed in Bretton Woods for their own currency. Thus, the citizen of the country received domestic currency, that is, the quantity of money in circulation increased without the banking system of the country being able to do anything about it.[16] In this sense there were complaints all over Europe about the export of American inflation.

This viewpoint—protection against imported inflation—asserted itself with particular weight in summer 1971, for example, in the Federal Republic of Germany. One and a half years earlier, at the beginning of 1970, this was not yet a problem. They even lost from their reserves when the banks of the United States syphoned off short-term dollar claims from Europe. But beginning with that, the FRG became the main target of dollar inflows for three reasons. The first was the great economic power of the country. The second was its large trade surplus. And the third was that, for internal business policy reasons, the country pursued a strictly restrictive monetary policy, and this entailed a high rate of interest. The German government protected itself and with the aid of forward sales of the German mark it tried to make the impression as if the mark would be also devalued. This was in vain. Thus domestic voices became stronger which sought the way out through a revaluation of the mark (that is, an effective devaluation of the dollar in comparison to it). And, under the impact of such rumours, on May 5, 1971, within forty minutes after the opening of the exchange one billion dollars were sold for marks. The central bank ceased its purchases and tolerated that the market exchange rate of the mark should rise against the dollar.

But the devaluation of the dollar—the main reserve currency—entails many kinds of consequences. First of all, the devaluation directly reduces the real value of the reserves of central banks. This is an effective loss of capital and it is not easy for the central banks to accept this fact. On the other hand, the devaluation of the dollar was tantamount to the revaluation of the mark and this impaired the trade position of the Germans, above all towards the United States, but also towards those countries which—and such was, e. g., France, one of the main economic partners of the FRG—at that time did not yet agree and, even after December, agreed only to a small extent to revaluation of their currency (relative to the dollar). As a matter of fact, the devaluation of the dollar would have improved the trading position of the United States—although this had to entail inflationary impacts. It was no easy decision for Nixon to endanger the prestige of the dollar. Conflicts in monetary issues became sharp indeed between the United States and its partners. After difficult negotiations at the Smithsonian Institute, the United States succeeded in December in getting an agreement. But this was already an epilogue and the beginning of something new. In the meantime the United States took action. We can read the following in the Economic Report of 1972: "... by August the private and public pressures to convert the dollar into other assets—foreign currencies and ultimately reserve assets [i. e., gold] or their equivalent—became overwhelming. The United States suspended convertibility of the dollar [into gold] on August 15. Its value in terms of several major currencies started to float" (*Economic Report*, 1972, p. 148). The suspension of the convertibility of the dollar into gold was followed by its abolition. The monetary system prevailing for a quarter of a century ceased to exist.

[16] If instead of a private person some commercial bank of the country does the same, it would thereby increase its reserves and obtain the right for an additional issue of money, unless the central bank "freezes" these reserves by special order. The central banks were usually not inclined to do so.

11.4 MEASURES OF THE "NEW ECONOMIC POLICY". GNP AND PRICES (FEBRUARY 1971–JANUARY 1972)

Abolition of the convertibility of the dollar was, of course, only one item in the package of the "New Economic Policy" announced at the same time. And in the birth of this gift-package domestic political reasons also played a not insignificant role. To wit: looking ahead to the presidential election due in a little over a year, something had to be done, as it was clear that the lasting high uneployment, inflation, the falling exchange rate of the dollar would all reduce Nixon's chances for re-election. Although the economic experts of the administration identified the sharpening balance of payments problem as the most important factor, the political aspect was no less important in the choice of date.

Let us consider in turn the measures of the President and their justification! The list of proposed measures and of those immediately introduced is so long that we have to limit ourselves here to listing only the most important ones. They are: a 10 per cent investment tax-credit, its purpose being stimulation of the creation of new jobs. Abolition of the 7 per cent sales tax on cars in order to boost the manufacture of cars, the key industry of the US economy (it was implemented only in December, but retroactively). A 10 per cent surcharge was introduced on imports and the convertibility of the dollar into gold was suspended. In addition, tax reductions were introduced in order to boost consumer demand. And finally, the hardest and most immediate interference with the functioning of the economy; freezing of (the majority of) wages and prices for ninety days. The President called this "package" in his usual modesty ". . .the most comprehensive new economic policy to be undertaken by this nation in four decades". (*Financial Times*, August 17, 1971) The nature of the implemented and proposed measures was in such glaring contradiction with all that the President and his economic advisers had advocated and promised for a long time and even a few weeks earlier (there would be no economic stimulation, no price and wage controls) that the sarcastic statement of Tom Wicker, commentator of *The New York Times*, seems fully justified, that during the twenty minutes of his appearance on television the President did everything he had said he would not do, and almost everything for the avoidance of which his whole earlier economic policy had, apparently, been devised. (*The New York Times*, August 17, 1971) No doubt, the hard facts, namely, insufficient economic growth and the deriving high unemployment, lasting high inflation rate, continuous deterioration in the balance of payments, which justified the introduction of the new economic policy did exist and quite a few of them had appeared for a longer time and in an ever sharper form. Earlier, however, the President had spoken in spite of that about improvement and a turn and had disapproved precisely the methods which he now proclaimed as the only ones leading to success. No wonder that after the introduction of the new economic policy under such circumstances the American press wrote much about the President losing credibility. Our task is, however, not to moralize, but to examine to what extent the measures proved to be effective in solving or at least alleviating the three main problems listed.

In this respect doubts have arisen immediately after the publication of the measures on the part of such well-known economists as Okun and Samuelson, who, although approving of the wage and price freeze, were very sceptical as regards the stimulation of growth. And the trade-union leaders objected to the fact that the burden of the fight against inflation had to be again borne by the wage earners, while the growth of interest, dividends and profits was not restricted. (But the spokesmen of the trade unions hardly reflected on how profits could be constrained.)

Let us glance at the movement of the two most important comprehensive indicators characterizing growth and prices—the volume of GNP and the implicit price index of GNP—in the quarter immediately preceding August 1971 and a few following it. (Table 11.2)

Table 11.2

Volume and implicit price deflator of GNP
(percentage change over the preceding
quarter, at annual rate)

	2nd	3rd	4th	1st
	quarter of			
	1971			1972
Volume of GNP	3.0	2.8	3.5	7.6
GNP implicit price deflator	5.7	3.4	3.6	5.8

In the same period unemployment steadily fluctuated around 6 per cent. The data thus show that although economic growth accelerated by the beginning of 1972, but not to an extent that could have mitigated unemployment perceptibly. On the other hand, although the freeze (which was replaced from mid-November 1971 by a so-called stage II, allowing the rise of prices and wages between certain controlled limits), temporarily mitigated the rise in prices, the rate of inflation exceeded in the first quarter of 1972 the one experienced before the freeze. To this new rise the replacement of the price and wage freeze by stage II also contributed. Somewhat breaking the logical order of describing the events, we now review the substance of stage II.

As regards the trend of prices, profits and wages, the following general principles prevailed: *Prices*: the rise of costs after the last price rise or following January 1st, 1971, could be percentually built into prices. *Profits:* the profit margin must not exceed that of the best two years of the three fiscal years prior to 1971. This restriction did not need to be applied if the firm did not raise its prices relative to the base period. *Wages:* the general limit to wage rise was set at 5.5 per cent. Exceptions were made where there was an outstanding inequality, and in respect of those workers whose wages had been rising by less than 7 per cent in the last three years. The measure did not extend to those workers whose hourly wages did not attain $ 2.75. Taking into account also certain supplements, the upper limit to wage increases might attain 6.2 per cent.

In certain cases the price and wage increases were linked to preliminary announcement and permission—even those allowed within the above mentioned general framework. To wit, as regards prices, every firm transacting an annual turnover higher than $ 100 million had to announce its intention of raising prices 30 days before the implementation of the rise. Wage increases had to be announced in advance in the case of every unit employing more than 5,000 workers, and every wage

172

increase exceeding the generally allowed extent regardless of the number of workers involved.

Price rises in firms transacting a turnover above \$50 mn had to give notice posteriorly; and so did firms with more than 1,000 workers if they implemented a wage increase smaller than the extent generally allowed.

Units below the above mentioned limits were not obliged to make announcements, but were still observed. To sum up: the first group comprised more than 1,700 firms with 45 per cent of sales and 15 per cent of employees, the second 1 700 firms with 5 per cent of sales and 6 per cent of employees and the corresponding figures in the third group are: 1.5 million firms, 25 per cent of sales and 29 per cent of employees. Thus control was exercised over 75 per cent of sales and 50 per cent of employees. In other words by the end of 1972, 6.5 million firms transacting about a quarter of sales and with about half of all employees were exempted from control under various titles.[17]

More or less different regulation was applied in some special fields, thus in the health service, insurance, housing rents, construction and public utilities.

The most important deficiency of the control system, causing much difficulty later on, was that the agricultural raw products, import and export goods were exempted from price control. Perhaps it caused less trouble that firms employing less than 60 persons were also exempted. (*Economic Report*, 1973, pp. 150–152)

Also, the architects of the price and wage control system held the opinion that its efficiency depended above all on the voluntary support of those concerned. Therefore, it was deemed desirable that the government should not one-sidedly force the observation of the rules of price control, but also the representatives of the private sector should be included in the system. This was also reflected in the composition of the various administrative bodies created.[18]

The authors of the control system did not expect it to withstand the strong pressure deriving from the excess demand for some products or the inelastic supply of labour. When the system had been introduced (October 1971) it was expected to reduce the rate of inflation (measured by the consumer price index) to 2–3 per cent. (*Ibid.*)

After this digression let us continue with the fact that the not too great successes of 1971 forced the President to moderate his earlier optimism in his Economic Report published at the beginning of each year, and to restrict himself to the statement that the results of the first five months of the new economic policy were "extremely encouraging". In the same place he declared: "The objective of the controls [of the second stage] is a state of affairs in which reasonable price stability can be maintained without controls. That state of affairs can and will be reached. How long it will take, no one can say. We will persevere until the goal is reached, but we will not keep the

---

[17] Incidentally, the data also reflect the high concentration of the American economy; (1700 firms, 0.2 thousandths of all firms, transacted 45 per cent of all sales).

[18] The President transferred the authority received from the legislature to the Board of Cost of Living subordinated to the Treasury. The Board exercised its function through various commissions composed of private persons. The most important were the Price Commission, and the Wages Office which represented at the time of its formation the employees, the enterprises and the public in the proportion of ⅓–⅓. Four of the representatives of employees resigned in March 1972, objecting to the decision related to the wage rise of longshoremen of the Pacific ports. The Office was then reorganized. From then on, all members represented the public, but among them there were also a trade union official and an enterprise manager. (*Op. cit.*, p. 144)

controls one day longer than necessary." (*Economic Report*, 1972, pp. 4 and 6–7) Let us now examine with the aid of the Δp_c formula—controls notwithstanding—what factors had a role in the 1971 price rise and what their weight was. In that year the price level of consumer goods rose by 4.6 per cent. Within it, wage incomes would have raised the price level by 8.1 per cent, that of transfers by a further 2.7 per cent, and it worked in the same direction, though to a negligible exent (0.3 per cent), that the savings of wage earners diminished relative to the preceding year and almost fell to zero. But the rise in the taxes of wage earners reduced demand (1.5 per cent). The combined impact of the factors in the numerator would have raised the price level by 9.7 per cent, while the factors of the denominator reduced it by 4.9 per cent. We can thus see that it was mainly the strong rise in the nominal income of wage earners that provided a possibility for a rise in the price level, which could only partially be counterbalanced by the in itself considerable rise in the volume of consumer goods sold. Above we called the price-raising impact of workers' saving slight by its numerical value. However, if we take into account that in the preceding year this had a price-reducing effect to the extent of 3.2 per cent, we have to say that this shift was a factor not to be underestimated in the 1971 consumer price rise.

Thinking of the oligopolistic price formation, the same facts may be formulated—perhaps more correctly—by saying that the 9.7 per cent rise in the earnings of employees allowed, in spite of a 4.6 per cent rise in prices, 4.9 per cent more consumer goods to be sold to wage earners.

The rise of the more comprehensive indicator of price level Δp_c^* was essentially identical with that of Δp_c. Within the global movement the price-raising effect of government expenditure covered with receipts increased,[19] while the deficit diminished and the combined effect of the two (that is, total government expenditure) hardly changed.

On announcing his new economic policy, the President declared that the suspension of convertibility into gold would not mean a devaluation of the dollar. This declaration was unfounded. It only served to camouflage the actual situation since, as mentioned, the downward float of the dollar started immediately and by the end of the year the dollar was also formally devalued in the framework of the Smithsonian Agreement. However painfully this affected the prestige of the United States, in other respects it was still a positive development because it abolished the obvious overvaluation of the dollar persisting for quite a long time already, and thus could become the starting point for improving the balance of payments position. While the balance of payments deficit trebled from 1970 to 1971 (from about $10 bn to 30 bn), by 1972 already a $10 bn surplus came about. (*Economic Report*, 1974, p. 351)

11.5 THE ACTUAL 1972 FIGURES

The most successful period of the three years examined here was 1972. Exceptionally, even the majority of government forecasts came true, since, according to the objectives of the government, the rate of economic growth accelerated, and that of price rises became moderated, as shown by the data of the following table.

---

[19] The spending of the profit tax and of indirect taxes also has a price-raising effect.

Regarding the year as a whole, the volume of GNP increased by 5.7 per cent, and its implicit price index by 4.1 per cent, which is in both respects an indisputable improvement over the 3.0 and 5.1 per cent changes in 1971. The future was not so rosy, however, as had been expected on the basis of the welcome figures, since the very low price rise in the second quarter of 1972 was followed in the next two and a half years, with the exception of the first quarter of 1974, by an inflation of increasing rate every quarter, reaching its peak with a 12.6 per cent jump in the last quarter of 1974.

Table 11.3

Volume and implicit price deflator of GNP
(percentage change over the preceding quarter, at annual rate)

	4th	1st	2nd	3rd	4th
			quarter of		
	1971		1972		
Volume of GNP	3.5	7.6	7.9	5.3	6.4
GNP implicit price deflator	3.6	5.8	2.9	3.4	4.7

The protracted rise of 1971 turned into a real upswing in 1972. Besides the data relating to total GNP, the indicators of its major components also testify to this fact. Fixed capital investment which in 1971 lagged behind even the recession level of 1970, started to rise vigorously and in the third quarter its volume somewhat exceeded the pre-recession level. At the beginning of the year the advisers of the President reckoned with a lower fixed capital investment than that, mainly because capacity utilization had been relatively low in the manufacturing industry. Indeed, in this branch the *volume* of investment was not higher than in the preceding year. This phenomenon can be well understood and may be considered typical of the newer cycles. In the early 60's, e.g., the investment wave became important in manufacturing only in 1964, the third year of recovery, And as regards the period prior to 1972, the last wave of investment was stifled by monetary policy in 1970. The recovery of 1971 was not yet definite enough to allow the exploitation of excess capacities. And in the case of low capacity utilization only a large-scale obsolescence of equipment or some kind of revolutionary technological change can prompt an essential increase of investment activity. But neither was present.

Thus it was not in the manufacturing sector that investment became lively, but mainly in the electric energy and gas supply, in telecommunications and the aircraft industry. Investment in these branches, as was mentioned in connection with the year 1970, does not much depend on the short-term fluctuations of business. This time, however, many speculative circumstances stimulated investment. These were: allowing accelerated writing off as depreciation (tax savings!), the "job development credit" (tax allowance for the creation of new jobs), as well as the reduction of the sales tax on new cars. And now, under the impact of growing receipts, fixed investment by farmers also increased. Thus it happened that in the year as a whole fixed capital investment exceeded substantially that of the preceding year, by 8.2 per cent. Also the growth rate of personal consumption increased, particularly that of durables. Its volume exceeded that of the preceding year by no less than 11.4 per cent. Although the volume of housing construction increased at a smaller rate than in the preceding year, the 18 per cent growth showed that this economic sector, most sharply reacting to monetary and credit stimulation, remained in a state of boom. There was also a change in demand deriving from government outlays: the volume of government purchases of goods and services increased over the preceding year by 1.5 per cent, after a decline through three years. But it should be added that within the global increase the purchases of the federal government continued to diminish, although at a smaller rate than in preceding years (a decline of 1.7 per cent against 9.1 in 1970 and 6.2 in 1971).

The development of profits also loudly testifies to an upswing. The profit of non-financial corporations deriving from domestic business increased by almost 14 per cent in 1971 over the naturally low figure because of the recession in 1970, while in 1972 there was a real jump of almost 25 per cent. The rate of price rise slowed down, thus the jump in the growth of real profit over the preceding year was even stronger, and the rise in profit continued from quarter to quarter. In the last quarter it exceeded the sum of a year before by almost 30 per cent. It seemed that it was not without reason that the election of Nixon and the return of the Republicans to power was so warmly hailed by business circles. The growth of the profit of financial corporations was not so stormy. However, their profit did not fall even in the recession year.

But the profit of the corporations is only a part (about one-third in the early seventies) of the total profits computed by us. Their development and their components are illustrated in the diagrams for 1971 and 1972 in Chapter 7 (see pp. 110–115).

Although the figures speak for themselves, perhaps it will not be superfluous to call attention to the following facts. The current price data show that the rather substantial growth of gross after-tax profits in 1972 covers opposite movements. While material profit increased, paper profit diminished. An interesting feature of the government's fiscal policy was (and we shall return to this) that the government deficit, still an important profit-raising factor in 1971, turned into a deficit in 1972, reducing profits by 8.2 per cent.[20] It was similarly a factor reducing profits that the slight surplus of the balance of trade in 1971 also turned into a deficit. (Besides 1972, a trade deficit occurred in the last three years of the decade, and in 1978–1979 it was much higher than in 1972.) The main element in the growth of profits was that the overspending by wage earners strongly increased. Another major factor in the growth of profits was the increase in investment, first of all fixed capital investment, and, to a lesser extent, of stockpiling. The movement of data at constant prices hardly differed from those at current prices. This is only natural, since here we are investigating changes between 1971 and 1972, quite near to 1972 which served as the basis of the constant price indicators.

It was already mentioned that in 1972 there was some moderation in the price rise. The same may be said about the change in price level as measured by the Δp_A formula: it fell from 4.6 per cent in the preceding year to 3.9 per cent. Let us scrutinize the factors

---

[20] Let us remind readers that our data relate to the domestic deficit. For its definition see the methodological Appendix (pp. 285–286)

in the slowdown of the price rise. As regards the price coefficient of consumer goods, although the combination of factors in the numerator increased demand more (exactly by 1.3 per cent) than in the preceding year, this was overcompensated by the higher growth rate of the volume of consumer articles sold, and the 2 per cent greater price-reducing effect it released. It is worth noting that the increase in the demand-raising effect of the factors in the numerator developed as a result of highly interesting counteracting movements. To wit, the price-raising effect of wage incomes continued to increase also in this year, but it was overcompensated by the demand-reducing impact of higher taxes paid. The price-increasing effect of transfers also diminished. Yet the strong growth of overspending by wage earners worked towards raising prices to an extent which was 2.9 per cent greater than in 1971.

To sum up, we may even venture the paradoxical statement that the mitigation of the growth rate of price rises took place under the impact of improving business. This is indeed a paradoxical statement as prices are usually rising when business is good. But unemployment benefits diminished in absolute terms and the direct taxes on wage earners considerably increased (the weight of their price-reducing impact was the same as in the year 1969, said to have been good for business). And these two effects relatively reducing demand in good business may be obvioulsy attributed to the operation of the built-in stabilizers. It is also true that in times of improving business production usually also increases, but on occasion enterprises attained the growth of output and sales of consumer goods by slowing down the rate of increase in the price level. Of course, under oligopolistic conditions the rate of price increase might have been even much higher. At least one more factor has to be taken into account. The (moderated) price control had a significant positive impact, mainly beacause (see our computations on p. 55) the pre-tax net profit margin on the GNP level was even so somewhat higher than in 1971, and this fact greatly mitigated resistance to price control. (Inventories also increased, but this is a normal phenomenon in times of improving business.)

As regards the more comprehensive Δp_c^* formula, the following may be stressed regarding its factors. In the numerator, the impact of government outlays covered by revenues double in 1972 relative to the preceding year, but this was partially compensated by the price-reducing effect deriving from a smaller government deficit. Even so, the combined price-level-raising impact of total government outlays was 1.2 per cent higher than in the preceding year. The price-raising impact of the whole numerator increased from 8.6 to 10.1 per cent, mainly owing to a sudden growth in the overspending by wage earners, and this is 0.4 per cent more than in the case of the numerator of the Δp_c formula. However, as regards the denominator of the formula, the volume of government purchases showed a minimum growth in this year, after three years of continuous decrease, and thus exerted a price-reducing effect. Therefore, also the effect of the Δp_c^* formula's denominator increased more steeply than that of the Δp_c formula (of course, in a price-reducing sense).

The upswing showing in the growth of output and profits, as well as the mitigation of price rises and a considerable improvement of the balance of payments were indeed successes, but unemployment remained a concern. Considering the years as a whole, the rate of unemployment was 5.6 per cent.[21] The decrease relative to the preceding year was merely 0.3 percentage points. Unemployment decreased only very slowly during the year and reached 5.1 per cent only in December. The lasting high unemployment level caused Nixon headaches, particularly because of the presidential election due in November 1972. In this context the opinion of Professor Samuelson, who wrote in August that unemployment and inflation might still be important questions in the election campaign, could be considered well-founded. In the same article—written for British readers—he was of the opinion that it had been an important factor in the upswing that, in view of the presidential election, the government did everything it could to stimulate the economy. This was reflected in the high budget deficit and the increase of money in circulation corresponding to a 10 per cent yearly growth. He also expressed doubts whether the controls could contain inflation for some longer time. As regards the durability of the upswing, he believed that a victorious Nixon would apply the brakes at a first sign of accelerating inflation and thus "the next recession, like the last one, will be made in Washington..." (*Financial Times*, August 22, 1972).

The person of the Democratic candidate—Senator George McGovern—and the tactical mistakes he made secured the re-election of Nixon with a great majority. The economic experts of the President illustrated with great fanfare the economic perspectives to be expected after the victory. Pierre A. Rinfret, the president of a reputable financial and economic consulting bureau, and at that time an ardent Nixon follower and his unpaid special economic adviser, and main spokesman on economic questions during the election campaign, immediately on the eve of the election wrote as follows (let us quote him at length because of his entertaining tone): "... We believe that our growth from 1972 to 1976 will be dynamic, vigorous and different from what has gone before... Recently, many people on Wall Street have been espousing a singularly silly theory, to wit, that President Nixon will produce a recession in 1973 in order to solve inflation. That silly idea ignores some basic facts... This economic expansion cannot be curtailed until it reaches full employment. Neither inflation nor rising interest rates can stand in the way of a fully-employed economy... In my judgement, the next four years will be totally unlike the past four years. I look for vigorous, renewed expansion of our free-enterprise system under Richard Nixon. Nixonomics are goods economics."[22] (*International Herald Tribune*, November 3,

---

[21] This figure cannot be fully compared to those relating to earlier years. Namely, the adjustment implemented in January 1972 increased the civilian labour force and civilian employment in the statistics by more than 300,000 persons and unemployment by 32,000. The latter was equal to 0.07 per cent of unemployment in December 1971. (*Economic Report* 1974, p. 227)

[22] *International Herald Tribune*, November 3, 1972. Nixonomics was the name given to the President's economic views and economic policy.

1972) In one respect Rinfret was right: the following four years did indeed differ from the previous four!

Of course, even in the United States not everybody believed that the position and future of the economy would be as rosy as claimed by the adherents of Nixon. And it is also natural that the more critical views can be found among the economic experts closer to the Democratic party and who are generally more progressive, e.g., the opinion of Professor Samuelson, already quoted. Professor Heller (during the presidency of Kennedy, a member of the Council of Economic Advisers) pointed out that if the 5 per cent unemployment was accepted as normal, the country would lose annually about $35 bn in GNP, $10 bn in profits and $10 bn in federal taxes. He challenged the correctness of an economic policy which reckoned in the final outcome with a 5 per cent unemployment and, therefore, he warned against stepping hastily on the brakes. (*Wall Street Journal,* September 12, 1972)

To end our report on the year 1972, let us briefly characterize the fiscal and monetary policy serving as a background for the events. We have seen that Samuelson spoke about a large budget deficit. The deficit of the federal budget was significant: 17.3 bn dollars, corresponding to 1.5 per cent of the GNP in 1972. On total government level the deficit was only $ 3.5 bn, but of this 5.4 bn fell to the rest of the world. In the final analysis, the difference between government revenues and expenditures remaining in the country showed a 1.9 bn surplus. We may add that this official deficit of 3.5 bn was $ 14.8 bn less than in the preceding year. This fall was partly an automatic consequence of improving business—the category of "fiscal drag" relates precisely to this phenomenon. But state and local organs did not fully use the support granted by the federal government in 1972. This reduced the expansive effect of the federal budget. The decline in the federal budget deficit did not derive from reduced expenditure, but from the fact that revenues increased more than outlays, Business revived and federal income tax revenues increased by $ 20.6 bn. And the increase in revenue occurred in spite of the fact that the measure announced in August 1971 by the President—though somewhat mitigated by Congress—reduced revenues by about 4 bn dollars. On the expenditure side the steep rise continued, except for unemployment benefits. The latter diminished, even though slightly.

About monetary policy we may say that the rate of increase of the money in circulation was higher than in 1972 only on a single occasion since the Second World War. Namely, between December 1971 and December 1972 it was 8.2 per cent against 6.2 per cent in the preceding 12 months. Long-term interest rates generally moved downward, while short-term rates moderately increased.

CHAPTER TWELVE

1973: THE APPROACHING RECESSION

12.1 SOME INDICATORS OF REAL PROCESSES IN A QUARTERLY BREAKDOWN

We have reached the last year of period 1971–1973, the one laden with the most contradictions. As regards the domestic economy, first of all economic growth, the turn of 1972/1973 no doubt found the country in an advantageous position. It seemed that the optimism of the development forecast by the President in his economic report for 1973 did have some objective basis. We may read in the report the following: "I believe it *can* be a great year. (Italics in the original.) It can be a year in which we reduce unemployment and inflation further and enter into a sustained period of strong growth, full employment, and price stability." (*Economic Report,* 1973, p. 7) The optimism of the administration was shared to certain extent by the politically opposed distinguished economic experts as well. For example, Heller was of the opinion in his assessment of the situation, and in also giving a forecast in the *Wall Street Journal,* that the rate of economic growth would again be around 6 per cent in the year just started, and the price rise would not be high, not much above 3 per cent. He believed that unemployement would fall by the end of the year to 4.7 per cent. On the whole, he reckoned with a balanced growth. At the same time he pointed out that under the given conditions the leaders of the economy no longer faced simply the well-known problem of greater unemployment *or* higher inflation, but, as a third problem, they also had to reckon with the control system itself. To wit: the respective agencies would have to decide on the basis of their own value judgement what degree of controls and unemployment they would be willing to tolerate in order to reduce inflation, or what degree of inflation they would be ready to tolerate in order to reduce controls and unemployment. He stressed that monetary policy was compelled to walk the tightrope: it must be restrictive enough to constrain the pressure of demand and only allow a moderate rate of expansion, while, on the other hand, it must prevent a major rise in the rate of interest of mortgages, consumer and other credits, because only in this way can it secure the contribution of trade unions to help contain the rise in costs. He called attention to the fact that under the given conditions economic policy was operating with increased risk and greater uncertainty, and thus advantages to be gained from greater flexibility and quick actions were also greater. (*Wall Street Journal,* January 11, 1973)

As regards the real processes, the forecast of the Council of Economic Advisers— thus the "official" prognosis—was as follows. A 6.75 per cent increase in the volume of

GNP was expected as was a further strong growth of fixed capital investment, but some decline in housing construction. A similar decline was reckoned with in the volume of federal purchases. But as regards the actual development of the real processes, the picture changed from one quarter to the other and the last quarter would have given rise to concern even if more alarming phenomena had not arisen in the field of finances and prices.

The data of the first quarter still seemed to support the optimistic expectation in general. The growth rate of real GNP even accelerated relative to the last quarter of 1972: it rose from 6.4 per cent to 9.4 (at annual level and inclusive of imputations). The real growth rates of both consumer expenditure and fixed capital investment were high: 8.1 and 19.3 per cent, respectively.

As regards the sectoral pattern of fixed capital investment, the situation reversed relative to 1972. Then there had still been considerable excess capacity in manufacturing, though in certain branches bottlenecks began to appear relative to the improving situation. The good business of 1972 and 1973, the considerable growth of GNP, however, resulted already in bottlenecks in a whole series of industrial branches, mainly in the extracting ones. It thus happened that in this year the leading role in investment both in machinery and equipment and in plant construction already fell to manufacturing. Also the earlier lag now became felt, measurable by the fact that while from 1948 to 1968 the volume of investment in manufacturing increased on annual average by 2.8 per cent, between 1968 and 1973 this growth was only 1.9 per cent annually. The growth rate of housing construction, however, significantly diminished, though it still remained positive at 4.0 per cent. But the percentages listed already were such high rates of growth which, according to experience, the American economy could not sustain for long, which might be thus considered as signs of overheating.

Even more warning signs could be read from the data of the second quarter. Instead of growth the volume of GNP practically stagnated. The volume of the most volatile (if you like, most unstable) element of consumer expenditure, of the purchase of consumer durables, already fell considerably, by 6.2 per cent, and there was a similarly sharp decline in the volume of housing construction, by 14.4 per cent. It follows that total consumer expenditure also declined somewhat. The growth rate of the volume of fixed capital investment significantly diminished also but still remained at 7 per cent, which is characteristic of a good business period.

In the third quarter, although the growth rate of the volume of GNP was somewhat higher than in the preceding one, it lagged much behind that of half a year earlier, or even behind that experienced in the whole of 1972, and even behind that which could be considered realistic in the long run: it was merely 1.7 per cent.

Although the growth rate of consumer expenditure again became positive, real growth remained slight (1.9 per cent). The decline in the purchase of consumer durables continued, although at a lower rate than in the preceding quarter, together with a rapid fall in housing construction of 22 per cent. (Let us not forget that our data on quarterly changes are always at annual rates.) The growth of fixed capital investment continued at a still vigorous rate of 5.8 per cent.

Finally, in the fourth quarter, the growth rate of the volume of GNP was 2 per cent, somewhat but only insignificantly higher, the volume of consumers' purchases was, however, palpably lower by 2.4 per cent than in the preceding quarter, and the decline in the purchase of durable consumer goods attained 9.9 per cent. And the further, 25.9 per cent, fall in housing construction may indeed be called a crisis-indicator. In this quarter the volume of fixed capital investment also fell by half of one per cent, but this was temporary and as in the first quarter of 1974, it was replaced by growth.

It is worth stressing that—as we can see—beginning with the second quarter fixed capital investment and consumers' investments again moved in opposite directions. Such a thing is already a sign of an overstrained boom and, simultaneously, of impending recession. There is some similarity between this situation and the one called by Marx the phase of overproduction immediately preceding the crisis. (*Capital,* Vol. 3., p. 347)

We compiled some indicators of real processes for the four quarters of 1973 in a table, to examine what actually happened in greater detail. (*Table 12.1*)

Table 12.1

GNP, production of goods and changes in inventories during 1973
(bn of 1972 dollars)

	Quarters of 1973			
	1st	2nd	3rd	4th
1. Changes in GNP	27.6	1.3	5.2	6.3
2. Changes in the production of goods	20.6	−0.5	2.9	9.4
3. Changes in inventories	11.7	14.8	14.1	25.4
4. 3 as percentage of 1	42.4	1138.5	271.2	403.2
5. 3 as percentage of 2	56.8	−[a]	510.8	270.2

[a]In this quarter the indicator cannot be interpreted as the production of goods diminished.

It turns out from row 4 of the table that following the first quarter of 1973 only inventory accumulation was reflected in the indicator of economic growth to a major—though changing—extent. This is shown even more conspicuously in row 5. It is, as a matter of fact, this indicator that reflects the substance of the process, since there is no stockpiling from the other two kinds of commodities constituting GNP, i. e., services and construction (GNP consists of goods, services and construction), thus in this row we find a confrontation of inventories with the products that cannot be stocked at all. The other aspect of the economic process reflected by this is that the sale of goods to users peaked in the first quarter and then showed a declining tendency. This process indeed suspiciously resembles an unfolding overproduction. It is also indicative of this that, although the development of bottlenecks was no longer rare in 1973, as has been mentioned, it was precisely on this account that the weight of fixed capital investment shifted to manufacturing in the first quarter. Yet, in the final analysis the continuous process of improving capacity utilization in manufacturing, characterizing 1971 and 1972, stopped in the second quarter of 1973 and began to deteriorate slowly. But, as regards the significant growth of inventories, it cannot be considered simply unintentional and a sign of unsaleability. In fact, we can be sure that under the given conditions—i. e., accelerating inflation—protection against price rises and speculation must have played a not negligible role in inventory accumulation.

12.2 A NEW DOLLAR CRISIS: ACCELERATING INFLATION, RELAXATION OF PRICE AND WAGE CONTROLS

With the last sentence we have already indicated the most glaring phenomenon of 1973, i. e., inflation, accelerating despite every forecast. Before discussing it, however, we have to report on another fact similarly causing an unpleasant surprise.

In the 1973 Economic Report of the President, it was boastfully claimed that the whole world admired the American anti-inflationary policy. Then the statement followed: "Largely because of this change the rest of the world is willing to hold increasing amounts of dollars." (*Economic Report,* 1973, p. 63) This statement was dated January 25, 1973. Merely eighteen days later, yielding to international pressure, the dollar had to be devalued by 10 per cent. This was a serious blow to the international economic position and prestige of the USA. But it was not an exceptional phenomenon, merely an episode in the accustomed decline of the exchange rate of the dollar, which continued with some breaks, ever since the system of floating was introduced.

Furthermore, the boastful sentence, in which the President forecast that 1973 might be a great year, was followed by reservations: "But 1973 will be a great year only if we manage our fiscal affairs prudently and do not exceed the increases in Federal expenditures that I have proposed." (Op. cit. p. 7) (It will be worthwhile pointing out, at least in parentheses, that Nixon, the cunning politician, declined responsibility well in advance in case the proposed budget expenditures were exceeded because of the behaviour of Congress and this involved negative consequences.) The forecast of the Council of Economic Advisers concerning the development of the price level was that the rise in the implicit price index of GNP would move around 3 per cent and in the consumer price index it would be 2.5 per cent by the end of the year, or even lower, but it was considered as a precondition that food prices should rise more slowly than in the preceding year. But they had no reason to assume that the rise in food prices would slow down. In spite of this, in January 1973 the administration shifted to the third stage of price controls, summarily but aptly characterized by Professor McCraken—still chairman of the Council of Economic Advisers when the whole control system was introduced in August 1971—by the following words: "Phase 3 is a looser and more flexible program. It does provide more scope for more people to raise more prices." (*Wall Street Journal,* April 7, 1973)

As already mentioned, considering 1972 as a whole, the price rise was smaller than in 1971, but following the second quarter its rate accelerated every quarter. And this ill-boding tendency continued in the first quarter of 1973, when the growth of the implicit price index of GNP jumped to 5.8 per cent (at annual level), and rose to 7.0 per cent in the second quarter. Food prices increased particularly quickly, by more than 20 per cent in the course of the first two quarters.

But if the rise in prices accelerated already in the second quarter of 1972, how could the administration justify the relaxation of the control system?

This is discussed at length in the report of the Council of Economic Advisers, dated February 1974. Accordingly, in 1972 inflation was slight and also the rise in wage level became moderated. The situation seemed propitious for a considerable modification of the second stage of controls. This modification was all the more necessary, it was said, because express capacities diminished and it seemed that if economic growth continued at the expected rate, the control measures would increasingly disturb production, productivity, investment decisions and also the administrative costs of the controls would grow. This is why in January 1973, the milder stage III was initiated, with the intention that soon an end would be put to the period of controls. (*Economic Report*, 1974, pp. 88–94)

Now, with certain exceptions, the annual 5.8 per cent upper limit to nominal wages remained in force also in the third (and the fourth) stage. But, as has been emphasized, the prices of agricultural products, import and export prices, as well as the firms not employing more than 60 persons were exempt from the price controls and in stage III housing and other rents were added to the list. Beyond that, the obligatory advance notice of permitted price rises was abolished in most sectors of the economy, and even the obligation of posterior notice was maintained only for the biggest economic units. But also the rules relating to the profit margin were changed; the number of years was increased from which the two most advantageous ones could be chosen for setting the permitted profit margin. The rules for setting the profit margin were entirely dropped in respect of those firms where the average price rise did not exceed 5 per cent *per annum*. (The justification was that if a firm reduced per unit costs through increased productivity, it should enjoy the advantage of a higher profit margin.) It was a further change that price rises necessary for the efficient allocation of resources or for maintaining a satisfactory level of supply were permitted. Special measures were introduced in order to contain the rise in food prices. Thus, the system of compulsory control was maintained in the production and distribution of food (for both prices and wages) and a few such measures were also taken which were expected to increase supply[23] but the price of agricultural raw products continued to remain outside the controls. By spring, however, it became obvious that the three special preconditions serving as a basis for the economic forecasts of the administration had not come true. One of them, the much faster than expected rise in food prices has already been mentioned. And by spring the advisers no longer believed that this process would stop in the second half of the year.

Secondly, in the first half of 1973 the growth of production was faster than expected all the world over, although it pretty well corresponded to expectations in the United States. But the capacity situation was tense both at home and abroad, and bottlenecks emerged in growing numbers.

Thirdly, in the second sentence of his annual report the President boasted of a strong dollar. But, the fact was that the dollar was quite weak. The exchange rate of the weakened dollar came to a rest at this time, in early 1973. Prior to that the dollar suffered considerable exchange-rate losses. (Precise data cannot be given. By various index numbers the loss between May 1970 and July 1973 may be put at 22–36 per cent.) In consequence, the level of the purchase price of imported goods increased in terms of dollars. This raised final prices similarly to the price of agricultural raw products, also exempt from price control. The other aspect of the matter was that also goods falling

[23] For a detailed description of the control system applied in the new stage and its comparison with the one used in the preceding stage, see *Economic Report* 1974, pp. 89–91.

under price control were increasingly being exported, since they could be sold abroad at higher prices. This, too, increased the pressure on domestic prices.

In consequence of all that, according to public opinion polls, in February 1973 already 43 per cent of the population wanted a return to the system of price freezing and this also entailed the paradoxical consequence that, at the news of expected price freezing, prices were increased even more. Thus the administration was anxious lest the hitherto solid, about 5 per cent annual rise of hourly wages should turn into a faster wage explosion.

Nevertheless, they hesitated because—as they said—the main cause of inflation was to be sought in the market of articles traded at the exchanges, and it was their conviction that controls could be of only limited effectiveness there, since the prices of raw products were free. It was said that the output of these products should be increased, but they had no idea how this should be achieved. Nevertheless, beginning with March the rules of stage III were somewhat tightened in order to reassure wage earners and consumers, as it was said, that the government would do everything in its power to contain inflation. Thus, e.g., the price control of crude oil and its derivatives was tightened, and there was a similar measure introduced for meat prices. In early May the obligation to give advance notice of intended price rises was restored in respect of those large firms which wanted to raise the prices in force on January 10 by more than one and a half per cent. (*Op. cit.* pp. 92–95)

We know this was little. The administration was finally compelled to take more resolute measures. On June 13, a price-freeze was again ordered (this was the second one), with the qualification that it was not to last more than sixty days. It was also announced that the price-freeze only served to allow time for elaborating the methods of regulations to be applied in the following period. (The freeze did not affect wages; it related only to prices, the latter were not allowed to rise above the level they were at between 1–8 June.)

One might think the delay was needed to prepare a fourth stage tighter than the third or even the second one. But what actually happened was different. Since the freeze did not apply to agricultural products and imported commodities—mostly raw materials—even now, the frozen prices of products at a higher level of processing reacted in a way so as to reduce production. Cattle breeding, the production of poultry and eggs declined; the commodity supply in the retail trade of foodstuffs diminished. The advisers drew the conclusion that the freeze was less effective than the one introduced in August 1971. They declared: "Little could be done through the use of direct controls to stop the price surge without interfering with production and inducing additional exports." (*Economic Report,* 1974, p. 97)

It was under these circumstances that the fourth stage was introduced on August 14, but the tightening rules were very thriftily applied. To wit, in the areas falling under price control it was prohibited to charge a profit margin to the rise in costs that could be shifted onto prices, only the cost rises since the last quarter of 1972 could be taken into account in pricing, and in some industries the price level was set at a lower level up to which prices could be raised without special justification. On the other hand, the price controls were lifted in respect of animal nutriments, cement, public utilities, lumber, waste copper, motor cars, fertilizers, aluminium and, with the exception of copper, all non-ferrous metals, semi-conductors, but also coal delivered on the basis of long-term

185

contracts. This also projected the perspective of an early abolition of the whole system of price controls.

When scrutinizing price developments in the fourth quarter separate mention should be made of the oil price explosion which about quadrupled the price of this important energy source and raw material almost from one day to the other. In spite of the fact that the United States covered the overwhelming share of its crude oil needs from domestic production, this surge in price had grave consequences. As mentioned, export and import prices were exempt from price controls. In consequence, these prices rose thoughout the period analyzed in this chapter at a rate much faster than other prices.[24] But the rise in export and import prices had been up to that time on the whole of an identical rate, while in the decade in question they already differed considerably and the growth of import prices exceeded by far that of export prices. The first was 41.8 per cent, the latter "only" 27.6 per cent (let us not forget: at annual rate!). Thus the international terms of trade took a highly unfavourable turn for the United States— similarly to the situation in many leading Western countries. This had a necessarily grave negative impact on the balance of trade and, through this, to some extent on the movements of profits, the balance of payments and the position of the dollar.

12.3 THE WHOLE OF 1973: FISCAL AND MONETARY POLICIES, PRICES AND PROFITS

Let us pass now to the analysis of indicators characterizing the whole of 1973. The 5.5 per cent growth in the volume of GNP hardly lagged behind that expected or the one attained in the preceding year. But, from the quarterly data we know that this may be attributed only to the high level attained in the first quarter. The growth rate of personal consumption—in a way characteristic of overinvestment periods—lagged behind the growth of GNP and also significantly declined relative to the preceding year, amounting to 4.2 per cent. Within that, although the growth rate of purchases of consumer durables remained high, it fell to 9.5 per cent from 13.4 in the preceding year. The growth rate of non-durables and services, showing generally minor fluctuations, also somewhat diminished. The volume of housing construction already showed a 3.7 per cent absolute decline. However, the growth rate of fixed capital investment further increased—in harmony with all forecasts—and attained 12.1 per cent. The volume of stockpiling jumped by more than three quarters relative to 1972. Through its purchases, the federal government exerted a mitigating effect on overheatedness also in this year, and expenditure on this item diminished by 5.4 per cent. In this the armistice in Vietnam actually coming about at the beginning of the year certainly had a part. The volume of military purchases fell to the same extent, but the decline in the volume of total government purchases was minimum. Unemployment fell from 5.6 to 4.9 per cent on annual average. But the declining tendency turned into a rise in the last two months.

[24] For example, in the first quarter of 1973, when the growth of the implicit price index of GNP was 5.8 per cent, the same indicator was 13.2 per cent in exports and 13.4 per cent in imports. The deviation continued to increase, the corresponding figures for the third quarter were 7.5, 27.8 and 21.6 per cent.

The various price indices show the following percentual changes over the preceding year:

Implicit price index of GNP	Δp_c^*	Δp_c	Consumer price index	of which: food	Wholesale price index
5.8	6.1	5.9	6.2	14.5	13.1

All price indices testify to an accelerating rate of inflation and illustrate, at the same time, the ineffectiveness of price controls.

Naturally, government economic policy was not restricted to modifications of the control system—effected three times in 1973 alone—but it also deployed other weapons from its armory. Throughout the year, the aim of monetary policy was to reduce the growth rate of the quantity of money and the volume of credit, while the extent of restrictions and the instruments used varied in the course of the year. Transition to a more restrictive monetary policy was reflected by the fact that the growth of the quantity of money fell from 9.5 per cent in the second half of 1972 to 4.5 per cent by the second half of 1973. In the first half of the year there was an attempt to restrain the growth of the quantity of money in circulation through open-market transactions. This was the purpose of the raising of the FED discount rate on several occasions, from 4.5 per cent at the beginning of 1973 to 7.5 per cent by mid-August. Fearing that the growth of business credits would escape the control of both commercial banks and the FED, the latter, responsible for control, wrote an open letter to the big banks in April, asking them to exhibit restraint in granting credit. Monetary restrictions even increased in the third quarter so much that in the course of the summer the quantity of money increased even in absolute terms. And at the turn of June/July the FED raised the obligatory reserve rates of most institutions. The ceiling on the rate of interest of certificates of deposit on large amounts was abolished. This was expected to increase the impact of the rate of interest on the distribution of credits. The great demand for credit resulted, on the one hand, in rising costs of credit and, on the other, in record-high interest rates for most of the short-term credits by September 1973. In the last quarter of the year the quantity of money increased again but the growth rate of credit granting slowed to an acceptable level. And in December, in view of a weakening economic situation, the Federal Open Market Commission expressed its wish to shift to a less restrictive policy.[25] How great the increase in credits nevertheless was in 1973 as a whole is shown by the fact that corporations raised $ 61 bn credit in various forms, and the total of credits raised attained the record level of 178 bn. According to an official statement, the situation on the mortgage market was less tight than in 1966 and 1969 when housing construction also fell, but now it fell notwithstanding. (*Economic Report,* 1984, p. 86) Although, as we have seen, the federal government pursued a policy tightening credit, it supported the mortgage credit market, precisely in defence of housing construction. In the course of this support

[25] The directives of this Commission, having a central role in setting monetary policy, were published only 90 days after they had been taken.

187

various government agencies diverted substantial sums from the open market to the mortgage market, and the President announced measures called upon to support the mortgage and the housing construction sector in both the short and long runs. Nevertheless, the fall in housing construction was much graver than following the 1966 credit restrictions. As a matter of fact, in 1966–1967 the decline in housing construction lasted through four quarters, amounting to 23.4 per cent. The corresponding data for 1969–1970 are: 5 quarters and 15.3 per cent, but the fall following the peak of housing construction in the first quarter of 1973 was not only very protracted (lasting for two full years) but also sharp and deep having attained 43.6 per cent. It is natural that in this case the cause of the decline was not only and perhaps not even mainly the credit squeeze, but also other important factors played a role. In the course of analyzing the 1974–1975 depression we shall analyse these too.

Passing now to the examination of fiscal policy pursued in 1973, the following might be stated: the fiscal policy of the federal government was expressly and acknowledgedly restrictive. The domestic government surplus calculated by our own methods increased in 1973 by nearly 11 bn. Within that, the balance of the federal government essentially achieved equilibrium against a deficit of $ 11.9 bn in the preceding year. The activities of the state and local governments acted against this change; their surplus somewhat diminished. To make the order of magnitude of the total change of $ 9.0 bn tangible, we mention that this was 0.8 per cent of the 1973 GNP (without imputations), but 5.1 per cent of after-tax profits. The shifting of the simulating policy maintained throughout the major part of 1972 into a restrictive one may be well traced by means of the quarterly balances:

Domestic balance of the federal budget
Bn dollars at annual rate

1972	1973			
4th quarter	1st	2nd	3rd	4th
	quarters			
− 19.5	− 4.1	0.5	1.5	1.2

As can be seen, in early 1973 a sharp turn took place in the budgetary policy of the federal government and in three quarters of the year this restriction amounted to almost 21 bn dollars at annual rate. This amounted to 1.6 per cent of the GNP, but to 9.7 per cent of after-tax profits. This restrictive impact was somewhat mitigated by the smaller budget surplus of the state and local governments. Thus, in the final analysis, the total domestic government balance shifted between the last quarter of 1972 and the second one of 1973 by 12.1 bn dollars in the direction of restriction, which is a significant turn in half a year by any measure. In the second half of the year—owing to a further decline in the surplus of the state and local governments—the surplus of the total government balance started again to diminish.

The shift of the budget towards restriction was only partially a result of deliberate economic policy measures, partially it took place spontaneously, because of a faster than estimated growth of budget revenues. This was attributable in most part to the

188

fast rise of prices, resulting in an automatic increase of taxes and similar revenues. The "merit" of the government in the turn is that it succeeded in keeping the rise of federal budget expenditure between limits. As a result, for the first time since 1969 it occurred that expenditures were rising more slowly than the GNP. It was again proved that, in the short run, the revenues of the federal budget react quicker than its outlays to an unexpected increase in the rate of inflation. Thus, the acceleration of inflation acted through the spontaneous change in the budget balance towards its own mitigation.

Let us now turn to what we can understand more exactly from the developments of 1973 with the aid of our own methods, through the examination of the diagrams relating to price level and profits.[26]

Let us start with the factors in the change of the price level of consumer articles. From the figure illustrating it we may read that the 10.0 per cent price-raising impact of the factors in the numerator was counterbalanced to the extent of 3.9 per cent by those in the denominator. This is how the 6.1 per cent price rise—much greater than in the preceding year—was derived. The price-raising impact of the numerator somewhat increased over the preceding year, but the fall of the price-mitigating impact of the denominator from 6.9 to 3.9 per cent was even more important. It is worth mentioning that in the three-year period examined the fluctuations in the price-raising impact of the numerator were slight, the three data being 9.7, 11.0 and 10.0 per cent. The price-raising impact of wage rises significantly grew also in 1973: it attained 13.5 per cent over 11.5 in the preceding year and 8.1 per cent in 1971. The price-raising effect of transfer payments slightly increased and the price-reducing impact of wage taxes diminished significantly, by 5 per cent. The fact that the price-raising impact of the numerator was still less than in the preceding year, may be traced in the final analysis to the fact that overspending by wage earners diminished against the significant figure in the preceding year (this is the other aspect of the above-outlined decline in consumers' investment). Thus, while in 1972 the growth in overspending was an important price-raising factor, its reduction in 1973 became a price-reducing one and overcompensated the impact of the previously mentioned three factors. The denominator developed in an unfavourable manner: the price-reducing effect of the volume of consumer goods sold fell from 7.4 to 4.2 per cent. To sum up: the price-raising impact of the numerator lagged by 9 per cent behind that of 1972—mainly due to a considerable fall in overspending by wage earners relative to the preceding year. At the same time, the rise in price level was 50 per cent higher than in 1972, partly because of the not too effective price controls and mostly owing to the significant rise in costs. (Even so the net after-

---

[26] The reader may ask why we did not employ our special methods also for the analysis of individual quarters. The answer is that we did not apply them because we could not.

For drawing our diagrams we need data without imputations but these are not available in a quarterly breakdown. The changes of our own price level indicators and the official price indexes are very close to each other, but they could not be identical even in the case of perfectly exact computations, as they refer to prices of sets of goods of different composition. Thus, our Δp_c formula is wider than the official price index of consumption expenditure, because it also comprises the purchase of dwellings (homes), while our Δp_c^* formula is narrower than the implicit price index of GNP, because it does not relate to the whole of GNP, but, beyond consumption interpreted in the above sense, it only comprises government purchases, that is, it excludes investment and foreign trade. (We have just repeated that we work with categories not comprising imputations.) For the diagrams see pp. 114–117 in Part II and pp. 54–55; 65–66 in Part III.

tax profit margin was merely 0.1 percentage point higher than in 1972.) This is why the volume of the additional sales in 1973 had to diminish by more than 33 per cent. Production was less restricted; it was the inventories that increased significantly.

On the basis of the figure of the more comprehensive Δp_c^* price level indicator (see pp. 65–66 these things said above may be complemented by the following. The price-level-raising impact of government expenditure was on the whole of the same extent as in the two preceding years. Thus, this indicator of the price-impact of fiscal policy worked throughout the period of price controls towards raising prices and to an identical extent every year, in spite of every effort to the contrary. In the denominator the price impact of government purchases may be qualified as negligible in all the three years, in spite of having changed sign even on two occasions: in 1972 it turned from price raising into price reducing and in 1973 the reverse happened.

To conclude our investigations of 1973 as a whole, let us see the movement of profits, the key category of capitalists for judging the situation and thus for the development of business. The nominal domestic profit of non-financial corporations was higher by 6.9 per cent than in the preceding year. Their real profit remained on the whole identical with that of the preceding year, but its share within GNP diminished. And yet another thing: this profit moved throughout the year below the peak of the first quarter, and lagged behind by about 6 per cent in the last quarter. The fall in GNP was preceded also this time by a decline in corporate profits. (For the gross profit after taxes in the whole economy and its elements and the changes therein, as worked out by us, see the diagrams on pp. 110–117)

We stress only a few major interrelations that can be read from them. While profits continued to grow, the paper profit became negative both at current prices and in terms of volume. This can be traced back to two factors: first, to the restrictive turn in budgetary policy implemented by the administration in order to put a brake on overheated business, as a result of which the minimal government surplus of 1972 was replaced by a rather significant one, second, the considerable fall in overspending by wage earners already mentioned in connection with the factors in the development of prices. The decline in paper profit would have been even greater had the negative effects mentioned not been counterbalanced to a certain extent by the fact that the deficit of the balance of trade turned into a surplus. The determining factor in the strong growth of material profit was the investment boom. (It was already mentioned that a considerable part—almost 40 per cent—of the increase in the volume of investment derived from the growth in every kind of stock.)

Attentive readers who have perhaps compared the percentual growth at current and constant prices in our figures, could work out that the growth of the "implicit price index" of gross after-tax profit was 3.8 per cent. This is much lower than the rise in either our price level indicators, or of the implicit price index of GNP, or of the consumer price index, both to be found in official statistics, for the same period. That is, the acceleration of inflation bit much less into the profits of capitalists than into the expenditure of either the state or wage earners.

12.4 ILL-BODING FORECASTS FOR 1974.
"OFFICIAL" SCEPTICISM REGARDING PRICE AND
WAGE CONTROLS AND OUR OWN VIEWS

Could it be surmised and did at least the economic advisers of the President surmise that 1974 would be the year of recession? If so, did it figure in their plans to do something about it?

President Nixon's *Economic Report* dated February 1st, 1974, began with the following words: "The United States enters 1974 in a position of leadership in the world economy. The dollar is strong, we have constructive economic relations throughout the world, and we have the greatest freedom of action resulting from our great capacity to produce. We must take the responsibilities and opportunities this position of leadership gives us." (*Economic Report*, 1974, p. 3) This sounded very self-confident, but it continued by saying that in 1973 difficulties were greater and progress smaller than had been expected, although the results were more important than the events causing disappointment.

What then were the results? Employment, productivity and output increased and so did the per capita after-tax real income of consumers. The President recorded as a result without qualification that employment exceeded every earlier figure, although unemployment still attained 5 per cent. A prominent place was given in the list of result to the fact that—first of all through the floating and the *de facto* devaluation of the dollar—the formerly significant deficit in the balance of trade turned into a surplus.

Then the greatest failure was mentioned: although inflation could be slowed down by the end of 1972, in spite of the uncomfortable rise in food prices, in 1973 the rise in consumer prices approached 9 per cent.

The acceleration of inflation, continued the Report, was not independent of the results listed. According to the Report, the rapid progress toward full employment, the growth of net exports, and the falling exchange rate of the dollar all supported inflation. But the lag of food production behind demand also contributed to this. The boom in other countries raised the price of raw materials for industry, and the OPEC countries raised the price of crude oil. The year 1974 began with the fact that to the triple problem of inflation, unemployment and the balance of payments was added a fourth: that of energy, the oil embargo coupled with the rise in crude oil prices.[27]

The Report of the President identified a triple task:

1. the moderate slowdown of the economic boom must not be allowed to accelerate due to the energy shortage;

2. the rise in fuel prices must be prevented from exerting an unwanted inflationary effect on other fields of the economy;

3. after the initial trouble caused by the energy shortage the economy had to be put on the path of increased economic expansion coupled with greater price stability. (*Op. cit.* p. 6)

As we know, these promises remained just that.

---

[27] The lifting of the oil embargo was then justly expected. And the report of the Council of Economic Advisers estimated the additional cost burden of the United States deriving from the price rise of oil at not quite 1 per cent of the GNP.

The tasks were followed by the enumeration of instruments to be used in the interest of their implementation and a tentative list of partial objectives. Three from the latter deserve to be mentioned.

1. In spite of the fact that the same list also comprised that in the short run a decline in production and employment would become unavoidable, President Nixon still provided for a moderately restrictive fiscal policy.

2. The President promised a "progressive" elimination of price and wage controls.

3. The President urged—as if certain preparations had been made for what actually happened instead of greater economic expansion—adjustment in the system of unemployment benefits that would better protect those losing their job in order that the secondary impacts of unemployment should have a lesser impact on the economy. (*Op. cit.* pp. 6–7)

We repeat that the above were taken from the report of the President himself. The Report of the Council of Economic Advisers was more pessimistic and, characteristically, the problem of inflation was given more definite emphasis. The Report started with the history of the last eight years and laid down that the American economy had to live with an inflation mostly already built into the system. First of all, said the Report, both workers and employers were already accustomed to a large-scale rise of nominal wages which reflects that they expected a fast-rate rise in prices. And this expectation could be moderated only gradually. This trend was also built into the level of rates of interest. The public was highly sensitive to inflation and reacted to all news confirming expectations concerning price rises. Whoever in this situation undertook to fight inflation, had to prepare for a long struggle. But this fight had to be undertaken, inflation had to be contained and the costs involved also had to be borne in order to avoid even higher costs of an even greater inflation.

The Report then listed what the American people wished besides averting inflation. Characteristically, the first place was taken by the need to maintain the "defence" of the country at an adequate level. Then came environmental protection, better care for the underprivileged, improvement of the health services, and the raising of the quality of life, which all required more private consumption. But, as it was added, the American economy had to face at the same time unusual obstacles to a faster increase of production.

The Report continued by assessing future perspectives. It laid down that 1974 had begun with a fast-rate inflation and an early stage of slowdown in the growth of production. It was unavoidable, it was said, that a large-scale rise in prices and wages should take place in the first half of 1974. It could not be known beforehand what would follow as this also depended on economic policy in 1974. But it was hardly doubted that the slowdown of the growth of production felt in the fourth quarter of 1973 (real growth at annual level moved around 1 per cent) would continue in the first half of the year and even an absolute decline was conceivable. But, it was said, there were also signs indicating a lasting expansion, such as, e.g., the planned increase of fixed capital investment by business.

As regards future prospects, the Report discussed first of all the possible impact of the energy situation. This was condensed into four points. It was of the opinion that the first, the limitation of production capacity due to the oil shortage, was not a grave danger. The second was taken more seriously: namely, that the shortage of oil and gasoline and the rise in the prices of the latter might reduce demand for motor cars, for such related things as motel services and other facilities connected with tourism, as well as the purchase of homes. The third point qualified the developments in the first two points as transitory. Accordingly, the limited availability of primary energy and the decline in demand would be counterbalanced by a shift in production towards the less energy-intensive branches, or perhaps by the fact that the oil-exporting countries would increase their demand for American goods. But it was thought that the impact would be lasting and that the drying up of cheap sources of energy would reduce the living standards of the American people through deteriorating terms of trade.

Finally, the fourth point discussed the problems related to the balance of payments and other international relations. Accordingly, every oil-importing country would suffer from the events related to oil—and their majority would be more gravely hurt than the United States. At any rate, demand and production would slow down—if not decline in absolute terms—in the majority of countries having business ties to the United States—with the exception of the oil exporters—and this would affect the domestic economy in several ways. It would moderate the rise in industrial raw-material prices. Also, the rise in the exchange rate of the dollar in the fourth quater of 1973 would reduce the dollar prices of goods quoted at the world exchanges. Domestic oil prices would be lower than abroad. This was one aspect of the matter. On the other hand, the recession to be expected abroad and the fall in the exchange rate of foreign currencies would impair the chances of American exports and, most likely, this would be the prevailing tendency. Most countries would have a deficit in their balance of payments, while the oil-exporting countries would invest their surplus money in claims or real assets outside their country. Turned into investment these surpluses might stimulate growth by drawing away means from consumption. But they might entail grave repercussions if investment aspects were diverted in wrong directions. Namely, the industrial countries might answer with restrictions to the deterioration in their balance of payments and such one-sided measures might lead to recession both at home and in exports.

According to the title of the subsection in the *Economic Report,* the list of objectives provided for 1974 was to follow, yet the text did not outline objectives but briefly surveyed conceivable development paths. It ended with two statements. According to the first, the development path characterized as the most advantageous one was nothing else but the opinion of the authors of the Report about the possible way and to what it would lead if economic policy successfully proceeded along that path. According to the second stament it was highly uncertain whether the outlined path was indeed passable and also whether the economic policy contemplated would really lead onto this path. (Op. cit. pp. 21–28)

* * *

Western economists generally place strong emphasis on the impact of expectations on the course of the economy and we are of the opinion that they are mostly right. But this Economic Report could by no means be called optimistic. True, the Council of Economic Advisers treated the slowdown or possible decline in real processes lightly, as a transitory phenomenon, and put the emphasis on inflation. Referring to it, the President promised a moderately restrictive budget. But did the advisers actually believe that if they talked about a possible absolute decline, would not almost everybody firmly believe in the inevitability of an absolute decline? Was it not the "trade-off" between inflation and unemployment, related to the Phillips-curve, that was on the minds of the President and his advisers? Did not 1970 repeat itself in a much graver form? Was it not intended to "discipline" primarily the workers by increasing unemployment at a time when it was already around 5 per cent? Why did Samuelson's 1972 forecast come true?

It was justly said that the rest of the world had to struggle with difficulties much greater than those of the United States and that a decline was very likely to occur there. But did the President not boast of the leading position of the United States? Did the American administration have to assess to what extent the European decline may influence the economy of the United States and not rather to what extent the maintenance of domestic economic growth with powerful incentives could help out the countries wich were compelled to view the USA's passivity, or an economic behaviour even worse than that?

And finally, why is inflation such a great evil that it is worse than unemployment? Can a capitalist country not live well for a longer period with an inflation of around 10 per cent? It can, as indicated by the economy of Japan. Of course, it is true that the Japanese economy is much more controlled through the direct instruments of state monopoly capitalism than that of the United States. If, however, inflation was really public enemy No. 1, why were price and wage controls abolished?

We have already reviewed the opinion of the Council of Economic Advisers about the problem. They were of the opinion that for them price control was not a suitable means of containing inflation. It was true, they said, that in 1972 inflation had been milder than the year before, but whether it had been milder than it would have been without controls was questionable. As regards 1973, agricultural prices were growing faster than at any time since 1917. As a result, retail food prices were responsible for 51 per cent of the inflation. A further 11 per cent was contributed by the energy prices charged to consumers. The rise in prices was faster—and let us add: naturally!—than either in the early period of price controls, or in the periods without controls. And the economic advisers asked the question whether inflation would have grown faster without the 1973 price controls. But they did not answer the question. They said that in 1973 it is more difficult to believe in the controls being effective in containing inflation than they had believed in 1972.

In a theoretical case—they argued—wage control puts a brake on demand, price control eases the inflationary expectations; supply may increase on the basis of the principle of small profits and quick returns and thus finally equilibrium may come about with constrained prices. But in the United States, they said, beginning with 1973, and in fact in the greater part of 1973, almost half of both prices and wages fell beyond the scope of controls, and if the controls resulted in a commodity shortage at some points, there was ample opportunity for incomes to flow to uncontrolled fields. Under such conditions there developed imbalances and shortages emerged, but the system was unable to bear this for a longer time. In the final analysis, those could buy who were ready to buy at higher prices. Here and there this price control contained prices, only to find higher price rises at other places. There was no sign that the controls contained spending. But, according to them, output did not grow faster in 1973 than on the average in the past. In fact, the advisers were not even sure whether the control system increased output through restricting the wage level. About the third stage they said that the order according to which in that stage the enterprises determined for themselves the permitted rise in prices was interpreted by public opinion in the sense that controls would soon come to an end. Consumer prices, it was said, increased in early 1973 precisely on this account.

Affirming repeatedly the correctness of loosening the controls, the authors of the Economic Report nevertheless emphasized that in stage III those branches contributed more significantly to the growth of inflation to which controls did not extend from the outset, or in which there was no significant difference between stages II and III, than those for which stage III introduced looser rules. But, in *our* opinion, this hardly proves anything beyond the single fact that the system of controls as it was implemented could not be really effective. The heart of the matter was that already stage II was all too liberal. This stage should have been essentially tightened for the sake of really effective control. But it seems that such requirement is alien to the free economy based on free enterprise in the United States. It was not even simply the resistence of large monopolies that put up an obstacle; if they have to, they can adjust to national interest. But the government was impotent, e.g., in face of the fact that, although the net income per farm in 1973 increased on the average by 24 per cent at constant prices, yet farmers, primarily animal breeders, started to reduce their supply. They behaved according to the model of oligopolistic competition, not according to that of a perfect one, although not merely a small number of producers were competing. The myth of the maximum promotion of public welfare by the free enterprise system, and the illusions of a well controllable capitalist economy were disproved. And the US economy—with the effective help of the administration and leaving their allies to fend for themselves— sank into a state in which the "free people of the free world" had to learn that they can simultaneously suffer from high unemployment and high-rate inflation. And the administration continued to consider inflation the main bogey, and unemployment only a second-rate discomfort. But this is already the subject of the next chapter.

THE 1974–1975 ECONOMIC RECESSION

CHAPER THIRTEEN

1974: THE UNFOLDING OF THE RECESSION

We have reached the most exciting section of the historical–analytical part of our book, which was rather problematic for the researcher, but provided many opportunities to draw theoretical conclusions.

In 1974–1975 the United States underwent the gravest economic recession of the three and a half decades following the Second World War. As regards its depth, extension, length[28] and the negative impact on the situation of American workers, this recession outdid every recession of recent decades. Below, we are going to publish ample data on all this. Therefore, we start this section by comparing the economic structure of 1973 with the structure of the first year of the 1957–1958 recession. (This was the gravest recession after the Second World War prior to 1974–1975, and the last quarter of 1973 may be considered either the peak of the boom or the beginning of the recession.)

13.1 COMPARISON OF THE ECONOMIC STRUCTURES OF 1957 AND 1973

From Table 13.1 a few structural changes during the one and a half decades preceding the recession can be seen. The share of personal consumption somewhat exceeded that of sixteen years earlier. If home purchases are also included in personal consumption and imputations are neglected, the corresponding shares are 63.3 and 62.8 per cent. But the role of durables increased between the two dates both within GNP and personal consumption. This means that within personal consumption (and within global demand) the weight of a highly unstable kind of demand, sensitive to crises, has increased. The share of the type of demand least sensitive to depression—services—has also increased somewhat. Within private investment (excluding changes in inventories) the share of housing construction increased, but the change was slight. The weight of housing construction increased somewhat also within GNP. More important, the ratios of business fixed capital investment and consumers' investment significantly shifted in favour of the latter. While in 1957 to 1 dollar of fixed capital

---

[28] Researchers of the leading business research institute of the United States, the National Bureau of Economic Research, put the peak before the recession at November 1973, and its trough at March 1975. Thus, according to them it lasted 16 months. (Zarnowitz, V. and Moore, G. H. 1977, p. 473)

investment there fell 1.2 dollars of consumers' investment, in 1973 the latter figure was already 1.4 dollars. Within fixed business capital, however, the weight of similarly unstable elements, such as the purchase of machinery and equipment, also increased.

Table 13.1

Major indicators of the structure of GNP production and utilization (in percentage of GNP, on the basis of data expressed in 1972 dollars)

Items	1973	Internal proportions	1957	Internal proportions
	By types of demand			
1. Personal consumption	62.2	(100.0)	60.9	(100.0)
2. Durables	9.9	(15.9)	7.3	(12.0)
3. Non-durables	25.0	(40.3)	28.6	(47.0)
4. Services	27.2	(43.8)	25.0	(41.0)
5. Gross private investment	16.7		14.3	
6. Non-residential fixed investment	10.6	(100.0)	9.7	(100.0)
7. Structures	3.7	(34.7)	4.1	(42.6)
8. Producers' durable equipment	6.9	(65.3)	5.6	(57.4)
9. Residential construction	4.8		4.4	
10. Changes in inventories	1.3		0.2	
11. Government purchases	20.4		23.5	
12. Net exports	0.7		1.3	
13. Trend-like part[a]	65.0		63.9	
14. Cyclical part[a]	26.6		21.6	
15. Irregular part[a]	8.4		14.5	
	By types of product			
16. Final sales	98.7		99.8	
17. Material production	57.0		59.0	
18. Production of goods	46.1	(100.0)	47.3	(100.0)
19. Production of durables	19.1	(41.6)	17.0	(36.1)
20. Production of non-durables	26.9	(58.4)	30.2	(63.9)
21. Structures	10.9		11.7	
22. Services	43.0		41.0	
Addenda:				
23. Consumers' investments	14.7		11.7	
24. Auto product	4.1		3.8	

[a] For interpretation see pp. 197–198.

From the point of view of the ensuing recession, the data given at the end of the first part of the table—grouped according to types of demand—about the trend-like, cyclical and irregular components are of particular importance because of the shifts in their shares. The group developing smoothly, almost without fluctuations, comprises beyond the two elements of personal consumption (purchase of non-durable consumption goods and services) the purchases of state and local government. The cyclically moving component comprises the purchase of consumers' durables, business fixed capital investment, changes in inventories and housing construction. And the one

197

showing irregular movements consists of the purchases by federal government and exports. We find that the share of the cyclical group sharply increased, mostly at the expense of the irregular group, but also at that of the trend-like one. The diminishing weight of the irregular one can be traced mostly to the absolute and relative decline in the federal purchase of goods and services. Of course, the significant growth of this group increased in itself the sensitivity to recession. But the most important structural change that occurred between the two dates was that the ratio of government purchases fell significantly.

Before going into the details of the matter, it will be timely to examine, again compared to 1957, the weight of government expenditure in the economy of the country. (See Table 13.2)

Table 13.2

Main indicators of the economic role of government

Items	1973		1957	
	Bn 1972 dollars	in percentage of GNP	Bn 1972 dollars	as percentage of end product
Total government expenditure*	395.6	32.0	201.7	29.6
Federal expenditure*	225.8	18.2	127.4	18.7
State and local government expenditure	169.8	13.8	74.3	10.9
Government purchases of goods and services**	252.5	20.4	160.1	23.5
Federal	96.6	7.8	89.8	13.2
of which: military	69.5	5.6	79.0	11.6
State and local	155.9	12.6	70.3	10.3
In percentage of all purchases of this kind				
Government purchases of material goods	63.8	9.1	50.3	12.5
Purchases of durables	16.1	6.8	18.7	16.1
Structures	30.8	22.8	22.4	28.0
Fixed capital investment	36.2	21.6	24.6	27.2
In percentage of total personal income				
Personal incomes from government	250.4	25.1	90.4	17.5
Wages and salaries	140.6	14.1	60.7	11.7
Transfers***	109.8	11.0	29.7	5.7

Complementary data

Items	millions	in percentage of total	millions	in percentage of total
	employment		employment	
Government employment	14.8	17.4	10.8	15.3
Military employment	2.4	2.7	2.8	4.3

* To exclude double counting, without grants by the federal government to state and local organs.
** Including government wages and salaries.
*** In official statistics we only find the government purchases of goods and services—inclusive of the wages of government employees—in 1972 dollars. The other transfer payments are only available in current dollars. Since they mostly become consumption expenditures, we converted them to 1972 dollars with the implicit price index of the latter.

As can be seen, the proportion of total government expenditure to GNP increased. But behind this increase we find a Janus-faced process. On the one hand, the share of personal incomes from government sources significantly increased within total personal income. This growth may be attributed to two factors. In spite of an absolute decline in the personnel of the armed forces, the number of government employees increased, and so did the ratio of their incomes to GNP. The almost doubling of government transfers was particularly important. On the other hand, however, the volume of material goods purchased by government significantly diminished within all purchases of this kind.

But, beyond this Janus-faced phenomenon, another one may also be observed. The ratio of government expenses increased relative to GNP in a way that the share of the expenses of state and local organs increased while that of the federal government fell. (We have already mentioned that the total of federal purchases of goods and services significantly diminished even in absolute terms.) The federal government was pushed back by local organs also in the purchase of goods and services–above all because of the fall in military expenses in both absolute and relative terms.

In order to make evident the importance of the diminishing weight of government and mainly federal purchases, we have to consider that in the USA, where the share of government ownership is negligible, one of the most important stabilizing feature of the strengthening state monopoly capitalism is that government purchases represent a steady market for a rather considerable part of output. By 1973 this stable market dwindled in relative terms with the " de-escalation" and eventual end of the Vietnam War, due to the decline in military purchases.[29] From the aspect of the stabilization possibilites of government economic policy this picture was little changed by the growing share of state and local government purchases. It should be seen, namely, that the many thousands of state, county, city and township organs do not and cannot have a unified budget and revenue policy that would take into account national interests and thus their impact on the shaping of business is uncertain. This is all the more so, since the states and local organs are obliged to keep their budgets balanced on annual level, independent of the actual business situation. This is all the more worth mentioning as these organs cover an ever increasing part of their expenses from aid made available by the federal government; the share of these was 10.6 per cent in 1957, but already 22.5 per cent in 1973.

The narrowing of the steady market created by government purchases became particularly grave because in the sector exerting the biggest impact on business and showing particularly great fluctuations, that of durable goods, the government purchases declined even in absolute terms, and their share fell to less than half of that of 1957. The reason was only partly the diminishing military purchases. The role of government also fell considerably in fixed capital investment. The same may be said about its role in construction.

Thus the share of government demand considerably fell within total demand in both

---

[29] The share of government purchases in GNP was highest at the time of the Korean War, in 1953: 27.3 per cent. It approximated this value in the recession year of 1958: 24.9 per cent. It hardly lagged behind the latter figure at the peak of the Vietnam War, in 1968: 24.6 per cent. Following that it declined every year till the trough of 1973.

areas (construction and durables) important for the shaping of business in general and in the 1974–1975 recession in particular.

While the direct market role of the state diminished, its impact on employment and personal income formation, and thus on the indirect shaping of the market, increased. We can render this statement even more exact. Government appared on the market, beyond its direct purchases, also through the mediation of others. Its direct purchases as well as those mediated through government wages and transfers amounted in 1957 altogether to 21.1 per cent of the GNP and in 1973 to 25.5 per cent. This may be estimated by adding to the direct purchases by government—not equal to the statistical notion of "purchases of goods and services", because the latter also comprise wages which had to be left out of account to avoid double counting—the consumption from government, assuming that, deducting taxes, financial payments and savings, the same portion of these incomes is spent on consumption as in the case of personal incomes in general. (This is a rather significant increase. But the weight of direct government purchases fell from almost 50 per cent in 1957 to 39 per cent, and within it the role of the federal government significantly diminished: in 1957 it was still 65.7 per cent, while in 1973 only 39 per cent, and the latter was only 3.9 per cent of GNP against 6.4 per cent in 1957. The federal government in 1973 purchased less material goods also in absolute terms than in 1957:$ 21.5 bn against 28.5 bn. These purchases corresponded to 3.1 and 7.1 per cent of all material goods.)

We may thus establish that the weight of the government in the market shifted towards an indirect role, while within direct purchases the share of federal expenses considerably diminished. We shall still have an opportunity to examine the role of this fact in the economic strategy position of the administration.

13.2 TOPICAL PROBLEMS AT THE TURN OF 1973/1974

It may be stated *ex-post* that, as a matter of fact, at the turn of 1973/1974 the US economy was already in a recession. We have seen that the President and his advisors also felt something similar. The harmful consequences of the "oil crisis" already became felt, e.g., in the production of cars, a key industry of the country, where as a result of the rise in gasoline prices production had to be strongly reduced because of falling demand. But it is also worth noting that in spite of this the price of the new cars introduced in October 1973 was about 400 dollars higher than earlier. Yet the President's advisors were still of the opinion that "the situation at the beginning of the year does not appear to presage a very long or severe slowdown." (*Economic Report,* 1974, p. 23)

Of course, this sentence did not reflect great optimism, either. Its relative optimism only served perhaps the objective of still having the fight against inflation in the centre instead of the recession. But a considerable number of experts outside of government were much more pessimistic. They pointed out that the situation was highly complicated and difficult, and the government had to be very ingenious if it was to cope with these problems with any success. The real danger was precisely—as pointed out by, for example, Mullaney, an expert of *The New York Times*—that the Nixon administration was "sitting" on the problems so long until it is too late to deal with them effectively. Its critics characterized the Nixon administration by saying that it only reacts to events, instead of controlling them actively through planning and foresight. *(International Herald Tribune, January 14, 1974)*

It was also in the first months of the year that Professor Heller analyzed the relationship between the oil situation and economic prospects in 1974 in the *Wall Street Journal*. He emphasized that the oil crisis meant the loss of 600,000 jobs and, in order that the economy could again grow in the second half of the year, the economic policy of the administration had to cope with two decisive tasks. With its energy policy it had to get consumers to reduce their oil consumption, and its economic policy had to focus on the fight against recession. It is worth quoting his statement that "...given a proper response to the energy crunch, the economy's key problem as 1974 wears on will be a shortage of demand, not of fuel.' (*Wall Street Journal*, January 8, 1974).

Finally, for characterizing the situation that developed by the turn of 1973/1974, let us also mention that the stock exchange, still playing to a certain extent the role of economic barometer to this, reflected a situation not at all rosy but laden with problems. This became manifest in the fact that in early January 1974 the Dow Jones index fell by 53 points in three days.

13.3 MONETARY POLICY IN 1974

We attributed the coming about of the mild recession in 1970 to the then restrictive monetary policy. Even then monetary policy could not stop the rise in prices, instead it curtailed the growth of production. But the price rise of those times, measured by the price index of consumer goods (Δp_c) hardly exceeded 4.5 per cent annually. But from 1973 to 1974 the prices of consumer goods rose by almost 10.5 per cent, and also the implicit price index of GNP increased by nearly 10 per cent. If we consider that— except for a large fall in the volume of purchases—rapid inflation can hardly occur without a not negligible increase in the quantity of money in circulation, we have to see that monetary policy can hardly be held primarily responsible for the 1974 recession, since inflation was rapid and the volume of sales had not yet fallen seriously. But monetary policy cannot be relieved of responsibility altogether.

In the 7–8 years before the recession the volume of GNP increased on the annual average by about 4 per cent. But there was inflation at the same time. The price sum of GNP, apart from short-term fluctuations, increased parallel to the M_2 indicator of the quantity of money which, in addition to banknotes and bank account money, also comprises the stock of deposits tied up for shorter or longer periods (with the exception of long-term deposits of large amounts, separetely regulated). Between 1970 and 1974, M_2 increased by about 10 per cent p.a., but the FED—true to its old practice—stepped again on the brakes at the worst moment, even if not very resolutely. For a year, between December 1973 and December 1974, it allowed M_2 to rise by merely 7.3 per cent. This was 1.6 percentage points less than in the preceding year, and 3.8 percentage points less than in 1972. As it turned out, this rise was not enough to cover even the loss of M_2 *in real value*.

We might believe that owing to this restriction inflation ought to have indeed slowed down, while in reality it attained a record level. But we are now interested in another aspect of the matter, namely, how this monetary restriction contributed to the development of the recession.

It contributed directly and mainly through the tense situation developed on the credit markets. This tension became stronger partly independently of the instruments directly applicable by the FED. Thus, in the course of the year the amount of those large deposits increased by 42 per cent which had been placed for some longer time and on which banks paid high rates of interest. But this engaged bank reserves, reducing the possibility of creating bank account money. There were similar consequences when the public increased its cash holdings. (The latter, namely, reduce bank reserves.)

This much is true in any case. But in analyzing what happened in the last resort and the role of monetary policy in it we cannot proceed by separating causes from consequences. In the processes actually taking place causes and consequences become indistinguishably intertwined and we can only speak about mutual influences and mutual adjustment.

Inflation reached a two-digit stage, although the rise in nominal wages did not contribute more tangibly to the price rise than in 1972 when inflation was 4 per cent, and contributed less than in 1973 when there was a 6 per cent price rise. In addition, the taxes and savings of wage earners took much more of the nominal earnings than in earlier years. Only transfers increased so that their price-raising impact grew by one percentage point.

This derived from the jump in unemployment, the latter from the decline in production, and production had to decline since prices were rising so steeply that real demand dropped. This is already a circular argumentation: we are saying that the rise in prices caused prices to rise. True, we can retreat a step. We can say that the profit margin fell to a low in spite of the steep price rise: it became lower than at any time in the 10 years examined. But one of the main reasons for the decline in the profit margin was a very high, about 14 per cent, increase of per unit wage costs. This followed not so much from the rising nominal wage level but from the fall in production. As is expectable in such cases, labour productivity diminished and fixed costs increased. For the time being, they still refrained from large-scale dismissals. Thus, looking for the causes of the recession we again come back to the recession as a cause. And it is a similarly circular reasoning if we state that perhaps the main cause of inflation was the taking root of inflationary expectations. (The rise in oil prices increased inflation directly by about only 2 per cent.) And in such rapid inflation turnover would have required more money than was made available. It followed that rates of interest reached record levels. In an inflation, namely, the lender cannot rest satisfied with a low rate of interest even if demand for credit was slack, and the borrower paid the high nominal rate of interest, since its real size is not so high. In fact, this time most rates of interest were still lower than the annual rate of inflation. Above all, those people lost who held their money in savings institutions. Of course, this was their problem. But mortgage credits, construction credits can be primarily gotten from the savings institutes. Their portfolio was full of older mortgages bearing lower interest, thus they could obtain new lendable funds only with difficulty. Thus, in the last resort, those planning to build or buy a home were the ones to suffer. The events experienced at the beginning of the 1970 recession repeated themselves: construction fell and this was no longer the private affair of those wanting to get a home; it significantly contributed to the decline in production.

Another matter worth mentioning is that government debt also increased, and this, together with the restrained issue of money, also significantly contributed to the private credit squeeze and to the rise in interest rates—with the gravest consequences for consumer credit and mortgages. But this already takes us to the role of the budget, the subject matter of the next section.

13.4 FISCAL POLICY, BUILT-IN STABILIZERS AND THE MARKET STABILIZING ROLE OF GOVERNMENT IN 1974

The part of the 1975 report of the Council of Economic Advisers which analyzed the most advantageous road but which was not at all passable for sure, finally set the economic policy goal to prevent in the first months of the year a prolongation of the decline and, in the later part of the year, to support an upturn, but without stimulating too quick a revival. In this—as manifest in the budget submitted by the President—fiscal policy was given the role of mitigating the slackening of the economy in 1974 but not to stimulate it so much as to make economic growth faster than the average rate. Accordingly, they figured that the balance of the federal budget would show a deficit of $ 4.6 bn, instead of the 0.6 bn surplus in 1973. It was stated—wisely, as a matter of fact—that "in view of the uncertainties facing us, it is extremely important to be prepared with fiscal measures to support or restrain the economy if it is clearly running outside the general track described here for 1974." (*Economic Report,* 1974, pp. 29–30 and 31)

Let us scrutinize how this idea was realized, and what was attained with it in the course of the unfolding recession. The report of the Council of Economic Advisers in February 1975 declared concerning the results—referring to the paradoxical behaviour of the taxation system caused by inflation—that the system of taxation pushed the budget much more in the direction of restriction than had been expected a year earlier. Let us see whether this restrictive effect can be shown.

The balance of the revenues and expenditures of the federal government developed as follows (bn dollars, quarterly data at annual rate, minus sign indicates a deficit):

1973 IV	1974 I	1974 II	1974 III	1974 IV	1973	1974
quarters					whole year	
− 5.3	− 5.5	− 7.6	− 8.0	− 21.7	− 6.7	− 10.7

Before speaking about the importance of the above figures, a remark on methodology is in order. This set of figures covers a field somewhat wider than the federal budget, and comprises final data published years later and modified several times. But this little changes our conclusion that we can unambiguously deduce from a comparison of these figures with the data to be read in the first paragraph of this section. To wit, that instead of producing a shift of $ 5.2 bn from 1973 to 1974 in the direction of stimulating the economy, the shift in the federal budget was only 4 bn. The essential thing still is that the 5.2 bn had been planned for the case that though the economy would somewhat slacken in the first half of the year, it would revive in the second. But in reality, as time went on, the economic situation turned only worse. Thus, the budget exerted a less stimulating effect on an economy developing much more unfavourably than expected. And the data relating to the full year show to some extent an even more advantageous picture than the real one. If, namely, the quarterly data are scrutinized, it is found that between the fourth quarter of 1973 and the third of 1974 the stimulating effect was only 2.7 bn. The deficit became more important in the last quarter, but even then it was about 3 bn less than in the fourth quarter of 1972, in a period of strong upswing in the economy. But the total impact of the budgetary means of the government is not influenced by the federal revenues and expenses alone, the monetary management of state and local bodies also have an impact. It has to be taken into account that the monetary movements directed abroad have no influence on the development of the domestic economy, thus they have to be deducted from the deficit. This is how we arrive at the domestic deficit (or surplus) of the government. This is illustrated below (similarly quarterly data at annual rate, bn $):

1973 IV	1974 I	1974 II	1974 III	1974 IV	1973	1974
		quarters			whole year	
11.5	9.9	9.3	7.2	−10.2	12.7	4.3

These data already reflect some stimulation, since to the growing federal deficit the diminishing surplus of the state and local bodies was added. Thus the stimulating impact comes to 8.4 bn from 1973 to 1974, and to 4.3 bn between the fourth quarter of 1973 and the third one of 1974. Between the third and the fourth quarters the shift is already considerable—17.4 bn—and the deficit in the fourth quarter of 1974 is already a significant surplus expenditure relative to the 2.3 bn surplus in the fourth quarter of 1972. However, in order to see the change between the fourth quarter of 1973 and the third one of 1974, one has to take into account that the sum of 3.4 bn was only 0.3 per cent of the GNP in the fourth quarter of 1973. We may thus safely state that, at least in the course of the three quarters of a year when recession was unfolding, the course of decline was not palpably prevented by the balances of either the federal or the total budget.

Let us also see in detail how the market-regulating role of the state was asserted in this decisive period. Let us start with government purchases of goods and services. (Quarterly data, at annual rate, in 1972 dollars.) Their sum was growing in the 3 quarters following the peak in the fourth quarter of 1973 by 2.6 per cent. For comparison we add here that in the three quarters following the peak this indicator had increased in 1957–1958 by 4.6 per cent. By then the recession came to an end.

The government purchases of durables diminished between the fourth quarter of 1973 and the third of 1974 by 1.7 bn, in the fourth they already started to rise. These purchases by the federal government first fell from $ 9.1 to 7.3 and then rose to 8.2 bn.

In the same period the government expenditure on construction diminished by not quite 1 per cent, federal expenditure by 9 per cent. Federal construction on the whole remained behind that of sixteen years earlier throughout the period of the recession. In the two areas most afflicted by recession (durables and construction) the development of government demand increased the difficulties, instead of stabilizing the market, it acted as a factor sharpening sales problems. (True, the fall in government demand in these sectors was much smaller than that in private demand—in business and consumers' investment.) For comparison, in 1957–1958 government purchase of durables had increased in three quarters by 4.2 and construction by 9.9 per cent. Altogether the direct market purchases of the government (purchases of goods and services less government wages) rose in the first three quarters of the recession from $ 112.5 bn to 116.2 bn, but—and this is perhaps worth mentioning—by the first quarter of 1975 (the trough of the recession!) they even somewhat diminished. Thus, on the whole, direct government purchases did have some market-stabilizing impact, but this asserted itself only on the market of non-durable goods and services hardly or not at all affected by the recession. For comparison, sixteen years earlier direct purchases had increased in three quarters by 10.3 per cent and extended to every main group of commodities.

Examining the indirect market role of the government (based on the wages paid and transfers), and its total role, we find that the former increased through the five quarters of the recession by 8.7 per cent, and the latter by 6.3 per cent. But the comparison shows 1957–1958 to have been more advantageous also in this respect, in three quarters the increase had been 9.6 per cent and 10.0 per cent, respectively.

Looking somewhat ahead, it is worth noting that in 1974–1975 the indirect market role of the state was overwhelming from among the two effects (86.8 per cent), in 1957–1958 the ratios of the two had been almost identical (direct impact 51 per cent, indirect impact 49 per cent).

The shift towards *indirect demand* influences the market-stabilizing ability of the state unfavourably in several respects. First of all, the state hands out money to people in the form of wages and transfers, on the one hand, and takes away, on the other, by levying taxes, and the activities of these two hands are not at all well harmonized in every case. They cannot be, since the state and local bodies paying almost two-thirds of the wages and transfers are motivated by many view-points—sometimes diametrically opposed ones. Furthermore, the households save more or less from the sum remaining after taxes and the movement of savings—at least of those by workers—is of pro-cyclical impact. Direct government purchases are more effective instruments of market stabilization, because they mostly assume the form of orders and relate to definite quantities. (The increase of merely monetary demand does not necessarily entail a growth in the volume sold.) The change is illustrated with two absolute figures more clearly than any indicator of growth or percentage distribution: in three quarters in 1974–1975 government increased demand by 11.1 bn dollars, while in 1957–1958 this had been 14.3 bn during the same time.[30] Thus, in this later recession the government expanded the market less even in absolute terms than it had sixteen years earlier. If we

[30] This, too, as everywhere if not indicated otherwise, should be understood at annual rate, in 1972 dollars.

add that in the first case the market expansion by the state balanced the decline in other components of GNP relative to the quarter immediately preceding the depression to the extent of 45.1 per cent and to 27.1 per cent in the other, it becomes clear that the market-stabilizing role of the state asserted itself much less in 1974–1975 than in 1957–1958.

The Government levies taxes and allocates money incomes. The ratio of the two significantly influences the development of disposable personal income. As was shown by one of the authors (Molnár, 1970, pp. 238–39) in the sixties the most important change in the capitalist recession after World War II was that a given decline in output and investment entailed a much smaller decrease in disposable income than had been the case earlier. It is mostly this phenomenon that prevents the strong evolution of cumulative processes releasing a deepening of the recessions. A few years later we investigated this process in a broader context. (P. Erdős and F. Molnár, 1969, pp. 907–923)

Let us now scrutinize the problem also from the aspect of the recession just examined. It happened that in the last quarter of 1973 the government handed out with its right hand (we think it justified to call 'right' the hand that gives) 140.7 bn dollars in the form of wages and salaries[31] and 108.2 bn in the form of transfers (altogether 248.9 bn) to individuals and at the same time levied 145 bn in personal income tax and dues, etc. It was thus the source of $ 103.9 bn net personal income. Three quarters later the net impact still was only 106.9 bn.

At the end of three quarters afflicted by recession the state levied personal taxes in higher real value than at the peak of the business cycle. Owing to rapid inflation the direct taxes otherwise acting as built-in stabilizers had a paradoxical effect. In the course of the significant increase in nominal wages and salaries accompanying inflation many people got into higher income brackets from the view-point of taxation, even though their real income diminished, and this significantly increased taxes. The state did nothing against this. In this period, economists and government experts regularly underestimated the expectable depth of the recession as well as the rate of inflationary price increase. They had to replace their forecasts continually with more pessimistic ones. (Okun, 1975, pp. 214–216) It thus happened that the average federal tax burden on on-transfer personal incomes rose from 12.2 per cent in 1973 to 13 per cent in 1974, the year of recession. In addition, the contribution of wage earners to social insurance was also increased.

But let us return to our figures. We have seen that in the third quarter of 1974 the government contributed 3.0 bn more to the personal incomes than at the peak of the cycle, but in the meantime incomes from other sources diminished by more than 23 bn and this was compensated by a net increase in incomes from government sources to the extent of only 15 per cent. Since the tax burden increased and wages shrank, the compensation derived exclusively from the increase in transfers. For comparison, in 1957–1958 wages paid by government had increased by 1.5 bn and transfers by 6.2 bn,

[31] Of course, in terms of 1972 dollars, as every other data of this computation. American statistics publish these only in current dollars. Since these incomes are spent on consumption, we converted them to 1972 dollars by division by the implicit price index of consumer expenditure. So they are comparable to other data, primarily to the disposable incomes published also in this manner.

while taxes had diminished by 2.9 bn, thus the net increase in incomes from government sources had been 10.6 per cent (in absolute terms three times the amount of that in 1974–1975), and this had compensated by over three-quarters the fall in other personal incomes. The result had been that disposable personal incomes fell by only 3 bn instead of the 20 bn in 1974.

13.5 THE DEVELOPMENT OF PRODUCTION AND DEMAND IN 1974

In the first quarter of 1974 the most comprehensive indicator of output (in the wider sense, thus also comprising services) began to decline. The rate of decline then was 3.9 per cent.[32] In the second and third quarters this rate became somewhat more moderate, but in the fourth it soared to 5.5 per cent. Between the last quarters of 1973 and 1974, GNP fell by 3.5 per cent, and in the whole of 1974 its volume lagged by 1.4 per cent behind that of the preceding year.

From among the indicators of production we only stress that the decline in construction was almost 16 per cent within a year and 13 per cent from 1973 to 1974. Construction activity was much more gravely afflicted by the recession than durable goods, which is quite an unusual phenomenon in the post-war period, one of the distinguishing features of the recession.

Data on purchases, that is, on the development of realized demand, provide a possibility for a more detailed orientation.

Purchases for personal consumption (computed without purchases of homes) essentially stagnated in 1973. More exactly, the peak was in the third quarter of 1973 and this was followed by decline through two quarters and a rise in a further two, only to decline again—for the last time in the course of this recession—in the last quarter of 1974. The decline between the last mentioned quarter and the corresponding period of 1973 was 1.7, while between 1973 and 1974 it was 0.9 per cent. Within personal consumer expenditures the purchase of durables peaked already in the first quarter of 1973, and then fell at varying rates through five quarters. This was replaced in the third quarter of 1974 by a slight increase, but it was followed in the last quarter of the year by the sharpest fall of the whole period of recession—33.8 per cent at annual rate—reaching at the same time the trough. At that time the volume of these purchases was 16.5 per cent lower than at the peak; 1974 as a whole lagged behind 1973 by 7.6 per cent.

The purchase of non-durable consumer goods also peaked in the first quarter of 1973. Following it, until the trough in the fourth quarter of 1974, there was decline in five quarters and a rise in two. On the whole, the volume of this kind of demand lagged in the last quarter of 1974 by 2.2 per cent behind the same quarter of a year before.

The volume of services bought by consumers was rising throughout the recession, even if more slowly.

Although the market of durable goods is made up by consumers' purchases to major extent, due to its importance we have to discuss also the purchases of these goods for

---

[32] Our data are based also henceforth on volumes given in 1972 dollars, at annual rate, and the percentual changes are also meant at annual rate.

investment purposes.[33] Their volume peaked only in the second quarter of 1974. This was followed by a stagnation through the next quarter and then by a decline through five quarters, attaining the trough merely at the end of 1975. In the last quarter of 1974 the sales of these goods lagged behind the volume of a year earlier by only 3.1 per cent, and as regards the year as a whole, 1974 was 3 per cent above the 1973 level. No doubt it has to be qualified as a particular feature that in the year of the unfolding of the recession more was invested into machinery and equipment than in the previous year which qualified as one of overheated business. This is yet another contribution to the fact that this recession was mainly one of consumers' investment. Although it is true that the total private fixed capital investment including also investment constructions attained its peak earlier (in the first quarter of 1974), the two troughs nevertheless coincided. The volume of fixed capital investment in the last quarter of 1974 was 6.3 per cent lower than in the corresponding period of 1973. In 1974 as a whole, however, it remained essentially on the level of the preceding year. From this we might also conclude that the decline actually experienced in this field can be traced back to the decline in investment construction. Indeed, the volume of the latter had its peak already in the third quarter of 1973, in the last one of 1974 it already lagged by more than 12 per cent behind the level in the last quarter of 1973, and in 1974 as a whole it was 6.6 per cent less than in the preceding year.

Housing construction—similarly to the purchase of consumer durables—attained the peak already in the first quarter of 1973 and then sharply declined through two full years every quarter. The extent of the decline was 26.5 per cent in one year, that is, till the last quarter of 1974, and 24.6 per cent from 1973 to 1974.

From what has been said it follows that also the volume of consumers' investments had their peak in the first quarter of 1973, and fell similarly sharply through two years. This fall was in the fourth quarter of 1974, 16.3 per cent relative to a year earlier, and 13.2 per cent from 1973 to 1974. A comparison of this pair of data with the similar ones of fixed capital investment supports those said about the nature of the recession.

The third component of private investment, the accumulation of inventories, deserves particular attention because of its special development. We find, namely, that after the peak in the fourth quarter of 1973, when its volume soared very high—to more than 25 bn in terms of 1972 dollars—the extent of inventory accumulation showed a diminishing tendency throughout 1974, but remained always positive, that is, stocks continued to grow during the evolution of the depression. This is an unusual phenomenon, since in every serious post-war recession, both in 1948–1949 and in 1957–1958, stocks had started to diminish with the decline in GNP also in absolute terms, and the reduction continued through 3–4 quarters, although these recessions had taken place in a shorter time than the 1974–1975 recession. This phenomenon, slowing down the fall in GNP, was by all means related to the accelerating inflation, to seeking protection against further price rises. Thus it could not last long.

The volume of net exports increased in 1973 every quarter and this continued in the first one of 1974. In the next two quarters it essentially stagnated, but in the last one net exports again increased and jumped almost 40 per cent higher than a year earlier.

[33] Looking back on rows 2 and 6 of Table 13.1 on p. 197 we can establish that the ratio to each other of purchases of investment goods and consumer durables was 1:1.4 in 1973.

Considering 1974 as a whole, it was more than double of the preceding year. We face here the surprising phenomenon that external economic factors (the price explosion of oil and raw materials, the oil embargo) by all means had a negative impact, deteriorating the balance of trade, the latter still showed a surplus and had a mitigating effect on the moderation of demand in the course of the evolution of the recession. (In this the devaluation of the dollar had an important role.)

Government purchases were already discussed in connection with the market stabilizing role of the state (pp. 203–205).

The trend-like group of demand further increased in the course of the year—in conformity with its nature—and a minimum decline, tantamount to stagnation, was to be found only in the last quarter. As against that, the cyclical group, after stagnation in 1973, began to fall strongly in the first quarter of 1974. This tendency prevailed throughout the year, and in the last quarter the volume of this group of demand was already 16.7 per cent lower than a year before, and in 1974 it lagged 10 per cent behind the 1973 level. The irregular group remained in the second quarter on a level identical with that of the first one, but then continued to grow, essentially smoothly.

From what was described above we can draw the conclusion that in the course of 1974 the recession developed with increasing force almost from quarter to quarter. At the same time, we may also establish that in this process it was not at all the decline in fixed capital investment, but, looking at the matter from the aspect of demand, primarily that of consumers' investment that played the main role. No doubt, it contributed to the evolution of the recession that the market regulation role of government demand in compensating the decline in private demand hardly asserted itself, if at all.

To partially explain the above development of consumers' investment let us mention that the volume of disposable personal incomes showed only a minimum increase in 1973, then diminished through five quarters beginning with the first one of 1974, and in the last quarter it was already 2.9 per cent lower than at the peak a year before. In 1974 as a whole, it lagged behind that of the preceding year by 1.5 per cent.

To conclude this section, let us have a look at the development of an indicator generally considered characteristic of the relationship between production and demand, how the former reacts to the latter. We are thinking of the exploitation of productive capacities. Although this indicator is available only for manufacturing, and although this branch contributed in 1973 only 24.5 per cent of the total GNP, yet, since it is most sensitive to business fluctuations, showing the biggest fluctuations, it may be considered as a good barometer of business.

In manufacturing the utilization of capacities stagnated in the last three quarters of 1973 around 87.7 per cent. The fall in capacity utilization started together with the decline in production, in the first quarter of 1974, when it fell to 85.7 per cent. In the next half a year decline was slow, but accelerated in the last quarter. Then it was only 79.7 per cent, that is, it stood 8 percentage points lower than a year before. Considering the whole of 1974, capacity utilization was 3.2 percentage points worse than in the preceding year.[34]

[34] The data are computed by using the index of the Federal Reserve Board. See *Economic Report* 1978, p. 305.

The ever worsening production and employment situation in 1974 also led to a deterioration in the position of wage earners. This was perhaps most conspicuously indicated by the steep rise in unemployment, particularly in the second half of the year. The number of unemployed increased from 4.5 mn in January to 6.6 mn in the last month of the year. These absolute figures correspond to annual rates of 5.0 and 7.2 per cent. Parallel to the rapid growth of unemployment a paradoxical process also took place, namely, in the first half of the year the number of non-agricultural wage earners even continued to increase; in spite of the palpably developing recession it attained peak level in September, almost 800,000 higher than in January. As a matter of fact, industrial output did not yet diminish in that period, thus in this sector, generally most sensitively affected by recessions, there had been no lay-offs and the managers of capitalist firms expected that the recession would be slight and end soon. On this account, and also because of problems emerging in some fields in connection with skilled labour, they made efforts to keep the labour force, particularly those with skills. But in the second half of the year, although for the time being at a slow rate, lay-offs started and employment declined by December by 1.1 mn relative to September and by about 300,000 relative to January. Thus, considering the year as a whole, the main source of growing unemployment was not so much those dropping out of work, but rather those seeking first employment in vain. Owing to slackening business, also the weekly number of hours worked by a worker diminished. This in itself acted towards reducing wages. Real earnings were even more reduced by the increasing inflation with which wage rises did not keep pace. The deterioration in the position of wage earners is definitely shown by the development of disposable weekly wages which, owing to the perverse functioning of the taxation system, fell by 4.6 per cent between the first and the last months of the year, and, considering the whole of 1974, were 5 per cent lower than in the preceding year.[35]

The sum of nominal wages and salaries paid out continued to rise in spite of slackening business; their sum was 8.2 per cent higher in the last quarter of 1974 than it had been a year before. In real terms (deflated by the implicit price index of consumers' expenses) there was already a decline of 3.3 per cent.

13.7 NEW PRESIDENT—OLD ECONOMIC POLICY

As amply shown by the data reviewed in section 4 of this chapter, the recession had robustly evolved in the first quarter of 1974. Almost all indicators relevant from this aspect deteriorated month by month, quarter by quarter. Parallel to that another process took place, not an economic one, yet with very harmful impacts on the economy. The position of President Nixon was increasingly shaken by the unfolding Watergate affair. The harmful impact on the economy was manifest in that the defence of his own shaken position—later proved untenable—took more and more of the

---

[35] The source of the data used in this section: *Economic Report* 1977, tables on pp. 221–227.

attention of the President and thus he could devote less attention and energy to the deterioration of the economic situation.

The only significant economic measure of this period was the complete liquidation of the remnants of price and wage controls in April, which, of course, further aggravated the situation by giving free way to inflation.

The economic experts of the President—at least as it can be judged from their public declarations—did not lose their optimism in spite of the worsening of the situation. Stein, chairman of the Council of Economic Advisers, still believed in May that the real growth rate of the economy would reach 3–4 per cent in the second half of the year and the rate of inflation would fall to 6 percent—measured by consumer prices. (*Neue Zürcher Zeitung,* May 13, 1974) The delusive optimism, so it seems, reached beyond government circles and even beyond the boundaries of the country, since the *Neue Zürcher Zeitung,* known for its excellent economic analyses, even at the end of July put a question mark after the title: "Economic recession in the United States?" It was under such circumstances that in early August an unprecedented event took place: The President was compelled to resign ignominiously.

The change in the person of the President might have been a good opportunity to replace the impotent and successful economic policy by a new and better one. This possibility and expectation was expressed in an open letter in the *Wall Street Journal* to Gerald Ford, the President taking office, by Professor Heller, the reputed economist already quoted several times in this book.

Stating that the first problem was inflation, he immediately called attention to the danger that, following bad tradition, the economic advisers of the President would seek the solution in strict monetary policy and in trimming the budget. (The conservative Stein was replaced as chairman of the Council of Economic Advisers by the even more conservative Greenspan, directly related to business circles.) He pointed out that the price to be paid would be grave unemployment and asked the justified question why the "game plan", which had so miserably failed in 1968–1971, would work in 1974–1975. He established that an economic policy reducing demand would not lead to success, only measures stimulating supply would bring an easing of the situation. The many kinds of excessive government regulations leading to raising prices had to be abolished, while the rise in productivity must not be prevented by a policy delaying the upswing. The results of the anti-inflationary policy had to be compared with the costs involved by it, which also meant that the burdens of this fight ought to be distributed in a socially more just manner. (*Wall Street Journal,* August 12, 1974)

The letter had no effect. Also a mistaken assessment of the situation might have contributed to this, since at the end of August one of the heads of the most respected business research institutes of the country, the National Bureau of Economic Research of New York, an acknowledged expert on the problem, Geoffrey Moore, declared that if matters did not turn much worse, there would not be any recession. (*International Herald Tribune,* September 1, 1974) Incidentally, the same institute and the same authority put the beginning of the recession, *post festum,* at November 1973.

Under such conditions it almost seems self-explanatory that Ford's new team, about whom even the *Neue Zürcher Zeitung* wrote that they constituted a strengthening of the conservative element, remained true to themselves and the result of the economic summit held at the end of September was an economic policy which pushed the economy into an even deeper recession. No wonder that it attracted criticism by both political parties. Ford's economic program, published in early October, also had elements corresponding to the given situation—as, e.g., the extension of unemployment benefits—but it also comprised such which was the worst possible thing in the given circumstances: the introduction of a 5 per cent surtax on both enterprise and personal incomes. On the whole, it was a lopsided program, devoid of courageous initiative. The poor results are well-known.

CHAPTER FOURTEEN

1975: THE TROUGH AND TURN IN THE RECESSION

14.1 ASSESSMENT OF THE SITUATION BY THE FORD ADMINISTRATION
AT THE BEGINNING OF THE YEAR
AND ECONOMIC POLICY IDEAS FOR 1975

The first sentence of the 1975 Economic Report testifies to the fact in the half a year between the President's taking of office and the submission of the Report to Congress the "penny had dropped". The sentence reads as follows: "The economy is in a severe recession."[36] This statement was by all means true. It also correctly identified the key problems of the economy. These were recession, inflation and the energy problem. As a main task it denoted the restoration of equilibrium in the economy, upset in many respects, and it suggested adequate fiscal and monetary policy—complemented by other initiatives—as the main tools. No doubt, it was also a correct recognition that the tasks to be solved could not always be reconciled.[37] In January, the President already also submitted his proposal providing for a $ 16 bn tax reduction as a tool of the fight against recession, which we may safely call a crisis. And the Council of Economic Advisers stated in its detailed analysis: "The momentum of the decline is so great that a quick turn-around and a strong recovery in economic activity are not yet assured. But prompt action on the Administration's proposals to stimulate the economy should hasten the end of the recession and contribute to the pace of recovery during the second half of the year."[38] From among the proposals aimed at stimulating the economy—beyond the tax reduction mentioned, to the implementation and consequences of which we shall return—we would mention the investment tax rebate, an energy program of several components, the increase of deficit spending, more efficient aid to the unemployed, and expansion of public works. (It should be noted that the estimated deficit of the federal budget for the fiscal year of 1976—Oct. 1, 1975 to Sept. 30, 1976—was 51.9 bn dollars, against 34.7 bn in the preceding year.)

It seems—at least in the knowledge of later developments—that by then experts were already too pessimistic in respect of both the assessment of the momentum of the recession and the effectiveness of the proposed measures. Namely, the decline in GNP attained the trough in the first quarter of 1975. And, as regards the impact of the measures, they believed they could mitigate the fall in the real GNP relative to the preceding year by 0.5–1.0 percentage points, but even so, in the average of 1975, output

---

[36] *Economic Report* 1975, p. 3.
[37] *Op. cit.*, pp. 3–8.
[38] *Op. cit.*, p. 19.

would lag behind 1974 by about 3 percent.[39] (In the end this decline turned out to be 1.3 per cent.)

The quotations testify to a decisive turn in the economic policy approach of the Ford administration; the weight of economic policy shifted to the fighting of recession. In September of the preceding year their standpoint was still that the only problem of the country was inflation, and its demand-pull kind at that. (This standpoint had been represented by Greenspan, chairman of the Council of Economic Advisers, Secretary of the Treasury Simon and by Friedman, the "pope" of the monetarists.)

The change in direction is also worth stressing because at that time not only the United States, but also the other advanced capitalist countries were in the deepest post-war recession and all looked to Washington to see how and with what results the blow afflicting all of them was fought. They were of the opinion—not without foundation—that the fight would be decided mostly there, and it depended on whether in 1975 recovery would start or the recession would turn into a worldwide one—the first since the thirties.

This is how also Professor Samuelson put the question in the respected British *Financial Times,* in his usual article for the New Year. His answer sounded optimistic—precisely because of the shift in the American economic policy approach—and he was of the opinion that in the second half of 1975 the American economy would again take the road to growth. According to him, those who prophesied a new Great Depression, did not remember what the Great Depression really had been like. There would be serious economic and political problems, but there would be no Great Depression.[40]

14.2 A ROUNDABOUT TURN IN FISCAL POLICY: THE 1975 TAX REDUCTION AND SUPPORT OF THE TURN BY MONETARY POLICY

As mentioned, in Janury 1975, President Ford proposed a 16 bn dollar tax reduction. This tax reduction was intended to be temporary, lasting a year and, as a matter of fact, it was aimed at compensating taxpayers (individuals to the amount of 12 bn, and firms to the extent of 4 bn) for the "excess taxes" paid on account of the already discussed paradoxical behaviour of the taxation system in consequence of the high, two-digit inflation rate.

In the course of the usual skirmishes between the President and Congress the original proposal underwent significant modification and by April, when it was enacted, both its nature and its sum changed. It no longer meant merely a compensation, but brought changes in the structure of the taxation system itself, while the sum in question increased to about $ 25 bn. Some of the measures were meant for a year, others for several years or were lasting ones. According to information published by the Treasury of the United States at the end of March, the annual sum of tax reductions affecting individuals was 18.1 bn, while that relating to firms 4.8 bn. Pensioners obtained a one-time grant of 50 dollars per head, amounting altogether to

[39] *Op. cit.,* pp. 20–27.
[40] *The Financial Times*, December 31, 1974.

1.7 bn. At the same time, certain allowances were withdrawn from the oil industry which increased budget revenues by 1.6 bn a year. (Fellner, 1975, Appendix, pp. 37–42.)

Experts were of the opinion that the tax reduction compensated individual taypayers for their surplus payments caused by inflation in the preceding years. (*Op. cit.* pp. 8–9)

We cannot know for sure what would have happened without the tax reduction. A reduction of taxes may even lead to increased inflation. Though argumentation of the *post hoc, propter hoc* type is always risky, this reduction of taxes had indeed a favourable impact—as it will turn out from our following analysis. Naturally, it changed in the most direct manner the revenues of the federal government, thus also its balance and the total government balance, and highly significantly at that (the data to be listed are again quarterly ones at annual rate). In the second quarter, the revenues of the federal government fell from 287.2 bn in the first quarter to 254.3 bn. Corresponding to the nature of the reduction, the decline primarily affected personal taxes: their sum fell from 137.4 bn to 99.6 bn. Since, simultaneously with the decline in revenues, expenditure increased almost exactly by the same amount as in the preceding quarter, the deficit of the federal government increased from $ 48 bn to 99.9 bn. And the total (domestic) government deficit increased from 38.1 bn in the preceding quarter to 87.8 bn, as the surplus of the state and local organs somewhat increased. (The rise was 130 per cent!) A nominal change of such amount was quite unprecedented in the history of the country.

The deficit of the federal government shown in official statistics (not the one we have called domestic) increased in the second quarter of 1975 by 51.9 bn as a result of diminishing revenues and simultaneously growing expenditure. This could only partially be attributed to the tax reduction. If the fall in revenues had been entirely a consequence of the tax reduction—but this assumption would cause an upward distortion—only 63.3 per cent of the increment in deficit could have been traced back to this measure. But the law on tax reduction also contained such not strictly tax measures which increased the outlays of the budget. Their sum was estimated at $ 2 bn.[41] A further part of the increment of outlays can be traced essentially to two factors, namely, the automatic increase in payments related to various programs and to the increased support allocated by the federal government to state and local bodies. The production-stimulating impact of fiscal policy was also mitigated by the fact that the purchases by the federal government of goods and services increased only insignificantly at current prices and essentially remained on the earlier level in terms of volume. Even if we do not look at the quarter immediately following the tax reduction, but confront the whole of 1975 with the preceding year, the growth in the volume of government purchases did not even attain 2 per cent. The growth in government demand for durable goods, strongly affected by the recession, was very slight and it even decreased in the case of construction, although this branch was most gravely hit by the recession.

Ceteris paribus, the increase in government deficit increases the after-tax gross profit

---

[41] Publication by the US Treasury on March 29, 1975. See Fellner, 1975, Appendix p. 39.

by its own amount. But nothing ever happens *ceteris paribus*. The increase in profits deriving from higher deficit is greatest, that is, the number of countervailing factors is smallest, if the increment of the deficit is spent altogether on domestic purchases of goods and services. In this case, namely, we have to reckon only with the effect of the import increment usually necessary for increased production and this reduces the trade surplus, thus also profits. This time it was not the most advantageous case that actually occurred. What happened was that the increased deficit appeared practically exclusively in the growth of disposable personal incomes. Both the tax reduction and the rise in transfer payment acted in this sense. But the rate of savings jumped from 6.4 per cent to 9.7 per cent from one quarter to the next, because almost 60 (!) per cent of the increment in incomes had been saved. Something similar must have been true also for the wage earners, since—according to our estimates—their savings in the whole year were higher than in the preceding one. But the increment of the savings of wage earners reduces profits—*ceteris paribus*—by its own amount and thereby hinders the revival of business. We might thus say that as regards the turn in the economy the tax reduction was not as effective as it could have been had it not been exhausted by the increase in personal incomes, but would have resulted at least partially, or even in most part, in a growth of government purchases.

For the sake of fairness, two comments are in order. It is certain that in general, and even more so in a recession, it is more popular or more acceptable to reduce taxes than to increase government purchases. By what right does the government increase its much criticized "waste" precisely when everybody else is compelled to tighten his belt? Such a thing could not have been "sold"—to use an Americanism—not even to an adequately manipulated public, but we may safely say that the business world and economists would not have accepted it either. As a matter of fact, few of them know the interrelations—formulated in Kalecki's theory or deriving from it—on the basis of which, e.g., capitalists and their representatives in Congress could understand that it was better also for them if the government rather spent the sum, with which it would otherwise reduce their taxes, on the building of hospitals and schools.

On the other hand, a significant increase in government purchases is usually coupled with higher military expenditure. What actually happened was still better than that.

In view of the recession and unemployment, in 1975 the FED did not resort to monetary restrictions. What it did was that, in principle, it set the limit of money outflow at 7.5 per cent p.a. in respect of M_1 and at 10.5 per cent p.a. for M_2. These figures were significantly higher than the 1974 ones. Nevertheless, what actually happened was that the growth of M_1—at annual rate—somewhat lagged behind that of the preceding year—which was of a restrictive nature—by merely 1 per cent. It was not the FED that forced this, it just happened that way. Namely, the greater part of 1975 was already characterized by revival, but GNP still moved at a very low level, and also the rate of inflation slowed down. Already these two developments put a brake on the demand for money. From this aspect, at least three important events also contributed. The first was that the tax reduction involved not insignificant tax refunds and this entailed an abundance of money even without new credits. The second was that the rise in nominal wages slowed down. The total earnings per man-hour increased by 7.6 per cent, against 10.6 per cent in 1974. (In the second and third quarters the wage rate of the production costs even diminished, although in the first quarter it rose—at annual rate—by almost 10 per cent and in 1974 as a whole by more than 14 per cent.) (*Economic Report*, 1976, pp. 74–75) And the third event was a large-scale reduction of stocks, and this, too, significantly reduced the demand for credit, thus for money.

The quarterly data show a rather considerable fluctuation. In January, M_1 even decreased, and the growth rate of M_2 slowed down between December 1974 and January 1975. In the second quarter the growth of M_1—at annual rate—was 11.7 per cent, while in the third—precisely when the price of GNP was rising steeply—the growth of the stock of money slowed down. And this picture did not undergo significant modification even in the fourth quarter. Interest rates, however, increased but slightly in the third quarter over the levels in the first and second quarters, thus relatively slightly in view of the fact that the rate of interest on commercial credits fell from a level approaching 12 per cent in the second quarter of 1974 to 7 per cent.

To sum up, this time the FED pursued an accomodating monetary policy.

14.3 REFLECTION OF THE 1975 TURN IN THE DEVELOPMENT OF OUTPUT AND DEMAND

The curve of production (GNP) fell in the first quarter of the decade much more sharply than in any earlier quarter of the depression; the rate of decline attained 9.1 per cent (at annual rate, at 1972 prices). With this output reached its trough, and in this quarter it lagged 5.7 per cent below the peak in the fourth quarter of 1973. The decline, continuing with varying acuteness through five quarters was followed in the next two quarters by a rise, although the rate became significantly mitigated by the last quarter of the year (the corresponding rates are 6.4, 10.5, 2.6 per cent). Even so, production did not attain the peak of two years before and remained below that by 1.2 per cent. As regards the year as a whole, GNP was 1.3 per cent below the level of the preceding year and 2.7 per cent below that of two years earlier.

The turn in business showed unambiguously also in the production of durables which are decisive from this aspect. Its curve moved synchronously with that of GNP, but both its fall in the first quarter (36.6 per cent!) and the following turn (13.8 and 19.9 per cent rise in the second and third quarters) were much sharper than the corresponding movements of GNP. But in the fourth quarter their growth completely stopped. At the trough the output of durables was 14.6 per cent lower than at the peak in the second quarter of 1973, and in the fourth quarter it was not only significanly below the peak (by 6.9 per cent), but also 5 per cent below the level of a year earlier, reflecting already a decline during the recession. As regards the year as a whole, the level of output of these goods was 6.8 per cent below that of a year earlier and around 10 per cent below that of two years earlier.

Up to now we have written about production, and not about the volume of purchases. The following data provide information about the latter.

Purchases serving personal consumption started to rise, after a fall through five quarters, already in the first quarter of 1975, earlier than any other important type of demand. In this quarter the rate of growth was still slight, accelerating in the next and remaining significant in the last two (7.0, 5.0 and 5.9 per cent). In the last quarter it was already considerably higher than at the trough a year earlier, and even exceeded the peak of the third quarter in 1973 by 3 per cent. Considering the year as a whole, the level of consumption was 1.8 per cent higher than in the preceding year and 0.9 per cent higher than in 1973. Within this expenditure, the purchase of consumer durables started to grow similarly in the first quarter of the year, and at a rather fast rate. This significantly accelerated in the next two quarters and was considerable even in the last quarter of the year (11.8, 22.8 and 16.5 per cent, respectively). Since, however, the fall in demand was very sharp in 1974, this indicator lagged behind the peak value even in the last quarter of 1975.

Similarly to the item of consumption just discussed, the purchase of non-durable consumer goods also started to grow in the first quarter of 1975, though only to a minimum extent. In the next quarter this rate accelerated, but slowed down again in the last two quarters. In spite of this, in the last quarter of 1974 it was merely half a per cent lower than the highest pre-recession level. As regards the year as a whole, it exceeded the level of the preceding year by 0.9 per cent, but remained below that of 1973 by the same percentage.

Also the volume of services bought by consumers increased every quarter in the course of 1975 at a steadily rising rate.

The purchase of durables for business investment fell in the course of 1975 every quarter, but the rate of decline became already significantly modified in the second half of the year. (In the first quarter it was 17.3, in the last only 1.9 per cent.) From all types of demand this was that which attained the trough the last—with a fall of 16.7 per cent. Total fixed business capital investment developed similarly in terms of volume. The decline was steepest in the first quarter, but became minimum by the last one. Then, at the trough, it lagged below the peak of seven quarters before by 16.6 per cent. In 1975 as a whole, fixed capital investment was 13.0 per cent less than in the preceding year and 13.3 per cent less than in 1973. We can thus see that this type of demand, widely held to be the main motor of short-term economic fluctuations, fell the latest from among the important groups of demand, and was also the last to start to recover in 1976!

The steep fall in housing construction continued in the first quarter of 1975, but with this it came to an end as well. The 30.5 per cent fall in this quarter was followed by a moderate growth in the next, and a strong one (of more than 30 per cent) in the second half of the year. At the trough, the volume of housing construction was 43.6 per cent below the peak of two years earlier, and lagged 34.4 per cent behind it even in the last quarter of 1975.

From what has been said it already follows that the group of consumers' investment attained its trough similarly in the first quarter of 1975, although by then the decline was already slight, since the largest component of the group as regards volume, the purchase of consumer durables, already started to rise. Even this included, in this quarter the volume of consumers' investment was almost one quarter less than at the peak, and even in the fourth quarter it lagged almost 15 per cent behind the peak, in spite of the rise in the preceding quarters of the year.

In respect of the third element of private investment, inventory accumulation, there was a great change precisely in the first half of 1975, and not upwards, but downwards; in the course of the recession this was the first period in which stocks already diminished, and at a considerable rate at that. The rise, still continuing in the last quarter of 1974, was now replaced by a fall of $ 19.4 bn. This shift reduced GNP by $

26.2 bn in a quarter and was a main factor in that the fall of GNP was sharpest precisely in this quarter. From the 28.1 bn of the latter no less than 93 per cent may be attributed to the shift. The reduction of inventories continued in the next quarter at a rapid rate, then became slight in the third quarter and somewhat accelerated again in the fourth.

The volume of net exports continued to grow in the first two quarters and attained 27.4 bn by the second. In the next half year it somewhat diminished, but still remained on a high level and was a positive factor in the recovery.

Examining the three large groups of demand, we may establish that the trend-like group increased in every quarter, if at a fluctuating rate; it was slowest in the first and fastest in the second. The cyclical group—true to its name corresponding to its nature—fell steeply in the first quarter of 1975 (49 per cent), slowly in the second (2.8 per cent), while it rose steeply in the third (43.2 per cent) and practically stagnated in the fourth. The volume of this group of demand lagged behind the peak by 27.1 per cent at the trough and by 18.7 per cent even in the last quarter of the year. Regarding the whole of 1975, it was 13.8 per cent lower than in the preceding year and 22.4 per cent lower than in 1973. The irregular group perceptibly increased in the first two quarters, somewhat diminished in the third and stagnated in the fourth. The odd movement in the second quarter, which was not anti-cyclical, may be attributed to the movement of the government deficit, in connection with the already mentioned tax reduction.

From the above reviewed data on the development of output and sales in 1975, and as we have already stated, it may be unambiguously said that 1975 was the trough year of the recession, then that of the turn of the initially rather slack recovery. Both output and sales started to rise in terms of volume. We speak about recovery precisely when both output and sales begin to grow. At the first moment it may seem that there is nothing to ponder concerning the simultaneous start in the growth of these two categories. As a matter of fact, there are in this context problems really worth considering. We have to report, as far as it is possible, on the main springs of the recovery.

We have already mentioned several times that it is a widespread view, accepted also in university curricula, that it is the revival of investment, not of consumption, i.e., precisely of the production of (and demand for) investment goods that can lift the economy out of the trough. As regards the recessions of the *classical* type, this is the standpoint also of Péter Erdős, one of the authors of this book. But the recession presently examined was not of the classical type.

It also turns out from Table 14.1 relating to the use of GNP, that in the turn, in the starting of the recovery, fixed capital investment not only did not play a positive role through a relatively long period, lasting three quarters, but with its decline it precisely hindered the turn and put a brake on the momentum of the emerging recovery.

In similar cases, Western economists usually say that the revival of consumers' demand was the main pulling power in the initial unfolding. This formulation is in harmony with Keynesian theory. Namely, for Keynes the direct cause of recession or stagnation was always the insufficiency of "demand". This can be traced even more clearly in the reasoning of his followers, than in Keynes' own work. In their view, consumers' demand may as effectively complement deficient investment demand as the growth in investment demand can complement too low consumer demand. But, first of all, by increasing demand in the first and direct sense of the word increase in monetary demand should be meant, that is, that people (or organizations, institutions) spend more money on purchases than before. In principle, this may have two effects: either the volume of sales increases, or prices will rise. These two processes may take place even simultaneously, but either of the two may occur without the other. We can only

Table 14.1

Distribution of the use of the increment in GNP between the
1st and 4th quarters of 1975

Items	Billions of 1972 dollars	Percentage distribution
GNP	56.3	100.0
Personal consumption	33.9	60.2
Durables	13.3	23.6
Services	13.1	23.3
Fixed capital investment	− 5.9	− 10.5
Residential construction	6.0	10.7
Changes in inventories	14.2	25.2
Net exports	1.7	3.0
Government purchases	6.4	11.4
Federal purchases	1.4	2.5
Addenda:		
Consumers' investment	19.3	34.3
Auto product	11.4	20.2

speak of improving business if the volume of both output and sales increases. To restrict ourselves to demand: business is improving if not only nominal, but also real demand grows. But whether real demand indeed grows depends not only on the amount of demand in terms of money and not even only on the side of demand alone, but also on the side of supply. And if the total volume of goods for sale is considered to be the supply, and if also stocks are sufficiently large, then real demand depends beyond nominal demand also on prices. Thus, if recovery has indeed occurred or started, and not in the investment sector but in the consumer sector, then the statement that increased demand was the main factor in the evolution of recovery is somewhat hazy and requires more accurate analysis.

Secondly, if indeed not only nominal demand increases, but also the volume of commodities sold, while production is not yet increasing, then we cannot speak of a real recovery. In such cases it is the disinvestment of inventories that balances the growth in the volume of sales.

Thirdly, it is not at all the same in which sector output and, together with it, "real demand" increased. If more investment goods are produced and bought than earlier, this clearly increases the volume of profits. The same is true if more consumer goods are produced and the surplus is consumed by capitalists. If, however, this surplus (or part of it) is bought by workers out of their current incomes, then this additional production and purchase increases profits only if the savings by workers were previously greater and now became smaller. (This follows from Kalecki's profit formula.) As a matter of fact, if with growing production and real consumption profits do not develop at least relatively more favourably, then this growth can hardly be accompanied by any lasting recovery.

Having said all that by way of introduction, considering that everything is related to everything else and that the dilemma of the hen and the egg can never be resolved, let us answer the question about the main factor in the recovery.

Of course, it is clear from Table 14.1 that the lion's share of the increment of "real demand" fell to personal consumption (60.2 per cent). And if the purchase of homes is also included, this component accounts for more than 70 per cent of the increment. But the real value of the most important direct source of this demand, of disposable personal incomes, even diminished slightly in the first quarter of 1975 (by 2.5 per cent). This reduction was somewhat more pronounced than that of consumers' expenditure. The two indicators did not move synchronously. Consumers' outlays preceded disposable income by a quarter in the periods of both decline and recovery. This, too, can be explained. It followed first of all from those measures, belonging to the sphere of monetary policy, which modified the conditions and possibilities of purchases on credit in a favourable or unfavourable direction. On the other hand, this running ahead followed from causes affecting the size of *savings*. The impact of the latter can be well seen precisely in the period investigated. Although in the first quarter of 1975 the real value of disposable income fell by 5.3 bn, the ratio of savings to disposable income fell from 7.5 to 6.4 per cent and this corresponds to an 8.5 bn fall in savings, thus to an identical amount of increase in outlays.

In the next quarter, under the impact of the tax reduction, disposable personal incomes soared by 44.3 bn, accelerating the expansion of consumers' purchases, but not at all at the same rate as that of incomes, because the rate of savings went high again (to 9.7 per cent). In the third quarter—as the once only impact of the tax reduction ceased—disposable income again fell somewhat, but the growth of consumption continued, if at a slightly slower rate, made possible again by a significant drop in the rate of savings. By the last quarter of the year, matters were again "put in their proper place" as both disposable income and consumers' purchases increased, the latter at a somewhat faster rate as the savings rate continued slowly to diminish.

The latter data are related to the disposable or actually spent *real* incomes, although these incomes are primarily money incomes, that is, nominal ones. The question still awaits an answer why the nominally growing incomes became greater also in real terms. The explanation must be found, of course, in the trend of prices, more exactly in the causes affecting the trend of prices. If we also take into account that we are investigating a profit-motivated capitalist economy, we end up comparing prices and costs. Let us compare the figures of our Δp_c diagrams for 1974 and 1975 (pp. 54–55). In earlier years the growth in nominal wages contributed more to inflation and transfers, less than in 1975, but the price-raising combined impact of the two components was more than counterbalanced by the changes in the taxes and savings of wage earners— two factors reducing inflation. If consumption in either 1974 or 1975 had not changed relative to the preceding year, then inflation would have been below 8 per cent in 1974 and above 9 per cent in 1975. But the volume of personal consumption soared in 1975. If prices developed according to the laws of free competition, we ought to say that the jump in consumption should have reduced the price level by about 3 percentage points. But the price level changes owing to monopolistic considerations. For a better understanding we have to turn to our profit diagrams. Figure 7.6 (p. 117) shows in the diagrams relating to 1974 and 1975 that while the real value of profits significantly diminished in 1974, by 1975 it already increased over 1974. And this 1.5 per cent increase came about so that while the real value of material profit even diminished by 19 per cent of the profit in the preceding year, paper profit increased by 20.5 per cent. The 5.3 per cent net-export increase, usual in recession years, contributed to this extraordinary increase in paper profit, while the deficit increase contributed by 23.4 per cent, although the savings of wage earners somewhat slowed this growth. Thus increasing deficit was an important factor in preventing a further decline in profits. And this jump in the deficit acted unambiguously towards improving business by increasing demand and, as we have seen, precisely consumer demand.

Was the increase in consumer demand indeed the main factor of improvement? No, the matter is not that simple! But the turn of a fall in profit into a small growth in profit and the decrease in wage cost per unit of product made it possible that, in spite of a more moderate increase in price level than in 1974, the profit margin should not diminish. In fact, as can be seen from Table 5.1 (p. 67) in this year the profit margin even increased slightly. Even so, it was lower than in any of the 10 years examined— with the exception of 1974. But the beginning of the year still fell into the period of recession. Capitalists do not like the recession and its slackening sales, either. Under such conditions they comforted themselves with the fact that the rise in prices set by them compensated them only for the rise in costs. It came as a present that the nominal purchasing power of wage earners, the greater part of which became effective demand, did not grow simply from additional wages increasing the costs of enterprises, but to a considerable extent was due to the jump in government deficit. Since price rises were relatively moderate, they did not carve into real profits in the manner described in section 5.8 of this book (pp. 62–64). If Washington was made primarily responsible for the recession, we may justly establish now that the push resulting in recovery also came from Washington—through the automatic increase of transfers and the discretionary measure of a tax reduction implemented at the right moment. But the pressure of the recession was needed lest the nominal additional income pumped into the economy should be wasted merely through a price increase. (All this will be discussed further in section 15.1 of the next chapter.)

To conclude this section let us briefly scrutinize the capacity utilization of manufacturing. This indicator, too, bottomed in the first quarter of 1975, when it stood at 70.9 per cent, 16.9 per cent lower than at the peak in the third and fourth quarters of 1973. Then it improved every quarter, rising to 76.9 per cent by the fourth quarter, which was still almost 11 percentage points below the peak.[42]

[42] The data are computed by using the index of the Federal Reserve Board. See *Economic Report* 1978, p. 305.

222

14.4 IMPACT OF THE TURN ON UNEMPLOYMENT AND REAL WAGES

Although, as we could see, according to the testimony of the indicators of output and quite a few others, the recession bottomed in the first quarter of 1975, and in the next quarter already several signs of recovery could be perceived, unemployment and some other indicators characterizing the situation of wage earners lagged behind the general picture. Unemployment continued to rise in the first months of 1975, and peaked in May 1975 with 8.3 million (9.0 per cent). From then on, unemployment eased relatively quickly, in the last month of the year it was about 700,000 less than at the peak, and its rate fell to 8.3 per cent. Considering the year as a whole, it was still very high: 8.5 per cent, against 5.6 per cent in the preceding year.

In the course of 1975 the nature of unemployment changed in certain respects. While, namely, in 1974, 45 per cent of the unemployed had been without jobs because they lost their jobs, in 1975 this rose to 55 per cent. The duration of unemployment also increased. And in this respect there was no improvement in the course of the year, since the average length of unemployment was 16.9 weeks even in the last month of the year, against 10.8 weeks in January.

Employment (measured by the number of non-agricultural wage and salary earners) moved on the whole in a direction opposite to unemployment and started to rise only one month earlier than when unemployment began to diminish. After smaller setbacks, the growth attained 1.6 mn by the end of the year.

Improvement of business also showed in the number of weekly hours worked. From the March–April trough this indicator rose to 36.4 hours by December, thus contributing to the increase in earnings. Also the deceleration of the price-increase rate acted so as to contribute to raising real wages. Thus, the weekly real earnings started to rise after the trough of July. With smaller fluctuations they rose above the trough by the last month of the year, but were still only slightly higher than in January. Considering the year as a whole, they lagged 2.8 per cent behind the preceding year, and 6.9 per cent behind the 1973 level. Owing to the tax reform intended to counterbalance the perverse effects of the tax system, the disposable real wage developed more advantageously: in the last month of the year it was already about 4 per cent higher than in January, but as regards the year as a whole, it was still lagging behind the preceding year and much more behind the figure of two years before (by 5.4 per cent).

We have already mentioned that owing to inflation the nominal sum of wages and salaries increased every quarter in 1974. But in the first quarter of 1975 the decline in production was so sharp, and by then also the rate of layoffs increased to such an extent that the sum of wages diminished in current dollars in spite of the inflation. Computed in real purchasing power, at 1972 dollars, this fall was rather sharp (7.0 per cent) and continued slowly even in the next quarter. In the second half of the year this indicator also started to rise again: in the last quarter it was already slightly above the level of a year before.

CHAPTER FIFTEEN

DISTINGUISHING FEATURES OF THE 1974-1975 RECESSION AND SOME LESSONS

15.1 THE MAIN DISTINGUISHING FEATURE OF THE RECESSION: INTERTWINING OF INFLATION WITH RECESSION

Since the directors of economic policy in the United States "succeeded" in 1974-1975 in realizing what earlier had been thought impossible—namely, to steer the economy into the gravest recession of the post-World War II period and at the same time allowing it to be subject to rapid inflation—we may state without hesitation that the main distinguishing feature of the recession was double-digit inflation coupled with a sharp decline in output.

No doubt, the whole post-war economic development has been characterized, for various reasons, by inflationary tendencies. The increased economic role of government worked in this direction, together with the huge budget deficits, the functioning of some built-in stabilizers, etc. This tendency was sharpened by some unfavourable events of the seventies: bad harvests in other parts of the world in 1972, then in the USA itself in 1974 which strongly pushed food prices upwards. Of course, the quadrupling of oil prices in 1974 had a big role in this and so had the simultaneous exaggerated business upswing in the main capitalist countries in 1973, etc.[43] Inflation was increased by the fact that, at the most unfortunate moment, in April 1974, the Nixon administration abolished altogether the price controls which were introduced in August 1971 and then gradually loosened, thus clearing the way for the assertion of factors pushing prices upwards. The course of the inflation is illustrated in Table 15.1

Table 15.1

Major indicators of inflationary price movements
(half-year data at annual rate, seasonally adjusted)

	1974		1975	
	June	Dec.	June	Dec.
Consumer prices	12.2	11.6	6.6	7.0
Wholesale prices	18.1	23.8	0.5	8.6
of which: energy prices	82.1	26.2	5.4	20.9
Implicit price deflator of GNP	10.5	12.5	7.3	7.0

Source: Federal Reserve Bulletin, July 1976: Prices in recession and recovery, pp. 557—565; *Economic Report* 1975 and 1976; various issues of *Survey of Current Business*

[43] For details, see Prices in Recession and Recovery. *Federal Reserve Bulletin*, July 1976, pp. 557–565.

The data of the table show that—on account of the causes listed, first of all the rise in oil prices, and the abolition of price controls—the steepest rise in prices fell to the period when output declined most sharply. According to the earlier—one might say century old—logic, the rise in prices ought to have increased profits and thus improved business. The nominal gross profit of non-financial corporations indeed increased between the fourth quarter of 1973 and the third of 1974 (by more than $ 20 bn), but in the last mentioned quarter almost half of their profits derived from the higher prices of their stocks. Deducting this, their nominal profit diminished by 18.8 bn. In real terms the decline was, of course, even greater (how much cannot be really established in lack of a proper price index). As a matter of fact, at a time of such a large rise in prices the growth of nominal profit did not at all stimulate capitalists to increase fixed capital investment, but all the more to accumulate inventories. Later (in the first quarter of 1975), when it turned out that there was no adequate demand facing the swollen stocks, this turned into a large-scale reduction of stocks, sharpening the fall in production, the recession. But when, for reasons discussed earlier (pp. 217–223), total demand started to rise in the second quarter of 1975, the continuing reduction of stocks cleared the way, as it were, before the increase of production, that is, it promoted the recovery of the economy.

In harmony with the causes explained by the authors, inflation, paradoxically, did not boost the purchases of consumers fearing further price rises. Wage and salary earners were afraid of the fast growing unemployment. Also their real wages diminished. These reasons may presumably explain why the rate of saving was abnormally high during the recession. The negative impact of inflation on the operation of the income tax system as built-in stabilizer has already been mentioned.

The harmful consequences of inflation were heightened by the fact that the FED— leaving other circumstances out of account—applied a restrictive monetary policy to fight it. It did not take into account that the rise in oil prices increased the cost of oil products used in the country by about 37 bn p.a. by the end of 1974, which in itself increased the demand for money by 2.6 per cent.[44] Even if we cannot agree with the exaggerated statement of Burns made in his speech in October 1975, that "the basic cause of the recession was our nation's failure to deal effectively with the inflation that got under way in the mid-sixties and soon became a dominant feature of our economic life",[45] it may be said on the basis of the above that through several objective and subjective factors inflation worked towards deepening the recession.

We believe that for exploring the internal connections of this process the Δp_c and Δp_c^* indicators presented in Part II of this book and used for the quantitative analysis of the factors in yearly price changes can be successfully applied. (See Table 15.2)

In addition to the components of the Δp_c and Δp_c^* formulae in the closer sense we also put into the table a few other data. As a matter of fact, the first three of these are parts of the formulae, only they are not explicitly shown, while the second three present the movements of some factors exerting significant effects from the side of costs.

It first of all strikes the eye that the rate of inflationary price rise attained in 1974 the highest value since the war, a frightening double-digit level. This was in the year when

[44] Perry, 1974, p. 223.
[45] Burns, 1976, p. 6.

Table 15.2

Adjustment of price level and realized demand in 1974 and 1975

Item	Percentage			
	change over preceding year	contribution to price increase	change over preceding year	contribution to price increase
	in 1974		in 1975	

A: Δp_c

Item	in 1974 change	in 1974 contrib.	in 1975 change	in 1975 contrib.
1. Wages	10.0	11.5	6.4	7.6
2. Government transfers	18.6	3.0	26.4	4.8
3. Less: taxes paid by wage earners	13.9	4.7	0.4	0.2
4. Less: savings by wage earners		2.2		2.9
5. Numerator	7.7	7.8	9.2	9.2
6. Personal consumption	−2.2	−2.4	0.7	0.8
7. Less: consumption by capitalists	−0.7	−0.1	0.4	0.1
8. Denominator	−2.4	−2.4	8.7	0.7
9. Δp_c (5/8)	10.4		8.4	
10. Δp_c (5—8)		10.1		8.5

B: Δp_c^*

Item	in 1974 change	in 1974 contrib.	in 1975 change	in 1975 contrib.
1. Business wages	10.3	8.3	6.3	4.5
2. Government expenditures covered by revenues	11.8	5.7	2.1	1.1
3. Government deficit		1.0		6.8
4. Less: taxes paid by wage earners	13.9	4.0	0.4	0.2
5. Less: savings by wage earners		1.8		2.5
6. Numerator	9.2	9.3	9.7	9.7
7. Personal consumption	−2.2	−2.1	0.7	0.7
8. Government purchases	1.9	0.3	2.4	0.4
9. Less: consumption by capitalists	−0.7	−0.1	0.4	0.04
10. Denominator	−1.7	−1.7	1.0	1.0
11. Δp_c^* (6/10)	11.2		8.6	
12. Δp_c^* (6—10)		11.0		8.7

C: complementary data

Item	in 1974 change	in 1974 contrib.	in 1975 change	in 1975 contrib.
1. Income of wage earners (A: 1 + 2)	11.0	14.6	9.1	12.4
2. Disposable income of wage earners (A: 1 + 2 + 3)	10.0	9.9	12.1	12.2
3. Total government expenditure (B: 2 + 3)	14.3	6.7	16.0	7.9
4. Productivity*	−2.8		1.8	
5. Hourly remuneration**	9.4		9.6	
6. Wage cost per unit of product	12.5		7.7	

* Output per man-hour in the private sector. Source of data in rows 4—6 of part C: *Economic Report* 1978, pp. 300—301.

** We use the term remuneration because the data also comprise extra-wage benefits—e. g. the social insurance contribution paid by employers.

the recession was evolving and in 1975, when output hit the trough and unemployment the peak, it was only about 2.5 per cent lower, but even so much higher than in 1973, a time of overheated business. What we said about the failure of adjustment, the turning of the function of the denominator into its reverse, the suicidal success of capitalists in shifting costs holds true the most for the year 1974. But let us look at the details! The growth of wages and thus their contribution to price rises became somewhat moderated relative to the preceding year, but remained high and was the most significant factor in the change within nominal demand. With unemployment growing, though for the time being only slightly, the price-raising impact of transfers also increased. But the price-reducing effect of savings by wage earners and of taxes somewhat strengthened.

The growth in nominal demand, reflected by the changes in the numerator, had on the whole a 2.3 per cent smaller price-raising impact than a year earlier. But capitalists wanted to shift the rise in their costs onto consumers; they increased prices mercilessly and thus the volume of realized consumer demand (essentially, the consumption of wage earners) diminished.

As regards the more comprehensive price-level indicator it is worth adding that the price-raising impact of its numerator did not diminish, since the effect of the items just examined was completely counterbalanced by the price-raising effect of the strong (14.3 per cent) growth of government expenditure. In its bulk this derived from the growth of expenses covered by revenues, while the price-raising effect of the deficit continued to remain slight.

The last rows of our table contribute somewhat to our understanding of the cost increases. It is well known that in these years the raw material and energy costs of production were rising fast. But our figures in the table also testify to the fact that the movement of the other factor of costs, i.e., per unit wage costs also changed in an unfavourable direction. But the primary reason was not a growth in hourly wages, but a decline in productivity and this was mostly caused by the constraint on production. The growth rate of labour cost per unit of product doubled relative to the preceding year, because, while the growth of hourly labour cost increased from 8.2 to 9.4 per cent, productivity fell by 2.8 per cent against the previous 1.9 per cent growth. The fall in productivity was unprecedented in post-war economic history. For example in the 1958 recession year productivity increased at about the same rate as it fell in 1974. At annual rate, 1975 was still a year of recession.

In 1975 curious things happened to the components of the numerator of the Δp_c formula. The rise in the growth rate of wages, and thus in its price-raising impact became moderated to a rather significant extent. Transfer payments increased—of course, first of all because of a jump in unemployment benefits—by more than 25 per cent, and the price-raising impact of this attained 4.8 per cent. The combined price-raising impact of the two items was 12.4 per cent and this was 2.2 per cent milder than in the preceding year. Thus, in spite of the compensating effects of unemployment benefits and other transfers, the recession slowed down the growth of the total nominal incomes of wage earners. However, the price-reducing impact of their taxes practically disappeared in consequence of the already-mentioned large-scale tax reduction of April 1975. As a result, the disposable nominal income of wage earners increased the most rapidly in 1975, when unemployment rose the highest in the whole post-war period, and as a consequence, also the price-raising impact of the nominal wage rise was the strongest in the whole period examined. Although the savings of wage earners and thus their price-moderating impact also increased somewhat, this could counterbalance the former but to a minimum extent. Thus, in the final analysis, the price-raising impact of the numerator rose from 7.8 to 9.2 per cent over the preceding year. We have already mentioned that the moderation of the growth of Δp_c was caused by the changes in its denominator. We now complement what has been said with a somewhat more accurate analysis. Two factors had a role in that capitalists as sellers contributed to the mutual adjustment of demand, supply and prices not exclusively by raising prices, but by also increasing sales. One of these facilitated this, while the other motivated them. It was not wages but the development of productivity that played the main role during the preceding year in raising costs, and now in slowing down the growth rate. Namely, while hourly labour costs still continued to grow somewhat[46] there occurred a favourable turn in labour productivity. The 2.8 per cent decline was replaced by a 1.8 per cent growth. The capitalists had less to shift onto buyers than in the preceding year. On the other hand, the swelling of inventories and the wish to get rid of the growing burden of the entailed costs (interest, storage, etc.) motivated them to sell the greatest possible volume with more moderate price rises. This is proved by the fact that in 1974 retail stocks still increased more than $ 8 bn, while in 1975 only by 0.3 bn. The stocks of wholesale trade and manufacturing fell noticeably by 1975.[47]

In connection with the more comprehensive price level indicator it is worth stressing that the price-raising effect of growing government expenditure increased in its numerator. Within that, the growth rate of outlays covered by receipts fell to a fraction of that of the preceding year and, accordingly, their price-increasing impact also dwindled from 5.7 per cent to 1.1 per cent. At the same time, the role of the deficit increase as a factor in pushing up prices became very strong (6.8 per cent) which is also important from the viewpoint of global price changes. The fact that fast rising government expenses could be less and less covered by receipts was, naturally, a necessary consequence of the tax reduction already mentioned several times. Thus, the tax reduction, bringing undoubtedly positive results from the viewpoint of getting out of the recession, led to rising prices through two channels. Together with the significant increase in transfer payments — similarly to be evaluated in a positive sense as an anti-cyclical stabilizer — it was a main cause in that the recession, with the concomitant unemployment, slowed inflation to a highly unsatisfactory extent. As a matter of fact, the Nixon-administration let this jinn, so difficult to control later, out of the bottle precisely as a cure for this evil.[48] This can be illustrated also numerically. The price-raising impact of the deficit increased from 1974 to 1975 by 5.8 percentage points, while at the same time the price mitigated impact of taxes paid by wage earners fell from 4.0 to 0.2 per cent; this is altogether a price-raising impact of 9.6 per cent.

The denominator of the Δp_c^* formula regained its role in moderating price rises even more than that of Δp_c.

[46] This only seemingly contradicts the said fall in the sum of wages, because the latter may be traced to a decline in employment and in the hours worked.

[47] *Economic Report* 1978, p. 310.

[48] The saying "medicina prior morbo" is indeed applicable.

Let us now devote a few sentences to the real income of wage earners.

The sum of real wages [49] of wage earners diminished in 1974 by 0.4 per cent and by a further 1.8 per cent in 1975. The decline in the real value of the sum of wages paid in the business sector was even more pronounced, attaining 2.8 per cent in two years. But the combined real sum of wages and transfers continued to rise, if to a minimum extent, also in the recession years, by 0.6 and 0.7 per cent, respectively. And as regards finally the disposable real income of wage earners, the minimum decline in 1974 was replaced by a rather considerable 3.4 per cent rise in the next years. In 1975, the disposable real income of wage earners — as a result of the recovery unfolding in the second half of the year — 3.1 per cent higher than in 1973. But, let us not forget, the real consumption of wage earners in 1975 was still lagging behind the volume of that of two years earlier by 1.6 per cent. [50]

The investigaton of the period 1974-1975 also proves that all the measures and processes that were favourable for the recovery of economic activity, raising demand, and thus for fighting the recession, at the same time supported the increase of prices and hindered the slowing of inflation. This contradiction was finally eased by the rise in labour productivity. To wit, relying on the firm base of a significant 3.5 per cent increase in productivity in 1976, the mutual adjustment of the price level and realized demand could take place in a manner whereby the rise in prices was considerably moderated — by about three percentage points — and at the same time the disposable real income of wage earners increased by 5.2 per cent and their real consumption by 7.2 per cent.

15.2 A FEW FURTHER CHARACTERISTICS OF THE RECESSION

In earlier post-war recessions industrial output in the closer sense mostly fell steeply when the decline unfolded, while the fall in GNP was slower and more moderate — primarily owing to the fact that services are crisis resistant. As against that, by the third quarter of 1974 the volume of GNP already lagged behind the peak by 2.1 per cent, but industrial production essentially stagnated in these first three quarters of the recesion, and a real fall began only in September 1974 and lasted till March 1975.

As a matter of fact, in the decline during the recession it was the steep fall in construction activity that played a dominant role. In this important sector of material production the decline lasted two years and a quarter and attained 27.7 per cent, and that was almost ten times as much as during the 1957-1958 recession, although the duration of the decline was the same. Between the peak and the trough (the fourth quarter of 1973 and the first of 1975) the reduction of construction accounted for 31.7 per cent of the fall in the volume of GNP and for no less than 39.3 per cent of that in material production.

This extremely sharp fall in construction was but a partial phenomenon of a further distinguishing sign of this recession, of the fact that a decisive role was played in it by the lasting and strong fall in consumers' investment. Namely, the decline in

---

[49] We arrived at the real data by deflating with the p_c indicator.

[50] See Table 6.4, part A, row 8, p. 78.

construction was to a major part (65 per cent) in the reduction of housing construction and not from the slackening of construction serving business fixed investment. In the 1957-1958 recession the situation had been the reverse: the decline in construction was almost entirely in the latter. The decisive role of consumers' investment in this recession is shown by the fact that the decline in this group of demand not only preceded that of GNP and of fixed capital investment—this was a usual phenomenon in post-war recessions — but, on the one hand, this decline was strong and long lasting (it continued for two full years and attained 24.6 per cent, while in 1957-1958, although it lasted longer, it only fell by 16.6 per cent). On the other hand, and this is the decisive point, it accounted for 29.4 per cent of the decline in the volume of GNP between the peak and the trough, against the not quite half as big share of business fixed capital investment, i.e., 14.7 per cent. The corresponding data in 1957-1958 had been 15.8 and 26.6 per cent. (It looks as if the same figures traded places.) The fall in the total output of consumer goods was — due to the decline in *durable* goods — not much less in terms of percentages (12.2 per cent) than that of total industrial output, while in 1957-1958 the difference between the two had been much greater (5.7 and 13.5 per cent). This, too, testifies to the outstanding role of the fall in demand by "households".

Last but not least, we have to mention the changed role of external, world economic factors. Even in our days, it is in all certainty correct to consider the American economy as one the external relations of which are relatively less strong than those of the other advanced capitalist countries, and thus its fate is determined by internal developments: its booms and recessions alike are of domestic origin. But it is an undeniable new feature of the seventies that the importance of external relations considerably changed for the US economy. This change can hardly be characterized adequately by quantitative indicators, yet it is an important circumstance that the share of foreign trade in the American GNP is no longer 4-5 but 8-9 per cent. But, parallel to their growing weight, foreign economic relations began to have an increasingly negative impact on the American economy. They caused difficulties. Let us just recall the large balance-of-payments deficit in the early seventies and its role in President Nixon's about-face in August 1971, or its role in the devaluation of the dollar in late 1973 and the ensuing lasting decline in exchange rates. The negative foreign economic impacts definitely asserted themselves also in the recession having taken place in the middle of the decade. Consider, e.g., the harmful consequences of the price explosion in raw materials and oil. True, the devaluation of the dollar had a positive impact on the balance of trade, presumably this, too, was a component in that the balance of trade continued to improve during the recession and had a profit-raising, anticyclical role. But, as the other side of the coin, more expensive imports were an essential reason why inflation did not abate significantly during the recession.

Let us not forget that this recession — for the first time after the Second World War — was part of a worldwide recession afflicting all developed capitalist countries, with all its negative consequences.

In part III of this work we have already investigated in Chapter 7 (pp. 104–118) the changes in profits and their components for the whole 1968-1978 period, on the basis of *annual* data. As everywhere in this book where there was a possibility, we used for our computations data eliminating imputations. But such data are available only at annual rates; US statistics do not comprise quarterly data without imputations. We nevertheless shall attempt to trace the development of profits from quarter to quarter. We cannot take into account each of the factors affecting profits, and the margin of error of our estimated data will grow somewhat. We still believe that even so we shall succeded in presenting a few important connections, for shorter periods as well.

United States statistics mention four different types of income, the lion's share of the sum of which we consider net profit. They are: corporate profits, "propietors',, income (including the profit of non-corporate business and the income of people free-lancing), people's rental incomes, and net interests. The data relating to these are available in official statistics also in a quarterly breakdown but imputations are not eliminated. Therefore, we had to undertake this task ourselves.[51]

Through the data thus obtained we may get a rather accurate picture about the quarterly changes in profits during the recession and we may trust that, in a qualitative sense by all means, but with a slight error also in quantitative terms, we can describe realistically what actually "happened" to profits. This is given in Table 15.3. We also included the data on after-tax profits,[52] not only because we used such data in Part III, but also because this offers an opportunity to examine the impact of taxes as well.

Let us examine the message of the table. We may establish first of all that corporate profits stagnated, and even diminished somewhat already in the year of overheated upswing, i. e., in the course of 1973. This decline became very pronounced in the quarter when the curve of GNP already turned downwards, i. e., in the first quarter of 1974. But the nominal sum of other profit-like incomes increased throughout 1973 and, although it started to diminish already in the first quarter of 1974, it still remained well above the level of a year earlier. But this could not hinder the fall in total profits. This occurred only in the first quarter of 1974, but then it was sharp: at annual rate, before taxes, it amounted to 22.6 per cent. But the fall in after-tax total profits was 33.0

---

[51] We proceeded as follows. From each of the kinds of income of profit nature we "eliminated" as many percentages of imputations as were comprised by the annual data. The error thus made is presumably very small, because the ratio of imputations changes from one year to the next only to minimum extent, and this is certainly true also for quarters, and also because corporate profit—in a sense the most important and mostly also quantitatively the greatest part of total profit—does not at all comprise imputations; while the other part of profits, proprietors' income of about equal size to the former, comprises merely two per cent imputation.

Beyond theoretically unclarified problems, it may be probably traced to this fact that when we read in American economic literature about profit, or the rate of profit, mostly or exclusively the corporate profits are meant. And the bulk of profit computed by excluding imputations—almost 90 per cent of it—is made up of these two items.

[52] To work them out, the sum of taxes levied on corporate profits is available from official statistics, and the taxes paid after other incomes of profit nature were worked out with the methods also described in the Appendix.

Table 15.3

Net profits between 1st quarter 1973 and 4th quarter 1975

(seasonally adjusted data at annual rate, excl. imputations,* at current dollars, and index numbers: 1st quarter 1973 = 100)

Period	Corporate profits				Other profit-type incomes				Total profits			
	Pre-tax		After-tax		Pre-tax		After-tax		Pre-tax		After-tax	
	billion dollars	index	billion dollars	index	billion dollars	index	billion dollars	index	billion dollars	index	billion dollars	index
1st quarter 1973	101.1	100.0	52.1	100.0	112.6	100.0	92.1	100.0	213.7	100.0	144.2	100.0
2nd quarter	98.1	97.0	48.3	92.7	117.5	104.4	96.3	104.5	215.6	100.9	144.6	100.3
3rd quarter	97.8	96.7	50.3	96.5	122.8	109.1	100.5	109.1	220.6	103.2	150.8	104.6
4th quarter	99.3	98.2	50.7	97.3	126.9	112.7	103.7	112.6	226.2	105.8	153.9	106.7
1st quarter 1974	90.1	89.1	40.7	78.1	123.3	109.5	100.5	109.1	213.4	99.9	141.2	97.9
2nd quarter	86.3	85.4	33.8	64.9	119.3	106.0	96.8	105.1	205.6	96.2	130.6	90.6
3rd quarter	80.1	79.2	22.9	44.0	120.2	106.7	97.0	105.3	200.3	93.7	119.9	83.1
4th quarter	77.6	76.8	27.2	52.2	119.7	106.3	96.4	104.7	197.3	92.3	123.6	85.7
1st quarter 1975	75.0	74.2	33.6	64.5	115.7	102.8	93.0	101.0	190.7	89.2	126.6	87.8
2st quarter	88.2	87.2	43.1	82.7	122.0	108.3	103.3	112.2	210.2	98.4	146.4	101.5
3rd quarter	110.1	108.9	54.3	104.2	129.8	115.3	106.3	115.4	239.9	112.3	160.6	111.4
4th quarter	110.3	109.1	53.4	102.5	130.9	116.3	107.1	116.3	241.2	112.9	160.5	111.3

* Adjusted for changes in value of inventories and depreciation allowance.

per cent at annual rate. The tax system no longer worked as a built-in stabilizer but as a pro-cyclical factor.

In the course of 1974 profits fell quite drastically from quarter to quarter, but the rate of the decline slowed down in the last quarter, and after-tax profits of corporations even started to rise. What actually happened was that while in the first three quarters corporations paid growing amounts of taxes on their diminishing profits, in the last quarter their tax burden was mitigated by a substantial sum, $ 7 bn, although this still happened before the tax reform. We may offer the following explanation. Our data, relating to the size of profits, neglecting harmony with the national income statistics of the United States—the yet unrealized profit deriving from the rise in stock prices, but firms are under obligation to pay taxes also on profits of such origin. The profit deriving from rising prices of stocks still increased in the first three quarters of the year (in the third quarter this rise was no less than 54 bn at annual rate) and already fell in the fourth (to not quite 40 bn).

In the next quarter, the first of 1975, at the trough of the recession, the pre-tax profit—also taking into account the adjustment on account of the price rise of stocks—was still further declining (at an annual rate of 13.3 per cent), but the after-tax profit already started to increase slowly (at an annual rate of 9.7 per cent). The cause of this divergence was also the reduction of the tax to be paid on account of the price rise of inventories.

The tax reduction introduced in the second quarter of 1975 had, of course, a considerable impact on the development of profits. In this year both types of profit already started to rise, and this was only enhanced by the tax-cut. It goes without saying that following a tax-reduction the after-tax profit increases faster or diminishes more slowly than the pre-tax profit. But this is only one of the effects. In this second quarter after-tax profits already increased also (by 63 per cent at annual rate, while pre-tax ones by only 45 per cent). In this growth a large role was played by the fact that, due to the tax-reduction, the government deficit—a factor increasing profits—was also rising. While during the recession corporate profits fell more steeply than other profits, beginning with the second quarter of 1975 the former were rising faster than the latter, although even in the last quarter of 1975 the ratio to the latter ones lagged behind that of two years and three quarters before.

The slighter fluctuation of other, mainly proprietors' incomes may be traced to the fact that many of the non-corporate, mostly small firms belong to the service sector, and, as we have seen, this was hardly or not at all affected by the recession. The decline in non-corporate profits was entirely caused by the fall in *farm* incomes during the recession: between the fourth quarter of 1973 and the first of 1975 this amounted to $ 18.3 bn, which was 103 per cent of the total fall in other profit-type incomes during the same period. This decline was partially counterbalanced by the slowly continuing rise of rents and interests during the recession. But the profits included here started to rise two quarters later than those of corporations. It further seems that the recession bit into the profits of financial corporations (mostly banks) more than into that of other corporations.

Unfortunately, what has been said up to now relates to data at current prices, thus they are bound to make a more favourable impression on the reader than the facts warrant. This distortion was reduced by our procedure which eliminated the profit from the change in the value of inventories. Namely, the sum of the—unrealized—profit deriving from the rising prices of stocks became very significant. Thus, e.g., in the last quarter of 1973, when the accumulation of stocks was at its peak, from the domestic-pre-tax profit of $ 75.8 bn of non-financial corporations 19.1 bn (i.e., a quarter) derived from the revaluation of stocks. The rate of inventory accumulation already became moderated in the third quarter of 1974, but prices were rising faster and thus already no less than 48 per cent of these profits derived from rising prices. As against that, in 1975 the rise in prices was also more moderate while stocks also diminished strongly, thus the price rise of stocks did not exceed 12 per cent of the profits of non-financial corporations. A realistic picture could only be obtained from a knowledge of real profits. But we do not know what price indices we ought to use for the deflation of the various types of profits to get a volume of profits that would reflect reality. For lack of a better procedure we shall deflate the after-tax sums of profits used in the course of the above computations by the implicit price index of GNP in order to get a picture at least approaching reality. This is found in Table 15.4.

Table 15.4

Net real after-tax profit between 1st quarter 1973 and
4th quarter 1975
(seasonally adjusted quarterly data at annual rate,
excl. imputations; bn 1972 dollar and index numbers;
1973 1st quarter = 100)

Quarter	Billion 1972 dollars	Index numbers
1st quarter 1973	140.1	100.0
2nd quarter 1973	138.2	98.6
3rd quarter 1973	141.5	101.0
4th quarter 1973	140.5	100.3
1st quarter 1974	126.9	90.6
2nd quarter 1973	114.2	81.5
3rd quarter 1974	102.0	72.8
4th quarter 1974	102.1	72.9
1st quarter 1975	102.0	72.8
2nd quarter 1975	116.2	82.9
3rd quarter 1975	125.3	89.4
4th quarter 1975	123.3	88.0

It can be seen that real profits had been practically stagnating already throughout 1973, and fell sharply in the first three quarters of 1974. The rate of decline may be safely said to amount to tumbling in the first quarter; at annual rate it was 38.6 per cent. In the next two quarters the rate of decline in the volume of profit eased at a diminishing rate, and then stagnated in the last quarter of 1974 and in the first one of 1975 at the level of the third quarter of 1974. In this recession lasting three quarters the volume of profits dwindled to less than three quarters of that in the first quarter of 1973 and—although it already started to rise in the second quarter of 1975— even in the last quarter of the year it lagged 12 per cent behind the level of two years and three quarters before. When it bottomed out, the volume of corporations' after-tax profits (in the third quarter of 1974) was merely 38 per cent of the peak attained in the first quarter of 1973.

Unfortunately, it cannot be verified completely satisfactorily whether the impact of paper profit was always anti-cyclical every quarter. Although for two components of paper profit, net exports and government deficit quarterly data are available from official statistics, we could not estimate the overspending or saving by wage earners in a quarterly breakdown.

The data on net exports and on government deficit are to be found in Table 15.5.

Table 15.5

Some elements of paper profit between 1st quarter 1973 and
4th quarter 1975
(seasonally adjusted quarterly data at annual rate, excl.
imputations, bn current dollars)

Quarter	Net exports	Government deficit	Total
1st quarter 1973	1.7	− 12.3	− 10.6
2nd quarter 1973	4.3	− 14.4	− 9.8
3rd quarter 1973	10.0	− 13.2	− 3.2
4th quarter 1973	12.7	− 11.5	1.2
1st quarter 1974	10.4	− 9.8	0.6
2nd quarter 1974	3.2	− 9.3	− 6.1
3rd quarter 1974	2.4	− 7.2	− 4.8
4th quarter 1974	8.2	10.2	18.4
1st quarter 1975	15.5	38.1	53.6
2nd quarter 1975	24.3	87.8	112.1
3rd quarter 1975	20.9	50.1	71.0
4th quarter 1975	20.9	52.5	73.4

The data of the table testify to the fact that these two elements of paper profit generally exhibited an anti-cyclical behaviour also on a quarterly basis. In 1973, the year of overheated business, this group still diminished profits as a result of restrictive fiscal policy, though by an ever smaller amount. In the last quarter of the year this was replaced, as a result of a somewhat less restrictive budget surplus and a rather significantly growing export surplus, by a minimal profit-raising effect. In the next year the trade surplus first declined and then rose again. But in the last quarter of the year— much more under the automatic impact of declining business on both the revenue and the expenditure sides of the budget than as a result of deliberate economic policy measures—the budget surplus already turned into deficit. What finally happened was that in the last two quarters these two elements of profit increased profits by about fifteen times as much as in the same quarter of the preceding year, and this $ 18.4 bn was significant even in absolute terms. This tendency gathered momentum in the first half of 1975. The profit deriving from these two components attained—mostly as a consequence of a deliberate economic policy measure, the tax cut of April 1975—in the second quarter of the same year a peak with the unprecedented amount of 112.1 bn! On the whole, this group added 122.7 bn dollars more to profits in this quarter than in the first one of 1973, and from this 22.6 bn derived from the higher trade surplus, while 100.1 bn from the shift in the budget balance from surplus into a large deficit. When the once only impact of the tax reduction was over in the second half of 1975, this sum fell but it was still 73.4 bn in the last quarter of the year.

Let us examine these also at constant prices. For lack of anything better, we again use the implicit price index of GNP for deflating the data in current dollars. (Table 15.6)

Table 15.6

Net exports plus government deficit between 1st quarter 1973 and fourth quarter 1975
(quarterly data at annual rate, in bn 1972 dollars)

Period	1st	2nd	3rd	4th	1st	2nd	3rd	4th	1st	2nd	3rd	4th
						quarters						
		1973				1974				1975		
Billions of 1972 dollars	− 10.3	− 9.4	− 3.0	1.1	0.5	− 5.3	− 4.1	15.2	43.2	89.0	55.4	56.4

Of course, the rapid inflationary rise in prices moderates the sum of changes between individual periods, but the tendency is unambiguously the same as what can be read from the data at current prices. For numerical illustration it will suffice that in the second quarter of 1975 these two profit components contributed 95 bn (1972) dollars more to the volume of profits than in the previous year.

Let us examine the relative importance of the profit deriving from these two components in comparison to total profits. (See Table 15.7)

Table 15.7

Share of net exports and government deficit in after-tax profits
(per cent, based on data in current dollars)*

Period	1st	2nd	3rd	4th	1st	2nd	3rd	4th	1st	2nd	3rd	4th
						quarters						
		1973				1974				1975		
Percentage share	− 7.1	− 7.0	− 2.1	0.8	0.4	− 4.7	− 4.0	14.9	42.3	76.6	44.2	45.7

* Since the same price deflator was used for both series of data, in principle it is the same whether the shares are computed from data at current price or at 1972 dollar prices. The data at current prices were chosen because they are official ones; their accuracy does not depend on how luckily we chose the price deflator used.

236

The development over time of the data in the table is startling. The percentual ratios, particularly in some periods, are striking. In the first three quarters of 1973 these two profit components had reduced total profits by a few percentages and had a similar effect in the first three quarters of 1974—not too disturbing. But in the second quarter of 1975 the source of more than three quarters of profits was already the trade surplus and the government deficit, i.e., 16.6 and 60, thus altogether 76.6 per cent. The latter is in itself surprising. If we accept that the movement of profit has a central role in the business cycle, the above data convincingly prove not only that the movement of the profit component group which we have called anti-cyclical is really anti-cyclical in itself, but also—and this is the really important thing—that in the single serious post-war recession this group had a highly important impact in quantitative terms on the development of profits and through that on the whole business cycle.

But we should like to give a picture of the anti-cyclical effect of *total paper profits*. For this we ought to know the development of the third item of paper profit, the savings or overspending by wage earners during the recession. In part III, Chapter 7 (pp. 118–120) we said that this component of profit showed a pro-cyclical movement and thus mostly moderated the anti-cyclical impact of the above examined other two profit components. Unfortunately, its quarterly development cannot be worked out, not even approximately.

But something can still be concluded about the combined impact of these three elements of paper profit. We know that in 1974 the three combined took $ 6.2 bn from profits and that, within it, the profit-reducing effect of savings by wage earners was 7.9 bn. In 1975, however, these components contributed $ 47.4 bn to profits, in spite of the fact that the profit-reducing effect of the saving by wage earners amounted to 29.8 bn (see Table 7.4 on p. 129). Thus the annual data show that the fluctuations on the savings of wage earners, and the turn from overspending into saving from 1973 to 1974, and much more so to 1975 did not at all mean such a great change as that of the government deficit alone, and much less if net exports are also included. The data on savings in official statistics (including imputations and, of course, also savings by others than wage earners) testify to the fact that in the first quarter of 1975 both the rate and the absolute amount of savings diminished. In the next quarter, obviously under the impact of the tax reduction, they again jumped high and their sum was about 25 per cent higher than the 1975 average. If we assume that the savings of non-wage-earners moved in a similar manner, we find that this sum could have been about $ 24-25 bn in the first quarter of 1975 and $37-38 bn in the second. If we deduct this from the sum by which government deficit and the export surplus increased profits in the same quarters (let us remember: 53.6 and 112.1 bn), we still get huge amounts: about 29 and 75 bn dollars. Thus, even taking into account the profit-reducing impact deriving from the pro-cyclical movement of savings by wage earners, we may maintain our statement that the anti-cyclical group of profit components (more exactly of paper profit), and, above all, the government deficit reflecting a resolute turn in fiscal policy, exerted an important anti-cyclical effect on the development of profits, and through that on the whole business cycle also during the recession.

We examined the role of paper profit and its main elements and found that it was important in the 1974-1975 recession. We are of the opinion that it is worthwhile taking a small détour to scrutinize whether this was a new phenomenon, or can similar tendencies also be found in earlier recessions.

We computed the net total profits, without imputations, for the most important recession of post-war times before 1974-1975, i.e., for 1957–1958. In this period the current price sum of profits—both before and after taxes—attained the peak in the third quarter of 1957 (with $ 95.6 and 66.6 bn) and its decline lasted for merely half a year—as that of GNP. The trough was in the first quarter of 1958 (with $ 87.9 and 63.4 bn). Then profits started to grow: in the third quarter of 1958 the nominal after-tax profit attained and then surpassed the peak before the decline while the pre-tax profit was reached in the fourth quarter. Thus the fall in profit lasted only for a short time and was not significant either in absolute or relative terms ($8.1 bn or 4.8 per cent).[53]

The important components of paper profit showed the following course. (Table 15.8)

Table 15.8

Some components of paper profit between 1st quarter 1957 and 4th quarter 1958
(bn current dollars, at annual rate)

Item	1st	2nd	3rd	4th	1st	2nd	3rd	4th
	quarter				quarter			
	1957				1958			
Net exports	6.8	6.4	6.2	5.8	2.9	2.4	2.8	1.8
Government deficit	− 5.8	− 3.8	− 3.3	1.4	8.1	12.4	12.1	9.6
of which: federal	− 6.5	− 5.0	− 4.7	− 0.6	5.6	10.0	10.1	7.9
Total	1.0	2.7	2.9	7.2	11.0	14.8	14.9	11.4

The data of the table show that in the period between the peak and the trough of the cycle (from the third quarter of 1957 to the first of 1958) the two components of paper profit increased together significantly, by $ 8.1 bn. Without it, the fall in profit would have been much more pronounced and, presumably, the recession would have been also deeper and longer. The combined growth of these two elements also had a considerable role in the recovery after the trough, since in the following half year they amounted to a further 1.9 bn, and this was almost 120 per cent of the increment of net after-tax profits. This was necessary, too, since fixed capital investment bottomed only in the third quarter of 1958. That is, the growth of the elements of paper profit taken into account overcompensated the decline in other components of profit, continuing

---

[53] If we work with profit at constant prices (using for deflator the implicit price index of GNP), the picture is not so favourable: net after-tax profit attained its peak already in early 1956, and fell to the third quarter of 1957, considered as the peak of the cycle, by 2.5 per cent, and till the trough by 7.7 per cent.

even after the trough of the recession. It is worth mentioning that this anti-cyclical impact derived entirely from the development of the government balance, since—as opposed to its behaviour in 1974–1975—net export was deteriorating in the course of both the recession and the recovery and thus it did not increase but diminished profits. As against that, the government balance, still showing a surplus in early 1957, changed through following one and a half years always in a profit-increasing way and the turn from surplus into deficit between the peak of business and the trough of the recession increased the sum of profits by $ 15.4 bn, and during the recovery by a further $ 4 bn. Within the government balance the decisive role was played by the federal budget: in the two periods mentioned its profit-raising impact was 10.3 and 4.5 bn. The importance of the government deficit is shown by the fact that its share in the total net after-tax profit was 4.4 per cent at the peak, 17.4 per cent at the trough and 23.1 per cent at the beginning of the recovery. This had an anti-cyclical effect in all certainty also in the 1957–1958 recession, which it is worth stressing also because the Republican Eisenhower administration then in power certainly did not pursue a deliberate Keynesian economic policy and did not introduce such a major mesaure as the tax reduction of 1975. Yet the institutional changes having taken place in the preceding decade, the built-in stabilizers, etc. still had a considerable anti-cyclical impact.

And what was the situation at the time of the Great Depression? The volume of GNP fell between 1929 and 1933 by almost 33 per cent and this was accompanied by an almost 25 per cent reduction of prices (measured by the implicit price index of GNP). And the important elements of profit and paper profit developed as shown in Table 15.9., which we are going to analyse.[54]

Table 15.9

Some components of paper profit, 1929—1935
(at current prices, excl. imputations, bn dollars)

Item	1929	1930	1931	1932	1933	1934	1935
Net after-tax profits	24.5	18.9	12.4	6.0	5.6	9.5	12.4
Net exports	1.1	1.0	0.5	0.4	0.4	0.6	0.1
Government deficit	−1.0	0.3	2.8	1.7	1.4	2.4	2.0
of which: federal	−1.2	−0.3	2.1	1.5	1.3	2.8	2.6
Net exports plus government deficit	0.1	1.3	3.3	2.1	1.7	3.0	2.1
Federal deficit in percentage of after-tax profits	−4.9	−1.6	16.9	25.0	23.2	29.5	20.1

Accordingly, the sum of net after-tax profit did not attain even a quarter of its peak value.[55] From the elements of paper profit, net export did not play an anti-cyclical role; it diminished somewhat itself. But, surprisingly, the government deficit—primarily the federal one—did have some anti-cyclical role even then. Turning from surplus into

[54] Because adequate quarterly data are lacking we are using for our analysis annual data, but also the annual changes were very large and thus they are suited for highlighting the major tendencies.
[55] The picture is somewhat more favourable at unchanged prices: profit "only" fell by 68.5 per cent.

deficit in the first two years of the depression it reduced the fall in profit by $ 3.3 bn. But, in consequence of the irrational economic policy of the Hoover administration, in the worst years (1932—1933) it had a profit-reducing effect (over the preceding year). The movements in the preceding two years followed from spontaneous, one might say, random factors. In the weak recovery of 1934 the federal deficit had a profit-raising effect of 1.5 bn relative to the preceding year (Roosevelt was inaugurated in March 1933), and this amounted to almost 40 per cent of the annual increment of profits. But this was not the consequence of a consistent policy either, proven by the fact that in producing the 1937–1938 recession the turn of the federal deficit of 1936 (3.6 bn) into a small surplus in the next year had a decisive role and this took almost 4 bn of the profit just starting to grow, but still lagging much behind the value of 1929. For judging the paper profit, the last row of Table 15.9 deserves attention. We can see that at the trough of the recession and during the recovery a considerable part of net after-tax profits, about 20-30 per cent, came from the federal deficit. The anti-cyclical role of this factor becomes even more conspicuous if we consider to what extent it counterbalanced the negative impact of the profit component most afflicted by the recession, i.e., fixed capital investment. We have reached the not uninteresting result that between 1929 and 1932, when the fall in net fixed capital investment was sharpest, this was significantly counterbalanced by the growth in government deficit. It seems that paper profit, or more exactly, an important element of it, i.e. the government (federal) deficit played an anti-cyclical role not only in the post-war decades, but already in the course of the last crisis of the "classical type", and the recovery following it. This could be traced partly to deliberate economic policy, partly, however, to spontaneous factors.

15.5 COMPARISON OF A FEW PROPERTIES OF THE 1974–1975 AND THE 1957–1958 RECESSIONS

Let us examine to what extent the 1974–1975 recession—no doubt the gravest one in the three decades following World War II—showed features similar to those of earlier post-war recessions, and in what respects it differed from them. Molnár outlined in 1963 (English ed.: 1970) the new features characterizing the post-war cycles of the United States and distinguished them from the earlier cycles—particularly from those of the inter-war period:

1. The recessions repeated themselves rather frequently.

2. They were relatively mild and short. Personal consumption hardly diminished during the recessions, and the decline in fixed capital investment never attained an extent whereby capital stock and productive capacity would have also diminished.

3. Recessions did not suddenly erupt, but the decline in output was preceded by stagnation through about half a year, and the phase of depression was either completely missing or quite short.

4. The major fall in output was restricted to durable goods.

5. Exept for the 1948–1949 recession, the recessions were accompanied by rising prices.

6. The recessions were not accompanied by the spectacular financial events well known from earlier periods (collapse of the exchanges, bank failures, credit crisis, etc.). (Molnár, 1970, p. 224)

240

Table 15.10

Distribution of the decrement of GNP in the 1974—1975 and the 1957—1958 recessions

Item	Decrement between			
	4th qu. 1973 and 1st qu. 1975		3rd qu. 1957 and 1st qu. 1958	
	bn 1972 dollars	percentage distribution	bn 1972 dollars	percentage distribution
Gross national product	71.0	100.0	22.2	100.0
by type of demand				
Personal consumption	8.7	12.3	4.2	18.9
Durables	11.7	16.5	2.9	13.1
Non-durables	6.0	8.5	3.3	14.9
Services*	−9.1	−12.8	−2.1	−9.5
Gross private capital investment	77.2	108.7	16.9	76.1
Fixed capital investment	32.4	45.6	6.5	29.2
Business fixed capital investment	14.7	20.7	5.9	26.7
Structures	8.1	11.4	0.6	2.4
Producers' durable equipment	6.6	9.3	5.2	23.6
Residential construction	17.7	24.9	0.6	2.7
Changes in inventories	44.8	63.1	10.5	47.2
Net exports*	−7.6	−10.7	4.7	21.2
Government purchases*	−7.3	−10.3	−3.6	−16.2
Federal purchases*	−1.6	−2.3	−0.3	−1.4
State and local purchases*	−5.7	−8.0	−3.4	−15.3
Trend-like part*	−8.8	−12.3	−2.1	−9.5
Cyclical part	88.9	125.3	19.8	89.6
Irregular part*	−9.2	−13.0	4.4	10.9
by type of product				
Final sales	26.2	36.9	11.8	53.1
of which: Material production	85.9	120.9	21.1	94.8
Production of goods	58.7	82.7	22.1	99.5
Durables	33.4	47.0	21.3	95.9
Non-durables	25.4	35.8	0.8	3.6
Structures	27.2	38.3	−1.0	−4.5
Services*	−14.8	−20.9	1.2	5.2
Addendum: Consumers' investment	29.4	41.4	3.5	15.8

* A minus sign indicates that the change moderated the decline in GNP

We are of the opinion that the statements then made still hold. The decline in personal consumption, though bigger than in 1958, might be called mild even in 1974–1975. As regards the fall in the output of durable and non-durable goods, there was a significant difference in favour of the latter. This does not indicate a major change in the "recession model" developed in post-war times. What then was the reason for the 1974–1975 recession having been much graver than the earlier ones?

For the analysis let us first see the role of the individual components of output and utilization in the global decline of GNP in this recession and in 1957–1958. Comparing the data relating to the two periods in Table 15.10, we may say the following.[56]

First of all, we may establish that the weights of end uses and stockpiling were different in the two periods. The first had a major role in the fall of GNP in 1957–1958, the second in that of 1974–1975. The decline in personal consumption had been responsible for a much greater part of the decline in the earlier recession than in the later one. Within that, the role of the purchase of durable goods was on the whole the same in both periods, while the decline in the purchase of non-durable goods in 1974–1975 was much smaller than it had been sixteen years earlier. Services mitigated the decrease of GNP in both cases to a similar extent. There is a conspicuous difference in the role of private investment including housing construction; it was 109 and 76 per cent, respectively, of the decrease of GNP. The difference may be attributed precisely to the fact that housing construction had not diminished significantly in the earlier recession, while it fell considerably in the later one. In 1957–1958 it had been responsible for merely 2.7 per cent of the reduction of GNP, but in 1974—1975 it caused a quarter of it. This is a new proof of the fact that the 1974–1975 recession may be traced first of all to the decline in consumers' investment and not to that in fixed business capital investment, since in 1957–1958, 41.4 per cent of the fall in total GNP was caused by consumers' investment, while in 1974–1975 this had been only 16 per cent. A further difference is the changed role of government purchases (inclusive of wages). These were growing during both recessions, but while in 1974–1975 their growth, interspersed with reductions, balanced merely 10.3 per cent of the decline in GNP, in 1957–1958 this had been more than 16 per cent. In both recessions, the contraction was essentially restricted to material production and in 1974–1975 the volume of services even increased.

It is worth calling the reader's attention to the difference in the role of the cyclically moving type of demand. This group caused in 1974–1975 a decline corresponding to 125 per cent of the total decline in GNP, which was compensated to the extent of 25 per cent by the growth of the trend-like and the irregular groups together. The decline in the cyclical group was 90 per cent of the total in 1957–1958. Also, the role of the irregular group was significant, while the trend-like group was growing also in this recession and partly counter-balanced the decline in the other two groups. The cause of the difference is that while in 1974-1975 net export increased demand, sixteen years earlier it had reduced demand.

The data of Table 15.11 reveal that the peaks and troughs in the movement of several important components of demand and production do not coincide with the peak and the trough of the movement of total GNP. The table illustrates the length and percentual size of the toal decrease in the main indicators.

Within personal consumption, the purchase of durable goods declined in 1974-1975 more steeply than it had in 1957-1958, but this decline lasted a full year less; at that time, namely, the production of durables (and of housing construction) had attained

---

[56] Looking at the absolute data we should not forget that the volume of the whole economy increased to 1.8-fold between the two recessions. Thus we have to make the comparison first of all on the basis of the percentual distributions.

Table 15.11

Decline in the major indicators of the consumption and production of GNP in the 1974—1975 and the 1957—1958 recessions (based on data in 1972 dollars)

Item	Decline			
	in 1974—1975		in 1957—1958	
	duration through quarters	extent per cent	duration through quarters	extent per cent
Gross national product	5	5.7	2	3.2

by type of demand

Personal consumption	5	2.3	.1	1.4
Durables	7	16.5	11	15.3
Non-durables	7	3.1	2	1.7
Services*	there was no decline		there was no decline	
Gross private capital investment	6	37.1	10	24.9
Fixed capital investment	9	22.3	10	11.7
Business fixed capital investment	7	16.6	8	13.3
Structures	7	21.0	10	10.1
Producers' durable equipment	6	16.7	4	19.3
Residential construction	8	43.6	11	20.3
Changes in inventories	5	—	9	—
Net exports*	1	0.6	5	65.3
Government purchases*	1	0.1	there was no decline	
Federal purchases*	1	0.6	2	1.7
of which: military	7*	8.9*	2	2.9
State and local purchases	1	0.1	there was no decline	
Trend-like part*	1	0.2	1	0.1
Cyclical part	7	27.1	10	21.5
Irregular part*	there was no decline		4	5.7

by type of product

Final sales	6	2.6	2	1.7
Material production	5	12.1	2	5.2
Production of goods	5	10.2	2	6.8
Durables	7	14.6	10	20.4
Non-durables	5	7.4	3	1.0
Structures	9	27.7	9	3.0
Services*	there was no decline		1	0.7
Addenda: Consumers' investment	8	24.6	11	16.6
Auto-product	8	41.4	11	43.1
Disposable personal income	5	3.7	2	1.2

*The decline in these purchases already started in 3rd quarter of 1968. Our data relate to the period between the 1st quarter of 1973 and the 4th of 1974. Following that, military purchases started to grow steadily.

the peak already in 1955. This was followed by a sharp decline, but during the recession itself it was already slight.

The decrease in the personal consumption of non-durable goods lasted much longer in 1974–1975 than in 1957–1958, but the percentual rate was slight again and the volume of services did not fall in any of the recessions.

The decline in business fixed capital investment was of similar extent in both recessions, but in 1957–1958 it lasted for two years while in 1974—1975 for only one and a half years. Reduction in the purchase of productive equipment was of similar proportions, but in 1974–1975 it was more protracted.

It is a difference worth mentioning that while government purchases had not diminished in the earlier recession, they fell in 1974–1975, even if transitorily and the reduction was minimal.

In the later recession the fall in GNP lasted much longer and in terms of percentages it was about one and a half-fold of that in 1957-1958.

To our surpise, the decrease of the cyclical part from among the types of demand lasted for a much shorter time than it had sixteen years earlier, but in terms of percentages it was much more pronounced—as expected. The trend-like group proved in both cases to be recession resistant. The behaviour of the irregular group has already been analysed.

The decrease in material production was much more protracted in this recession and the perctentual fall almost double of that in 1957–1958. It was a conspicuous feature of the 1974–1975 recession that the percentual decrease in construction was ten times as much, but it lasted as long as in 1957–1958 (related to the decline in consumers' investment—more precisely in housing construction—after 1955, as has been already mentioned). It is a very important difference in comparison with 1957–1958 that in 1974–1975 the not too large decrease in disposable personal income lasted much longer, but a one per cent decrease in GNP entailed a 0.7 per cent decrease in disposable income, while in 1957–1958 this ratio had been 0.4 per cent.

15.6 MAJOR FACTORS IN THE SEVERITY OF THE 1974-1975 RECESSION

In the preceding section as well as in section 1 of Chapter 13 we listed some statistical data; in sections 1 and 2 of the present chapter we reviewed some properties of the recession while the economic policy behaviour of the federal government we analysed in Chapters 13 and 14. Referring to all these we can briefly summarize the factors and circumstances under the impact of which this recession became the gravest among all post-war recessions. To sum up in one sentence: all the listed properties which distinguished this recession were negative in nature. However:

1. The structual changes in the economy, having taken place in the 10-15 years before 1973 caused a significant growth in the ratio within GNP of the cyclically moving, that is, of the most unstable type of demand (see Table 13.1, row 14). Further, the share within GNP of manufacturing, which generally declines more than GNP in a recession, and, within it, the production of durables, somewhat increased.

2. The relative weight and structure of government expenditure changed in an unfavourable manner. The recession struck the country at a time when the process that

started with the de-escalation of the Vietnam War had not yet ended. As a result of this and of the economic policy of a government reflecting conservative economic views and which was asserted for five years beginning with 1969, a shift occurred in favour of the indirect role of government expenses, on the one hand, and, on the other, in favour of the local organs not pursuing (and incapable of pursuing) a comprehensive anti-cyclical policy. Thus the weight of government demand considerably diminished precisely in the two fields most afflicted, the production of durables and construction. Thus, by the beginning of the recession the instruments and possibilities of the state for anti-recession interference objectively weakened: it had less ammunition.

3. As distinct from earlier post-war recessions, the significant decline in the two decisive types of demand, i.e., business fixed capital investment and consumers' investment, mostly coincided, and this was not counterbalanced by the third main type of demand, that on the part of government.

4. Through several transmissions, and not least because of the reversal in the operation of an important *built-in stabilizer,* the progressive tax system, in the period prior to the tax reduction the situation was aggravated by high rate inflation, hardly abating even during the recession.

5. Consumer demand, making up the bulk of total demand, got between the pincers, as it were. On the one side was the reduction in disposable income, on the other the unusually high savings of frightened consumers—of course, mostly wage and salary earners. In order to save a higher portion of their smaller real income they, naturally, had to strongly reduce their purchases.

6. The impact of the world economy gathered momentum and also turned unfavourable. The American recession took place as a part of a worldwide decline in the developed capitalist countries.

7. Last, but not at all least, the wrong, weak and ill-timed economic policy of the federal government was a major factor in the deepening of the recession.[57] To a certain extent it was also expectable that the Republican administration would not come up to expectations, since historical experience suggested that on similar occasions its main concern was always inflation and not the fight against unemployment. In addition, precisely in the decisive period, in the first half of 1974, the Watergate affair also contributed to the impotence of the administration. On the whole, it may be established that the performance of the highest representatives of economic policy making was inexcusably weak.[58]

While the severity of the recession also had external causes, it should be obvious that the internal ones were decisive.

[57] The activity of the Ford Administration and, within it, of FED Chairman Burns was briefly but sarcastically and aptly criticized by Samuelson. (Samuelson, 1975)

[58] It can also be shown numerically by how much the diminishing weight of the state in the economy, and the non-use of the smaller ammunition—the incorrect economic policy—worsened the situation. (See Perry, 1975, p. 228 and Molnár, F. 1977, pp. 675–687.)

FROM RECESSION TO DECLINE AMIDST INFLATION
(1976–1979)

Although in the five-year period between the end of the gravest post-war recession and the decline starting in the second quarter of 1980, and of a depth and length that could not yet be judged at the time of writing this book (September 1980), no such spectacular events or turns occurred in either the world or the American economy or in economic policy as in the years examined in the previous three sections of our book (1969-1975), this period cannot be considered simply calm, problem-free either and thus uninteresting for economic analysis. This is borne out by a statement made by Samuelson in August 1978. We have already quoted him several times, not only because of his reputation and sometimes deep insight, but also because he is witty. He was of the opinion that "although it is never easy to understand what is happening in the American economy, the situation at the present time seems especially confusing and even pradoxical". (Samuelson, 1978)

CHAPTER SIXTEEN

GENERAL CHARACTERISTICS OF THE PERIOD

The recovery starting in 1975, accompanied by a moderation of inflation, again provided an opportunity for the American administration to project with its official optimism the perspective of long-term growth free of graver inflation and approaching "full" employment. In reality, however, a new cycle started of a type already familiar in the seventies, beginning with significant recovery and ending in a recession enhanced by the government. But it started under much more ill-boding circumstances than the earlier ones.

Several important countries of the capitalist world emerged from the 1974-1975 recession with much greater difficulty than the United States, and this also had an impact on the latter. One of the not insignificant reasons was the rise in crude oil prices which led to grave disturbances in international financial relations. The United States was also among the victims, though to a lesser degree than other countries.

Thus in the course of the period under investigaton GNP increased at an ever slower rate and began to diminish in the course of 1980. Inflation, measured either by the implicit price index of GNP or by that of consumer prices, increased, on the contrary, ever more steeply and in 1979 the price rise of the consumer basket again ran into two digits. Throughout the whole period, economists complained that the volume of private investments essentially lagged behind that previously experienced during recovery, and particularly behind the required level. Consequently, the gap between the theoretically possible and the attained volume of output became ever wider. Despite a certain improvement, unemployment thus also remained high throughout the period. But this was only half of the troubles. Due to insufficient investment — and other reasons that had remained mostly unclarified — the growth of productivity also lagged behind the averages experienced in earlier recoveries, and in 1979 it already began to diminish. Essentially at the same time, corporate profits also started to fall together with real wages which by 1979 fell already below the 1975 level.

And yet another ill-boding circumstance was the shaken trust in Keynesian economic policy and the significant gains made by monetarist theories.

The first year of the period examined still fell to the presidency of the Republican Ford, but in 1977 the Democrat Carter occupied the White House. In itself, this change might have promised good things to come. For illustration we have Table 16.1, a continuation of the table which we showed commenting Nixon's inauguration.

Table 16.1

Average yearly percentual change in the major economic indicators
(based on data in 1972 dollars)

Items	1953—1960 Republican	1961—1968 Democratic	1969—1976 Republican
	administrations		
GNP	2.6	4.6	2.4
Personal consumption	3.2	4.3	3.3
Durable goods	3.8	6.7	4.7
Fixed capital investment	3.0	6.3	1.0
Residential construction	3.4	2.5	1.4
Consumers' investments	3.6	5.2	3.7
Government purchases	1.0	5.2	0.2
Federal purchases	− 2.0	4.4	− 3.5
Military purchases*	− 2.7	3.7	− 5.4
Industrial output	3.4	6.1	2.5
Per capita disposable income	1.3	3.2	2.2
After-tax corporate profits**	3.0	6.2	− 1.9
Weekly real wages	2.2	1.6	0.0
Employment	1.1	1.8	1.8
Output per man-hour	2.7	3.6	1.5
Implicit price deflator of GNP	2.1	2.3	6.2
Consumer price index	1.4	2.1	6.3

* Official statistics publish this item only at current prices. We arrived at the data by deflating with the aid of the implicit price index of federal government purchases.

** The Department of Commerce only gives the data at current prices. We arrived at the data by deflating with the implicit price deflator of GNP.

It can be seen that the 1969–1976 period of Republican administration outdid even the most pessimistic expectations. It was decisively this fact that helped the Democrat Carter to victory. But Carter took power at the time of the advance of monetary theory, one might say its ideological terror.

It will be instructive from this viewpoint to quote, freely or verbatim, excerpts we find characteristic in the Economic Reports of the President, in chronological order.

We start with the 1977 Report, which was still President Ford's. We quote excerpts from the Report written in a tone of "official optimism":

"The past year was a year of sound economic achievement. A year ago I said that my ... goal was 'to create an economic environment in which sustainable noninflationary growth can be achieved'. While much remains to be done, we have built a very solid foundation for further economic gains in 1977 and beyond. The recovery has continued to produce substantial gains in output and employment. Unemployment remains much too high, but the marked reduction that we see in inflation as well as in inflationary expectations represents significant progress towards regaining the stable noninflationary prosperity that has been our goal." (*Economic Report*, 1977, p. 3).

At any rate, Ford also perceived an essential deficiency, namely, the slack private investment activity. He intended to implement an economic policy stimulating investment. "Investment has grown more slowly than would normally be true at this stage of a recovery." In order to fully implement the goals "the present policy of moderation in fiscal and monetary affairs and of relying on a restored vitality in the private sector must continue. ... The creation of permanent, meaningful and productive jobs for our growing labor force requires a higher level of private investment." It was not budget expenditure that had to be increased. "We must recognize that making governmental expenditure the principal arm of demand management has undesirable consequences ... It weakens incentives, reduces efficiency, leads to lagging standards of living, and carries inevitable risks of inflation. It is much better to provide fiscal adjustments through tax reductions than through Federal spending programs."(*Op. cit.*, p. 10) Such a tax reduction had to be implemented whereby inputs serving the stimulation of consumption would be counterbalanced by those increasing investment. "A stronger spur to investment in productive plant and equipment is necessary for the further improvement in production and employment in 1977 and beyond." (*Op. cit.*, p. 4)

But, being a good Republican, Ford also took care that social welfare and similar expenses directly helping the situation of masses of people should not come to the fore. Namely, it followed that, unfortunately, "we persist in the belief that we can always tolerate a little larger Federal deficit, or the creation of a little more money, especially for the sake of programs which seem to promise clear and readily definable benefits." But this was "a kind of self-deception that we must learn to resist. ... We must restrain the growth of Federal expenditures. If we do not we shall have to resign ourselves to higher taxes or to high employment deficits with their inflationary consequences." (*Op. cit.*, p. 9)

And in the fields of social insurance and health Ford did not at all wish to tolerate damnable socialism. Let wage earners pay for them in advance. "I have emphasized the need to maintain a fiscally sound social security system and repeatedly rejected proposals to fund increased benefits out of what are called general revenue...

Funding our social security benefits through specifically designated payroll taxes strengthens the discipline that should govern these decisions... Individuals, businesses and unions, confronted with the higher costs of private health insurance have begun to exert curbs on the systems for delivering health and medical service, and their influence should be salutary. I hope we will not choose to fund these costs through a comprehensive national health insurance system, since this will only weaken the incentives for improvement and efficiency that are now emerging." (*Op. cit.,* p. 10)

But 1977 was already a year of the Democrat Carter. At the end of January the President already made public his package plan for the stimulation of the economy, providing for tax reduction, increasing public employment, etc. But not even three months passed when two important elements of the plan — the $ 50 per capita tax reduction and the investment-stimulating measures were dropped.[59] Carter began his first Economic Report, in 1978, by listing the difficulties and then, speaking about how to continue, he set, among others, the following tasks: "We must continue to move steadily toward a high-employment economy in which the benefits of prosperity are widely shared... We should rely principally on the private sector to lead the economic expansion and to create new jobs for a growing labor force... We must contain and reduce the rate of inflation as we move toward a more fully employed economy. (*Economic Report*, 1978, p. 5) The international situation was not at all rosy. "The American economy is completing three years of recovery from the severe recession of 1974–1975. Recovery in most other nations has lagged far behind our own... Our inflation rate is also lower than in most other nations around the world." (*Op. cit.,* p. 3) However, as there were still 6.5 million fully and 3.25 million partially unemployed in the country, this was a problem which the United States had in common with other countries. "Businesses are still hesitant in their long-term investment planning, and the stock market remains depressed despite the substantial increase in business profits... concerns about the future have deterred business investment in new plants and equipment. As a consequence, economic growth has stagnated in many countries, and the rise in capital stock needed to increase productivity, raise standards of living, and avoid future inflationary bottlenecks in not occurring." (*Op. cit.,* p. 4)

Among the causes of the deficiencies listed we find the deep recession of 1973–1975 and the grave inflation; the problems of energy supply and energy prices; fear from government controls; the high costs of capital goods and the depressed atmosphere of the exchanges. True: "Industrial capacity is ample now. But without a substantial increase in investment over the next few years, problems would build for the future." (*Op. cit.,* p 16)

Yes, inflation! And fighting it necessitates "gradually reducing the share of our national output devoted to Federal spending. ... Adopting more effective programs to reduce the current rate of inflation and prevent a reacceleration of inflation as we approach high employment." (*Op. cit.,* p. 6)

But Carter knew that this required the consensus of the population, and made the

---

[59] According to an expert opinion: "The improvement in business conditions was the official reason for abandoning the rebate. However, the rebate was not popular in the Senate and might well have been defeated had it come up for a vote." (Pechman, 1977, p. 44)

appeal: "I am . . . asking the business community and American workers to participate in a voluntary program to decelerate the rate of price and wage increase. This program is based on the initial presumption that prices and wages in each industry should rise significantly less in 1978 than they did on average during the past two years." (*Op. cit.*, p. 19) But in vain did Carter acknowledge the behaviour of the population approvingly in the following year, this "initial presumption" did not come true at all.

The Economic Report of 1979 listed it among the successes that unemployment diminished, disposable real income increased, business profits significantly increased, and business investment also recovered. (As a matter of fact, fixed capital investment did not grow at a faster rate at all than in 1977 and investment in equipment actually slowed down.) But then the President moved to the problem of inflation. He established it as a fact: the problem of inflation became acute and to a considerable extent this followed from the unsatisfactory growth of productivity. (*Economic Report*, 1979, p. 3) Inflation came to the fore in the Report again and again. From the "four principles" of the "economic and budgetary program" proclaimed by the president, the first was that "reducing inflation must be our top economic priority." (*Op. cit.*, p. 3) Then, a few paragraphs later: "It is for all these reasons that reducing inflation must now be the primary concern of economic policy." (*Op. cit.*, p. 7) Then followed a specification of tasks: "The budget for 1980" (i. e., the budget of the fiscal year beginning with October 1, 1979) "must be very tight, and I intend to make sure that a fiscal policy of firm and measured restraint is maintained." (*Op. cit.*, p. 4)

In this context the President also made declarations intended to reassure the public: "We will not reduce inflation at the expense of the most vulnerable members of our society." (*Op. cit.*, p. 3) Or: "We will *not* try to wring inflation out of our economic system by pursuing policies designed to bring about a recession." (*Op. cit.*, p. 7) But against these mild tunes the general tone remained: "Firm, sustained and carefully applied fiscal and monetary restraint must be the first element in our effort to reduce inflation." (*Ibid.*) And finally a wise statement which only shows that the road to hell is paved with good intentions and promises: "Twice in the past decade inflation has accelerated and a recession has followed, but each recession brought only limited relief from inflation. . . . Stop-and-go policies do not work." (*Ibid.*)

In the 1980 Report of the President we already find the following self-consoling statement: although many had expected a recession for 1979, output continued to grow, consumers' savings diminished, while their outlays did not, and inventories also remained moderate. Yes, but the inflation! "Last year world oil prices more than doubled. . . . Higher oil prices were the major reason for the worldwide speedup in inflation during 1979 and the dimming of growth prospects for 1980. . . . The Nation's output of goods and services which had been predicted in last year's Economic Report to grow by $2^1/_4$ per-cent over the 4 quarters of 1979, rose by less than 1 per cent . . ." There was "a sharp decline in productivity." (*Economic Report*, 1980, p. 3)

As regards the prospects, the President was of the opinion that "we face a difficult economic transition in the next year or two. According to my economic advisers, our economy is likely to undergo a mild recession early this year." (*Op. cit.*, p. 5)

Would then at least moderately stimulating measures be necessary to avoid the ill-famed stop-and-go? It seemed not, as "to fight inflation . . . fiscal and monetary restraint" was needed: ". . . the budget will have to remain tight" and ". . . monetary

250

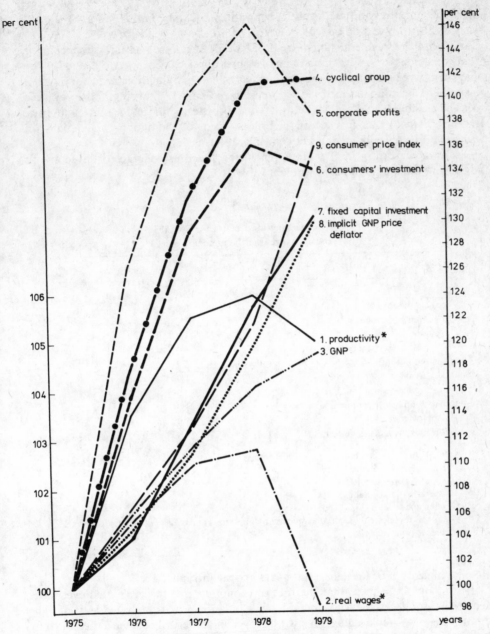

Figure 16.1 Major indicators 1975–1979 (index numbers: 1975 = 100)

policy will have to continue firmly in support of the same anti-inflationary goals."
What is this if not a stop-and-go policy? (*Op. cit.,* p. 4.)

And what else? General statements like "we must pursue measures to encourage
productivity growth..." (*Op. cit.,* p. 5) Measures concerning energy, food and fodder,
which would reduce sensitivity to the impacts of external inflationary factors. And if
government again abandoned the economy to recession? What should the governed
do? There should be "... restraint by the private sector in its wage and price
decisions." (*Ibid.*) But, in view of the critical needs of the nation, "...outlays for
defence will increase by over 3 per cent in real terms."

Let us now scrutinize the development of the most characteristic economic
indicators over the period as a whole. (Table 16.2)

Table 16.2

Major economic indicators between 1976—1979

(percentual change over the preceding year)

Item	1976	1977	1978	1979
GNP^a	5.9	5.3	4.4	2.3
Fixed capital investment^a	4.8	8.6	8.4	6.0
Gross after-tax profits	7.8	5.2	2.8	..
Corporate profits^a	25.7	11.7	4.2	−5.1
Disposable personal income	3.7	4.2	4.6	2.2
Industrial output^b	10.8	5.9	5.7	4.2
Productivity^c	3.5	1.9	0.5	−1.2
Implicit price deflator of GNP	5.1	5.9	7.3	8.9
Capacity utilization in manufacturing^d	79.9	81.9	84.4	85.7
Unemployment^e	7.7	7.0	6.0	5.9
Okun's "inconvenience indicator"^{f}	13.5	13.5	13.7	17.2

^{a} On the basis of data computed in 1972 dollars.
^{b} Federal Reserve Board index.
^{c} Output per man-hour.
^{d} In percentage of total exploitation.
^{e} In percentage of civilian labour force.
^{f} Sum of the percentage of unemployment and the annual percentual change of the
consumer price index.

Some indicators of the same four years appear in Figure 16.1.

It turns out from these that the rate of economic growth decelerated ever more
definitely throughout the whole period, while inflation was strongly accelerating. The
upward trend was replaced by downward movement in regard of some indicators only
in 1979. But, as regards economic policy, we find a sharp dividing line already a year
earlier. In consequence of the developments in 1978, in his 1979 Report the president
laid special emphasis on the fight against inflation and, in this context, on constraint of
budget expenses, and, in view of the failure, a year later he declared the same to be the
top priority. Thus, we have an acceptable justification for dividing the discussion of the
period to be examined into two sub-periods, each lasting two years.

CHAPTER SEVENTEEN

THE ECONOMIC SITUATION IN 1976–1977

17.1 PRODUCTION AND DEMAND

Following the trough in the first quarter of 1975 recovery started slowly in the economy. The volume of GNP[60] exceeded the pre-recession peak already in the first quarter of 1976. In the course of the two-year period final consumption increased at a somewhat slower rate than GNP (5.4 and 4.7 per cent), since — as is usual in this stage of recovery — stocks were considerably repleted. From the increment of GNP between the last quarter of 1975 and the last of 1977, 12.4 per cent fell to this component. But the output of material goods increased faster than GNP; between the quarters mentioned it rose by 13.3 per cent. Construction activity was growing even faster — by 13.5 per cent — while output was growing most rapidly in the production of durable goods. But while in respect of durables we may speak about a real upswing, as their output already exceeded the pre-recession peak already in the second quarter of 1976 and remained steadily rising also afterwards, the growth in construction started very sluggishly and its level remained below that of two years earlier even at the end of 1977. The production of non-durable goods and services was growing — as usual — much slower than that of the items mentioned, in the eight quarters it was 9.7 and 8.0 per cent, respectively.

Let us look at these in a grouping by types of demand!

From the cyclical, trend-like and irregularly moving types of demand (for the definition see Chapter 13, pp. 197–298 the first one developed very rapidly (28.6 per cent), the second was average (8.2 per cent), while the third fell significantly (by 10 per cent). In other words, as was also expectable, the latter moved anti-cyclically mainly because net export fell between the two end points of the period from $ 22.2 bn to 5.8 bn.

Personal consumption (excluding the purchase of homes) increased faster than GNP in the two years, and the purchase of durables was growing particularly rapidly, by 19.0 per cent. Housing construction was rising even faster than that, by 42.1 per cent. It follows that the rise in consumers' investment was steep indeed: it attained around 25 per cent.

We know that economists were not satisfied with investment activity. Although business fixed capital investment was rising faster than both total GNP and personal consumption—by 17.8 per cent—and as much can be expected in a recovery from

---

[60] Our quarterly data are also in these two chapters expressed in 1972 dollars, at annual rate, and so are the changes.

recession, but much more slowly than consumers' investment. This was not sufficient also because the base serving for comparison of fixed capital investment was the trough in the fourth quarter of 1975, while consumers' investment started to grow already half a year earlier. Investment construction was particulary slow in growth: even in the last quarter of 1977 its level lagged well behind the peak in 1973, i. e., by 13 per cent. This is precisely the explanation for the unsatisfactory development of construction activity.

The biggest item of total demand after personal consumption, i.e., government purchases, hardly increased through these eight quarters, merely by 2.2 per cent. Within that the growth of federal purchases was somewhat more rapid, in spite of a slight decline in military purchases.

We can get a most expressive picture of the recovery in some factors between the fourth quarters of 1975 and 1977 by analysing the internal proportions of the increment of GNP. The information is contained in Table 17.1.

It can be seen that, in contrast with what we saw in 1970–1971, the decisive part of

Table 17.1

Distribution of the increment of GNP between the 4th quarters of 1975 and 1977

Item	Billions of 1972 dollars	Percentage distribution
by type of demand		
GNP	133.4	100.0
Personal consumption	89.8	77.3
Purchase of consumer durables	22.7	17.0
Fixed capital investment	19.9	14.8
Residential construction	17.8	13.3
Changes in inventories	10.5	12.4
Government purchases	5.8	4.3
Federal	4.5	3.4
Military*	−0.9	−0.7
Cyclical group	76.8	57.6
Trend-like group	68.5	51.3
Irregular group	−11.9	−8.9
by type of product		
Goods	73.2	54.9
Durables	36.9	27.7
Non-durables	36.3	27.2
Structures	14.7	11.1
Material production	87.9	65.9
Services	45.5	34.1
Addenda:		
Consumers' investment	40.5	30.4
Auto product	11.7	8.8

* Published in official statistics only in current dollars. Conversion was made with the implicit price deflator of federal purchases.

254

the increment in demand was for consumption goods, and within it for consumers' investment, not only in the period immediately following the recession, but also during the two years of recovery examined in this chapter. The role of fixed capital investment was only somewhat greater than that of the change in inventories. The share of consumers' investment in the increment of GNP was conspicuously high (more than 30 per cent), double that of fixed capital investment. The share of the latter was surpassed by the increment in the purchase of consumer durables alone, and was approached by that of housing construction.

The growth in real consumption was made possible first of all by the increase in the disposable income of the population. Employment increased and thus also more flowed into the economy and, for the time being, this increment was not yet counterbalanced by the not too fast rise in price level. Thus disposable personal income increased during the eight quarters by $ 80 bn (at 1972 prices). On the other hand, the increase of consumers' investment was, of course, accompanied by a decline in the rate of workers' saving. According to our own computations, the $ 23.4 bn saving of wage earners (in 1972 dollars) turned into an overspending of 16.1 bn by 1977.

The table also shows that among that factors boosting the recovery a rather small role fell to government purchases. It seems that economic policy-makers were of the opinion that they had done everything in their power with the tax reduction in April 1975.

17.2 PROFIT AND PRICES IN 1976–1977

About the movement of profits we get the following picture on the basis of their most important and most volatile part, i.e., corporate profits. Their volume,[61] which, as could be seen in section 3 of Chapter 15, started to rise steeply after the first quarter of 1975, maintaining its momentum till the first quarter of 1976, while this was followed by a one-year stagnation, was interspersed with downward fluctuation. Thus, in the first quarter of 1977 the volume of corporate profits was the same as a year earlier. This was again followed by an upswing and by the third quarter of the year the volume of profits not only exceeded the trough in the first quarter of 1975 by almost 90 per cent, but even the peak in the first quarter of 1973, by 23.8 per cent. In the fourth quarter a minimum decline followed, to be traced to the fact that the part of profits attributable to the revaluation of stocks on account of accelerating inflation increased, while our figures eliminate its effect. A similar, though not so strong, rise is shown by the movement of the second biggest item of profits, of proprietors' incomes: their volume was already 10.7 per cent higher in the last quarter of 1976 than at the trough (but still 17.5 per cent lower than at the peak).

We may get a deeper and more detailed insight into the factors determining the movement of profits through our diagrams showing the movement of the factors in the sum and the annual changes of its components. (See figures 7.3–7.6 in Chapter 7, pp. 110–111 and 117) In this respect the following may be stated.

After-tax gross profits increased in terms of volume (at 1972 dollars) by 28 bn (or 13.5 per cent) from 1975 to 1977. More detailed information can be found in Table 17.2.

---

[61] We arrived at the volume data in 1972 dollars by deflating the data appearing in official statistics only in current dollars by the implicit price index of GNP.

Table 17.2

Distribution of the increment of gross after-tax profits
1975—1977, and contribution of individual profit components

Item	Billions of 1972 dollars	Percentage distribution	Percentage contribution
1. Gross after-tax profits	28.0	100.0	13.5
2. Gross material profits	48.1	171.8	23.1
3. Gross investment	41.6	148.6	20.0
4. Depreciation (capital consumption)	5.1	18.2	2.5
5. Net investment	36.5	130.4	17.6
6. Changes in inventories	22.9	81.8	11.0
7. Net fixed capital investment	13.6	48.6	6.5
8. Capitalists' consumption	6.5	23.2	3.1
9. Paper profit	− 20.1	− 71.8	− 9.7
10. Net exports	− 23.0	− 82.1	− 11.1
11. Government deficit	− 37.1	− 132.5	− 17.8
12. Less: savings by wage earners	− 39.5	− 141.1	− 19.0
13. Less: statistical discrepancy	− 0.5	− 1.8	− 0.2
14. *Addenda:* Net after-tax profits	22.9	81.8	11.0
15. Gross fixed capital investment	18.7	66.8	9.0
16. Net material profit	43.0	154.6	20.7

Material and paper profit also had effect of an opposite sense on the changes in total profit in the course of this revival. The first one greatly increased profits, but changes in the latter offset more than 40 per cent of the first. Thus, the whole of paper profit also played now an entirely anti-cyclical role—this time putting a brake on the revival. This may be attributed entirely to the changes in only two components of paper profit, earlier (p. 120) given the name—now deserved—of anti-cyclical group namely, net exports and government deficit. Their combined effect changed reduced profits in the course of the two years by no less than 60 bn (1972) dollars. The lion's share may be traced to a drastic fall in government deficit. This may only partly be attributed to built-in stabilizers working in this sense in this phase of the business cycle; it came about mainly in consequence of the economic (fiscal) policy behaviour of the administration. The deterioration of the balance of trade, usual in this phase of the cycle, was enhanced by the continuing rise in oil prices.

The third component of paper profit that may be considered cyclical, i.e., the savings by wage earners, greatly contributed to the rise in profits. The considerable overspending and this increased profits by almost $ 40 bn.

All components of material profit changed between 1975 and 1977 in a way so as to increase profits and, if the counter-effect of paper profits had not asserted itself, the volume of profits would have grown by 23.1 per cent instead of the actual 13.5. From among the elements of material profit the greatest effect was exerted by the changes in inventories, reinforced by gross fixed capital investment and capitalists' consumption. It is worth pointing out that the turning of wage earners' savings into overspending contributed more to the increment of profits than the growth of fixed capital investment (39.5 and 18.7 billion in terms of 1972 dollars). In the case of net profit this

Table 17.3

Price level indicators and changes in their components: percentual contribution to the changes in the numerator and the denominator 1973—1975

Item	Percentual change 1977—1975	Percentual contribution		
		1977—1975	1976—1975	1977—1976
	A: Δp_c			
1. Wages	24.0	27.8	−13.1	13.0
2. Transfers	16.9	3.5	1.9	1.5
3. Less: taxes paid by wage earners	33.9	11.1	5.6	4.9
4. Less: savings by wage earners	−182.0	−6.4	−3.5	−2.6
5. Numerator	26.6	26.6	12.9	12.1
6. Personal consumption	13.9	15.3	8.3	6.5
7. Less: consumption by capitalists	9.6	1.0	0.5	0.5
8. Denominator	14.3	14.3	7.8	6.1
9. Δp_c	(10.7)[b]	12.3[c]	5.1[d]	6.0[e]
	B: Δp_c^*			
1. Business wages	24.5	20.0	9.4	9.5
2. Government expenditure covered by revenues	29.4	13.6	6.9	6.0
3. Government deficit	−81.0	−4.7	−3.0	−1.6
4. Less: taxes paid by wage earners	33.9	9.3	4.7	4.2
5. Less: savings by wage earners	−182.0	−5.4	−3.0	−2.2
6. Numerator	25.0	25.0	11.7	11.9
7. Personal consumption	13.9	13.1	7.0	5.6
8. Government purchases	3.5	0.5	−0.1	0.6
9. Less: consumption by capitalists	9.6	0.9	0.5	0.4
10. Denominator	12.7	12.7	6.5	5.8
11. Δp_c^*	(11.0)[b]	12.3[c]	5.1[d]	6.1[e]
Addenda:				
12. Total government purchases (B: 2+3)	17.1	8.9	3.9	4.6
13. Total consumption (B: 7+8)	8.8	13.6	6.9	5.0

[a]Contribution to the percentual change in the numerator and the denominator and, approximately, to that in Δp_c and Δp_c^*
[b]5/8
[c]5—8
[d]6/10
[e]6—10

phenomenon is even more striking. It was thus not without reason that they complained about insufficient investment!

As regards the quarterly changes in gross after-tax profits, this time we shall throw a glance merely on the development of paper profit elements that can be directly read from statistics, i.e., domestic government deficit and net profits. Their sum was the greatest in the second quarter of 1975 (deficit $87.8 bn, export surplus 24.3 bn), that is, $112.1 bn. By the last quarter of 1976 the deficit fell to 23.6 bn and net exports to 3.2 bn, (altogether 26.8 bn). Though slowing down, this process continued in the next year, too. In the fourth quarter of 1977 the deficit was $ 15 bn, and the surplus of the balance of trade turned into a large deficit of $ 18.1 bn (making 33.1 bn altogether). Thus, the changes in these items through two and a half years reduced profits by 115 bn (current) dollars. This process became in itself a not negligible obstacle to a stronger upswing even independently of the economic policy of the government.

Let us now pass to the trend in prices. The diagrams illustrating the factors in our Δp_c and Δp_c^x formulae can be found in Part II (figures 5.1 and 5.2 on pp. 67, 68) It turns out from them that the 8.4 per cent price rise of 1975 became moderated to 5.1 per cent by 1976. The difference is 3.3 percentage points. What happened was that the demand-increasing impact of the growth in the sum of nominal wages was greater than the demand-reducing effect of the rise in wage taxes and the demand-modifying impact of the overspending by wage earners was more than 3 percentage points stronger than the demand-reducing impact of the moderation in transfer payments, and thus the rise in nominal wages exceeded that of the preceding year by 4.5 percentage points. Enterprises, however, put up with the fact that their net after-tax profit margin should exceed that of 1975 by merely 0.4 percentage points. (Cf. Table 5.1 p. 67) It may be attributed to this fact that the volume of consumer goods purchased by wage earners increased 7.8 per cent over the preceding year or, arguing the other way round, the 7.8 per cent increase in the sale of wage-goods was only made possible by the fact that the enterpises held back the rate of price increases by 3.3 percentage points.

The changes between 1975 and 1977 are shown in Table 17.3.

Similarly to the price indices in official statistics, our own price level indicators also increased in 1977 more rapidly than in the preceding year. The most important factor in the growth of nominal consumer demand (the numerator of the Δp_c formula) was the rise in the sum of wages, and this was of equal size in both years. In this respect, the second most important factor in boosting demand was the turn in the savings of wage earners into overspending, although even so its weight was only about a quarter of that of the rise in wages. The price-raising role of transfers—compared to during the recession—strongly diminished, first of all because of a decrease in unemployment benefits, and this slowing tendency continued in 1977. Also the rise in wage earners' taxes significantly mitigated demand (more in 1976 than in 1977). Finally, nominal demand increased 12.1 percentage points in 1977, less than in 1976. But the labour costs per unit of product increased (outside agriculture) by 6.3 per cent in 1977 against 4.7 per cent in the preceding year. The reason was that while the rate of growth of remuneration per man-hour was somewhat moderated relative to the preceding year, the growth of productivity fell from 3.5 per cent to 1.6 per cent.(*Economic Report*, 1980, p. 247)

At the same time, enterprises increased their profit margin by 0.5 percentage points in 1977 against 0.4 in 1976. The growth in costs, and the slight rise in the profit margin caused a price rise of altogether 6 per cent, 0.9 percentage points higher than in 1976, and this, together with the slackening growth in nominal demand, reduced the growth in the volume of wage goods sold to 6.1 per cent, against 7.8 in the preceding year. (Not only the wage rate increased, the wholesale price of raw materials also rose by about 12 per cent and that of intermediares by 6 per cent between 1976 and 1977.)[62]

[62] *Economic Report* 1978, p. 322.

CHAPTER EIGHTEEN

CHAPTER EIGHTEEN

1978–1979: SLACKENING UPSWING AND ACCELERATING INFLATION— AT THE THRESHOLD OF RECESSION

18.1 ECONOMIC POLICY ENDING IN RECESSION

The tools for implementing the economic targets of the Carter administration were indentified in the 1978 *Economic Report* as follows: urgent adoption of the energy program; reduction of federal expenditure relative to GNP through careful and prudent fiscal policy; tax cuts and tax reform; balancing the budget at the fastest possible rate allowed by the strength of the economy; fight against structural unemployment; promotion of business capital formation; more effective measures to fight inflation and international economic policies promoting economic recovery of the world and the expansion of world trade. (*Economic Report,* 1978, pp. 5–6)

The proposed tax reform would have reduced the tax burden by $ 25 bn, and within it, corporate tax significantly by reducing the progression of taxes and making the investment tax credit permanent (*Op. Cit.,* pp. 74–75). All this should have taken effect on October 1st, 1978, but Congress voted the tax bill into law only in mid-October, (together with the energy program), diluting the reform and reducing the sum of the tax cut to $ 18.7 bn.

We have already seen the substance of the anti-inflation program: Carter asked the business community and the wage earners to participate voluntarily in a program aimed at slowing down the rate of price and wage increases. In this respect the *Economic Report* also comprised numerical forecasts: it was of the opinion that in the next few years the average growth of GNP might be 4.5–5 per cent, and the rate of inflation could be reduced to below 6 per cent—if the requests of the President were met. And from Table 16.2 (p. 252) it turns out that these targets were not attained in 1978, and much less so in 1979.

Here we have to mention an event of 1978 which may have an impact on the long-term formation of American economic policy. Congress voted into law the "Full Employment and Balanced Growth Act".[63] This was—at least according to the intention of its authors—a completion and extension of the Employment Act of 1946 (for a review of this Act, see p. 35). The new Act firmed up the old one in three respects. It explicitly stated the economic priorities and tasks of the nation; it asked the President to define and Congress to consider the targets based on the priorities; and

---

[63] In American literature we meet it under the name of Humphrey-Hawkins Act, after its initiators.

prescribed new rules of procedure, and new requirements for the President, Congress and the FED in order to improve the harmonization and development of economic policies. It declared "rational price stability" a national goal. Ceding to the strengthening monetarist influence aimed at reducing government interference it raised the requirement that the share of government expenditure in GNP should regularly decrease , and that in solving the tasks set by the law primarily the private sector should be relied upon. It separately stressed that a balanced federal budget compatible with the realization of other targets was a national political task. (*Economic Report* 1979, p. 107)

The Act also specified that government should set targets for the economic indicators of key importance (employment, unemployment, output, real income, productivity and prices) for five-year periods, in an annual breakdown. The President was to propose in the budget estimates expenditure and revenue levels in harmony with these.

The Act also prescribed for the FED to report on the tasks and plans of monetary policy to Congress twice a year. Congress would consider the policies of the President and the FED together. According to the Act in the first Economic Report of the President to be drawn up according to the guidelines, for 1983 a 4 per cent unemployment and a 3 per cent rise in the consumer price index was to be provided for. Beginning with the 1980 *Economic Report* the President was justified to change the provisions if he thought it necessary. But if he changed the provision for unemployment he had to specify by the end of which year he expected the new target to be fulfilled. (*Op. Cit.* p. 108)

It is a positive feature of this Act that it demands a more concrete specification of the tasks and this obliged the government to undertake some planning. The effort at coordinating the activities of the various high level organs is a part of this. But even these positive features would only be useful if the whole Act were not permeated by the

Table 18.1

Economic targets, 1979—1983

Item	1979	1980	1981	1982	1983
	level in fourth quarter[a]				
Employment (millions)	97.5	99.5	102.6	105.5	108.3
Unemployment (per cent)	6.2	6.2	5.4	4.6	4.0
	percentual change from fourth quarter to fourth quarter				
Consumer prices	7.5	6.4	5.2	4.1	3.0
Real GNP	2.2	3.2	4.6	4.6	4.2
Disposable real income	2.8	2.3	4.4	4.4	4.0
Productivity[b]	0.4	1.1	1.8	2.0	2.1

[a] Seasonally adjusted

[b] Total real GNP divided by the number of hours worked. *Source: Economic Report* 1979, p. 109.

260

spirit of the monetarist counter-revolution. The demand of a return to budgetary orthodoxy is definitely of a regressive nature; the emphasis on reliance on the private sector is utopistic, since it almost amounts to a declaration that the fate of the capitalist economy has to be left to its own spontaneous mechanisms. We have to know, of course, that these spontaneously working mechanisms sooner or later force a deviation—by otherwise threatening economic and mainly political failure—from the dogma of a balanced budget, but a dogma institutionalized by law makes it at any rate difficult to implement such a turn at the right time.

Complying with the Act, the *Economic Report* of 1979 published the above table.

The same *Economic Report* was compelled to acknowledge that targets set in the preceding year were not realized. As for as that goes, the targets set on the basis of the new Act shared the same fate. This was acknowledged in the 1980 *Economic Report* and—using the authorization mentioned—the President set new targets. He put off the reduction of unemployment to 4 per cent to 1985 and the reduction of the rate of inflation to 3 per cent three years later than that. (*Economic Report*, 1980, pp. 9–10)

Recession was "predicted" by many already in 1979, and even in 1978, but this proved to be exaggerated pessimism for some time. Merril Lynch Economics, drawing up forecast with a big econometric model, expected, e.g., a recession for the first half of 1979 in a forecast made in November 1978, and estimated the annual increase of GNP at only 1.1 per cent.[64] The same firm, together with several other large institutions engaged in forecasting, expected even at the end of 1979 that recession would begin already in the first quarter of 1980. (*Op. Cit.*, Jan. 8, 1980) It was also clear that there was a close relationship between inflation and the danger of recession. The director of the Wage and Price Stability Council of the President, B. Bosworth, announced in Autumn 1978 that inflation was inevitable if the anti-inflationary measures did not succeed. (*International Herald Tribune*, Oct. 14–15, 1978)

We are of the opinion that the economic policy of the Carter-administration failed and ended in the 1980 recession primarily because it did not stick to its promise "that the inflation from the past cannot be cured by policies that slow growth and keep unemployment high". (*Economic Report,* 1978, p. 17.) Although this was promised in the course of the primary contest for the Democratic nomination, yet the judgement of Senator Kennedy was not cheap electioneering, but a statement containing a grain of truth that under the Democratic administration there was Republican inflation for a further three years, Republican rates of interest for a further three years and Republican economics for again three years. (*The New York Times*, January 29, 1980) And the mild judgement of non-American experts was that " ... on the revenue side, no attempt was made to offset the fiscal drag". (*OECD Economic Outlook,* 27, July 1980, p. 73)

Of course, the trouble was bigger than this. Getting caught in the pincers of an indeed strong, mostly external inflationary pressure (the price rises of oil) and fiscal orthodoxy, they chose the wrong way. At the same time when the price rise drained the consumers by 55 bn dollars, (according to their own computations, see *Economic Report* 1980, p. 29) i. e., 3 per cent of their after-tax income, they also had to suffer from

[64] See Conference Board Statistical Bulletin, December 1978, p. 8.

the restrictive fiscal policy. This was reflected by the fact that the so-called high-employment balance turned between 1978 and the second half of 1979 from a deficit of $7 bn into a surplus of 13 bn. We can read the admission in the report of the Council of Economic Advisers, that "the magnitude of this restraint" caused by the two factors "had no parallel in any post-war year—including 1974, when the first big OPEC price increase rocked the economy". (*Ibid.*)

The fall into sin is, however, of an earlier origin. This is reflected on the fiscal policy side by the following data. The (domestic) deficit of the federal government was $45.9 bn in 1976, the last year of the Republican administration. In the Carter years it first fell to $37.6 bn and then to 15.3 bn, turning into a 3.5 bn surplus in 1979. The turn was particularly sharp in the last two years. To wit: in the last quarter of 1977 there was a deficit of 43.8 bn, which fell to 8.3 bn in the course of the next year. The change was smaller in terms of quantity in the next half a year, but it was a qualitative one: the second quarter of 1979 already showed a surplus of 7.9 bn. Then, it seems, they realized that one can have too much of a good thing, and by the fourth quarter the surplus fell to 0.7 bn. But this could no longer help, it could not reverse the factors working towards recession which had already gathered momentum, since, in the final analysis the total (domestic) deficit of $20.9 bn in 1976 turned into a surplus of 27.9 bn by 1979, reducing profits by $48.8 bn—with all the consequences involved.

18.2 PRODUCTION AND DEMAND IN 1978–1979

The start was bad in 1978. Owing to the extremely severe winter and the coal miners' strike the rate of growth of GNP fell to a very low value in the first quarter, to 1.9 per cent (here and henceforth at annual rate). As if by reaction, in the next quarter it jumped unusually high (8.3 per cent), but in the following one and a half years it showed a declining tendency, whith fluctuations: in the last quarter of 1970 it did not even attain 1.5 per cent, and in the second quarter of 1980 the recession started with a 9.1 per cent fall.

The slowdown of the growth rate of production showed first of all in the production of material goods. The situation was about the same in construction. The slowdown was particularly sharp in the production of durables, from 16.8 to 6.3 per cent. Even the growth of services slowed a little.

Examining the situation by types of demand, the following may be established. The slowing down of the growth rate affected all types and groups of demand, but its extent greatly differed; with some of them even an absolute decline occurred. But let us look at each in turn.

Personal consumption (excluding the purchase of homes) definitely lost its momentum: growth between the two end points of the period (the last quarters of 1977 and 1979) was only 6.2 per cent, between the last quarters of 1978 and 1979 only 1.7 per cent and in the last quarter of 1979 merely 1 per cent. Within this the sharp negative turn in the purchase of consumer durables it is particularly striking: in eight quarters it only increased by 3.1 per cent (in the preceding eight ones by 19 per cent!) and even this occurred in a manner whereby between the end of 1977 and that of 1978 the growth was still 6.8 per cent, but already in the course of the next year a 3.5 per cent decline

262

followed. A great role was played in that by the falling demand for cars, as reflected by the stagnation of automobile production in 1978, and its 15.6 per cent fall in 1979. Housing construction presented an even more hopeless picture, as its growth already stopped at the end of 1977, stagnated in the the following year, declined in 1979 every quarter and in the fourth quarter it was already 7 per cent below the level of a year before. The result was an unfavourable development of consumers' investment: in the last quarter they stood at the same level as two years earlier. In the course of 1978 there was still a 4.7 per cent growth, but this was replaced by a decline in almost every quarter of the following year, amounting altogether to 4.7 per cent.

As regards fixed capital investment, their volume increased through the eight quarters by 13.7 per cent—rather strongly, yet significantly more slowly than in the two preceding years. But even here we find a great difference between 1978 and 1979: the rate fell from 10.5 per cent to 3.0, and in the last quarter of 1979 there was a very small decline.

Except for the second quarter of 1979 the accumulation of inventories showed a diminishing tendency and in the last quarter of 1979 it merely amounted to 15 per cent of its value two years earlier. It should be noted that the relative low level of stocks may be considered undoubtedly a favourable circumstance in view of the expectable gravity of the recession unfolding in 1980.

Instead of mitigating the general slackening of demand, government purchases increased at a decreasing rate—by merely 2 per cent in two years—while federal purchases even diminished. But military procurement again started to grow.

The changed character of development is also reflected in the fact that the growth rate of the cyclical group of demand (2.8 per cent) did not reach even one tenth of the value in the preceding two years. Also the growth of the trend-like group slowed somewhat, from 8.2 per cent to 6.3. But the earlier negative role of the irregular group was replaced by an 11.9 per cent growth. The reason was that the deterioration of the balance of trade changed and improved, and this trend was only slowed by the new major rise in oil prices in 1979.

In the slackening of personal consumption, and particularly in the reduction of consumers' investment a role was played by the fact that following the first quarter of 1979 the disposable personal real income already started to decline and in the last quarter it was slightly higher than a year earlier. The slackening of consumption and the decline in some of its elements was not more pronounced because the unfavourable development of disposable income was counterbalanced by the continuing fall in the rate of savings and this indicator sank by the last quarter of 1979 to an extremely low value, 3.4 per cent, something not seen for decades.

We hope to gain a deeper insight into the driving forces of the outlined processes again by analysing the structure of the increments in the fourth quarters of the relevant years. (See Table 18.2)

The data of the table unambiguously show (particularly if compared to the similar table on p. 254) what changes were taking place in the role of the factors determining economic movements. The role of the cyclical group became quite slight, and the main factor in growth was the trend-like group, even if only to a small degree. The booster role of consumers' investment became quite spent, while that of fixed capital investment increased. The weight of government purchases also increased somewhat,

Table 18.2

Distribution of the increment of GNP between the fourth quarters of 1977
and 1979

Item	Billions of 1972 dollars	Percentage distribution
	by type of demand	
GNP	79.4	100.0
Personal consumption	54.9	69.1
Purchase of consumer durables	4.4	5.5
Fixed capital investment	18.1	22.8
Residential construction	−4.2	−5.3
Changes in inventories	−8.8	−11.1
Net exports	14.0	17.6
Government purchases	5.4	6.8
Federal purchases	−1.4	−1.8
Military purchases[a]	3.5	4.4
Cyclical group	9.6	12.1
Trend-like group	57.0	71.8
Irregular group	12.8	16.1
	by type of product	
Production of goods	31.6	39.8
Durables	16.2	20.4
Non-durables	15.4	19.4
Structures	6.4	8.1
Material production	38.0	47.9
Services	41.4	52.1
Addenda:		
Consumers' investment	0.2	0.3
Auto product	−7.6	−9.6

[a] In official statistics this is only given at current prices. Conversion was
made by using the implicit price deflator of federal purchases.

although this was not the general slowdown. The weight of federal purchases—except
for military ones—even diminished.

Looking at it according to product types, the leading role was taken by services; the
importance of every element of material production definitely diminished. In this
context, it is worth mentioning that the decline in construction can be traced back
entirely to the absolute fall in housing construction, while investment construction
continued to grow. All this testifies to the fact that, similarly to what had happened in
the period immediately preceding the 1974–1975 recession, and contrary to the
widespread theory, the direct cause releasing the recession was not fixed capital
investment at this time either. The immediate cause of the decline in total demand, and
thus of the evolution of the recession, was the fall in consumers' investment.

In consequence of the outlined changes in production and demand, naturally, the
utilization of the productive capital assets also turned unfavourable. This indicator

attained the peak in the first quarter of 1979 (with a utilization rate of 86.7 per cent), and fell to 84.6 by the last quarter of the year. It is to be noted that the peak was now 1.2 percentage points below the maximum attained prior to the recession, in the third quarter of 1973 (*Economic Report,* 1979, p. 231 and 1980, p. 251).

We can state that the development of production, demand and capacity utilization unambiguously indicated an impending recession. After five years of expansion this happened as a result of the economic policy of a Democratic administration—for the first time in over 30 years. Thus the optimistic expectations of the Carter-administration (see p. 259) proved illusory.

18.3 PROFITS AND PRICES IN 1978–1979[65]

We start the examination of the movement of profits again by taking corporate profits. Their sum fell somewhat in the first quarter of 1978, but grew again through the next three quarters, attaining the peak in the last quarter of the year. Then, in the course of 1979, it was slowly declining, and its volume not only remained below the value in the last quarter of a year before, but was lower than two years earlier. Also the other main type of profit, proprietors' income, showed a declining tendency in 1979 and thus their combined volume[66] was, in the fourth quarter of 1979, 8.3 per cent lower than a year earlier, though somewhat higher than two years earlier. As regards 1978 as a whole we can gain an insight into the relative importance of the factors in the movement of profits through our own profit indicators. In that year gross after-tax profits still increased by 2.8 per cent (in 1972 dollars), though much more slowly than in the two preceding years (7.8 and 5.2 per cent). The changes in the individual elements of profit contributed in the following manner (+ = increasing, − = decreasing impact): gross material profit + 6.7 per cent, paper profit − 3.4 per cent. It can be seen that the movement of paper profit was now also anti-cyclical, similarly to the preceding two years, and neutralized the favourable influence of the growth of material profit almost by half. Within the latter, both gross investment and the changes in capitalists' consumption had a positive effect. It is worth mentioning that a decisive part of the positive contribution of net investment (4.8 per cent out of 5.2) derived from net fixed capital investment, while the role of stockpiling was very slight. From among the elements of paper profit the role of government deficit remained strongly negative (− 6.6 per cent), while that of net exports turned positive, if only to a minimum extent. Overspending by wage earners had had a significant positive impact in the preceding two years (+ 10.9 and + 7.5) and now this dropped significantly to 1.8 per cent.

The following can be said about 1979. On the basis of the above-outlined development of corporate profits and proprietors' incomes, it may be taken for sure that the volume of gross after-tax profit diminished, probably by a half or one per cent

[65] When writing this chapter (August 1980) the data necessary to work out our own profit and price indicators for 1979 were not yet available.

[66] Official statistics publish these data only at current prices; we worked out the volumes in 1972 dollars by deflating them with the implicit price index of GNP.

at annual rate. The decline between the last quarters of the two years may have been more than that: 2–3 per cent, essentially because of the fall in corporate profits. And as regards the components of profit: material profit increased, because from its elements both investment and the volume of consumption by capitalists continued to grow, even if at a slower rate. But the negative impact of paper profit increased by all certainty, for the following reasons. The volume of government deficit changed from -6.6 bn (1972) dollars in the preceding year to -16.9 bn, that is, the surplus increased. Namely, the domestic balance of the federal government changed from a significant deficit (though decreasing through the earlier years) into a surplus of a few billions. True, the volume of net exports changed from -6.8 bn in 1978 to -3.7 bn in 1979, but the growth in profit attributable to it only neutralized but about one third of the profit-reducing impact of the 10.3 bn change in government deficit. The balance was thus played by the third element of paper profit, the savings by wage-earners, in this case by their over-spending. While regarding the two former factors we were able to rely on official data, in this respect we have only our own estimations. We know as much that both the purchase of consumer durables and housing construction (and by all certainty: the purchase of homes) definitely fell in 1979. (See section 18.2 of this chapter.) According to general experience this is usually accompanied by a reduction of overspending, in some cases turning into saving. Further, from official statistics we also know that in 1979 the net growth of both consumer (instalment) credits and of mortgage credits connected with the purchase of homes slowed down. (*Economic Report,* 1980, pp. 280–282) This, too, supports the reduction of overspending. Thus we have sufficient reason to assume that the scales tipped towards the profit-reducing effect, the negative impact of the paper profit unambiguously overcompensated the positive effect of the slight growth in material profit. As regards the volume of profit, we think a 1–2 per cent decline is likely.

Thus, in the last resort the anti-cyclical effect of paper profit prevailed throughout the whole period, primarily because of the first decreasing government deficit which later turned into a surplus. The latter alone reduced profits between 1975 and 1979 by 78.5 bn (1972) dollars. Between the second quarter of 1975 and the fourth of 1979 the changes in anti-cyclical profit components took around 150 bn (current) dollars of profits of which 115.7 bn could be attributed to the above described movement of the government deficit. A fiscal policy having such an impact on profit was bound to lead to recession.

On the basis of our price level indicators Δp_c and Δp_c^* we may state the following for 1978 (see the corresponding diagrams in Chapter 5 of Part Two, pp. 54–55 and 65–66 and the numerical data in Tables 6.5 and 6.6). The nominal demand-raising effect of the numerator was moderated in the case of both indicators—by equally 0.5 per cent. This reduction came about in spite of the fact that the price-increasing effect of wage rises strengthened. This effect was, namely, overcompensated by a more moderate rise in the overspending by wage earners (by 1.5 and 1.8 percentage points), while the price-moderating impact of taxes and the price-raising one of transfers, (as well as of government expenditure in the Δp_c^* indicator), remained essentially unchanged. The enterprises kept their profit margin at the level of the preceding year in the deteriorating situation. (According to our own computations the profit margin interpreted at GNP level fell by one tenth of a percentage point, but such a slight difference does certainly not exceed the margin of error in our computations.) But this meant that our Δp_c indicator signals a 6.8 per cent price rise and the Δp_c^* indicator one of 7.2 per cent, 1.1 and 1.4 percentage points higher than a year before. In consequence, the annual growth of the volume of commodities sold, figuring in the denominator of the Δp_c^* formula, fell from 6.2 per cent in 1977 to 4.2 per cent.

The official statistics reveal (among other things) the following price rises. The implicit price index of GNP increased between December 1977 and the same month of 1978 by 8.2 per cent and in the next twelve months by 9 per cent. The rise in the consumer price index jumped from 9.0 per cent to 13.3, again transgressing the scary double-digit zone (the price rise is 11.3 per cent even when the whole of the two years are compared). Wages cannot be blamed for the increasing inflation even with deliberate malice. But the development of labour productivity had much to do with it. Although between the last quarters of 1977 and 1978 it still showed some rise, in the next year it already fell by 2.1 per cent and thus it lagged behind the level of two years before by 1.3 per cent at the end of 1979.[67] It thus happened that while hourly wages increased in the course of the two years to the same extent, the rise in wage cost per unit of product increased from 8.3 per cent to 11.3 between the last quarters of 1977 and 1978.[68] The price rise was also prompted by external factors. From among them the most important was the doubling of the world market price of crude oil in the course of 1979. As a result, the energy element of the consumer price index jumped by 35.6 (!) per cent and that of producer prices by 62(!) per cent between the last quarters of 1978 and 1979 (*Economic Report,* 1980, p. 27). The slowly declining exchange rate of the dollar worked in the same way—even if to an incomparably smaller extent.

To conclude, a last datum. In the private sector of the economy (not counting agriculture) the weekly real wages already stagnated between the last months of 1977 and 1978, and fell by 5 per cent in the following twelve months. Considering 1979 as a whole the fall was 3.1 per cent; a greater decline only occurred in 1974 and 1975. The result was that the real wages of the bulk of American wage earners were in 1979 somewhat lower than four years earlier, in the crisis year of 1975.

[67] Much energy was devoted to exploring the causes of the unfavourable development of productivity. One of the most recent and comprehensive works is by E. F. Dension, the well-known researcher of growth problems: *Accounting for Slower Economic Growth*, The Brookings Institute, Washington, D. C., 1979.

[68] Source of the official data on prices, productivity etc. are the tables in the statistical appendices to the *Economic Report* of 1979 and 1980.

CHAPTER NINETEEN
A FEW CONCLUDING REMARKS

19.1 OUR NEW ACHIEVEMENT IN PRICE AND PROFIT THEORY

In the introductory pages to this book we have already indicated that we wanted to confront the views of *Wages, Profit, Taxation* with the concrete reality of the economy of a country. Only in this manner can it be established whether the model applied in that book did not abstract from such aspects of contemporary capitalism whose neglect would lead directly to false conclusions. This means at the same time that our present work may be considered, to a certain extent, as a revision, or, if you like, as the critique, of *Wages, Profit, Taxation*.

As indicated by the subtitle of the volume, the results of our present book of theoretical interest relate to the theories of price profit and business cycles.

It seems that as regards price theory only a few essential statements can be found in our present work which had not appeared also in the earlier book. Apart from the statement on the inverse relationship between the price level of consumer goods and the real profit attainable through their sales, only some shifts of emphasis occurred.

Above all, the meaning of the relationship illustrated with the Δp_c formula had to be formulated more cautiously than before. In this formula not only the price level but also the volume of products sold may be regarded as dependent variables. The formula interprets the mutual adjustment of nominal demand, the price level and the saleable volume of products. It also turned out that the positive and negative savings of wage earners have a greater role in the development of nominal demand than can be read in *Wages, Profit, Taxation*, just as the difference between government transfers and wage taxes has a greater role, and not only in the development of prices but also that of profits—by influencing the government deficit. As regards the theory of profit, the following may be considered new results. The separation of material profit from paper profit on macrolevel, the revealing of the specific properties and role of the latter; the statement that—as distinct from material profit—the development of paper profit does not depend on the decision of capitalists; presentation of the interrelations among the components of macrolevel profit, as well as of their impact on the development of total profit; distinction within the macrolevel profit of the groups of trend-like, cyclical and anti-cyclical profit components; clarification of the role played by the individual components of profit in the mechanism of business cycles and, within the latter, identification of the anti-cyclical nature of the movement of paper profit.

In the course of our investigation we have met with an abundance of facts which allow us to draw conclusions, valid for the "model country" of contemporary capitalism, the United States, but very likely for a whole group of countries, about the causes and course of present-day business fluctuations.

We begin to characterize the business fluctuations of the examined decade with two general statements. The first is that the recessions were either not too deep, or even mild. The second is that there were no periodical crises of the classical type. These are statements valid not only for the seventies but for the whole post-war period.

As regards the first statement, we have to establish that all the structural changes that had saved the economy earlier from deeper crises, now also worked towards a mitigation of recessions. Such changed conditions are, to mention only the most important ones, the increased weight in the economy of the unproductive sector, within it of government and of services in general. (We already referred to our earlier study, in which, through the example of the 1957–1958 recession, we investigated quantitatively and in a wider context, the role of cumulative process in recent recessions with particular attention to the role of structural changes, built-in stabilizers and discretionary government measures in mitigating the deepening of the process of recession.) (See P. Erdős and F. Molnár 1969)

It was primarily due to the structural changes that the 1974–1975 recession and, naturally, even more so the 1969–1970 one, were expressly milder than those of the interwar period or than the so-called reconversion crisis between 1944 and 1947 in the course of returning to peace economy. (In the latter, the fall in GNP attained 17.4 per cent.) This model of business recession to be characterized by a not too large decline in production has become permanent.

As regards the second statement, first of all it should be remembered that one of the characteristic features of the classical type crises was a more or less regular periodicity. But today we cannot speak about periodicity in the classical sense. Between the 1957–1958 recession and the beginning of the next one of 1960–1961 there were three years, between the 1969–1970 recession and the former one nine years, between the latter and the 1974–1975 recession five years, and between the last quarter of 1974 and the first one of 1980 five and a quarter years passed. However we look at it, we do not find two such dates between which the "regular" 7–12 years had passed. Thus not even the concept of intermediary crisis can be justly related to any of them.

Secondly, we used to characterize the classical type crises as overproduction crises. As much is true that overproduction also has a role in today's recessions. In the sectors suffering from the greatest fall in production and demand—e.g., in housing construction—this factor not infrequently has a determining role. This is testified, e.g., by the fact that as a result of building activity in 1971–1973 (2 million dwellings annually), at the end of the last mentioned year no less than 650 thousand homes and owner-occupied dwellings remained unsold in the hands of the construction firms. (Renshaw, 1946, p. 43) On the other hand, in the 1974–1975 recession such events appeared, not at all characteristic of overproduction, as bottlenecks in agriculture and a few other fields of the economy, that had come about in 1973. But, in connection with the crises of the classical type, we can frequently meet with such statements that,

269

through annihilating considerable forces of production, such a crisis temporarily solves the accumulated contradictions. Molnár (1970, 244–245) formulated a similar statement in such terms that in earlier crises when production declined, that is when a "narrowed reproduction" was taking place, net accumulation became negative. Of course, this was true even in the period of crises of the classical type only in the case of really deep crises, and not every one of the classical was really deep. But Molnár emphasized that in the post-World War II recessions this did not happen even exceptionally, and this he formulated in such terms that extended reproduction and accumulation had parted company. This means that the stock of fixed capital continued to grow even during the crisis, and so did productive capacity, since investment did not fall to such extent as not to cover the (physical and moral) obsolescence of fixed capital.

Expanded reproduction separated not only from accumulation but also from gross investment. True, it had occurred in the preceding century, too, that overproduction had been first felt in the market of consumer goods, but in the typical cases the avalanche had been started by a decline in fixed capital investment. But after World War II the phenomenon has become permanent that in the evolution of recessions the decline in total demand and production starts with a fall in consumers' investments. (Thus, fixed capital investment continues to grow for a time after the beginning of the recession.) Similarly, it is the beginning of the growth of consumers' investment that starts the recovery after the recession, while the movement of business fixed capital investment only follows consumers' investment with a time lag of half a year or a year. All these testify to the fact that in the period following World War II we may speak—at least as regards the United States—about a series of recessions of identical type—in spite of certain distinctive features of the 1974–1975 one.

But the last-mentioned occurrence, the asynchronous movement of reproduction and fixed capital investment is a paradoxical phenomenon, almost incredible to those thinking in terms of the theory of crises of the classical type. In this scope of ideas it seems axiomatic not only that capitalist economy is a profit-motivated economy and that the decline in profit entails the contraction of the whole economy, but also that profits have to grow or diminish together with the growth or decline of investment. And it is true that if the volume of profits diminishes, then besides the effort to sustain the profit margin, the volume of sales and then of output also has to diminish. And if the volume of profit is the sum of investment and the consumption by capitalists—and this much was true with good approximation also at the time of crises of the classical type—then, since the consumption by capitalists is rigid in the short run, investment and the volume of profits are bound to move together. But then it is indeed baffling how an asynchronous movement of reproduction and investment is possible.

A resolution of the paradox is made posssible, of course, by the recognition of the significantly increased role of paper profit. The savings or overspending by wage earners significantly influence the size of total profit. Thus, the profit margin and even the absolute size of profit may also diminish when investment does not yet diminish, since a possible decline in the overspending of wage earners or its turning into net savings will reduce profit. But this possible decline almost becomes regular in improving business—and precisely around the peak of the business cycle promoted by economic policy and the accompanying inflation—when, in the interest of putting a brake on inflation, credit granting is restricted, rates of interest are raised, that is, a restrictive monetary policy is implemented. In such times, the use of consumer and mortgage credits declines by necessity and wage earners are forced to reduce consumer investments. It is this partial phenomenon of the "political cycle" that causes the initial decline in the margin of the volume of profit. This decline will sooner or later also hinder investment. It is in this manner that the crisis of non-classical type is born which is not started by overproduction, nor by the periodical fall in fixed capital investment, but by monetary and credit restrictions and, mostly, by restrictive fiscal policy. It should also be clear that the new fetish of consumer investment cannot replace the fetish of fixed capital investment. The prime mover of the mechanism of decline and recovery is not the change in consumers' investment. Although the latter develops cyclically, monetary policy has a controlling role in both the decline and the recovery, while the relatively lasting nature of the decline already follows from the general decline and the fear of it. But it is also affected by fiscal policy measures, namely, if these have a serious impact on the disposable income of wage earners—as, e.g., the tax reduction of 1975.

The latter example related to the recession-mitigating effect of the budget. It was an example of the case when inflation remained moderate in spite of the growing deficit, but such a situation is an exception. Otherwise, a growing deficit usually increases inflation. Of course, inflation may become graver also for other reasons, particularly under the pressure of costs in oligopolistic conditions, and—through the "perverse" impact of fiscal effects, the growing tax revenues in spite of recession—it reduces the disposable incomes relative to the rate of price rises, accelerates the decline in sales and deepens the recession. Apart from this "perverse" effect, although the growth of the deficit stimulates business, it does so mainly if the additional government spending is aimed at material expenses. Wage outlays are less effective in this respect, because their direct impact increases not real but mostly only nominal demand, and partly not even, that because a part becomes (temporarily) annihilated in the course of the recession in the form of savings. Recession is, of course, aggravated by the rise in import prices because—through the price rise released—it reduces the volume of commodities sold on the one hand, and reduces profit through the deterioration in the balance of trade on the other. If until now we have written about the outbreak and deepening of the recession, let us add for the sake of completeness that contemporary recessions end, as it happened in 1975, generally without an increase in investment. Besides government deficit, a role is played in that by consumers' investment, that is, by the stimulating financial and credit policy, as well as by the decrease in the savings of wage earners or by their turning into overspending. In such cases profit already starts to grow in spite of the fact that investment does not yet increase. Of course, this, too, can only be unterstood by taking into account paper profit.

What can we then say about the causes releasing the typical business fluctuations in the United States? In a rather schematic way we may say that they are brought about by three groups of factors: (1) the autonomous movement of the economy, (2) random shocks, and (3) the economic policy cycle called political cycle by Kalecki. (For these three groups of causes, see Molnár, 1979, p. 208.)

In this chapter not much has been said as yet about the autonomous movement of the economy, but, naturally, this also has an important role. Thus, in connection with

271

what happened in 1973–1975, to the phenomena of autonomous movement can be ranked the development of fixed capital investment; the characteristic fluctuations in the savings by wage earners independent of the credit possibilities; partly, and not in every respect, the development of consumers' investment and, last but not least, the growing inflationary pressure even independently of government interference. Also, the insufficiency of fixed capital investment in 1976–1979 belongs here.

Random shocks in this period—instead of wars and natural calamities were the oil price explosion and the following oil embargo, and then the repeated doubling of oil prices in 1979.

19.3 POLITICAL CYCLE AND KEYNESIAN ECONOMIC POLICY

The cyclical changes in economic policy have been analysed in detail. But in fact we are dealing with much more here, namely, real political cycles. Kalecki, as if he had seen the future, projected the possibility and even the likelihood of such a political cycle already in 1943. He wrote that in view of the deficit there would be some economists who would declare that the situation was obviously unhealthy. The pressure of these and of big capital would prompt the government to return to the orthodox policy of reducing the budget deficit. But this would lead to depression and in the depression the policy of government expenditure would regain its rightful role. (Kalecki, 1980, p. 144)

In the period investigated, American big business found on the eve of three recessions the economists who found the situation unhealthy—characterized by relatively low unemployment and by 1979 not so low unemployment, and by high real wages very moderately rising relative to inflation between 1976 and 1978 and declining in 1979—and who, under the pretext of fighting the unbearably high inflation (in 1969, 5.0 per cent, in 1973, 5.8 per cent, measured by the implicit price index of GNP), led the country into a recession with their economic policy. It is timely to note here that the repeated fall in consumers' investment, classified above as belonging to the group of autonomous movement, came about mostly in consequence of the discretionary economic policy decisions dictated by political considerations and embodied in monetary and fiscal policy measures. Then in 1975, when the trouble was already great indeed, they resorted to the largest budget deficit ever seen (primarily not by increasing expenditure, but by reducing taxes).

With these last sentences we have arrived at the problem of the more or less Keynesian economic policy. What we want to say about it does not relate to the whole of the post-World War II period, but rather to the period discussed in this book. Namely, it has turned out that in the seventies such process took place in the economies of the United States and other developed capitalist countries in which the tools of the monopoly-capitalist state, based on the Keynesian theory and previously used with success, became blunted. In the contemporary capitalist economy there is an irreconcilable contradiction between the anti-cyclical measures, on the one hand, and the efforts at relative price stability, at containing inflation, on the other. Under inflationary conditions Keynesian economic policy meets with several objective and partly insurmountable obstacles and becomes much less effective than earlier.

The substance of the matter is that it could not be achieved, nor was it possible to achieve that if, in consequence of some government measure, nominal demand increased by a definite amount this should result in a higher volume of output and not in a higher price level. It happened mostly the other way around. Primarily, the reason was the unfavourable development of labour productivity throughout the seventies and the oligopolistic price formation mechanism. These failures were reflected by the fact that the trends gathered momentum in Western views on economics, which, discarding even the positive features of Keynes's theory and the economic policy based on it, turned back to the economic policy of "laissez faire" ideology and wanted to push those directing economic policy—not without success—towards radically reducing government interference.[69] It will perhaps not be considered exaggerated immodesty if we remark that the p_c formula and the new concept introduced by us, the paper profit, separated from total profit, may be considered appropriate tools for analysing these failures. It turned out precisely from the analysis of the latter concept that paper profit played a significant anti-cyclical role through its impact on the development of profits—in spite of the fact that the behaviour of wage earners, dictated by business fluctuations, was pro-cyclical. This anti-cyclical role evolved as a result of international economic relations and the effects of economic policy—mainly fiscal policy—measures. (It is a fact, at any rate, that the broad tax reduction of 1975 played a highly positive role in fighting the recession.) We may thus say about the Keynesian recipes that they cannot be considered as a panacea, having many drawbacks and they only work if the patient takes them, or, if necessary, is forced to do so. But there repeatedly arise situations when he must take them.

Let us finally state regarding the recent recessions that the not too deep nature of contemporary recessions follows from the lasting—and continuing—structural changes in the economy, and the relative gravity of individual recessions depends first of all on concrete operative economic policy measures—or precisely on their not having been taken. Finally, though we have not referred to it in our text, it is timely to establish that both from our data on the profit margin and from relevant literature a lasting tendency of a falling rate of profit seems to emerge. As a result of this and of the permanent energy concerns (as well as of the urgent demands of environmental protection) a lasting deceleration of the growth rate may be expected.

---

[69] To this current may also be counted the new theory of "reasonable expectations".

APPENDIX

A METHOD FOR THE ESTIMATION OF THE INCOMES, CONSUMPTION AND SAVINGS OF SOCIAL CLASSES, BASED ON THE STATISTICAL DATA OF THE UNITED STATES OF AMERICA

A.1 INTRODUCTORY REMARKS

In solving the problem indicated in the title, US statistical data were used.[1]

In these statistics—beyond data on several hundreds of (aggregate) categories of the United States—we also find aggregate national economic balances, in the form of uninterrupted time series from 1929 to these days, in an annual and even quarterly breakdown. It is thus from these that we have to derive the "facts". Of course, these statistics do not and cannot rely altogether or even predominantly on "vouchers". This is so not because and not even primarily because there is nothing to guarantee that the data supplied by enterprises are not distorted by real or assumed interests or because the sanctity of business secrets prevents thorough checking, but because the data also comprise the economy of millions of "small people", from whom no detailed data can be requested. Precisely on this account, a considerable part of the data published is derived from assumed partial interrelations or from estimates arrived at through balance-identities. (Although this does not prevent those compiling the data from publishing mostly six-digit figures, while unquestioned inexactitude, called "statistical discrepancy" already appears in the third digit.) We have to put up within this situation, and from the point of view of their compilers these national economic balances of the official American statistics may excellently reflect that economy even so.

We have said that the models serving as raw material of our models may well reflect the reality of the American economy from the viewpoint of their compilers. We repeat:

---

[1] We should not fall into the error of believing that if we study a national economic statistics compiled with good professional conscience and accurately, then we are examining facts reflecting reality without qualification. It is well known, e.g., that price index numbers or the indices showing changes in national income develop differently depending on weighting and on the identification of goods. They do not establish unambiguous facts, but indicate how indicators relating to certain facts change if we take into account certain partial facts that can only be defined inexactly, in some manner to be exactly defined separately, e.g., by weighting. A statistical time series, even one based exclusively on creditable vouchers, cannot eliminate the well-known deficiences of the index numbers relating to populations with changing weights. It characterizes, namely, with a single scalar quantity such a thing which, in principle, could only be imagined as a multi-dimensional vector. If for example it bears the title "national income", this means so much, in the best of cases, that the time series relates to something that — similarly to innumerable other time series more or less deviating from it — may be called, not without good reason, the change over time of the national income.

from their point of view. But we have different points of view precisely in respect of the most essential interrelations. The US statistics contain a huge amount of data, but we do not find e. g., for surplus value, the rate of surplus value, the profit margin or the rate of profit, the part of taxes paid by capitalists or by wage earners, the personal consumption by wage earners or capitalists, etc. It is precisely the most important data on the incomes of social classes that are missing. These statistics only take into account the existence of different classes to the really inevitable extent, but we have to confront the laws of own political economy based on class categories—formulated with different degrees of concreteness, but all too abstract relative to the richness of reality even in their most concrete form—through the data of bourgeois statistics with what actually happened in the 1970s. It is easy to see that this is not a simple task.

A.2 ON THE DIFFICULTIES OF THE PROBLEM

In this Appendix we wish to show, through a single detail, the tools with which we assume to solve our problem sufficiently satisfactorily.

The economies of the developed capitalist countries were characterized in the seventies by such, almost incessantly accelerating inflation which seems to have played a highly significant role in the sudden decline and recession starting in 1974. This inflation could finally only be slowed down but not eliminated by the recession itself and by anti-inflationary government intervention. The simultaneous occurrence of economic recession and a general price rise which—apart from times following major catastrophies—seemed to be a square peg in a round hole prior to World War II in the economy of the United States, became a recurring phenomenon, at least since the 1954 recession. But it was only in the seventies that a significant recession coincided with a significant inflation. Obviously, we have to clarify the mutual impacts of production (and trade) and inflation, thus, among other things, we have to clarify the relative importance of the major factors maintaining and at times accelerating inflation.

It was our Δp_c formula relating to the price level of consumer goods that seemed best suited for a theoretical analysis of the latter problem. But there are no statistical data available on a number of elements figuring in the formula, such as the size of taxes paid by wage earners, saving by wage earners, personal consumption of wage earners, and some elements of wages of lesser weight. We had to find a way of showing these at least approximately. Without them, the Δp_c formula could not have been written in terms of actual figures.

The first difficulty we met was that the theoretical formula reckons simply with workers and capitalists, while in reality the boundary between classes is somewhat blurred. The compilers of the US statistics, of course, did not intend to depict real class divisions, but we, too, would be in great trouble if we had to draw such unambiguous lines ourselves—even if we had perfect knowledge of all imaginable data. But US statistics offers something to hold on to: it published money incomes by types of income. Yet the matter is not that simple. Namely, the series of data relating to incomes and consumption also comprise imputations. Thus, e. g., one who lives in a rented flat pays a housing rent, therefore—concludes the Western economist—one who lives in his own home, "pays", rent to himself. This imputed housing rent is part of his income. (Also allocations in kind are considered imputed incomes in American statistics.) However, if we wish to use the Δp_c formula, we have to think in terms of market sale and purchase, i.e., we have to use data without imputations. To tell the truth, we frequently lost our way in the labyrinth of American national accounts, but finally we succeeded fully in solving the task of excluding imputations. We succeeded, e.g., in working out the sum of wages and salaries in individual years without imputations.

But the category of "wages and salaries" means a type of income in American statistics and not an unambiguous class-income. The car-manufacturer Ford also gets a salary from his company, not only dividends or similar remuneration; his salary is also included in the total of salaries. (Wages and salaries are not separated, they appear in combined form.) From the other aspect, American statistics record also profits and their certain components as well. But in these statistics the shoe-shine boy or the poorest farmer are equally entrepreneurs; their incomes are equally of a profit nature. Another problem is that in theory we consider interest to be a part of profits, an income of capitalists. In the United States many workers have savings deposits and receive interest on them. We thus had to make a compromise. We had to set out from the fact that the workers who cannot be counted as capitalists are many and there are not many Fords. Therefore, we hardly commit too big an error if we assign the total sum of "wages and salaries" to those who receive wages and salaries, and not *also* a salary. We gave the incomes of a profit nature mostly to those not living on wages and salaries (they are not necessarily capitalists, since they belong in considerable numbers to intermediate groups, but, for the sake of brevity, we shall still call them capitalists and their income profits.) And we accorded a part of the interests to wage and salary earners—the total of net interest is a small sum. (We shall report on the details later on.)

This summary procedure may raise doubts concerning the applicability of data derived in this manner for analytical purposes; we are working with data the exact meaning of which we do not know. As a matter of fact, this is not even the main difficulty. That is still ahead. Thus, e.g., in the Δp_c formula we do not need the total of wages and salaries, but only the part spent by wage earners on consumption. Thus we have to deduct from the total the personal taxes and social insurance contributions paid by wage earners. The same would hold for the "capitalists" if we needed their money income spent on their consumption, but we do not need it. (In another context it was still needed.) If we estimated these missing data by some "intuition" we would have committed, in all likelihood, much graver mistakes than what might derive from the former mentioned summary procedures.

It seems obvious that those compiling the "official" data may also have frequently met similar problems, though they no doubt have the advantage of possessing more or less mature estimation procedures. But where do they take these methods from? They obviously apply various econometric procedures. Behind these we always find theoretical assumptions about the interrelations between the economic variables in question, assumed behavioural equations. They stick to them as long as the time series arrived at with their aid prove to be more or less consistent with each other and the other data, but they are modified, should the need arise. We, too, wanted something similar. And we believe we have found, precisely in this seemingly hopeless situation, something to hold on to.

A.3 THE ASSUMED SCHEME OF BEHAVIOUR

The economists doing research into behaviour were caught unaware by the paradoxical phenomenon that the saving of the population were the highest precisely when the rate of inflation was highest and thus the depreciation of the sums saved was fastest.

We believe that this phenomenon can be well understood. We set out from the fact that a good part of wage earners have no opportunity (nor the necessary expertise) to invest their saving so that no loss is incurred, but in the uncertain world they do feel the necessity of having reserves they can use in case of trouble. But we also knew the ackward nature of the urge to save, widespread consumers' and mortgage credits. We consider the fact, causing surprise to many, that the saving of wage earners are governed not by inflation but by the state of business, not as a paradoxical form of behaviour but as one that may be justly expected of them.

The reader may know well this view of ours from the text, thus there is hardly any need to go over it again. We shall restrict ourselves to the essentials.

The sum of personal saving is known from statistics. From the data published by forms of income the income of wage earners could be correctly separated from that of non-wage earners. About the consumption of the latter we may, in our opinion, justly assume that if we deduct the outlays on durable consumer goods and on the purchase of homes from their total consumption, the volume of their remaining consumption is essentially rigid. More exactly, if the volume of GNP increases or decreases, it will also increase or decrease but at a slower rate than that of GNP. And the part not consumed of their income is their saving. Deducting this from the known amount of personal savings we get the savings by workers.

There are, however, two problems. The first one is that taxes are levied on incomes, and therefore we have to deduct direct taxes from incomes to arrive at the disposable incomes. Fortunately, relying on a (non-official) American publication we can estimate well what percentage of tax was levied on the different kinds of income. (Pechaman and Okner, 1974, p. 78) Thus we can establish the disposable income of non-wage earners in the individual years with rather good approximation, and if we knew, at least for a single year, how much they actually spent of it, we could also tell how much the saving by workers are in that and in any preceding and following year. But it was precisely this that we could not know. Therefore, we resorted to a hypothesis we thought likely. We assumed, namely, that, in the course of the period examined, the savings by workers were positive in the bad years and negative in the good ones. Let us examine to what extent this hypothesis brought us nearer to our goal—provided it held fast.

A.4 THE SUBSTANCE OF OUR PROCEDURE

Kalecki elaborated the following national economic balance scheme (Kalecki, 1975, p. 82).

We may also write this in the form of the following equation: consumption by capitalists less the saving by workers equals gross profit after taxes less gross

$$\text{Gross profit net of direct taxes} \quad = \quad \left\{ \begin{array}{l} \text{Gross investment} \\ + \text{Export surplus} \\ + \text{Budget deficit} \\ - \text{Workers' saving} \\ + \text{Capitalists' consumption} \end{array} \right.$$

investment less export surplus less budget deficit. Now, the size of gross investment, export surplus and budget deficit can be taken from official statistics, and the amount of gross profit can be approximately given in the way indicated. Thus the unknowns are: (1) consumption by capitalists, (2) deductions from profits and (3) saving by wage and salary earners.

Knowing this, we did the following. We varied the consumption by capitalists between certain extreme limits in a series of computations and assigned to every assumed amount of capitalists' consumption varying amounts of deductions from profit—again between certain extreme limits. Thus we arrived at quite a few hypothetic time series regarding the savings by wage earners. It turned out that only a few of these time series indicated positive savings in bad years and negative savings in good years. Beyond that, the time series satisfying this assumption and which are not totally untenable from other respects either, were situated within a narrow band.

In the preceding paragraph we mentioned deductions from profit of varying size. We did not speak about taxes, because, in order to arrive at the disposable income on non-wage earners we also have to deduct other items in addition to taxes from profits. But taxes were the single biggest item. It was really reassuring that it turned out that from the time series arrived at through trial and error those few coincided with our hypothesis, and also seemed most likely to hold from other aspects as well, in which the size of tax taken from said publication also figured. Therefore, we hope and justly believe that our models built on these data are usable, that is, suited to be used to analyze both qualitatively and quantitatively with acceptable accuracy what actually happened in the 1970s.

In actual practical computations all this proved much more complicated, but as regards the substance of the matter we did as described above. In the hope that the things hitherto described become more understandable and—perhaps—more credit-able, in the following we also describe in greater detail how we arrived at the figures.

A.5 DETAILED DESCRIPTION OF THE PROCEDURE

In building up our partial model we set out from the following national economic balance of Kalecki. In its original form, it is the following: (Kalecki, 1971, p. 82)

It was this scheme we had to fill in on the basis of data taken from American statistics.[2]

[2] If not otherwise indicated, the sources of the statistical data are: The National Income and Product Accounts of the United States 1929–1974. Statistical Tables. United States Department of Commerce (Bureau of Economic Analysis), Government Printing Office, Washington, D.C. (up to 1972); Survey of Current Business, July 1974 (for the years 1973–1976) and July 1979 (for the years 1976–1978).

Gross profit less taxes Wages, salaries and transfers net of taxes	Gross investment Export surplus Budget deficit Capitalists' consumption Workers' consumption
GNP less taxes plus transfers	GNP less taxes plus transfers

This scheme is, however, all too simplified in its original form. We had to bring it into harmony with the categories of the American national accounts.

Let us start with the left-hand side of Kalecki's balance. By gross profit Kalecki means every kind of capitalists' income, inclusive of depreciation allowances (that is why he calls it gross profit). American statistics record GNP and its various components, but do not divide the latter into gross profit on the one hand, and wages and salaries on the other. We had to perform this division with approximate accuracy ourselves. The components of GNP as a sum of incomes in American statistics are as follows: (1) compensation of wage and salary earners, (2) profit-type incomes, (3) net interests, (4) indirect taxes, (5) statistical discrepancy, (6) depreciation (capital consumption). From these we included in profits profit-type incomes and the overwhelming part of net interests. (More on this below.) The former is composed of corporate profits, proprietors' incomes (the incomes of non-corporate ventures—farmers, single-person firms, among them very small enterprises and free-lance professionals) and rental incomes. We "gave"—for the time being undefined—a part of net interests, to be denoted by p, to wage and salary earners.

Further, we included in the capitalists' income the lion's share of interests paid by government. These are paid, namely, mostly on government loans. The part q falling to wage and salary earners may only be small. Finally, the statistical item of "subsidies less current surplus of government enterprises" was also added to capitalists' incomes.

As regards wages and salaries, we included the compensation of employees and transfers. Both can be found in statistics. (Kalecki's balance only comprises government transfers, but among the incomes of wage and salary earners—called simply wages and salaries by Kalecki—also the transfers received from enterprises have to appear.)

From among deductions, Kalecki mentions only taxes. As a matter of fact, from gross incomes the following items have to be deducted:

1. the direct taxes on capitalists and capitalist enterprises from the profits. Here belong the corporate profit tax which appears in statistics, further the direct personal tax x paid by capitalists after their personal income (dividend, interest) and on their receipts from non-corporate ventures (tax on income and wealth, etc.).

In addition, capitalists also pay a personal social insurance contribution, y. Thus, to the capitalist incomes listed, we added depreciation allowances, deducted the corporate profit tax as well as the sums x, y, q, and p, and thus we arrived at the sum called in Kalecki's balance "gross profit less taxes".

2. From wages and salaries we had to deduct the direct taxes paid by wage earners. Statistics gives the sum of total personal taxes and, deducting from it x, we get the

direct taxes paid by wage and salary earners. Further, from their compensation we have to deduct the obligatory social insurance contribution paid by the employers, which they do not get at all. This, too, can be taken from statistics. Also the social insurance contribution by the workers themselves had to be deducted. This is the total insurance contribution less y. Thus we arrive at the disposable income of wage and salary earners which corresponds in Kalecki's scheme to the category of "wages and salaries less taxes".

In addition to the disposable income of capitalists and workers the left-hand side of the balance also has to include some numerically small items which, however, belong to the completeness of American statistics, namely, those government transfers which we did not take into account among the incomes of wage and salary earners (e.g., transfers to abroad), as well as the statistical discrepancy appearing as a separate item in statistics, due to inaccuracies. With these, the left-hand side of the balance indeed adds up to the item "GNP less government revenues plus government transfers". (What Kalecki calls "taxes", correspond in reality to total government revenues.)

The procedure was easier on the right-hand side of the balance. In statistics we find the balance of foreign trade, the sum of gross investment, the budget deficit (the difference between government expenditure and revenues), as well as the global amount of personal consumption which, at this stage of the investigation, cannot yet be separated into consumption by workers and capitalists (or by wage earners and non-wage-earners). We note here that we consider the sum spent on the purchase of houses (homes, owner-occupied dwellings and so-called mobile homes) as consumption, since a house is the biggest and most durable kind of consumers items. (Robinson, 1970, p. 270) Fortunately, in American statistics—which under housing construction lumps together the purchase of homes and the building of rented apartments, though the first is consumption mostly from wages and salaries and the latter capital investment—in the table showing the division of GNP without imputations the sum spent on the purchase of homes is to be found not under investment but in the row of personal consumption, thus it is in the form wanted for our purposes.

On this basis, we present Kalecki's balance on p. 264. in terms of categories corresponding to American statistics (without imputations).

For illustration we also compiled this balance for the year 1972, without imputations, at current prices, in billions of dollars. (See p. 285.)

It turns out from the balance that, since x, y, q and p appear in the disposable incomes of capitalists and wage earners with opposite signs, they do not appear in the sum totals. The equilibrium of our balance does not depend on whether we estimated these items, directly not available from official statistics, correctly or incorrectly.

We only needed this balance to check with its aid whether we interpreted the categories of the American national accounts correctly. In fact we need a balance derived from it, in this, however, the x, y, q, and p amounts will also appear in the sum totals.

I.

1. Gross[a] income of capitalists[b]
2. Deductions from capitalists' incomes[c]
3. Disposable income of capitalists (1—2)
4. Income of wage and salary earners[d]
5. Deductions from the income of wage and salary earners[e]
6. Disposable income of wage and salary earners (4—5)
7. Other government transfers[f]
8. Statistical discrepancy

10. Gross domestic private investment
11. Surplus of the balance of trade
12. Deficit in the balance of government revenues and expenditure
13. Personal consumption[g]

---

9. GNP less government revenues plus government transfers $(3+6+7+8)$

14. GNP less government revenues plus government transfers

a) Interpreted inclusive of capital consumption.

b) More exactly: incomes of capitalist firms and of those not living on wages and salaries. Its elements are: corporate profits, proprietors' incomes, personal rental incomes, depreciation allowances, the greater part of net interest, difference between government subsidies and the current surplus of government enterprises, interest received from government.

c) Its elements are: profit tax of corporations, direct personal tax of capitalists (x) and personal social insurance contribution (y), the part of interest received from government and of total net interest falling to wage and salary earners $(q+p)$.

d) Its elements are: compensation of workers and other employees, transfers received from enterprises and government, the share of workers from the interests mentioned $(q+p)$.

e) Its elements are: direct taxes of wage and salary earners (total direct tax less x), from total compensation the social insurance contribution paid by employers, personal social insurance contribution of wage and salary earners (total contribution less y).

f) Transfers abroad and wages not yet paid out.

g) As distinct from the original balance of Kalecki, at this place the consumption by workers and by capitalists is not separated, and also comprises the purchase of homes.

From the former we arrive at this balance if we deduct both from the left-hand side and the right-hand side of the former one the disposable income of wage and salary earners. But in order that we have on the left-hand side only the disposable income of capitalists after the deduction—as in Kalecki's original balance—we have to transfer item 7, "other government transfers" and item 8, "statistical discrepancy" to the right-hand side. Merging the former with item 12, "deficit of government revenues and expenditure" we form the item: "modified deficit of government revenues and expenditure". So that the right-hand side of the new balance should agree with the right-hand side of Kalecki's corresponding balance, we have to deduct now the disposable income of wage and salary earners from the right-hand side of the former balance. We know, however, that the item "personal consumption" is equal to the sum of consumption by capitalists and wage and salary earners. Wage and salary earners

284

use their disposable income for personal consumption, savings and transfers abroad. In consideration of these, the new balance (excluding imputations) can be written in the following form:[3]

II.

1. Gross income of capitalists   286.6
2. Deductions from capitalists' incomes $(41.5 + x + y + q + p)$
3. Disposable income of capitalists (1—2)
   $245.1 - x - y - q - p$
4. Income of wage and salary earners $817.1 + q + p$
5. Deductions from the incomes of wage and salary earners $231.9 - x - y$
6. Disposable income of wage and salary earners (4—5) $585.2 + x + y + q + p$
7. Other government transfers 2.4
8. Statistical discrepancy 1.7

10. Gross domestic private investment   138.2
11. Surplus of the balance of trade -3.3
12. Deficit of government revenues and expenditure   3.5
13. Personal consumption   696.0

---

9. GNP less government revenues plus government transfers $(3+6+7+8)$ 834.4

14. GNP less government revenues plus government transfers   834.4

1. Disposable income of capitalists

2. Gross domestic private investment
3. Surplus of balance of trade
4. Modified deficit of government revenues and expenditure[4]
5. Consumption by capitalists (c_c)
6. — Savings of wage and salary earners (S_w)
7. — Transfers abroad by wage and salary earners
8. — Statistical discrepancy

[3] Namely, (consumption by capitalists + consumption by wage earners) — (consumption by wage earners + their savings + their transfers abroad) = consumption by capitalists — savings and transfers abroad of wage earners.

[4] Transferring item 7 on the left-hand side of Kalecki's balance to the right-hand side and merging it into item 12.

If we now attempt to fill in this balance with the factual data of a given year—1972, this time—the following may be written (bn current dollars, data excludes imputations):

1. $245.1 - x - y - q - p$

2. 138.2
3. -3.3
4. 1.1
5. c_c
6. S_w
7. -1.0
8. -1.7

We could not fill in the items "consumption by capitalists" and "savings of wage and salary earners" because these cannot be found in such form in official statistics. But we can also write the balance in the form of the following equation: S_w + statistical discrepancy $(1.7) = 110.1 - (x + y + q + p) - c_c$, where $(x + y + q + p)$ can also be denoted by e (= estimated data). The same equation may also be written for the years 1969–1975, and thus we get the following time series:

F_1 time series:

1969: $S_{w69} - 3.3 = 93.8$
1970: $S_{w70} - 2.1 = 80.2$
1971: $S_{w71} + 1.3 = 84.7$
1972: $S_{w72} + 1.7 = 110.4$ $-(x_t + y_t + q_t + p_t) - c_{ct}$
1973: $S_{w73} + 2.6 = 108.4$ where the subscript t indicates that the data
1974: $S_{w74} + 6.6 = 100.3$ should be taken into account with their actual
1975: $S_{w75} + 4.4 = 90.2$ value in the given year

The sum $(x_t + y_t + q_t + p_t)$ will be called in the following e_t.

From among the four items adding up to e, the personal tax of capitalists is by far the biggest (x). Its size can be approximately estimated by using the above mentioned American publication discussing tax burdens, which gives the percentage of total personal tax falling in a given year to the different kinds of incomes. With its aid we worked out the size of x for every year. In respect of y, official statistics give the social insurance contribution of the self-employed, that is, of the owners of "one-man firms" and of the freelance professionals. We augmented this amount by a fraction of the so-called complementary health insurance contributions. As regards net interest, we assumed that wage and salary earners get 30 per cent of the total (this is p). From the interest paid by the government, mainly interest on state bonds, we gave 10 per cent to wage and salary earners (q), and even this seems too much. In the last resort, the x seeming to be the most reliable is 75–80 per cent of the whole e_t, therefore the error in the estimation of $(y + q + p)$ is presumably much smaller than that in the case of x.

In view of this remark it should be clear that it would only have been seeming accuracy if we had aimed at separately assessing these three items by relying on different assumptions. Instead, we took for 1972[5] instead of the x estimated at \$ 30 bn, seven different values from 21 bn to 39 bn and moved these for the years 1969–1975 in conformity with the series of indexes derived from the original estimates (that is, we obtained seven different assumed time series).

Similarly, we estimated the value of consumption by capitalists (c_c) at 60 bn in 1972 (without the purchase of homes, and at 66 bn inclusive of it) and concluded from that on their corresponding consumption in the individual years—using the official data on total consumption, total purchase of homes and total purchase of durable consumer goods. But this was only one of the variants, since we constructed the estimated time series in altogether 15 variants, beginning with 50 bn (without home purchases) in 1972 up to 75 bn in the same year and assuming 4, 6 and 8 bn spent on the purchase of homes. That is, combined with the former mentioned 7 variants we worked with altogether $7 \times 15 = 105$ variants. But, as can be seen from the time series F_1 we needed not e and c_c separately but their sum and from the 105 variants only a few proved to be essentially different in respect of this sum.

In the preceding we have already mentioned that the saving by workers S_w is a function of e and c_c. We present here a few diagrams of the function S_w belonging to different e and c_c values. (See diagrams 1–4.)

In the first three diagrams we illustrated S_w with the aid of one unchanged value of c_c each (in the first one with a high value of c_c, in the second with a medium value, and in the third with a low value). In the fourth diagram we linked the capitalist consumption deemed most likely with different values of e.

A.7 OUR FINAL CONCLUSION

In Diagram 1 only the lowest curve ($c_{c72} = 61$, $e_{72} = 39$) corresponds to the assumption that the net saving of wage earners is negative in the good years (1969, 1972 and 1973) and positive in the bad ones (1970, to a certain extent 1971 and, naturally, 1974 and 1975). But in this diagram the overspending obtained for 1969 is much greater than the one derived for the overheated 1973 and this somewhat challenges the accuracy of the diagram.

In Diagram 2 only the highest curve ($c_{c72} = 83$, $e_{72} = 21$) could be taken into account, but here we do not find any overspending in 1973, and the S_w of about 40 bn arrived at for 1975 amounts to a realistically high portion of the total "personal" savings of 69 bn (which also includes the savings of non-corporate business units).

From the curves in Diagram 3 the medium one ($c_{c72} = 71, e_{72} = 30$) would be most suitable but no essential overspending can be found for 1973.

The medium curve of Diagram 4 ($c_{c72} = 66$, $e_{72} = 30$) seems to be suited in every respect. Although saving is low in 1970, the 1970 recession was by far not as deep as the one in 1974, also the level of unemployment was much lower, real wages did not fall, thus wage earners had no reason to strongly increase their savings for fear of the future.

---

[5] We chose this year because statistics takes into account the volumes at the prices of this year.

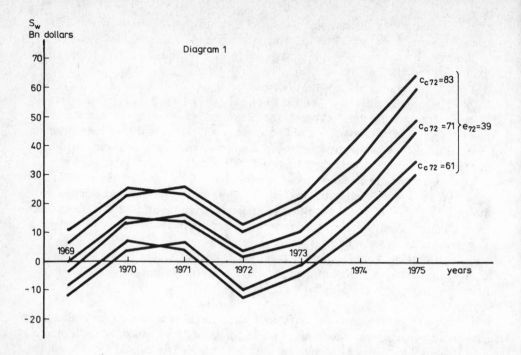

Diagram 1

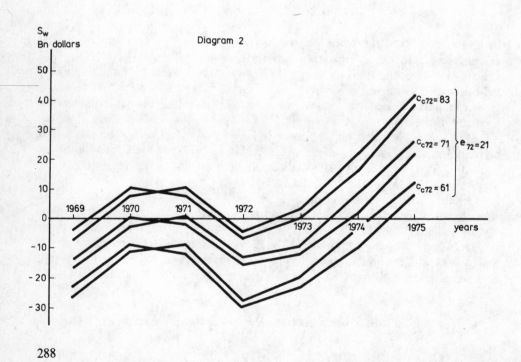

Diagram 2

288

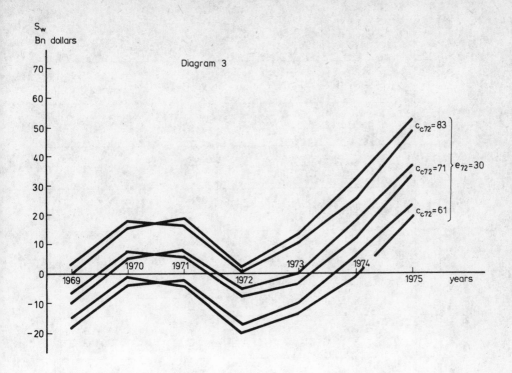

Diagram 3

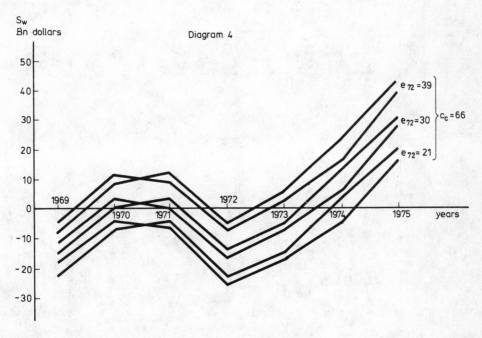

Diagram 4

289

Table A.1

Kalecki-type balance-sheet No. 1
data excl. imputations, bn current dollars

Item	1968	1969	1970	1971	1972	1973	1974	1975	1976	1977	1978
Left-hand side											
1. Proprietors' incomes	61.9	64.7	63.6	66.1	74.3	90.2	83.7	84.2	85.8	95.9	112.2
2. Rental incomes	8.1	7.9	8.3	9.0	10.0	11.1	11.6	10.9	11.5	14.3	15.4
3. Corporate profits	85.8	81.4	67.9	77.2	92.1	99.1	83.6	95.9	126.8	150.0	167.7
4. Profit-type incomes $(1+2+3)$[a]	155.8	154.0	139.8	152.3	176.4	200.4	178.9	191.0	224.2	260.2	295.3
5. Net interest	2.5	3.3	6.9	9.1	8.6	8.6	17.7	20.9	19.2	19.5	19.9
6. Depreciation (capital consumption)	60.6	67.4	74.8	81.5	86.8	96.2	112.7	133.9	147.3	160.5	176.6
7. Remuneration of wage and salary earners	517.0	568.6	606.4	647.6	712.4	796.4	872.4	927.3	1033.6	1152.3	1299.3
8. Transfers by enterprises	3.4	3.8	4.0	4.2	4.7	5.4	5.9	7.6	8.0	8.7	9.2
9. Indirect taxes	67.4	73.6	79.6	87.5	93.9	101.8	109.0	118.0	128.1	140.0	152.5
10. Less: government subsidies less current surplus of government enterprises	1.3	1.8	2.7	2.2	3.1	3.5	0.7	2.2	0.8	2.9	4.1
11. Statistical discrepancy	-0.6	-3.3	-2.1	1.3	1.7	2.6	5.8	7.4	6.1	7.5	3.3
12. Gross national product $(4+5+6+7+8+9+10+11)$	804.8	865.6	906.7	981.3	1081.5	1207.9	1301.7	1403.9	1565.3	1745.8	1952.0
Right-hand side											
13. Gross investment	102.7	116.0	111.8	118.9	138.2	169.3	170.3	146.2	183.4	224.8	262.9
14. Surplus of the trade balance	2.3	1.8	3.9	1.6	-3.3	7.1	6.0	20.4	8.0	-9.9	-10.3
15. Government purchases of goods and services	197.3	206.2	216.8	231.5	250.7	266.8	299.8	335.7	358.6	393.2	431.6
16. Personal consumption	502.6	541.8	574.9	629.4	696.0	764.5	825.5	901.6	1015.8	1137.6	1267.7
16[a] Consumption of wage earners	451.8	486.6	517.6	567.7	630.1	693.3	747.2	816.1	921.5	1033.0	1152.7
16[b] Consumption of non-wage earners	50.9	54.9	57.1	61.7	66.0	71.4	78.3	85.5	94.3	104.6	115.0
17. Gross national product $(13+14+15+16)$	804.9	865.8	906.6	981.4	1081.6	1207.7	1301.6	1403.9	1565.8	1745.8	1952.0

[a] Without interest from government

Table A.2

Kalecki-type balance-sheet No. 2
(data excl. imputations, bn current dollars)

Item	1968	1969	1970	1971	1972	1973	1974	1975	1976	1977	1978
Left-hand side											
1. Gross income of non-wage earners	229.8	236.8	234.7	255.5	283.9	319.5	323.7	362.5	411.6	461.7	514.8
2. Deductions from the income of non-wage earners	61.2	63.2	59.0	63.7	71.5	80.3	87.3	90.7	104.9	116.1	131.7
3. Disposable income of non-wage earners (1−2)	168.6	173.6	175.7	191.8	212.4	239.2	236.4	271.8	306.7	345.6	383.1
4. Income of wage earners	578.9	637.4	689.9	745.8	820.9	919.9	1021.1	1113.7	1235.5	1368.8	1531.8
5. Deductions from the income of wage earners	136.7	161.9	167.5	175.2	206.0	233.5	266.0	267.8	313.2	358.7	409.9
6. Disposable income of wage earners (4−5)	442.2	475.5	522.4	570.6	614.9	686.4	755.1	845.9	922.3	1010.1	1122.5
7. Other government payments*	2.8	2.9	3.2	4.4	5.4	6.4	7.5	7.6	7.7	8.7	12.4
8. Statistical discrepancy	−0.6	−3.3	−2.1	1.3	1.7	2.6	5.8	7.4	6.1	7.5	3.3
9. GNP − government revenues + government payments other than purchases	613.0	648.7	699.2	768.1	834.4	934.6	1004.8	1132.7	1242.8	1371.9	1520.7
Right-hand side											
10. Gross investment	102.7	116.0	111.0	118.9	138.2	169.3	170.3	146.2	183.4	224.8	262.9
11. Surplus of the trade balance	2.3	1.8	3.9	1.6	−3.3	7.1	6.0	20.4	8.0	−9.9	−10.3
12. Deficit of government revenues and expenditure	5.5	−10.7	9.4	18.3	3.5	−6.3	3.2	64.4	35.7	19.5	0.3
13. Personal consumption	502.6	541.8	574.9	629.4	696.0	764.5	825.4	901.6	1015.8	1137.6	1267.7
13a. Consumption of wage earners	451.8	486.6	517.6	567.7	630.1	693.3	747.2	816.1	921.5	1033.0	1152.7
13b. Consumption of non-wage earners	50.9	54.9	57.1	61.7	66.0	71.4	78.3	85.5	94.3	104.6	115.0
14. GNP − government revenues + government payments other than purchases	613.1	648.9	699.2	768.2	834.4	934.6	1005.0	1132.6	1242.9	1372.0	1520.6

* Transfers and interest to the rest of world

Table A.3

Kalecki-type balance-sheet No. 3

(data excl. imputations, bn current dollars)

Item	1968	1969	1970	1971	1972	1973	1974	1975	1976	1977	1978
Left-hand side											
1. Disposable income of capitalists	168.6	173.6	175.7	191.8	212.4	239.2	236.4	271.8	306.7	345.6	383.1
Right-hand side											
2. Gross investment	102.7	116.0	111.0	118.9	138.2	169.3	170.3	146.2	183.4	224.8	262.9
3. Surplus of the trade balance	2.3	1.8	3.9	1.6	−3.3	7.1	6.0	20.4	8.0	−9.9	−10.3
4. Government domestic deficit	2.7	−13.6	6.2	13.9	−1.9	−12.7	−4.3	56.8	28.0	10.8	−12.1
5. Consumption of non-wage earners	50.9	54.9	57.1	61.7	66.0	71.4	78.3	85.5	94.3	104.6	115.0
6. Less: savings by wage earners	−10.2	−12.1	3.5	1.8	−16.1	−8.0	6.9	28.9	0.0	−23.7	−31.7
7. Less: transfers of wage earners to the rest of world	0.8	0.9	1.1	1.1	1.0	1.3	1.0	0.9	0.9	0.9	0.8
8. Less: statistical discrepancy	−0.6	−3.3	−2.1	1.3	1.7	2.6	5.8	7.4	6.1	7.5	3.3
	168.6	173.6	175.7	191.9	212.4	239.2	236.6	271.7	306.7	345.6	383.1

Table A.4

Consumption of the two social classes in current dollar, excl. imputations

Year	Non-wage earners				Wage earners			
	Billion dollars	1968 = 100	annual change per cent	in percentage of total consumption	Billion dollars	1968 = 100	annual change per cent	in percentage of total consumption
1968	50.9	100.0	–	10.1	451.8	100.0	–	89.9
1969	54.9	107.9	7.9	10.1	486.7	107.7	7.7	89.9
1970	57.1	112.0	4.0	9.9	517.8	114.6	6.3	90.1
1971	61.7	121.2	8.1	9.8	567.6	125.7	9.7	90.2
1972	66.0	129.7	7.0	9.5	630.0	139.5	11.0	90.5
1973	71.4	140.3	8.2	9.3	693.3	153.5	10.0	90.7
1974	78.3	153.8	9.7	9.5	747.2	165.4	7.8	90.5
1975	85.5	168.0	9.2	9.5	816.1	180.1	9.2	90.5
1976	94.3	185.3	10.3	9.3	921.5	204.0	12.9	90.7
1977	104.6	205.5	10.9	9.0	1033.0	228.6	12.1	90.8
1978	115.0	225.9	9.9	9.1	1152.7	255.1	11.6	90.9

Table A.5

Consumption of the two social classes in 1972 dollar, excl. imputations

Year	Non-wage earners				Wage earners			
	Billion dollars	1968 = 100	annual change per cent	in percentage of total consumption	Billion dollars	1968 = 100	annual change per cent	in percentage of total consumption
1968	58.9	100.0	–	9.9	536.8	100.0	–	90.1
1969	60.0	101.9	1.9	9.8	552.5	102.9	2.9	90.2
1970	60.4	102.5	0.7	9.7	561.7	104.6	1.7	90.3
1971	63.1	107.1	4.5	9.7	589.2	109.8	4.9	90.3
1972	66.0	112.1	4.6	9.5	630.0	117.4	6.9	90.5
1973	67.7	114.9	2.6	9.4	654.7	122.0	3.9	90.6
1974	67.2	114.1	– 0.7	9.5	639.3	119.1	– 2.7	90.5
1975	67.5	114.6	0.4	9.5	644.0	120.0	0.7	90.5
1976	70.9	120.3	5.0	9.3	694.0	129.3	7.8	90.7
1977	74.0	125.6	4.4	9.1	736.3	137.2	6.1	90.9
1978	75.9	128.9	2.6	9.0	769.2	143.3	4.5	91.0

On the basis of all this we believe it may be stated that the consumption of capitalists may have been between $ 60 and 70 bn in 1972, while the value of e may be assumed to have fallen between 28 and 32 bn.

We analysed in our book business fluctuations and inflation. Thus, as a matter of fact, in these analyses not the absolute figures of some year, but their changes were important. Therefore, we may accept any intermediate figure between the 60 and 70 or the 28 and 32 bn dollars, since a wilful choice in this sense hardly modifies the percentual changes.

Actually we accepted the values $c_c = 66$ and $e = 30$ bn dollars for 1972.

In the following pages we present our (Kalecki-type) balances Nos 1, 2 and 3 for the years 1968–1978.[6] We also present the development of the consumption of the two social classes, estimated in similar manner, for the same period, both at current and at unchanged (1972) prices, (See Tables A.1–A.5)

[6] Kalecki also attempted to work out the profit for the United States for the years 1929—1940 (Kalecki, 1971, p. 90) but, partly because of the inadequacy of available statistics and partly because of the inaccuracy of the method applied, his results were not too convincing.

294

REFERENCES

Ackley, G.: The Contribution of Economists to Policy Formation. *Journal of Finance*, Vol. 21. May 1966.

Bailey, N.J.: The 1971 Report of the President's Economic Advisers; Inflation and Recession. *American Economic Review*, September 1971, pp. 217–621.

Burns, A.F.: The Real Issues of Inflation and Unemployment. *Challenge*, Jan.–Feb., 1976.

Burns, A.F. and Samuelson, P.A.: *Full Employment, Guideposts and Economic Stability*. American Enterprise Institute, Washington D.C. 1967.

Crockett, J., Friend, I. and Shavel, H.: The Impact of Monetary Stringency on Business Investment. *Survey of Current Business*, August 1967, pp. 10–26.

Denison, E.F.: *Accounting for Slower Economic Growth. The United States in the 1970s*. The Brookings Institution, Washington D.C. 1979.

Economic Report of the President, 1969–1980. Washington D.C. Government Printing Office, 1969–1980.

Eichner, A.S.: *The Megacorp and Oligopoly*. M.E. Sharpe Inc., White Plains, New York.

Erdős, P.: A Contribution to the Criticism of Keynes and Keynesianism, in: *The Subtle Anatomy of Capitalism*. Ed.: J. Schwartz. Goodyear Publishing Co. Santa Monica 1977, pp. 232–254.

Erdős, P.: *Contributions to the Theory of Capitalist Money, Business Fluctuations and Crisis*. Akadémiai Kiadó, Budapest 1971.

Erdős, P.: *Wages, Profit, Taxation*. Akadémiai Kiadó, Budapest 1982.

Erdős, P. and Molnár, F.: A tőkés gazdaság struktúrájának és a válsághajlam csökkenésének összefüggéseiről (On the interrelations between the structure of capitalist economy and a declining tendency to crisis). *Közgazdasági Szemle*, 1969, Nos 7–8., pp.907–923.

Erdős, T.: A tőkésországok nemzetközi gazdasági kapcsolatai és a gazdasági válság (International economicrelations among capitalist countries and the economiccrisis). *Társadalmi Szemle*, 1975, No.10, pp. 43–54.

Erdős, T.: *Egyensúly, válság, ciklikusság* (Equilibrium,crisis, cyclicality). Kossuth Könyvkiadó, Budapest 1975.

Fellner, W. et.al.: *Correcting Taxes for Inflation*. American Enterprise Institute, Washington D.C. 1975.

Gordon, R.A.: Economic Instability and Growth: The American Record. Harper and Row, New York 1974.

Harrod, R.: *The Life of John Maynard Keynes*. MacMillan St. Martin's Press. London–New York 1963.

Kalecki, M.: *Selected Essays on the Dynamics of the Capitalist Economy*. Cambridge Univ. Press 1971.

Kardos, T.: Külkereskedelmi mérleg és áruszerkezet a konjunktúra elemzésben (Balance of trade and commodity structure in business cycle analysis). *Külgazdaság*, 1980, No.10.

Keynes, J.M.: *The General Theory of Employment, Interest and Money*. MacMillan, London 1936.

Marx, K.: *The Capital*, Vol.III. Foreign Languages Publishing House, Moscow 1966.

Molnár, F.: *Economic Growth and Recessions in the United States of America*. Akadémiai Kiadó, Budapest 1970.

Molnár, F.: *Az amerikai gazdaság jelenlegi helyzete és néhány főbb problémája: Gazdaságelmélet, kelet-nyugati kapcsolatok, magyar és amerikai gazdaság* (The present situation of the American economy and some of its major problems, in: Economic theory, East-Westrelations and the Hungarian and American economies). Világgazdasági Tudományos Tanács, Budapest 1979, pp. 193–210.

Molnár,F.: The 1974–1975 recession in the USA: a lot of facts and some lessons. *Acta Oeconomica*, Vol.17, No.2, pp. 177–201.

Molnár, F.: Adócsökkentés és konjunktúra az Egyesült Államokban (Tax reduction and business upswing in the USA). *Közgazdasági Szemle*, 1965, No.9. 1059–1074.

OECD Economic Outlook, July 27, 1980. OECD. Paris 1980.

Okun, A.M.: A Postmortem of the 1974 Recession. *Brookings Papers on Economic Activity*, 1975, I. pp. 207–221.

Okun, A.M.: Measuring the Impact of the 1964 Tax Reduction, in: W.W. Heller, ed.: *Perspectives of Economic Growth*. Random House, New York 1968, pp. 25–49.

Okun, A.M.: *The Political Economy of Prosperity*. Norton and Co. New York 1970.

Pechman, J.A. and Okner, B.A.: *Who Bears the Tax Burden?* The Brookings Institution, Washington D.C., 1974.

Pechman, J.A. and Okner, B.A.: *Who Bears the Tax Burden?* The Brookings Institution, Washington D.C., 1974.

Perry, G.L.: Policy Alternatives for 1974. *Brookings Papers on Economic Activity* 1975, No.1, pp. 227–237.

Prices in Recession and Recovery. *Federal Reserve Bulletin*, July 1976, pp. 557–565.

Renshaw, E.F.: Productivity, in: *U.S. Economic Growth from 1976 to 1980: Prospects, Problems and Patterns*. Volume 1. U.S. Government Printing Office, 1976, pp. 21–56.

Robinson, J.: *The Accumulation of Capital*. ELBS and MacMillan, London 1973.

Samuelson, P.A.: A Cynical Economist's View of American Economic Prospects. *Financial Times*, August 16, 1978.

Samuelson, P.A.: Behind Ford's Plan. *Newsweek*, Oct. 20, 1975.

Samuelson, P.A.: Tough Year for the New Administration. *Financial Times*, January 1, 1969.

Stein, H.: *The Fiscal Revolution in America*. The University of Chicago Press, Chicago 1969.

Zarnovitz, V. and Moore, G.H.: The Recession and Recovery of 1973–1976. *Explorations in Economic Research* Vol.4., Fall, 1977, pp. 471–557.

STATISTICAL SOURCES

The National Income and Product Accounts of the United States, 1929–1974. Statistical Tables. A Supplement of the Survey of Current Business.

U.S. National Income and Product Accounts. *Survey of Current Business*, July 1976, July 1977, July 1978, July 1979.